Hong Kong New Wave Cinema (1978–2000)

Pak Tong CHEUK

To：吳曼霞女士雅正。

Hong Kong New Wave Cinema (1978–2000)

卓伯棠於香港

Pak Tong CHEUK

11-11-2010.

intellect Bristol, UK / Chicago, USA

First Published in the UK in 2008 by
Intellect Books, The Mill, Parnall Road, Fishponds, Bristol, BS16 3JG, UK

First published in the USA in 2008 by
Intellect Books, The University of Chicago Press, 1427 E. 60th Street, Chicago, IL 60637, USA

A catalogue record for this book is available from the British Library.

Cover Design: Gabriel Solomons
Copy Editor: Holly Spradling
Typesetting: Mac Style, Nafferton, E. Yorkshire

ISBN 978-1-84150-148-2

Printed and bound by Gutenberg Press, Malta.

CONTENTS

INTRODUCTION

In the short span of eight years from the late 1970s to the early 1980s, the Hong Kong film industry spawned a group of young directors aged about thirty. This brand new force consisted of about thirty people, including Ann Hui, Yim Ho, Tsui Hark, Allen Fong, Patrick Tam, Clifford Choi, Dennis Yu and others. Most of them had received film training overseas, particularly in the United States and the United Kingdom; then, at various points in time, joined several local television broadcasting institutions: Hong Kong Television (Television Broadcasts Limited), Rediffusion Television (the progenitor of Asia Television) and Commercial Television, the television unit of Radio Television Hong Kong. After gaining practical experience in film-making for several years in the television industry, many of them left and entered the film industry.

The infusion of so much indigenous new blood in the field of film was unprecedented in the 80-year history of Hong Kong cinema. Passionate about film and art, these new directors gradually got a feel for current social developments. They were familiar with what the audience liked and could make films with unique ideas, interesting themes, forceful images and unusual styles. Their works were widely accepted by the mass audience and also gained recognition from the news media and critics. This group of young directors, with their irrepressible attitude, was like a huge wave passing through a Hong Kong film industry that was then at a low tide, opening up a new terrain. People thus dubbed them 'The New Wave' of Hong Kong cinema.

Of all the Chinese communities around the globe, including mainland China, Taiwan and Singapore, Hong Kong was the first to produce its own New Wave films. Its emergence, to various degrees, stimulated the emergence of the Fifth Generation of mainland film-makers as well as Taiwan's New Cinema. It stimulated change in the film industries on both sides of the Strait. The aim of this study is to examine the causes of the emergence of the Hong Kong New Wave in the late 1970s, the New Wave's relationship with the television industry, the interaction between New Wave works and their far-reaching influence on the film industry. The content, style and aesthetic achievements of the New Wave films will be analysed, and larger questions, such as how pluralistic cultures encourage the making of films and how films respond to diverse voices in society, will also be addressed.

For the purposes of continuity and cohesion, the scope of this work is not limited to the period of the New Wave but also extends to the year 2000. Certain New Wave directors, namely, Tsui Hark, Ann Hui, Yim Ho and Kirk Wong, had been absorbed into Hong Kong mainstream cinema and still had an impact on the industry. Also, if their works are studied as a whole, from the period preceding the New Wave (that is, the works they produced while working in the television industry), the New Wave period and their subsequent works, a more comprehensive picture emerges.

The twelve New Wave directors discussed in this work are classified into two groups: core auteurs and non-core auteurs. The reason for this is that, among these New Wave talents, some, such as Lam Kuen and Ng Siu-wan, made only one or two films before leaving the film industry. Others, such as Rachel Zen, Wong Chi and Lee Pui-kuen, remained in the television industry, making no more films and exerting no influence on the general development of the New Wave. A few directors also emerged in an earlier period of the New Wave and had little in common with more significant New Wave directors. Leong Po-chih belongs in this category. There were also directors on the fringes of the New Wave, such as Johnny Mak. The discussion here will exclude the latter two groups of film-makers.

The twelve New Wave directors referred to here have been divided into core auteurs and non-core auteurs, according to the experimental spirit of their work and the extent of their impact. That is to say, the members of the first group made more experimental films than the second group. They also never stopped producing and, therefore, had relatively more influence than the second group. More importantly, throughout their works, they display a consistent vision of life. The film-makers of the latter group, in contrast, made films that were less experimental. Their influence was thus not as strong as that of the first group. Some of them even stopped making films after several productions or only made films intermittently. Also, the ideas and styles in their films are scattered and disorderly that do not amount to a coherent vision of life.

Chapter 1 of this study will explore the origins of the New Wave. Chapter 2 will consider the relationship which existed between the New Wave and the Hong Kong film and television industries. Chapters 3 to 8 will then focus on the core New Wave directors, whilst Chapters 9 to 10 will cover the non-core directors. Finally, Chapter 11 will conclude on the contribution and influence of the New Wave.

1

The Emergence of the New Wave

In 1978 a new force burst into the Hong Kong film industry like lightning on a clear day. These young directors were, on average, not over thirty years of age. A conservative estimate places their number at over thirty.[1] Born around 1950, most of them graduated from film schools in the United States or the United Kingdom and returned to Hong Kong in the mid-1970s. All at about the same time, they went to work for Hong Kong's television stations – which were dubbed 'Shaolin Temples'[2] – and underwent two to three years of training. In this way, they accumulated practical experience in making dramas and became proficient at the language of film. Then, without prior arrangement, they left the television stations and joined the film industry. Passionately committed to film, they made movies rich in feeling, with unique ideas and structures. This group of young people, like an irresistible force, stirred up a colossal wave when the film industry was at low tide and opened up new vistas. The influx of so much new blood into Hong Kong cinema was unprecedented. The media and the critics dubbed these new directors 'The New Wave' of Hong Kong cinema.

The Origin of 'The New Wave'

The term 'The New Wave' originated from the French New Wave Cinema.[3] In 1959, Truffaut and Godard, who were critics in *Cahiers du Cinéma,* made their first films, respectively: *400 Blows* and *Breathless.*[4] These two films not only injected vitality into the ossified forms of cinema, they also explored film as a subject in itself. *400 Blows,* a semi-autographical film, boldly included personal experiences and feelings. *Breathless* incorporated hand-held cinematography and the technique of 'jump-cutting' to deliberately create disharmony and depart from common motifs and conventions.[5] These two films proclaimed the birth of the French New Wave.

The first to name this group of young directors, who at the time were still working in television, as the 'New Wave' was a periodical of film and television criticism, *Da Texie*

(*Close Up*), founded by Tang Shuxuan. In the first issue, dated 1976, one article asserted that 'The three television stations are enthusiastically nurturing new directors. A new wave is rising that will force veteran directors to advance. In the long run, the new generation will sooner or later replace the current so-called big directors who only occupy a seat but produce nothing.'[6] That same year, *Ming Pao Monthly* also predicted that 'The young directors (in television) are unquestionably different from the veterans, namely King Hu, Li Hanxiang, and Song Cunshou, in terms of subject matter and style. They will make Cantonese films and there will be social overtones to their works. It is believed that in two years a "New Wave" in Hong Kong will arrive.'[7] Not surprisingly, the guess proved to be true. In 1978, Yim Ho, Dennis Yu and Ronnie Yu formed a company to make the film *The Extra*. Tsui Hark was also feverishly planning his feature *Dangerous Encounter – 1st Kind*. *Da Texie* published an article entitled 'A New Wave in Hong Kong Cinema – Revolutionists Who Challenge Traditions',[8] dubbing this group of directors who had moved from television to film as the 'New Wave' and expressing high expectations of them. These directors represented a new force and new orientation in Hong Kong cinema, and their appearance was a sign of its future vitality.

The Extra, produced in 1978, marked the beginning of the New Wave. Here, the sphere of cinema was taken as a metaphor for society. This film is about a freelance actor of bit parts from the lower class of society and his struggle for survival. Behind a light façade are tears and distress. The film is full of human feeling, rich detail and sharp images, which caused the audience to look at things with new eyes. That same year, the film won the first-runner-up award in 'the Election of Top Ten Movies'[9], which illustrates the extent to which it had won the respect of the critics. In 1979, the films *The Secret* (Ann Hui), *Butterfly Murders* (Tsui Hark), *Cops and Robbers* (Alex Cheung) and *The System* (Peter Yung) appeared one by one, creating momentum. They were warmly received by the public. In the same year, *Diyidai Shuangzhoukan* (*First Generation Biweekly*) conducted a series of interviews with these fledgling directors, and already referred to them as 'The New Wave'.

In the same year, the magazine *Xinyidai* (*A New Generation*) started a column called 'The Collective Images of New Wave Directors', which was overseen by Michael Fong and Clifton Ko. More than ten new directors, including Ann Hui, Tsui Hark, Alex Cheung, Yim Ho and Patrick Tam were interviewed. The 94th issue of the magazine contained these lines: 'We use the term "New Wave" to describe the current situation in the film industry of the emergence of a new force.... This term is generally recognized in the cultural domain. "New Wave" has become a general name to refer to this new breed of directors and their films. It has even sparked off a spate of discussions and interviews.'[10]

The term 'New Wave' was, therefore, given to this group of new film-makers by the broadcast media, whilst the films made by these directors were, quite naturally, referred to as 'New Wave films'.[11] However, the names of these young directors, who originally came from television, were already relatively well known before they began making feature films. For example, in the annual 'Appraisal of TV Programmes 1977' the results were as follows: the Best Feature Drama was *A House Is Not A Home* (TVB); the Best Anthology Series(s) were *Social Worker* (scriptwriter: Patrick Tam), *Seventeen 1977* (scriptwriter: Yim Ho), *Dazhangfu zhi 'club' nü* [Real Men: the Club Girls]* (scriptwriter: Michael Mak) and *Below the Lion Rock: The Wild Child* (scriptwriter: Allen Fong). Selina Chow Leong Suk-yi was awarded The Outstanding Television Worker. Among the winners, Patrick Tam, Yim Ho and Allen Fong would later become outstanding members of the New Wave. Also, Chow, who at the time was the head of programming for TVB, together with Wong Shek-chiu, the Chief Manager of Rediffusion TV (the former of Asia TV) and Cheung Man-yee, the head of the television unit of RTHK, contributed greatly to the development of Hong Kong's television industry.

The Road to Localization

The development of Hong Kong cinema has all along had a close and complex relationship with Mainland China. The relationship began in 1909 when the Asia Film Company in Shanghai shot *Stealing a Roast Duck* in Hong Kong. This was Hong Kong's first narrative film. The first locally produced short drama was made in 1913 by the Huamei (Chinese-American) Film Company, established by Lai Men-wei. The capital for this production came from Benjamin Brodsky, the founder of Asia Film.[12] This also makes it immediately evident that the connection between the Shanghai and Hong Kong film industries was a strong one. During the War of Resistance against Japan, and the civil war between the Communists and the Nationalists in the 1930s and 1940s, Hong Kong saw an influx of Shanghai film workers, both on- and off-screen. They worked together with local film-makers to expand Hong Kong's film industry. Most of them had the mentality of émigrés. To them, Hong Kong was only a transit station; they had no plans to reside in Hong Kong over the long term, and still set their sights northwards, towards mainland China. This attitude was depicted in Cai Chusheng's *Boundless Future* (1941). The film centres around mainland expatriates in Hong Kong of various backgrounds, who, oppressed by the capitalists, eventually return to the mainland to participate in the war against Japan.

Close Ties with the Motherland

The Great China Film Company,[13] founded by a group of film-makers from the mainland, produced films such as *Tongbing xianglian* [Compassion for Similar Misfortunes]* (1946), *Kulian* [Bitter Love]* (1946), *Changxiangsi* [The Long-lasting Love],* (1947) and *Geyou qianqiu* [Of Various Talents]* (1947),[14] with stories set in or related to the mainland. *Tongbing xianglian**, set in occupied Shanghai, is about various tenants in an apartment building, who ostensibly live in harmony, but who are in fact hostile to each other at heart. Again, set in Shanghai, the love tragedy *Kulian** tells the story of a Gong Qiuxia, a stage artist, who falls in love with a married man, Lu Yukun, and becomes pregnant. The lovers leave the city to live elsewhere. They constantly quarrel and finally divorce. Gong returns to Shanghai and works as a music teacher to raise their daughter, while Lu commits suicide. Another film, *Changxiangsi* is set in China during the war of resistance against Japan. After the husband of female protagonist Zhou Xuan joins the battle, not a single piece of news is heard of him. In a period of crisis, their friend Shu Shi looks after Zhou's family. Just as the two come to admire each other, Zhou's husband returns, having lost an arm. Sense tells them they ought to terminate their love relationship, and Shu Shi chooses to depart abruptly and silently. The next film under discussion, *Geyou qianqiu*, depicts Zhou Xuan, a female protagonist fighting for women to have equal opportunities for education. Persistent in pursuing her ideals, she opens a nursery to educate the next generation. This narrative is similar to the story of a character in another film, *Sannüxing* [Three Women] (1947). Here, one of the female characters, insisting on independence and autonomy, starts up a nursery and contributes unselfishly to society. All of these films, although shot in Hong Kong, deal with problems on the mainland, such as family ethics and the status of women.

In the 1950s, films made in Hong Kong started to portray the social problems of Hong Kong; however, the contents and spirit of these films were still interlinked with the motherland of China in the same way that the Chinese films of the 1930s and 1940s were. For example, *Renlun* [Human Ethics] and *Garden of Repose*[15] were both adapted from Ba Jin's novel *A Garden of Repose*. *Renlun*, focusing on family ethics, was a criticism of the upper class, particularly, of the feudal landlord class. The film describes a young master who leaves his family, but fails to make a living, and finally lands in prison. Likewise, *Garden of Repose* is a story about the younger generation rebelling against a large feudal family. *A Mother's Tears* (1953),[16] on the other hand, extols the value of mothers. This film is about a mother who endures all kinds of hardships to bring up three children. However, her dedication is not repaid. Her eldest son commits a crime and is sentenced to death, and her second child, a daughter, is killed in an accident. It is only the youngest, also a son, who can take care of her until her death.

Two other similar movies are *Parents' Hearts* and *Father and Son* (1954).[17] The former describes the relationship between two generations. The father works as a street singer to earn money for his son's education. However, his expectations for his son are not fulfilled, as the child 'awakens' to live a different life – he quits school and starts to work. The latter film portrays a father who sends his son to an exclusive school in the hope that he will become spectacularly successful. However, the child is subjected to a great deal of ridicule at school. The movie satirizes the idea of pushing the next generation hard in order to achieve excellence. These films show that the spirit of the realist movies of the 1950s can be traced back to the Chinese movies of two to three decades earlier, which focused on similar traditions of family ethics, and the unconditional sacrifices made by the older generation for the younger generation. The realist stories of the fifties have themes such as anti-feudalism and anti-capitalism, which are also closely linked with the leftist philosophies of the 1920s and 1930s, as well as with the establishment of the People's Republic of China.

First Step in Localization: Strongly Westernized Content

The 1960s was a time when the generation born immediately after the war reached adulthood. In Hong Kong, this young generation had a weak sense of nationhood and held neither long-term goals nor ambitions. They received a western education in the colony, and the society at the time was suffused with western popular culture. This was reflected in a handful of youth-oriented films, such as *Romance of a Teenage Girl* (1966), *I Love A-Go-Go* (1967), *Joys and Sorrows of Youth* (1969), *Social Characters* (1969) and *The Teddy Girls* (1969).[18] These films, which depicted social issues, especially the problems that young people were facing, were the first step in the localization of Hong Kong cinema. Woo Feng, the male protagonist in *Romance of a Teenage Girl*, was a youth who initially had ambition, but who gives up after a series of setbacks and becomes involved in drug trafficking and anti-social behaviour. With the encouragement of his girlfriend, Josephine Siao Fong-fong, he repents. In *I Love A-Go-Go*, Josephine Siao's adoptive father is a poor man, while her biological father is an immensely wealthy man. Her biological father wants to retain the right to raise Siao. This nearly kills Siao's poor adoptive mother, who has endured hardship for more than half her life to bring the daughter up. Siao eventually remembers the grace and virtue of her adoptive parents and decides to stay with them. The theme of this film is similar to that of a Mandarin movie, *Mambo Girl*.[19] In the latter, the female protagonist, Ge Lan, searches everywhere for her biological mother, but in vain. Finally, she returns to her adoptive parents. The message is that biological parents – one's own origins – are no longer very important, the implication being that ties to the motherland have been cut.[20]

In the *Joys and Sorrows of Youth*, everyone is tempted by money, to the point where humanity becomes distorted. Cheung Ching is the typical prodigal son. His father, who works as a jazz player, declares bankruptcy. The son becomes a delinquent and the daughter, Tina, is raped. She later becomes a call girl. Many other characters in the movie are triad members and extremely decadent.. Another film, *Social Characters*, likewise portrays a group of seven young boys and girls who live a wild life. They spend their days dancing and taking hallucinogenic drugs, the symbols of a decadent western youth culture. Lacking family warmth, and under the influence of a bad social climate, the female protagonist of *The Teddy Girls* becomes a delinquent. She is eventually sent to the youth rehabilitation centre. The film discusses the seriousness of juvenile delinquency and is strongly didactic. The 1960s was a period of rebellion and challenges to authority. It was also an era in which numerous protests and demonstrations swept from America to France to China and to Czechoslovakia in Eastern Europe challenging the bourgeois capitalist order.[21] Hong Kong was under a highly repressive colonial regime at the time. Although the economy was growing, the distribution of wealth was uneven and there were massive contradictions within society. Youth felt that they had no way out. Under such circumstances, the society was in crisis and on the point of exploding. The result was the 1967 leftist riots, where leftist and rightist political forces confronted each other. Hong Kong can be said to have pursued progress in the midst of serious contradictions at that time. What were reflected in the films mentioned above were gaps and conflicts between generations, the rebellion of youth and willful decadence. The influence of western popular culture on young people was so great that they lost their sense of self and their confidence in their native culture. This was one reason why the youth films of the 1960s failed to genuinely localize. Those who had been born and raised in Hong Kong were, culturally and politically, growing increasingly distant from China. Unlike their father's generation, there was no intersection with the nation. Even as the older generation gradually withdrew from the stage of history, the younger generation no longer had native memories of China and little national consciousness. In addition, as the economy prospered, and as Hong Kong became increasingly urban and international, a local consciousness naturally developed simultaneously.[22] That is to say, while a local consciousness emerged in the 1960s, it was not until the 1970s, when television entirely adopted Cantonese as the medium of communication (in Chinese channels), and when the programmes were localized and the New Wave emerged, that the task of the localization of cinema was completed.

The New Wave Completes the Work of Localization

In the early 1970s, Hong Kong's television stations had entered an era of locally produced programmes (for details refer to Chapter 2). Here, a programme worth highlighting is TVB's *Hui Brothers' Show* (1971), written and directed by Selina Leong Suk-yi. A mixture of comedy and popular music, the programme was inspired by a foreign television programme, *Laugh In*. However, because of cultural and linguistic differences, only the concept and form of the original were replicated, while the contents were totally localized. For example, a Cantonese song, "Tieta lingyun" [Eiffel in the Clouds], written by Sam Hui, was presented in the show, and, in fact, it was this song that sparked off the craze for Canto-pop.[23] The *Hui Brothers' Show* was hugely popular among young people and families. It was also an index of the localization of Hong Kong television programmes in the early 1970s in that it was an adaptation made by the TV producers in response to social changes. At the same time, localization was based on the practical needs of social development. Later, the appearance of the situation drama *Seventy-Three* (1973), which satirized social problems and current affairs, showed that the process of localization had sprinted ahead. In this regard, TVB definitely took the leading role.

Nearly the entire collection of TV programmes produced by the New Wave members during their television careers involved realistic topics. The few exceptions were Tsui Hark's martial arts costume drama, *Golden Blade Sentimental Swordsman*, Clifford Choi's *Wong Fei-hong* and *The Water Margin No. 6* and Terry Tong's *Bastard Swordsman* and *The Silver Sword Killer*. Those apart, the others were, without doubt, works about local experiences. For example, Allen Fong's *The Wild Child* is a work rich with autobiographical elements. *The Story of Yuen Chau Chai* tells a sad story about the Yuen Chau Chai in the Taipo area of Hong Kong, who are being forced to move out. Yim Ho's *Seventeen: 1979* and *Art Life* describe the struggles of a group of young intellectuals, who are facing ups and downs in their journey through life. Alex

Cheung's *Taxi Driver: The Trio* is a tale about the male protagonist's persistence in pursuing his dreams despite experiencing setbacks in life. Certain social issues are addressed in Ann Hui's *The Bridge*, which is a story of how the residents of Ma Chai Hang fought for their rights in a bureaucratic system. In addition, all of Hui's ICAC drama episodes are about the issue of corruption in the Hong Kong police as well as among Hong Kong residents. *Seventeen: Summer Break*, directed by Dennis Yu, explores the differences between various classes in society, and the spirit of ambition in women factory workers. Patrick Tam's *Seven Women* portrays a group of middle-class women in Hong Kong, focusing on the anxieties and distress that they encounter in their journey through life and on their self-confidence. These works explore people of all classes and various events that occurred in Hong Kong society at the time. Most importantly, they displayed a kind of self-confidence, which would also characterize the upcoming movies directed by the New Wave; for example, *Father and Son*. This film is about the personal experiences of the director, but it is also part of the collective memory of Hong Kongers in the 1950s and 1960s. *The Secret*, on the other hand, describes a mysterious murder that occurred in the Western District of Hong Kong Island. The film shows strong local characteristics. Equally, *The Spooky Bunch* brings forth the colourful superstitions and folklore of the outlying islands. In *Collis Killer*, the dilapidated house is reflective of the killer's fortunes later in life and is his sole refuge, where he can regain his confidence. *Nomad* shows the mixture of Chinese and foreign (Japanese), poor and rich, and the causal attitude of young people towards sex and love. It is a realistic portrayal of the modern metropolis that is Hong Kong. Thus, as early as during their careers in television, New Wave directors were creating works about local experiences. When they entered the film industry, they were to even more directly bring about the localization of Hong Kong cinema.

Reformists Not Revolutionists

This group of young scriptwriters-directors, coincidentally yet concomitantly, shifted from television to film within only a few years. This phenomenon did not by any means spring out of a vacuum. First, these directors had already made films (16mm) during their television days. Second, there was a shortage of talent in the film industry, and there was an enormous demand for new blood. Third, there was a demand, especially in Southeast Asia, for films. This was evident from the rise of independent film-making. Fourth, changes had occurred in the television industry. When Commercial Television closed down, certain young scriptwriters-directors were absorbed by rival stations, for instance, Terry Tong went to Rediffusion Television; while some others, such as Tsui Hark and Ann Hui, had earlier been hired away by independent film companies. Here the phrase coincidentally yet concomitantly is used because these young film talents did not have a common plan, a common creed or make declarations to draw up consensus among themselves. What occurred happened by chance. Put simply, they did not have an organization or a unified stance. They migrated to the film industry without any revolutionary intentions, and with no plans to subvert traditions or to achieve a clean break from conventional Hong Kong movies. Even though the periodical *Da Texie* had published an article entitled 'New Wave in Hong Kong

Cinema – Revolutionists Who Challenge Traditions', which was full of fiery vigour, the article was based on little more than the fact that Yim Ho, Dennis Yu and Ronnie Yu had established the New Force Company and were in the midst of producing the film *The Extra*. Of course, other directors such as Patrick Tam, Tsui Hark, Alex Cheung and Ann Hui were in the middle of preparing their first features. That article argued that, due to this influx of new talent, Hong Kong cinema would become even more vibrant, and that the new people were expected to bring certain changes and a new look to the industry. The emergence of this new force would be significant in the following ways: First, they were young and their youth signified energy, the courage to try new things and creativity. Second, most of them had returned from overseas with professional training. They took film seriously, regarding them as a vehicle for the personal expression of thoughts and emotions; that is, as creations rather than as products. Third, their television programmes involved sentiments rare in commercial films.[24] And, indeed, new scenes and ideas appeared, just as the writer of the above article foresaw: Appearing after *The Extra*, *Cops and Robbers* uses sharp images and illustrates the meaning of destiny. The murder in *The Secret* (1979) was narrated from various points of view, creating heart-stopping suspense. *The Butterfly Murders* (1979) uses scientific explanations to subvert mystical manifestations and shows a great deal of creativity. *The System* (1979) adopted a documentary style to capture police efforts to clear up the drug trade, and to comment on a bureaucratic system that made the efforts fruitless. *House of the Lute* (1979/1980) used symbolism to depict the terrifying aspects of changes of class. In these films, the courage to create and the spirit to experiment can be discerned. Furthermore, the films are full of quick wit and overflowing with feeling, and the personalities of the creators come through strongly. In their first features these New Wave directors 'completely abandoned "traditional" techniques. From subject matter, narrative method, and rhythm to method of acting, all deviated from customary styles. Most importantly, the films of the four key directors [Tam, Tsui, Cheung, and Hui] do not "just tell a story". Instead, they have a strong personal style and provide the audience with a totally new experience, an assault that takes a long time to subside.'[25] There are critics who discuss the Hong Kong New Wave in parallel with the French New Wave. 'On the artistic level, they may not comparable with the French New Wave of the late 1950s. However, in terms of the number of new directors, they did not lag behind the two years of French efforts.'[26] In fact, given that Hong Kong is a small place, in terms of the number of directors and films, the New Wave in Hong Kong was by no means inferior to, or was even definitely superior to, the French New Wave. In addition, 'The French New Wave was actually a product of an industrial system, just like the Hong Kong New Wave. The two were not different in nature. They were merely different with regard to the time of their emergence and the magnitude of their impact.'[27] Therefore, there is certainly no need to belittle ourselves.

A Debate over the 'Rupture' of the New Wave

The emergence of the New Wave shook the Hong Kong film world, and also led to controversies. The earliest was raised by Leung Nong-kong in a special issue of the

Hong Kong International Film Festival in 1979, 'Is the New Wave able to create a "rupture", to a certain degree, from Hong Kong cinema's past, or to open up new prospects? Is it possible for it to query the form of self expression in film, and to explore the relationship between ideology and activities that communicate meanings?'[28] A few critics suggested that the Hong Kong cinema of today was not about to undergo a fundamental break from that of the past. Nor would a new wave appear in the international sea. To expect such a phenomenon would be to ignore or deny the history of the development of Hong Kong cinema and the nature of the formation of the industry. Other critics even argued that the breakthrough made by this group of new directors was solely achieved during their period in television and was not successfully transferred to film. Hence, they claimed that the New Wave was found in television rather than in cinema.[29] In the same issue, other views were also expressed to the effect that the 'new directors' have gradually become our cultural prophets and that their works are attractive to a new generation of intellectuals. They are the subject of discussion in local cultural magazines and have also received attention at international film festivals. As early as during their days in television, their works unquestionably represented a sort of new creative sensibility; that is, social consciousness along with the experimental use of techniques employed in western films.[30] Of course, it is good to pose demands on the New Wave directors, but the demands should not be too idealistic, or they will be unrealistic and impractical. As I have previously argued, the New Wave directors never had the intention to overthrow or to make a clean break from traditions in Hong Kong cinema. Furthermore, they had no formal organization or common objective. Therefore, the claim that they represent a break from tradition or from the past is open to question. Film or art are human cultural activities and also a concrete manifestation of the deep-seated structure of human psychology. Cultural activities themselves, then, are the accumulation of human experiences, and the act of accumulation itself is a form of history. It is essential to understand that unless history utterly perishes, it cannot be absolutely discontinued. Film has a history of over a century and has many excellent traditions. The New Wave film-makers have gradually developed and progressed on the basis of the achievements and experiences of the previous generation. If such a foundation were absent, it would be unrealistic and unproductive to talk about the accumulation of knowledge, development and advancement. We must confront the historical facts of the Hong Kong film industry in order to acknowledge its continuity and to respect its trajectory if there is to be further evolution. A more important problem is that Hong Kong movies cannot survive by relying on the local market alone. Satisfactory local box office receives can usually barely cover the costs and it is necessary to rely on overseas markets, including those of Taiwan, Southeast Asia, Europe, North America and Korea. This explains why the 'market' is the primary consideration in Hong Kong cinema. This is a fact, and this is the reason why, in Hong Kong productions, a relative emphasis tends to be placed on the language of images, the level of entertainment and the international character of a movie. Thus, those critics who understand the nature of Hong Kong films have shown more tolerance of the New Wave. 'That Hong Kong cinema can still achieve so much when government support is inadequate, is no easy task.'[31] This is a fair comment.

To Express Oneself Via a Camera: A Wide Vision

Actually New Wave directors, as with most other directors, hope to be welcomed by a broad audience. In an interview, Tsui Hark makes this point clear, 'In the beginning of the New Wave period, there were some who chose to pursue unpopular topics. However, I have always wanted to be a commercial director.'[32] Kwan Wai-pang, a producer, wants to make films that are both entertaining and full of substance.[33] Yim Ho wants to focus her efforts on the popular in order to obtain balance between entertainment and art. Entertainment is the foundation of film, just as survival is fundamental to life. Only when one can survive can one talk about better and more meaningful ways to survive. That is to say, entertainment is the foundation of the existence of film; it is also the essence of the Hong Kong film industry.[34] Thus, no New Wave director can afford to give no weight to this element. This also echoes the practical attitude of such directors, who avoid grand discourses and aloofness. Yet being practical does not mean being unoriginal or unprogressive. On the contrary, these directors have similar backgrounds and experiences, are enthusiastic about film and art and are capable of mastering visual language. Moreover, their films are the expression of their vision of life and of real society. This corresponds to the idea of 'la camera-stylo' (the camera-pen) advocated by the French New Wave: an auteur (author) uses the camera to write,[35] to express his/her thoughts. 'Even if they are only reformists rather than revolutionists, their works, at least, offer a newness that can cause people to be full of hope.'[36] The Hong Kong New Wave, moving from the television industry, charged at a film industry that was just then at a low ebb, introducing new blood, new technology, new ways of narration and new concepts. All of these strengthened the industry and even raised its standards.

Whether in the television or in the film industry, the New Wave film-makers all quietly experimented and bravely opened up new vistas. They showed unprecedented courage and sincerity in their works with regard to subject matter, form of expression and content. Thus, they considerably enlarged the space for Hong Kong cinema and culture. Later, new directors exhibited their talent to the world. First, let us consider diverse characteristics of the New Wave productions. 1. An acute sensitivity responsiveness towards current problems in society: *The Story of Yuen Chau Chai, The Bridge*, the *Social Worker* series, *Dangerous Encounter – 1st Kind* and *Teenage Dreamers*. 2. Local scenes: the *Seventeen* series, the *Taxi Driver* series, *The Happening, The Wild Child, The Secret, The Spooky Bunch, Collies Killer, The Imp* and others. 3. Individual experience and collective memory: *The Wild Child, Father and Son, Ah Ying, Starry is The Night, Ordinary Heroes, Song of the Exile* and others. 4. The writings of women: *Seven Women No. 2, 7,* and 6; *ICAC: Three Women, Song of the Exile, Summer Snow* and others. 5. Concern for the nation, nationality and Chinese émigrés: *The Boy from Vietnam, The Story of Woo Viet, The Boat People, Homecoming, A Better Tomorrow III*, the *Once Upon a Time in China* series, *The Romance of Book and Sword, Prince Fragrance* and others. 6. The reconstruction of classical legends and the application of technology from a new perspective: *Green Snake, The Lovers*, the series *A Chinese Ghost Story, Zu – Warriors from the Magic Mountain, Evil Cat* and others. 7.

Explorations of the language of images and forms of narration: the *Seven Women* series, *CID: Four Moments of Life*, *Love Massacre*, *The Secret*, *Eighteen Springs*, *Ah Ying*, *Just Like Weather* and others. The above works also demonstrate the broadness of the directors' minds and visions. They were not revolutionists, but they were unquestionably reformists and innovators.

The Film Market and the Cinematic Cultural Environment during the Emergence of the New Wave

The Film Market and the New Wave

Hong Kong films attracted overseas attention, particularly in Southeast Asia and Taiwan, and later in Western Europe, from the 1950s onwards. As early as the 1950s and 1960s, the practice of 'selling unfinished movies' (?????) had already emerged, which enabled independent film-making companies to fulfill the demand from overseas markets, chief among them Singapore and Malaysia. Usually revenue from this source was about one-third of the cost of production, making it a key source of capital for Hong Kong films. In the 1970s, Bruce Lee's films were the key to opening up a larger overseas market, which continued to expand with the popularity of martial arts films. Revenue from overseas markets thereupon increased from one-third to two-thirds or even three-fourths of the cost of production.[37] After the mid-1970s, major studios such as the Shaw Studios began to decline and the number of productions dropped drastically. This allowed a host of independent companies to emerge, and to fill the gap in the market. These changes also facilitated the genesis of the New Wave. As for Taiwan, since the 1950s, the film market had been dominated by Hong Kong movies. In 1963, when *The Love Eterne*, a Shaw Brothers movie, was released in Taiwan, sales to Taiwan surged.[38] The only films that could contend with such a fad were the adaptations of Qiongyao's novels in the 1970s and the New Cinema of the next decade. Certain developments had a bearing on the dominance of Hong Kong films in Taiwan. Because of the anti-Communist policies of the Taiwan government at that time, Hong Kong movies were classified as 'national movies', thereby exempting them from the quotas imposed on imported foreign films. In addition, Hong Kong movies were allowed to participate in Taiwan's Golden Horse Awards for film.

Market-related factors also accelerated the rise of independent production companies. The independent companies spotted the marvelous work being turned out by the various members of the New Wave while the latter were working in television stations. The companies then called them up and made them offers. Thus, from 1978, these young film-makers became the darlings of the independent producers. For years, these television scriptwriters-directors had been overlooked by the film industry. Now they were being invited to invigorate the lifeless industry.[39] Thus, during a period of recession in the film industry, but with great demand from the market, the independent producers accepted these young directors into the film industry.

The New Wave films did indeed gain the attention as well as the approval of the public. Asked to select the top ten Hong Kong Films of the 1980s, local critics Kam Ping-hing, Law Kar, Wong Kowk-siu, Lau Shing-hon, Cheung Kam-mun, Lee Cheuk-to, Wong Oi-ling and Lit-fu chose the following: 1. *Homecoming*; 2. *Long Arm of the Law*; 3. *Dangerous Encounter – 1st Kind*; 4. *The Boat People*; 5. *Ah Ying*; 6. *Father and Son*; 7. *A Better Tomorrow*; 8. *Rouge*; 9. *Gangs*; 10. *The Club* and *Police Story*.[40] If *Long Arm of the Law* is also included in the list of New Wave productions, their work occupied the top six places. *The Club*, one of the top ten films, was also a New Wave film. Seventh-ranked *A Better Tomorrow* and eighth-ranked *Rouge* were closely connected with the New Wave. Tsui Hark was the producer of the former, while the latter was directed by Stanley Kwan, who had been strongly influenced by the New Wave works. As for directors, the top ten were: 1. Tsui Hark; 2. Ann Hui; 3. Allen Fong; 4. Ringo Lam; 5. Yim Ho; 6. John Woo; 7. Stanley Kwan; 8. Sammo Hung; 9. Michael Mak; 10. Peter Yung and Jackie Chan. Of the top five, four were New Wave directors. This testifies to the achievements and impact of the New Wave on Hong Kong cinema in the 1980s.

Film Culture and the Educational Environment

It was not until the 1960s that cinematic cultural activities began to be held in Hong Kong. Hong Kong City Hall was founded in 1962. A group of westerners initially organized *Diyi yingshi* [The First Screening Room]* and the Hong Kong Film Association to show European films that were relatively more artistic than mainstream films. These included French New Wave productions. They also promoted these films. The active members of this association were foreign professionals who showed very little interest in local films. In addition, the publications of the association were in English. On the whole, therefore, the mood was one of colonial selectiveness.[41] However, the promotion of European classic films was very much favoured by young students and intellectuals at the time. In 1966, they established *Daxue shenghuo dianyinghui* [University Life Film Society], which regularly ran film screenings and held writing and experimental film-making activities. The society also organized regular screenings, seminars and publications, supported by the *Zhongguo xuesheng zhoubao* [The Chinese Students Weekly] (the editors-in-chief were Law Kar and Luk Lei) and *Daxue shenghuo yuekan* [University Life Monthly]. In addition, quite a number of young people wrote film criticism for the film page of *Xuesheng zhoubao* [Students Weekly]. Those of them who later came to be affiliated with the New Wave were Kam Ping-hing, Ng Ho, Patrick Tam, Shu Kei, Wong Chi and others. At the time, the leftist *Qingnian leyuan* [Youth Playground] and the liberal *Xianggang qingnian zhoubao* [Hong Kong Youth Weekly] also published articles on film criticism.

In the 1960s the magazine *Theatre* was published in Taiwan. Qiu Gangjian, who was closely linked to the New Wave, was one of the founders, and Law Kar was the editor. The ninth issue of this periodical was a special issue that enthusiastically advocated the French New Wave. The publication also organized the first experimental film festival in Taiwan, sparing no effort to promote film culture. In 1972, *Influence*, the first formal film periodical on the island, began publication. I happened to be studying in Taiwan at the time, learning how to shoot films under the director Li Xing. Nevertheless, I was still able to take part in the work of establishing the journal, and this helped to strengthen the ties between the film cultures of Taiwan and Hong Kong. The Hong Kong New Wave's Patrick Tam, and those who had close ties with the community, such as Leung Nong-gong, Ng Ho, Law Wai-ming and others, were members of the editing committee of the journal, as well as contributing writers. Lau Shing-hon also quite often submitted writings to the periodical. That particular issue also had a considerable impact on quite a number of the early 1980s auteurs of Taiwan New Cinema, such as Zhang Yi and Wan Ren.

In the early 1970s, a fair number of publications discussing and critiquing culture, society and politics were published in Hong Kong; for example, *Haowei* [An Extra], *Xin sichao* [New Wave of Thoughts], *Qishi niandai shuangzhoukan* [The 1970s Biweekly] and others. In 1976, the film periodical *Da Texie* was founded in Hong Kong by director Tang Shuxuan, to function as a platform for film lovers. The periodical paid particular attention to the New Wave scriptwriters-directors in the television industry. It also set aside a considerable amount of space for reporting and critiquing their works. This publication can be said to have played a crucial role in the early formation of the New Wave during the television era, and in the consolidation of their forces. In 1979, *City Entertainment* succeeded *Da Texie* right after the latter ceased publication. *City Entertainment* took over the role of critiquing, interviewing and monitoring those of the New Wave who were in television and those who had moved to film. It became a friend of the New Wave, occupying an extraordinarily significant position. The editors-writers of these two magazines, such as Cheung Kam-mun, Shu Kei, Law Wai-ming and others, later worked for most of the New Wave members as scriptwriters, while Lee Kwok-chong took up major acting roles in *Seventeen: Art Life*, *Seventeen: 1977* and *The Boy From Vietnam*. Following the closure of *Daxuesheng dianyinghui* [The Film Society of University Students]*, the *Huoniao dianyinghui* [Burning Bird Film Society]* was established in 1974 to carry on the activities of its forerunner, such as screenings, seminars and publications. The Safeguarding Films Society, *Weiyinghui*,* founded in 1972, organized an experimental film festival. Later, with the sponsorship of the Urban Council, it held three exhibitions of experimental short film. In 1976, *Weiyinghui* held a ten-year retrospective of experimental films, in which upcoming New Wave members, including Ann Hui, Patrick Tam, Alex Cheung, Lau Shing-hon and Terry Tong, participated. Some others, such as John Woo, Cheung Shuk-ping, Fong Ling-ching and Chan Lok-yee, who had ties to the New Wave also had their films shown. In the 1960s and 70s, under the influence of American underground films as well as the French New Wave Movement, quite a number of young people in Hong Kong took up their cameras and produced short films of their own. After the mid-1960s, several young critics and film fans, including Shek Kei, Law Kar, John Woo, Kam Ping-hing, Patrick Tam, Ringo Lam, Ng Shing-foon and Xixi, made short feature films, expressing their feelings and thoughts about society, life and film.

In 1978, Hong Kong Film Culture Centre was established at the initiative of the New Wave participants Clifford Choi, Law Kar and others. It not only promoted Hong Kong films and Chinese films, but also ran a two-year certificate programme on film, in particular, Super 8mm film-making. In addition, there was a small library in which film screenings and seminars were held. In short, the Centre nurtured film talent in a non-academic environment.

At the time, no local post-secondary school institution offered a formal programme on film. This caused many young people in the 1960s and 70s to go overseas to study film. This also explains why most members of the New Wave studied film in America or England in the 1970s. In Hong Kong, it was not until the late 1970s and early 1980s that a film programme began to be offered, by the Department of Communication of Hong Kong Baptist College (now Hong Kong Baptist University). The programme, however, was not comprehensive, as it was merely being run by a committee under the Department. Only in 1991, when the Department was expanded to a School, was the first Department of Cinema and Television among all tertiary institutions in Hong Kong formally established. The aim was to train professionals in this field in order to respond to the demands of Hong Kong's media, which had developed extremely rapidly in recent years. In the mid-1990s, the Hong Kong Academy for Performing Arts opened its School of Film and TV; and in 1998, the City University of Hong Kong founded the School of Creative Media. This largely completed the plan to cultivate talent for film, TV and media that had been carried out in phases.

New Wave Enters the Mainstream and the Rise of Cinema City

In the 1970s, Hong Kong's economy expanded rapidly, leading to the formation of an extensive middle class. This class gradually grew and society became more diverse. The New Wave TV programmes reflected such phenomena, as well as increasing political-ideological confrontations between the leftist and the rightist in the 1960s, the social criticisms of intellectuals of such matters as the colonial system and consumerism. Patrick Tam's *Seven Women No. 2* and Yim Ho's *Seventeen: Art Life* and *1979* are examples of this. In contrast, the film industry became increasingly conservative and divorced from real life. Films were not reflecting the practical needs of society. Therefore, the industry began to decline. The rise of independent film-making was advantageous for the emergence of the New Wave. With respect to the political climate, after the arrest of the Gang of Four in mainland China, the pragmatist Deng Xiaoping came to power in 1979. Deng announced that China was entering a period of 'reform and openness'. The mood in Hong Kong turned positive. The New Wave was born in the year prior to this critical moment. *Jumping Ash*, a film made earlier (1976),[42] was filmed using relatively modern techniques, but was in spirit very far from the New Wave. Therefore, it can only be regarded as a warm-up production that came before the movement - a prologue and nothing more. Formally speaking, it does not qualify as a New Wave film.

Emerging in 1978 and subsiding in 1984, the New Wave can be roughly divided into four phases: First, the start of the New Wave: In 1978, *The Extra*, a work by the TV scriptwriter-director Yim Ho, marked its launch. In 1979, Ann Hui's *The Secret*, Tsui

Hark's *The Butterfly Murder*, Alex Cheung's *Cops and Robbers* and Peter Yung's *The System* burst onto the scene and provoked a reaction. The arrival of the New Wave was thus confirmed. Second, the period of full blossom: From 1980 to 1982. Over thirty New Wave films were made during this period, including *The Sword, Encore, Father and Son, House of the Lute, Dangerous Encounter – 1st Kind, The Happening, The Spooky Bunch* and others. During this time, the New Wave became the focus of the film industry. Third, the later stage: Between 1983 and 1984 the films *Ah Ying, Health Warning, Twinkle Twinkle Little Star, Hong Kong Hong Kong, Zu, Shanghai Blues, Love in A Fallen City, Homecoming* and others appeared. They were undoubtedly still highly creative, although perhaps somewhat less acute and vigorous than preceding New Wave films. This is not to say that the New Wave had already disappeared. Rather, it was gradually entering the mainstream and being absorbed by it. The members of the New Wave kept on creating, but in a different way. Since the beginning of 1985, they had already become part of mainstream cinema, which, in point of fact, was what they had desired. Ann Hui's latter works, such as *Eighteen Springs, Ordinary Heroes* and *As Time Goes By*, all showed her experimental spirit by exploring modes of narration and the subject of film itself, rethinking Hong Kong social and political issues of the 1960s and 70s, and representing personal experiences. Yim Ho's *Kitchen* was a return to the local, revealing intricate relationships between the individual, reality and the metaphysical. *Red Dust* was about the conflicts between a private romance and the fate of a nation, between individual desires and the national will. Furthermore, Tsui Hark and Kirk Wong worked on modernizing and innovating traditional ideas. These qualities of the New Wave proved that the spirit of the movement still prevailed. The principal reason why the New Wave subsided was the birth of Cinema City's comedies, which took over the principal market.

Founded in 1979, Cinema City was originally called the Fendou Film Company.* The company was founded by Karl Maka, Shek Tin and Wong Pak-ming. In 1980, with support from the Golden Princess film distribution company owned by Lui Kwok-kwan, the chief executive officer of the Kowloon Motor Bus Corporation, Fendou Film Company was renamed Cinema City Enterprises Ltd. Comedies were its hallmark. At the initial stage, so-called 'hoodlum comedies'(??????) such as *Crazy Crooks* (1980), *Laughing Times* (1980) and *By Hook Or By Crook* (1980) were made. The hoodlums refer to certain poor and shabby members of the lower class. These films were low-budget productions that did not make uses of big stars. They portrayed the hard times of the 1960s, when, to survive, the characters would even take advantage of friends. Unexpectedly, these films were well received and generated satisfactory returns at the box office. However, after a short while, the audience became bored with these poor fellows, and led to the decline of this genre. Cinema City then switched over completely to action comedy. The characters were now handsome men and beautiful women. The costumes were dazzling. Big stars, such as Sam Hui and Alan Tam, were invited to star in these productions. These modern comedies adopted the approach of easy watching, allowing no extreme views, no vulgarities and no dirty jokes.[43] They included *Chasing Girls* (1981), *All The Wrong Clues* (1981), *Aces Go Places* (1982), *Aces Go Places II* (1983), *Aces Go Places III* (1984), *Aces Go Places IV* (1984), *Aces Go*

Places V: The Terracotta Hit (1989) and others. These modern urban comedies each took in box office revenues ranging from 10 million to 30 million Hong Kong dollars,[44] which was a record, making them the most successful commercial movies made in Hong Kong. The victory of Cinema City reiterated the fact that the space for the survival of other types of movies, including New Wave movies, was shrinking.

The reason for the commercial triumph of Cinema City was that it focused on developing to the full the concept of the commodification of films. It paid attention to strategies for the packaging and distribution of its products and poured massive amounts of money on promotion. For example, such a torrent of money was spent on promoting *All The Wrong Clues* that those in the industry referred to the move as 'a suicide action'.[45] The standard promotion budget was in the range of 2 to 5 hundred thousand Hong Kong dollars, approximately one-tenth of the cost of the whole production. Cinema City broke this convention with the motto 'rather burnish the name than earn a dollar'. Taking an overtly aggressive approach,[46] it invested nearly 1 million Hong Kong dollars – almost equivalent to the production cost of an entire film. Moreover, they practiced a monopoly-like approach of controlling the production, promotion, distribution and release of a film. This led to a situation in which films other than those of Cinema City could hardly get a showing in its theatres. Those that did manage to appear on screen were given the worst periods for release. These practices completely violated the principle of fair competition. The space for independent productions to survive, including those of the New Wave, was thus squeezed. On top of this, Cinema City invented commercial formulas based on a precise calculation of the potential effects of a film; that is, formulas for writing scripts. One film would be divided into nine parts, each consisting of ten minutes. The creators would then calculate the time that should be taken up by each scene. Then, they would determine the appropriate proportion of three elements: special effects, gags, and action, to be included. After this was done, the plot would then be created. In this way, all of these elements could be guaranteed to appear in each scene. The first, fourth, seventh and ninth parts would respectively be designed as the beginning, the middle and the end, covering the 'rise-hold-twist-close' (*qi-cheng-zhuan-he*) [the various stages of a complete drama] process.[47] The fact that the elements of action, gags and special effects were to be found in every part would, it was expected, attract the audience. This kind of scientific calculation could certainly prove to be effective in the short run; at the very least it would offer a sense of freshness. However, film is, after all, not an absolute product. Rather, it is a form of art. It primarily communicates with the audience at an emotional level. A scientific calculation reduces a film to a formula or to an ossified form, lacking in creativity and personal style. Consequently, after *Aces Go Places IV* (1986), Cinema City began to appear exhausted and dried up. This process of withering was witnessed in the protagonist of the *Aces Go Places* series. In *Aces Go Places III*, the main character, 'Bald Inspector', a brave and confident man, finds the lost jewel in the crown of the monarch of the United Kingdom. This shows the British Government's reliance on Hong Kong and its people's tolerance of colonial rule. But in *Aces Go Places IV* (1986), Bald Inspector's wife and son are kidnapped.

When he tries to save them, he is nearly killed. This shows that the Inspector was not as valiant as before. In *Aces Go Places V: The Terracotta Hit* (1989), the Inspector loses his job and gets divorced. He is also engaged in a hostile relationship with his counterpart, Sam Hui, and then is arrested by the Chinese police, together with his new partners, Leslie Cheung and Nina Li. His treasure can only be regained if he collaborates with the Beijing government. As the narrative hints, Cinema City was running out of vitality, a vitality could not, as it turned out, be restored. No wonder that the film was identified as 'a work of death' for Cinema City in the 1980s.[48]

Of course, in some sense, the rise and fall of Cinema City was connected to the future of Hong Kong. Negotiations between China and Britain over issues concerning Hong Kong began in 1982 in a political climate full of ambiguity and uncertainty. People were anxious about their future, and many decided to emigrate. Cinema City, grasping this particular moment, produced fantasy comedies that exactly resonated with the escapist mood of the Hong Kong people. This was a reason for the tremendous popularity of these films. After the two governments of China and Britain signed the Joint Declaration in 1984, Hong Kong people realized that they had no say over their future. Their loss of self-confidence was reflected in films showing that the protagonists were unable to control their fate and therefore were forced to cooperate with Beijing. This was perhaps an allegory of the partnership between China and Hong Kong.

Cinema City's comedies were dominant soon after they first appeared and made fat profits. Thus, the company over-expanded, recruiting a large number of directors, including New Wave directors. More than ten directors joined forces with the company all at once. They worked either in a collaboration, such as Tsui Hark (*Working Class*), or in a satellite alliance, like Dennis Yu and Yuen Woo-ping (*Life Line Express, Cupid One** and *Musical Singers*, etc.). The box office reception of these films was only average; some others, for example, *Life After Life* and *Once Upon a Rainbow*, even flopped. 1984 could be said to be the heyday of Cinema City, when comedies such as *Happy Ghost, Kung Hei Fat Choy* and *Merry Christmas* were produced. It was precisely because of the dominance of Cinema City that the New Wave migrated to the mainstream cinema at an accelerated pace.

Based on the above factors, the causes for the decline of the New Wave can be summarized as follows. First, Cinema City chiefly relied on comedies and similar films, which echoed the Hong Kong people's frustrations and anxieties about the future, and were able to take audiences away from the New Wave films. The company's recruitment of some New Wave talent also dimmed the overall brilliance of the group. Second, the lack of mass support for New Wave works was partly caused by the strong personal style to be found in such films, and this was inherently incompatible with the emphasis on commercial, mass entertainment which prevailed in Hong Kong. It was understandable, therefore, that over the short term the New Wave would not find it easy to achieve recognition from a mass audience, as was evident by the generally low box office returns for their films, with some exceptions such as Ann Hui's *The Boat People*. Third, the inclination of the New Wave to move towards mainstream cinema also led to a dilution of the films. Finally, the growing power of producers during the 1980s meant that greater institutional control began to be exercised over personal creativity, and this caused the films produced to lose the individual style of the director, as well as the creativity and vigour of a work of art. Under the constraints of such a system, few talented New Wave directors were able to create anything of value.

Nevertheless, from its emergence in 1978 to its gradual absorption into the mainstream in 1985, the New Wave exerted a constant influence, and unquestionably brought something new to the Hong Kong cinema and television industries. The New Wave produced quite a number of films of extraordinary creativity that elevated the audience's sense of appreciation, and broadened their vision of cinema. The New Wave played a unique, noteworthy role in raising the quality of Hong Kong movies, in establishing a local culture, and in promoting Hong Kong films internationally, where they received serious regard and approval.

Notes

1. According to an informal estimate, 60 film-makers, excluding scriptwriters and technical staff, produced their first picture in this period. See Law Kar, '"The Shaolin Temple" of Hong Kong New Cinema'. *The Study of Hong Kong Cinema in the 1970s*. 8th Hong Kong International Film Festival. HK: Urban Council, 1984, p. 110. There were also other estimates of around 50 or 60. See Wong Chi. 'Vicissitudes of the New Wave: About Woo Viet'. *City Entertainment*. No. 178, p. 56.
2. Ibid., p. 110. At that time, the staff of HK-TVB referred to the station as the 'Shaolin Temple'. And, in the 'Five Stations Hill' period, the corridor outside the studio 'Enjoy Yourself Tonight' in Broadcast Drive, where the backstage staff and performers of that programme rested as well as practiced scripts was called the 'alley of wooden people'.
3. In 1959 and the early 1960s in France, Jean-Luc Godard, Francois Truffaut, Claude Chabrol, Jaques Rivette, Eric Rohmer and others wrote articles on film criticism in the magazine *Cahiers du Cinema*. Later, these critics even engaged in film-making, opening up a new aspect to film-making, which was termed 'The New Wave'.
4. *400 Blows* (Les Quatre Cents Coups) and *Breathless* (A bout de Souffle) were the pioneering works of the French New Wave.
5. Monaco, James. The New Wave. New York: Oxford University Press, 1976, p. 38.
6. Zhang Tian. 'Xindaoyan yizhupian' (The Left-Out of the New Directors). *Datexie* (Close-Up). No. 20. Hong Kong Datexie Press. 9 September 1976, p. 32.
7. Lau Shing-hon. 'Hong Kong Directors, the Cinema's Gain / Loss and Prospects.' *Ming Pao Monthly*. September 1976, p. 406.
8. Yi Jing. 'Xianggang dianying xinlangchao – xiang chuantong tiaozhan de gemingzhe' (Hong Kong New Wave Cinema – the Revolutionists who Challenge Traditions). *Datexie*. No. 63. Hong Kong Datexie Press. 18 August 1978, p. 2.
9. An election of 'Top Ten Movies' jointly organized by *Datexie Monthly* and *City Entertainment* in 1978.
10. The periodical *Xinyidai* (A New Generation) published an interview series, entitled 'The Collective Images of New Wave Directors', that appeared in consecutive issues from No. 89 (1 June 1979) to 97, which focused on the new blood in the industry. Starting issue

No. 98, the periodical presented another interview series, entitled 'The New Wave's Group-in-Waiting. The film-makers interviewed in this series included Allan Fong, Ng Siu-wan, Lau Shing-hon and Dennis Yu and others. These sentences are quotations from the article 'The Debates about the New Wave' (Clifton Ko). No. 94, 10 August 1979, p. 14.

11. Wong Chi. 'Vicissitudes of the New Wave: About Woo Viet'. *City Entertainment*. No. 178, p. 56.
12. Yu Mo-wan. 'The Deep Origins of Hong Kong Cinema and Shanghai Cinema'. *Hong Kong–Shanghai: The Twin Cities of Film*. 18th Hong Kong International Film Festival. 25 March – 9 April 1994, p. 88.
13. The Great China Film Company, financed by the Investment Film Distribution Company, was founded in 1946 by businessmen in the film industry, namely, Jiang Boying, Zhu Xuhua, Shao Cunren, Zhou Jianyun, Yan Youxiang, Xie Bingjun and others. It was closed in 1948. During the three years of its existence, Great China made 34 Mandarin films (*guoyu pian*) and 9 Cantonese films (*yueyu pian*) in a variety of genres. The company played pioneering and inspiring roles in the period following the war of resistance against Japan. See Shen Sai-shing, ed., 'A Draft of History of the Development of Hong Kong Cinema 1946–1976'. In *Spectator Magazine* (Guanchajia zazhi).* No. 3, 1976, p. 75.
14. *Tongbing xianglian** (dir. Zhu Shilin, 1946). *Changxiangsi** (dir. He Zhaozhang, 1947). *Kulian** (dir. Du Yu, Chen Shi, 1947). *Sannüxing** (dir. Yue Feng, 1947). *Geyou qianqiu** (dir. Zhu Shilin, 1947).
15. *Renlun**: a Union Motion Picture production (dir. Li Chenfeng, 1957). *Garden of Repose*. (dir. Zhu Shilin, 1963).
16. *A Mother's Tears* (dir. Qin Jian, 1955). *Autumn* (dir. Qin Jian, 1954).
17. *Parents' Hearts* (dir. Qin Jian, 1955). *Father and Son* (dir. Wu Hui, 1954).
18. The directors of these four films were, respectively, Chen Yun, Jiang Weiguang, Chor Yuen, Chen Yun and Long Kong.
19. *Mambo Girl* (dir. Yi Wen, 1957).
20. Law Wai-ming. *Law Wai-ming's Film Writings*. Hong Kong: Zhenzheng chuangzao chuban. July 1978, p. 42.
21. Fu, Poshek. 'The 1960s: Modernity, Youth Culture, and the Hong Kong Cantonese Cinema'. In Fu Poshek and David Desser, eds. *The Cinema of Hong Kong: History, Arts, Identity*. London: Cambridge University Press, 2000, p. 71.
22. Li Cheuk-to. 'Shadow of the Father – the Chinese Context of Hong Kong New Cinema in the 1980s'. *The Chinese Context in Hong Kong Cinema*. 14th Hong Kong International Film Festival. April 1990, p. 79.
23. Pak Tong Cheuk and Law Kar. 'Interview with Leong Suk-yi.' *Hong Kong New Wave – Twenty Years After*. 23rd Hong Kong International Film Festival. April 1999, p. 129.
24. Ibid., as item 8, pp. 3–4.
25. Sze Chai. 'Retrospective on the First Wave of the New Wave, Longing for the Second One.' *City Entertainment*. A special article offered with issue No. 202, p. 2.
26. Wong Kwok-siu. 'Hong Kong Cinema in the 80s'. *Hong Kong Cinema '79–'89* (combined edition). 24th Hong Kong International Film Festival. April 2000, p. 21.
27. Spoken by a French professor who teaches at an American university. In 'An Overall Look at the New Wave', A Seminar on the Special Topic of Hong Kong New Wave Cinema. HK: 23rd Hong Kong International Film Festival. 1999, p. 21.

28. Leung Nong-kong. 'Has "the New Wave" of Hong Kong Cinema Come into Existence?' *Hong Kong Cinema '79*. 3rd Hong Kong International Film Festival. 25 June 1979, pp. 9-11.
29. The two critics were Liu Wing-leung and Law Wai-ming. 'Re-Evaluation of the New Cinema'. *City Entertainment*. No. 63. 25 June 1981, p. 14.
30. Evans Chan. 'The Chapter of Unforgiving-ness - Notes of "the New Cinema"'. Ibid., as item 29, p. 16.
31. Ibid.
32. An interview conducted by Wong Ho-yin. 'Tsui Hark- an Ordinary Glutton for Work.' *City Entertainment*. No. 400. 11 August 1994, p. 27.
33. Ti Ko. 'Alex Cheung + Kwan Wai-peng = Cops and Robbers'. *City Entertainment*. No. 19. October 1979, p. 14.
34. Lau Fong, Chan Chi-leung. 'Interview with Yim Ho.' Chinese-Western Motion Pictures. March 1986, p. 23.
35. Monaco, James. *The New Wave*. New York: Oxford University Press. 1976, p. 5.
36. Law Kar. 'Fennu de huigu - tan yijiubayi, yijiubaernian de dianying' (An angry retrospective: discussing the films of 1981 and 1982). *Baixing banyuekan* (The People Semi-Monthly), 1982. See Jiao Xiongping, ed. *Xianggang dianying fengmao, 1975-1986* (A View of Hong Kong Cinema, 1975-1986). Taipei Times Press. May 1987, p. 364.
37. Leung Lai-kuen, Chan To-man. 'The Relationship Between Overseas Markets and the Development of Hong Kong Cinema 1950-1995.' *Years of Electric Shadows*. 21st Hong Kong International Film Festival. 25 March - 9 April 1997, p. 138.
38. Leung Leung. 'The Outward Development of Hong Kong Cinema - Hong Kong and the Two Sides of the Strait.' *Years of Electric Shadows* - A Report of the Seminar about Hong Kong Cinema. 21st Hong Kong International Film Festival. 12 April 1997, p. 28.
39. Ibid., as item 11.
40. 'The Top-Ten Hong Kong Movies in the 1980s - A Retrospective of Films in 1980s'. *Big Motion Picture*. 16 December 1997, p. 28.
41. Law Kar. 'Hong Kong New Wave Cinema: Undergoing Innovation in a Culture of Confrontation.' *Hong Kong New Wave - Twenty Years After*. 23rd Hong Kong International Film Festival. April 1999, p. 38.
42. *Jumping Ash* was a film directed by Leong Po-chih, and *Woo Fook* was another. Leong worked in advertising for a number of years after his departure from television. He is regarded as a predecessor, instead of a member, of the New Wave Cinema.
43. Law Kar, Shek Kei. 'Interview with Tsui Hark'. *Hong Kong Cinema in the 1980s*. 15th Hong Kong International Film Festival. April 1991, p. 94.
44. *Chasing Girls* made 10 million Hong Kong dollars at the box office, while *Aces Go Places* I, II and III, respectively, earned 26, 23 and 29 million Hong Kong dollars.
45. Ji Er. 'Xinyicheng celueshang de qichengzhuanhe' (The 'rise-hold-twist-close' process of Cinema City's Strategy). Jiao Xiongping, ed. *Xianggang dianying fengmao, 1975-1986* (A View of Hong Kong Cinema, 1975-1986). Taipei Times Press. May 1987, p. 161.
46. Ibid.
47. Clifton Ko. 'The Operation of the Hong Kong Film Industry, 1984-1989'. *Years of Electric Shadows* - A Report of the Seminar about Hong Kong Cinema. 10-12 April 1997, p. 13.
48. Shek Kei. 'Sense of Achievement and Crisis in Hong Kong Cinema in the 1980s'. *Hong Kong Cinema in the 1980s*. 15th Hong Kong International Film Festival, April 1991, p. 13.

2

The Interactive Relationship Between Hong Kong's Film and Television Industries

The emergence of Hong Kong New Wave Cinema in the late 1970s and the early 1980s can be said to have been a response to the social needs of the time. This was a time when the film industry was at a low ebb, while the television industry was growing rapidly. The need to respond to the demands of social diversity and localization fostered the rise of a group of young film-makers aged around thirty. Their works had an individual style and vision. Most important, they had a deep understanding of social needs and were close to the pulse of society. They were the pioneers of the New Cinema among Chinese communities all over the world, including mainland China and Taiwan. The aim of this chapter is to explore the reasons behind the rise of Hong Kong's New Wave cinema, especially in terms of the relationship between the film and television industries in the 1960s and 1970s. This is because the relationship between the New Wave films and the growth of television was unique to Hong Kong, when compared with the situation in mainland China and Taiwan.

Social and Economic Conditions in Hong Kong

The 1950s saw a massive influx of migrants from mainland China to Hong Kong, due to the change in the political landscape there. The immigrants included businessmen, entrepreneurs and labourers. In addition, capital from all over Southeast Asia flowed in. After about a decade of hard work, the foundation of Hong Kong's economy was established. The 1960s was a turning point for Hong Kong. From an economy largely based on entrepôt activities, Hong Kong gradually developed into a manufacturing centre. In addition, the population grew dramatically, from 2,226,000 in the 1950s to 3,130,000 in 1961. By 1966, the figure was 3,730,000, and in 1970 over 4,000,000.[1] In the 1980s, the population even reached 5,000,000. In terms of land area, Hong Kong had become the most densely populated area in the world.

Along with the rapid increase in population came a variety of social problems. Among these ills, housing was the most obvious one. Thousands of citizens could not afford their own houses or apartments and thus lived in wooden huts in squatter areas, where fires were a constant threat. In 1953 a great fire broke out at the Shek Kip Mei squatter settlement. Over 7,000 huts were burned and 60,000 people were made homeless. The government then began to resettle them in temporary housing and to build public housing estates. In 1964, 350,000 were settled, and in 1970, 1,100,000.[2] Social instability was thus alleviated.

The vast increase in population in the 1960s and 1970s swelled the number of labourers. The ratio of young people also grew annually. Consider the age range of 15 to 29. This rose from 20 per cent of the population in 1961, to 24 per cent in 1971, to 32.7 per cent in 1981. Members within this group made up a large part of the workforce. Those aged 15 to 64 comprised 68.8 per cent of the total population;[3] that is, two-thirds of the population could engage in labour and create wealth. In other words, the young people were an advantage to the development of Hong Kong's economy.

Moreover, free primary schooling was implemented in September 1971. In September 1978, this was extended to nine years of free schooling, meaning that children of the appropriate age could complete secondary school. The proportion of middle school and pre-matriculation students was 16.5 per cent in 1961; in 1981, the figure was 44.6 per cent. Likewise, the proportion of college students increased, from 2.4 per cent in 1961 to 6 per cent in 1986. That is to say, the number of mid-ranking professionals grew; and this undoubtedly represented society's greatest potential for expansion. In 1986 those who had received a middle-school education or above made up more than half of the population.[4] Perhaps the situation still lagged behind that in other well-developed nations; however, it was far better than in Third World countries. There is a positive correlation between Hong Kong's rapid economic expansion and the intellectual level of its people. With the abovementioned factors, from 1961 to 1965 Hong Kong's GNP grew at an average annual rate of 13.6 per cent, and the per capita income reached HK$4,757. Hong Kong was undergoing a gradual transformation towards industrialization, to stand at the forefront of developing countries.

From the above table,[5] it can be seen that Hong Kong's economy enjoyed significant surpluses except for two periods: 1959–1960, when a financial crisis was experienced worldwide; and 1965–1966, when there was a crisis in the property market and runs on banks.

Under this favourable situation of rapid economic growth some problems occasionally arose. For instance, in May 1962 there was an influx of people fleeing famine in the

Hong Kong's Balance Sheet
(in millions of Hong Kong dollars)

Year	Income	Expenditure	Balance
1959–60	664.6	710.0	–145.47
1960–61	859.2	845.3	13.9
1961-62	1070.5	953.2	77.3
1962–63	1253.1	1113.3	139.8
1963–64	1393.9	1295.4	98.5
1964–65	1518.3	1440.5	77.8
1965–66	1631.7	1769.1	–137.4
1966–67	1817.8	1806.1	11.7
1967–68	1899.1	1766.0	133.5
1968–69	2081.1	1873.0	208.1
1969–70	2480.1	2035.2	448.5
1970–71	3070.1	2452.2	615.7

Source: *Hong Kong Annual Statistics Report*, Hong Kong Government, 1960–72.

mainland; in 1966, riots broke out over fare hikes on the Star Ferry; in 1967, a labour dispute at the Sun Po Kong plastics factory, snowballed with the interference of leftists to a series of disturbances that extended into the following year.[6] From then on, the British exercised an authoritative and meritocratic kind of rule in order to depoliticize the society. But this could not bring to an end the rivalry between the two political forces, the Nationalists and the Communists. The ideological opposition between the leftists and the rightists throughout the decade remained a potential source of social frustration and instability. Amidst these contradictions, Hong Kong continued to advance socially and economically.

Ferocious Competition in the Television Industry

The First Television Station, Rediffusion Cable

Rediffusion Cable, the progenitor of Rediffusion Television, was launched in 1975. It was a cable black-and-white broadcast. Nearly all of its programmes, including dramas, documentaries and news, were imported from Britain, and all of these were in English.[7] Only some news reports and the weather reports were produced by the station itself. After operating for over two years, the station made little headway among the public.

It suffered from low subscription numbers and, therefore, a deficit. It was therefore forced to split into two parts: an English channel and a Chinese channel. The Chinese channel came under the supervision of the production manager of the Motion Picture and General Investment (*dianying maoye*) company, Zhong Qiwen, who worked as the programme director. Immediately after his arrival, he began producing new programmes such as shows on cookery, flower arranging, handicrafts, hygiene and health and a comedy, *Funny Life*. This new strategy gradually attracted an audience. Cantonese was the principal tongue but, at the same time, a range of Chinese dialects such as Mandarin, Hakka and Chaozhou were also incorporated in order to capture a wider viewership.

At the same time, the Chinese channel endeavoured to embrace talent from the domains of film and theatre. Those from the film world, both on-screen and off-screen, included Bu Wancang, Wu Hui, Zuo Ji, Siu Sang, Wong Tin-lam, Cheung Ching, Cheung Ying-tsoi, Ng Cho-fan, Wan Ying-kwai, Chong Yuen-yung, Lee Pang-fei, Pao Hon-lam, Chu Hark, Lee Heung-kam, Keung Chung-ping, Sek Sau, Leong Sun-yin and Miu Kam-fung. Those from the stage included Chung King-fai, Chan Yau-hau, Tam Yat-ching, Fung Tsui-fan and others. In the opening phase of the television industry, a sizable number of personnel were transferred from the film world – additional evidence of the ailing health of the film industry.

In addition, Rediffusion launched its own training programmes, with Bu Wancang in charge of cultivating new talent. The graduates included Lisa Wang, Lo Kwok-hung, Wong Suk-yi, Huen So-ha, Lee Si-kei, Lo Tai-wai, Sum Sum, Lee To-hung, Lee Ying and Leong Siu-ling. They later became well known in television, proof of the discerning judgement of the station's management.

Rediffusion's own productions included *I Am A Detective*, *Four Daughters*, *A Secret Visitor*,* *Husband and Wife* and others. There were also foreign imports, which were dubbed into Cantonese; for example, *The Untouchables*, *The Saint*, *Wagon Train*, *Knight The Saint** and *Mission Impossible*.[8]

Rediffusion thus abandoned the approach of merely purchasing foreign programmes; rather, it adopted a multi-pronged strategy of recruiting local talent, training new blood, dubbing English-speaking programmes into Cantonese and producing their own programmes. As a result, the number of subscribers climbed from a few thousand to nearly a hundred thousand. Financially, the station went from suffering losses to generating surpluses, making it possible for it to construct its own broadcast building on Broadcast Drive.

The Successive Entries of Hong Kong Television Broadcasts Limited and Commercial Television

In 1967, just when Rediffusion was celebrating the tenth anniversary of its establishment, Hong Kong's second television station, Hong Kong Television Broadcasts Ltd (HK-TVB), was launched, broadcasting in colour. TVB's entry broke the monopoly held by Rediffusion and opened a new page in the history of Hong Kong television. It also set the stage for keen competition in the industry. Competition meant progress, which was a good thing for the audience and for the whole of society. When TVB first began operating, all of its programmes were in black and white, with the exception of some imported colour programmes. In 1971, TVB began producing its own shows in colour; for instance, *Enjoy Yourself Tonight, Kao's Club* and *Sharp's Club*. But full colour programming was not achieved until Rediffusion Cable temporarily suspended operations in November 1973, renamed itself 'Rediffusion Television', and formally resumed broadcasting on 1st December with full colour programming.

Principally featuring singing and comedies, *Enjoy Yourself Tonight* was a live variety show. It had the longest run in Hong Kong television history, spanning from 1971 to the 1990s. Riding on the success of this programme, TVB enjoyed a surplus in the second year of its operation. It also triumphed over its rival, Rediffusion Television, with a regular viewer share of 80 to 90 per cent thirty years onwards. Not until after the mid-1990s, did the situation change slightly, with TVB's ratings retreating to 70 per cent and, sometimes, 50 per cent. However, after a short while, the figure would rebound to a decisive lead of 70 or 80 per cent.

In fact, in the first few years of the existence of HK-TVB's Cantonese-language channel, Jade, with the exception of the abovementioned three in-house programmes, the channel's airtime was filled with imported programmes; for example, English-language ones such as *Doctor Kildare, I Spy, The Lucy Show, Bonanza* and others,[9] and early Mandarin/Cantonese films such as *True and False Husband, The Revenge* (both Chaozhou-dialect pictures), *Cool Chau Mei, Wonderful Princess* and *Haunting Valley, Magic Pearl**.[10] This was not greatly different from what was on offer in Rediffusion Cable. What was different was TVB's move, in 1968, to make its first drama series, *A Dream Is a Dream,* released in fifteen-minute segments on a weekly basis. Set around the May Fourth Movement, the story was of a realistic type, was well organized, and was well received by the audience.

Local television gradually gained in popularity. Consider, as evidence, a list of the top ten programmes on HK-TVB, which was released in November 1970: (1) *Enjoy Yourself Tonight*; (2) *It Takes a Thief*; (3) *Tarzan*; (4) *Kao's Club*; (5) *Japanese Story*; (6) *Sharp's Club*; (7) *Night of Sharp*; (8) *Viceroys on Life*; (9) *News and Weather Report*; (10) *The Fugitive*.[11] Half of the programmes on the list were imports – numbers (2), (3), (5), (7) and (10) – but the list also showed that the audience was beginning to like watching local productions.

At that time, the drama series of both stations were still adaptations of stage performances or popular novels.[12] Since 1970, HK-TVB has presented drama series of all kinds, under an omnibus umbrella of titles; for example, 'Weekend Theatre', 'Sunday Theatre' and 'Jade Theatre'.[13] Among them, 'Jade Theatre' afterwards evolved into a long drama series. It also gained for the television enterprise a remarkable annual profit of not fewer than several hundred million Hong Kong dollars.

On 7th of September 1975, the third television station, Commercial Television (CTV), was established. The competition was no longer between two but three 'powers', and Kowloon's Broadcast Drive came to be known as the 'Five Stations Hill'.[14] In its early days, CTV adopted an educational function, as indicated in its license. Such a role was soon taken over by Educational TV (a branch of Radio-Television Hong Kong). Because their funds were limited, the task of staff training was turned over to Taiwan's Guangqi Station, and the Taiwanese broadcasting system was adopted. Producer Lu Zhizi from Taiwan was invited to make CTV's first period drama, *The Stories of Tsui and Tang*. Unfortunately, the production was not spirited enough, audience numbers dropped and so did morale. However, there was a turnaround in 1976, when CTV released a martial arts drama, *The Brave Archer*. The plot was not as thin and dull as its predecessor, and the series attracted nearly one million viewers, half that of the highest ratings in the history of Hong Kong cable television broadcasts, and surpassing Rediffusion's several hundred thousand viewers.

The Dominance of the Three Stations and the Gradual Localization of the Programmes

HK-TVB produced the epic *Romance of Book and Sword* (1976), featuring a cast including Adam Cheng, Lisa Wang, Lee Si-kei, Wong Suk-yi and Wong Yuen-sun. As an avant-garde production of the martial arts genre,[15] this drama opened up a spectacular new page in the history of Hong Kong television. In 1973, Leong Suk-yi, the head of programming for HK-TVB, was in charge of producing the situation comedy *Seventy-Three*. The series consisted of 30 episodes, each 30 minutes long, with one shown each week over a three-month season. The programme proved to be a great hit, mainly because of its social overtones, light-hearted style and refreshing presentation. *Seventy-Three*'s breakthrough set the stage for subsequent anthology series shot on film, namely, *Crossroad* and *CID* (both 1976), *Wonderful* (1977), *Seven Women* and others.

Meanwhile, in order to rescue the station from its inferior position, the general manager of Rediffusion Television, Wong Sek-chiu, promoted Johnny Mak to programming leader. Mak began the production of *Ten Sensational Cases* (1975), filmed on 16mm stock. The show was based on up-to-date news events. In addition, Mak employed on-location shooting. Taking one hour as a unit, the series emphasized bloody, sensational scenes of fighting, deception and killing. Verisimilitude was one of the prime concerns and sensationalism was another. This drama boosted audience numbers, surpassing those of Commercial Television, taking Rediffusion to second place in the market. Following this success, Rediffusion made other single-drama episodes, such as *Ten Assassins**, *Real Men** and *Ten Fraud Cases*, paving the ground for the use of 16mm film stock in television production.

Taking advantage of the success of *Ten Sensational Cases,* in 1977 Rediffusion launched a 'counter-attack' and made two large-scale martial arts dramas. HK-TVB, in the meantime, fought back with several 16mm anthology series, namely, *CID, Wonderful* and *Seven Women,*[16] as well as a period martial arts drama, *Heaven Sword Dragon Sabre.* As for CTV, it could manage to produce *Guangdong Heroes* to respond to the keen battle for viewers, despite a lack of capital and coordination. A battle over ratings broke out. The result was that TVB consolidated its position as the leading station, with Rediffusion in second place and CTV in third.

CTV was the big loser in this war: its capital was exhausted, income had dropped to zero; and advertising revenues could not cover expenditures. Faced with an immediate financial crisis, the Board of Directors of CTV had no choice but to recruit new investors. In 1977, the Lam brothers joined the business, and the station was able to continue operating. The new arrivals triggered off another round competition in 'Five Stations Hill'.

Television History's 'Battle of the Century'

On 1st February 1978, HK-TVB's Leong Suk-yi defected to CTV, bringing with her a number of key personnel.[17] This sparked off a bidding war for talent in 'Five Stations Hill'. Offers and counter-offers were made. Performers and technicians were lured from one station to another by attractive offers. What was being raised was not merely their wages, but also their value as professionals. The year 1978 was the year in the history of television when their status was at its peak. Following the new influx of talent from HK-TVB, CTV began intensive training and production efforts. It also launched wave after wave of propaganda attacks directed mainly at HK-TVB.

The 1st of July 1978 was the day CTV chose to launch it attacks. The station had already begun publicizing the effort in the media since the end of the previous month. It relied primarily on newspaper publicity to launch its attack. Such fortune-telling rhetoric (adapted from the Chinese Almanac) as the following appeared in newspapers: 'One should not entertain guests the day after tomorrow' (published on 29 June), 'One should not play mahjong tomorrow' (published on 30 June). The message was that one should stay at home to watch CTV's programmes. On 2 July, the slogans were 'No fighting tonight, but watch *The Golden Blade Sentimental Swordsman*', 'Don't go to bed early tonight', and 'Watch *The Night Person* at 11.30'. CTV's keen competitor TVB did not take all of this sitting down. Calmly, they observed CTV's strategies before responding accordingly. On 6 July, in a counter-attack, HK-TVB published an advertisement containing the motto 'HK-TVB's "Almanac" grants you everything you want'.[18] Simple, yet forceful and restrained, this advertisement demonstrated the spirit of one who was in a leading position.

Rediffusion Television, which had originally not been involved, also joined the advertising battle. On 16 July, on the front page of *Ming Pao Daily* the station published an advertisement that read, 'Wonderful programmes every day; no need to consult the programme almanac', exhorting the audience to enjoy Rediffusion's offerings. This publicity war among the three stations is regarded as the most vigorous in the history of Hong Kong television, then or since.

Starting in July, HK-TVB and CTV stood at loggerheads. Their roster of programmes is shown here:[19]

Date	CTV Programmes	HK-TVB Programmes
Sunday 7.30 p.m.	*Golden Blade Sentimental Swordsman*	*Glittering Stars*
9.30 p.m.	*Psychological Theatre*	*Best of World Cup, Below the Lion Rock*
Monday–Friday Evenings	*Romance of Celebrity*	*Rock Strong Man* (*Taxi Driver*)
Saturday Evenings	*The Henchman*	*Heaven Sword Dragon Sabre*

Source: *Ming Pao Daily*, 1, 2, 6 and 12 July 1978

As can be seen from the above, all of the programmes were in-house productions. CTV's *The Henchman* and HK-TVB's *Taxi Drivers* were anthology series shot using film. *The Golden Blade Sentimental Swordsman* was Tsui Hark's farewell work to his television days. *Romance of Celebrity* was a big-budget production that was partly shot in Hawaii and featuring Patrick Tam and other actors. Very shortly after the outbreak of the battle for ratings, CTV failed utterly, removing the threat to HK-TVB and confirming HK-TVB's premier status.

The causes of CTV's failure were diverse and cannot be explained simply by the notion that HK-TVB had an established audience. Nor could the blame be placed on one or two people alone. The truth is that television is a huge, collective industry. A programme, satisfactory or not, is the sum of the efforts of every member. Put in another way, any fault in any part, say, in directing or even in managing the props, has an effect on the quality of the programme. CTV's July programmes were not flawless. Consider, for example, *The Henchman*. The editing in this drama was judged to be too fast for the audience to follow. The shots were not comprehensible, as they shifted at an excessively fast pace. The director did not have a good grasp of tempo and that ruined the rhythm of the show. *Psychological Theatre* is another example. Every episode required the viewers to painstakingly follow the detective's reasoning, and often also to determine the truth and the identity of the criminal. It was perhaps too demanding for the average viewer.

In addition, of the three competitors, HK-TVB was the only one to have a budget surplus. It was on a solid financial footing and had an adequate repertory of talent. Even with the loss of personnel caused by Leong Suk-yi's departure, the station still possessed formidable power. Furthermore, its counter-offers to the defectors were often taken up. More important, after years of operating, a well-balanced production system had been established. From the conception to the completion of a programme, the required division of labour and the necessary resources were available. Scriptwriters and directors were given a great deal of authority, which enabled them to enjoy creative freedom. This system had been established by Leong when she worked for HK-TVB. It guaranteed that directors would have the chance to exercise their talents and have the courage to innovate. Furthermore, compared to its two rivals, HK-TVB had the largest pool of popular performers. To conclude, it was obvious that HK-TVB had won the championship in this 'battle of the century'. CTV, for their part, had been overly rash and had attempted to defeat a strong adversary in only half a year's time, clearly underestimating that adversary's strength.

CTV had only been operating for a little over three years, but had already spent HK $5,000,000. The station was eventually forced to close because of licensing and managerial problems and financial problems. This ended the competition in the television industry among three stations. The playing field was then left to HK-TVB and Rediffusion Television. Over the long term, Rediffusion incurred financial losses, which led to several changes in management. By contrast, after its first two years of operation, HK-TVB enjoyed complete dominance for more than two decades.

From Domestic Productions to Drama Series Made on Film

It had been several years since Hong Kong's television stations stopped purchasing foreign programmes and began making their own. Such a change was natural as the industry developed and prospered. Here, HK-TVB took the lead. Beginning with the *Hui Brothers' Show* in 1971, they then produced two other series, *Crossroads* (1972) and *Seventy-Three* (1973). The former, directed by Lau Fong-kong, was the first drama series in Hong Kong to be shot entirely using 16mm film. It was surprisingly well received, which encouraged HK-TVB to produce the single-drama episodes of *CID*, *Wonderfun*, *Interpol*, *Seventeen* and *I Am A Woman*.

Following HK-TVB's *CID*, in 1976, Rediffusion produced *Ten Sensational Cases* shot in film. The television unit of Radio Television Hong Kong also started projects such as *Below the Lion Rock* and *When We Were Young*. These dramas should not be overlooked, as they were painstakingly produced and of high quality. Young film buffs fell in love with these works. Thus, both directly and indirectly, the television stations trained quite a few talented people for the Hong Kong film-making industry

– Hong Kong's New Wave cinema (which emerged in 1978) was the best evidence of this.

In the history of Hong Kong television, the most popular long drama series was HK-TVB's 1976 production *Hotel*. Produced by Leong Suk-yi and Sek Siu-ming, it was also the first long drama series to consist of half-hour shows totalling 101 episodes. Set in a transitional period of the rapid expansion of Hong Kong's economy, the drama was about the growth and struggles of the middle class. At the time wealth was very unevenly distributed in society, being concentrated in the hands of a few tycoons and individuals; and the power play among them was also part of the story. The story was set in an extravagant hotel. A diverse range of characters appeared in the series, including the manager, all levels of staff and rich guests. They all had their own stories, intricate and unique. Starring Shek Kin, Deborah Leung and Chow Yun-fat, the conflicts among them reflected a genuine picture of society. The story's emphasis on the value of personal endeavour was an accurate portrayal of Hong Kong's development in the 1960s and 1970s. *Hotel* made a Chow Yun-fat, Cora Miao, Deborah Leung and a few other artists famous. It attracted a viewership of about 1,900,000, making it a phenomenal success.[20]

Following this hit, TVB again reached a new pinnacle in audience numbers with *A House is Not a House* in 1977. According to a survey conducted in November of that year, this drama topped the ratings with an audience of 2,400,000.[21] The show was about the changes faced by one family. The father, the breadwinner for the whole family, was jailed for a crime, and the entire family fell into a crisis. The eldest daughter, Lok Lam, was then forced to take up the challenge of supporting the family. In the male-dominated society of the time, Lok naturally encountered numerous difficulties. But this did not stop her from stubbornly forging ahead. She had a firm belief that her diligence would one day be rewarded. In her career she was tough, and in love she made her own decisions. She became the epitome of the strong career woman of the 1970s.

The dramas of the 1970s, both anthology series and long series, mirrored the social developments of the time. For this alone, these productions were profoundly meaningful. From them, one can trace the gradual advancement of society, and listen to the voices of the various interest groups, particularly that of the middle class, as Hong Kong society became more pluralistic in nature. The late 1970s was the liveliest period in history of Hong Kong television, and was also the peak period for social development in Hong Kong. As the entire society progressed, so also did the quality of its cultural artifacts, including its television.

A Quest for Identity: Hong Kong Films in the 1960s

During the 1940s and 1950s the ties between Hong Kong cinema and China were many and complex. For this reason, Mandarin-speaking movies (*guoyu pian*) and Cantonese-speaking movies (*yueyu pian*) developed in parallel. This was a marked characteristic of Hong Kong cinema, and it was not until the late 1970s that the situation changed. In fact, Hong Kong was gradually becoming detached from the motherland, but, in spirit, the city's cultural inheritance from China was still strong. In the realm of Hong Kong cinema, family dramas (emphasizing family ethics) and realistic movies were the mainstream. Such a situation began to change in the 1960s. This was because those born in Hong Kong in the immediate post-war period had come of age. They had received a western education and had been exposed daily to western culture. Moreover, they had reached the age of rebellion and were rebelling against the older generation and the authorities. At the same time, disoriented, they were searching for their identity and place in society. This led to the making of such movies as *Colourful Youth* (1966) and *Girls are Flowers* (1966),[22] which sparked off a craze for youth-oriented films.

At about the same time as the youth-oriented films, novel martial arts movies, also called 'new-style' martial arts movies, appeared; for instance, *Come Drink With Me* (1996) and *The One-Armed Swordsman* (1967). In the early 1960s, there were martial arts series with an emphasis on mystery and magic, such as *The Secret Book* (1961), *Buddha's Palm* (1964), and *Moslem Sacred Fire Decree* (1965). There were also many dramas focusing on the lives of working-class people; for example, *The Factory Queen* (1963), *Queen of the Market Place* (1964) and *Dim-Sum Queen* (1965). Comedies such as *Diary of a Chauvinistic Husband* (1966) and *Wise Wives and Foolish Husbands* (1969) were also made. In the second half of the decade, certain creative and meaningful movies, such as *Story of a Discharged Prisoner* (1967), *The Window* (1968) and *Teddy Girls* (1969), also appeared.

Young film workers of the time were living in a rapidly changing society. They had no choice but to absorb lessons from their seniors. On the other hand, they were also boldly learning from European and Japanese film-makers. Their experiments, although perhaps too impetuous and somewhat coarse, were a good beginning that eventually bore fruit. Looking at their films, it is possible see that they were very different from those of the 1950s and early 1960s in the following ways. (1) They were fast-paced; for example, *Broadcast Prince* (1966), where changes of scene were achieved with the use of sound. (2) They made sophisticated use of zoom-ins. In *She Is Our Senior* (1967), in the scene in which Kenneth Tsang is first introduced to his father, a zoom lens was used in editing, with marvelous results. (3) Split-screen compositions were also employed. One example of this is in *Waste Not Our Youth* (1967). With the scene showing the male protagonist, Sai-kit, looking at a pair of pens sent to him by the female protagonist, Mei-fun, the director juxtaposes the past (memory) and the present. Another example can be found in *Social Characters* (1969), where a split screen is used to demonstrate a strong contrast: Lisa quietly reads at home; on another screen, a seven-member gang dances wildly. (4) Sophisticated parallel editing was also employed. For instance, two lines of action intersect in the *Story of a Discharged Prisoner* (1967): the hero, played by Patrick Tse Yin, joins a party for discharged prisoners and is watching a performance; meanwhile, his younger brother becomes drunk and, step by step, falls into the trap set by the villain, played by Shek Kin. (5) Precise and delicate shots were also used. Examples include a gift-giving scene in *The Window* (1968), where the hero sends the heroine a Chinese musical instrument called a *pipa*; and a court scene in *Teddy Girls* (1969), where well-cut shots capture the responses of various characters. These illustrations are evidence of the director Long Kong's mastery of cinematic language.[23]

Towards the end of the decade, the number of Cantonese-speaking movies began to decline, whereas the number of Mandarin-speaking movies rose. In 1960, the figures were 166 to 68; by 1969, this had shifted to 63 to 95.[24] In 1971, the number of Cantonese movies made in Hong Kong even dropped to one; and the following year, to zero. There were many reasons for such a drastic drop. The chief ones were: (1) Television had just been introduced to households in Hong Kong, and its development was remarkably rapid. The percentage of households in Hong Kong with a television was 12.3 per cent of the non-boat residents (a total of 97,000 television sets) in 1968; 72 per cent (a total of 609,000) in 1972; and 90 per cent (a total of 860,000) in 1976.[25] Clearly, television was attracting away the audience for Cantonese cinema. (2) The amount of capital invested in Mandarin cinema allowed for extravagant, big-budget productions. For the middle class, who had become richer, and were enjoying a higher standard of living, this was a greater attraction. These films provided them with dreams of what they could aspire to, but could not yet obtain. (3) Cantonese movies, which were repetitive and hardly inspiring, could no longer satisfy this better educated audience, whose tastes and expectations toward movies had been raised. It was not surprising that they turned their eyes instead to western movies and Mandarin movies. (4) The cyclical nature of the market. From this perspective, it was not strange to see a decline in Cantonese cinema in the late 1960s and the early 1970s. But there was one advantage to reaching the trough of the market, and this was that this marked the turning point for a resurgence.

The Film Industry in the 1970s

In the 1970s, Hong Kong industries underwent a shift from labour-intensive to technology-intensive activities. Apart from the oil crisis in 1974 and the global recession in 1975, Hong Kong's economy experienced an annual two-digit rate of growth, the highest in the world. Details can be found in the table opposite:

As can be seen from the above chart,[26] in 1975, almost zero growth was recorded, while the GNP rose by over 17 per cent in 1976. The considerable fluctuation was due to the fact that Hong Kong is a small-scale, free economy open to external political and financial influences. However, this fluctuation also proved the matchless adaptability of the economic system.

From the 1970s, large fiscal surpluses began to be generated. In the financial year 1969–1970, the figure was HK $418 million; in 1973–74, HK $ 513 million; and in 1980–81, HK $65.96 billion.[27] Under such conditions of growth, the Hong Kong

Year	GNP Dollars (in millions)	Average Growth Rate (%)
1969	51,467	12.0
1970	56,361	9.5
1971	60,536	7.4
1972	67,197	11.0
1973	75,725	12.7
1974	77,309	2.1
1975	77,616	0.4
1976	90,967	17.2
1977	101,893	12.0
1978	110,824	8.8
1979	123,923	11.8
1980	136,775	10.4

Source: Mo, 55

government was able to carry out a public housing policy. In 1973, Governor MacLehose announced a 10-year housing scheme that eased the needs of 1.5 million people. By 1977, 2 million had been resettled. In 1978, nearly 2.2 million lived in public housing, 46 per cent of the total population.[28]

The Convergence of Mandarin Films and Cantonese Films

In the early 1970s, there was one year when no Cantonese film was produced in Hong Kong, while Mandarin films were on the rise. These two bodies of films had long been produced separately, particularly in the 1950s and 1960s. Each had its own audience; the audience for Cantonese movies was largely limited to Hong Kong, whereas that for Mandarin features included Singapore and Malaysia in addition to Hong Kong. Thus, the latter had an advantage. In the 1970s, fewer Cantonese films began to be produced as compared to Mandarin films. Consider, for example, the year 1970. Among the 118 films that were produced that year, 83 were Mandarin films and 35 Cantonese. In 1971, the ratio was 85:1 out of a total of 86. In 1972, the ratio was 87:0. In 1973, the ratio was 93:1, of a total of 94 (the lone Cantonese movie was *The House of 72 Tenants*, which was the box office winner). In 1974, the ratio was 80:21, out of 101. The highest-grossing films were the Cantonese productions, namely *Games Gamblers Play* and *Hong Kong: Seventy Three*. Together with *The 72 Tenants*, they were adaptations from television dramas. In 1975, the ratio was 69:28 out of 97. Again, the top box office hits were Cantonese movies, *The Last Message* and *ICAC Storms**. In 1976, the share was 59:36 out of 95. The two highest-grossing films were *The Private*

Eyes and *Jumping Ash*. In 1977, of a total of 87 films, the proportion was 42:45, with Cantonese movies occupying a greater share. Again, Cantonese films, namely *Money Crazy* and *Winner Takes All*, topped the box office. In 1978, the ratio was 24:75, for a total of 99. The two most commercially popular features were the Cantonese films *The Contract* and *Drunken Master*. The pioneer New Wave work *The Extra* was actually ranked ninth in terms of box office revenue. In 1979, the ratio was 23:86, out of a 109 films. *Fearless Hyena* and *The Servant*, both Cantonese movies, were the top two films in terms of monetary return. In 1980, the entire local production of 105 consisted of Cantonese features. The two streams of Cantonese and Mandarin productions merged to a single Cantonese stream. Cantonese films dominated the whole Hong Kong market. Even the long-established Mandarin film-making studios such as the Shaw Brothers and Golden Harvest gradually came to produce more and more Cantonese pictures until, in the early 1980s, the transformation was complete.

Such a change in Hong Kong film-making industry can be attributed to several factors: (1) The popularity of television. With the fast-growing economy, Hong Kong society became more prosperous and television sets more affordable. Furthermore, the keen competition among television stations pushed up the quality of television programmes. Those in Cantonese were particularly well received. (2) The emergence of a local consciousness. With the rapid growth of the economy and the rise in living standards, the confidence that Hong Kong people felt in their ability to handle both internal and external forces rose apace. (3) The rise of a middle class, amidst an increasingly pluralistic society enjoying freedom of speech, led to a push for social reforms and to Hong Kong people becoming the protectors of Hong Kong society.

Even when the domestic production of films was at a trough, Hong Kong people still flocked to watch movies. For example, in the years 1966 and 1969 movie attendance was 98,370,000 and 84,900,000, respectively. The comparable figures for Japan in those years were 106,000,000 in each year, for an average of two films per person, far behind the rate of 21 per person in Hong Kong.[29]

The table opposite[30] chronicles film viewership in Hong Kong and the changes throughout the 1970s.

In the 1960s, the average annual number of films produced was over 200; however, at the end of the decade, this had fallen to over 100, and then to fewer than 100 in the 1970s. But in terms of attendance, the level remained at approximately 60 million, which was considerable. This was proof of the viability of Hong Kong cinema. From 1981 to 1986, the number of theatres increased from 82 to 105. Small theatres began to emerge. This situation was certainly linked to the rise of independent film-making. Audience attendance went from 63,000 in 1981 to 66,000 in 1982, and back down to 60,000 in 1986. However, box office revenue boomed from HK $244,786,000 to HK $614,717,000, a nearly threefold increase. The increase was related to the price of tickets (in 1980, the price was about $8 to $10 per ticket; in 1982, $12; in 1983 and

Year	Total Number of Films Produced	Number of Films Shown in Theatres	Total Admissions
1970	147	118	74,000,000
1971	126	86	70,500,000
1972	130	87	71,270,000
1973	220	94	73,000,000
1974	178	101	70,000,000
1975	126	97	54,000,000
1976	120	95	54,300,000
1977	135	108	60,000,000
1978	130	114	65,000,000
1979	137	104	65,000,000
1980	142	105	63,000,000

Source: *Hong Kong Annual Report, 1969–1981*

1984, $15; in 1985, $18; and in 1986, $20). By contrast, the growth in revenue of foreign films was less than double, from 167,109,000 in 1981 to 264,013,000 in 1986. In other words, in that period, locally produced movies enjoyed an overwhelming dominance over imported ones. This was an indication that Hong Kong movies were being warmly received and was also a result of localization. (The above figures were obtained from *Hong Kong Annual Report* and *Entertainment News**.)

The Kung Fu Films of Bruce Lee

Bruce Lee had been a child star in Hong Kong cinema in the 1950s. After featuring in the Hollywood films *The Green Hornet* (1964) and *Marlowe* (1969),[31] on 31 October 1971, he accepted the invitation by Golden Harvest to join Luo Wei's production *The Big Boss* (1971). Immediately after the release of the film, the box office takings reached $3.19 million. Following this success, in the following year Lee participated in another film, *Fist of Fury*, which grossed $4.43 million. Also in 1972, he directed and starred in *The Way of the Dragon*, which broke the record for Mandarin movies, earning over $5 million. In the next year he suddenly died, after completing the film *Enter the Dragon* (directed by Robert Clouse). His sudden death at the age of 32 shocked the world.

Bruce Lee's kung fu pictures appeared when Hong Kong film-making was at a low ebb. His movies not merely reinvigorated the wilting industry, but also initiated a kung fu craze, which swept over Southeast Asia for the first time. For Hong Kong movies to enter the international film market was groundbreaking. Lee achieved the status of a superstar, becoming the hero/idol of millions of socially and ethnically marginalized people. Since childhood, Lee had been trained in Jeet Kune Do. In every one of his films, he demonstrated his talent in Chinese martial arts. All of his characters uphold justice, even at the price of life, and staunchly defend the Chinese people, who had long been subjected to discrimination and suppression. In *Fist of Fury*, Lee broke a tablet with the words 'Chinese and dogs are not allowed'. This was similar to his act in breaking up the placard of a Japanese martial arts school. In *The Way of the Dragon*, the hero employed Jeet Kune Do to defeat some westerners and a restaurant waiter named Little Kylin, in an expression of uncompromising manliness and national dignity. A parallel plot can be found in *The Big Boss*. At the beginning, the hero, Cheng Chiu-on (Bruce Lee), kept his promise to his dead mother to refrain from fighting, even when ridiculed. However, after the jade piece, an emblem of his mother, was shattered by an opponent, he rose up in fury and killed the drug traffickers. The message was simple, yet forceful. The reverence in which Bruce Lee was held by Blacks, Latin Americans and people in Third World countries, therefore, was understandable. These weak ethnicities had suffered humiliation and suppression from whites, who symbolized power.[32] Now, at the spiritual level, Lee was avenging them. It was thus natural for them to regard Lee as a hero, or even a god. For Hong Kong Chinese, he was no less significant.

Bruce Lee wrought miracles for Hong Kong cinema, despite the fact that he made a mere four or five films in barely three years. His contribution cannot be reckoned in terms of quantity but, apart from the abovementioned psychological impact, in the following aspects: Lee re-ignited the audience's concern for indigenous cinema, made it possible for Hong Kong movies to enter the international market for the first time and created a craze for kung fu movies, influencing later figures such as Jackie Chan, Lau Kar-leung, Sammo Hung, Yuen Woo-ping and others.

Michael Hui's Comedies and Television Programmes

With regard to the bonds between television and film in the 1970s, the earliest such direct links were the comedies of Michael Hui. As early as 1971, Hui produced a half-hour comedy called the *Hui Brothers' Show* for HK-TVB, the response to which was satisfactory. Along with *Enjoy Yourself Tonight*, it became the station's most popular show. Hui grasped the skill of making television comedies: namely, that the jokes should be of a certain quantity and frequency in order to attract an audience. After three years of training, Hui left the television industry to make his debut feature, *Games Gamblers Play* (1974). This film grossed HK $6,250,000, topping the box office list in that year. 1975's *The Last Message* garnered HK $4,550,000. *The Private Eyes*, made in the subsequent year, took in HK $8,500,000 and, in 1978, *The Contract* earned HK $7,823,000.

It could be said that Michael Hui's comedies and Bruce Lee's kung fu films were the two main streams in Hong Kong cinema and had a similar status. In the beginning, the structure of Hui's films was carried over from the television equivalent. They then improved, successfully shaping a distinctive genre in Hong Kong cinema. One advantage Hui had was that he was adept at scriptwriting, directing and acting. In particular, his acting was remarkable, and he came to be considered a first-class comedian. The leading roles in Hui's features were often archetypes of lower-class people. Consider, for instance, the arrogant older brother in the *Games Gamblers Play*; the self-loathing characters in *The Last Message*; and the cynics, particularly toward institutions or rulers, in *The Contract* and *Security Unlimited*. All of these creations were popular and widely recognized by the public. Although the *Games Gamblers Play* may now appear crude in terms of production, contain too much dialogue and have unsophisticated characters, it was unquestionably a pioneering work in the 'compacted comedies' of the 1970s.[33]

Another noteworthy HK-TVB comedy is the 1977 *It's Not So Simple*, directed by Chan Ka-sun. With Josephine Siao as the female lead, Lam Ah Chun became a household name with her 'unisex' appearance, characterized by an over-sized shirt, belled trousers, thick spectacles and mushroom-like short hairstyle. Thus, when Chan Ka-sun left HK-TVB in 1978, the iconic Lam reappeared in his 1978 film *Lam Ah Chun* and in Wong Wah-kei's 1979 sequel, *Lam Ah Chun Blunders Again*. In appearance, image and acting, the Lam Ah Chun of the films was basically adapted from the Lam Ah Chun of television. Without the television character, there would have been no film character. This was indicative of the growing connection between television and film.

The House of 72 Tenants and Cantonese Cinema

The corruption of the Hong Kong police was part of the climate of the early 1970s. The phenomenon was corrosive to both the foundations of society and to relationship between the police and the public. The Hong Kong government was therefore urged to found the Independent Commission Against Corruption (ICAC), which began service on 15 February 1974. It was in such a context that Chor Yuen made his movie *The House of 72 Tenants*, adapted from a stage performance of the same title, in 1973. The film was an unexpected hit, grossing over HK $5,600,000 and topping the box office.

The narrative revolves around 72 people who live in an old apartment. Their landlady, a money-minded woman concerned solely with her own interests, keeps forcing her tenants to move out. The tenants unite to rebel against both the landlady and the police – symbols of authority who, however, misuse their powers. After a series of confrontations, they triumph over the wicked characters. The film gave voice to the audience's dissatisfaction with oppression and the abuse of power. As a Cantonese-speaking film, it was not surprising that it also led 'the resurgence of Cantonese cinema'.[34] This also explains why the practice of dubbing Mandarin films or films of other dialects into Cantonese later became common. As a remake of a Wang Weiyi film of the 1960s, which was released in Rediffusion Cable, the audience should have been familiar with the story of *The House of 72 Tenants*. But it was still so well received, as if it were something fresh. This was because the film echoed the current social situation, and spoke out about the concerns of the average urban dweller.

The mid-1970s saw the decline of the big studios, which allowed independent film-making to come to the fore. It was also a period of continuous demand from Hong Kong, Taiwan, and some other regions in Southeast Asia for Hong Kong movies. Following Bruce Lee's pictures, more kung fu films were produced. Zhang Che's *Five Shaolin Masters* (1974), *All Men Are Brothers* (1975) and Luo Wei's *New Fist of Fury* (1976) are examples of the traditional type. At the same time, another sort of kung fu comedy, which revised the genre, emerged. These included, to name a few, Yuen Woo-ping's *Snake in the Eagle's Shadow* (1978), Lau Kar-leong's *36th Chamber of Shaolin* (1978) and Sammo Hung's *Warriors Two* (1978).

As was mentioned above, in the early 1970s, corruption was rife among policemen and government officials. This led to internal contradictions in society and to a worsening of social order. According to the Government's statistics, the number of cases of crime increased drastically from 37,778 in 1973 to 50,000 in 1974, or 40.6 per cent. The ICAC, which was established the next year, was so effective that a drop of 10.8 per cent was reported in 1976. In 1977, however, the number of crimes rose to 60,000 cases; then, in the subsequent year, it again declined, by 10 per cent, to 6,749 cases.[35] Immediately after the establishment of the ICAC, corrupt government officials felt under threat and triad members lost their police protection, explaining why the number of crimes dropped. But the fall did not last long; the number of crimes rebounded after several years. The gangster element was also reflected in a number of crime movies, namely *Bald-Headed Betty* (1975), *Ironside 426* (1977), *Hot Blood* (1977) and *The Rascal Billionaire* (1978). Although not notably successful commercially, these pictures helped to pave the way for the revved-up gangster films of the coming two decades.

The Blood Tie between Cinema and Television

In the 1970s, the development of Hong Kong's television industry was as rapid as that of the territory's economy as a whole. Recall that in the early days of the establishment of television stations, there was an influx of film talent, both on-screen and off-screen, which greatly sped up the development of television. However, after a decade, the situation was reversed. No only did television have an influence on film-making, it also transferred a great deal of talent to the film industry. The contribution made by HK-TVB is especially noteworthy. HK-TVB went from importing foreign programmes to producing its own television programmes (in the late 1980s and early 1990s. In this way, a great number of talented people, especially in the fields of scriptwriting, directing and acting were trained. In addition to the disturbances that rocked the television industry (Leong Suk-yi's migration to Commercial Television and its closure, hastened by the failure of its publicity campaign, and the termination of the film unit of TVB), talent moved from the broadcasting sector to the film sector, and that further revitalized Hong Kong cinema.

The years following the mid-1970s were the golden era of Hong Kong's economy. The middle class grew, calls for democracy became common, a strong local consciousness emerged, the society was dynamic, and the people were full of confidence. Television, as a significant and central channel of communication, reflected this context. Realistic and satirical television comedies such as the *Hui Brothers' Show* and *Seventy-Three* became popular, and films with a similar content, such as the *Games Gamblers Play* and *Hong Kong 73*, also achieved success at the box office. The film *The House of 72 Tenants* was a fair, if not exact, equivalent of its television version. The cast was fully made up of the actors and actresses who had appeared in the television version. As a Cantonese-speaking drama, the narrative focused on the life and psyche of the television audience and ordinary people. It would not be wrong to call this film an outgrowth or an extension of its television forerunner.[36] In the 1970s, the relationship between cinema and television was mutually supplementary and interlocking, and extremely close.

In Hong Kong's television industry, HK-TVB was the very first to use 16mm film in television productions. Its use began with the film director Lau Fong-kong, who transferred to television in 1972. In *Crossroad*, made for HK-TVB, he adopted film-making techniques that integrated drama and documentary. The results were vivid and lively, and the programme received good reviews. Because of this success, in 1975, HK-TVB followed this with two series consisting of half-hour episodes, *Wonderfun* and *Superstars*, both directed by Patrick Tam. These were followed by *Seven Women* and *Thirteen*. Through these television productions, Tam's talent became known and that laid the foundation for his later film-making career. In 1976, HK-TVB officially established a film unit headed by Lau Fong-kong. It solicited such film-makers as Ann Hui, Law Kar, Yim Ho, Dennis Yu, Chan Dzuk-dziu, Ng Siu-wan, Pak Tong Cheuk, Lam Kuen, Alex Cheung and Ho Hong-kiu. The unit produced such series as *CID* (1976), *Social Worker* (1977), *Seventeen* (1977), *Interpol* (1977), *The Detective Story* (1978), *Taxi Driver* (1978), *I Am a Woman* (1979), *The First Step* (1979) and others. Later the film unit came under the supervision of Lee Pui-kuen. As its major rival, Commercial Television had closed down and Rediffusion posed no significant threat, HK-TVB stopped investing massive amounts on film-stock productions. Thus, in 1979, HK-TVB formally dissolved its film unit and fully adopted videotape shooting.

With the exception of Alex Cheung, Lee Pui-kuen and Ho Hong-kiu, all of the directors in the film unit of HK-TVB were young directors who had studied in film schools overseas and then returned to Hong Kong. Apart from those in the film unit, film-makers such as Tsui Hark, Clifford Choi and Kirk Wong also worked for the station. One by one, when they were about thirty years old or so, they later left and devoted themselves fully to film-making.

Rediffusion Television also used film stock to make dramas. One example was the aforesaid drama series, Johnny Mak's *Ten Sensational Cases* (1975–76). Soon afterwards, Rediffusion also shot a series of reality-action dramas, namely *Ten*

Assassinations (1976), *Operation Manhunt II* and *Big Sister* (both 1977), in videotape. These television dramas, to a greater or lesser degree, had both a direct and indirect influence over movies such *Rules of the Family**, *Hot Blood* and *The Rascal Billionaire*. Mak made his entry to the film industry in 1982 and produced an array of theatrical action films such as the *Long Arm of the Law* and its sequels, drawing on what he had learned during his days working in television. The government-financed Radio Television Hong Kong (RTHK), for its part, was under much fewer constraints in terms of budget and production time than the commercial television stations, which had to compete fiercely with each other. With such advantages, RTHK produced the drama series, shot on film, *Below the Lion Rock*. The series was originally intended as a way of spreading the news about government policies and to help people solve problems. However, under the direction of some film-makers with their own ways of thinking, the propagandist element was reduced to a minimum, and several thoughtful works were produced. This landmark series was supervised by Wong Wah-kei, and later by Cheung Man-yi. Two episodes by Allen Fong, *The Wild Child* and *The Song of Yuen Chau Chai*, won him the Asia Broadcasting Society's Best Young Director Award. Fong demonstrated strong realism in most of his works. Moreover, another series, *When We Were Young*, made by such directors as David King, Lo Tzi-keung, Rachel Zen, Fung Yi-ching and others, was launched. It was this series that first brought Rachel Zen to the attention of the public

The ratings war initiated by Commercial Television made Tsui Hark famous. He found his direction during his tenure at CTV and waited for a chance to enter the film industry. Patrick Tam, likewise, became popular during his days with HK-TVB. He was not long at CTV; and his *Romance of Celebrity* was only a project made on contract terms. The closure of CTV hastened the entry of the two to the film industry. This breed of young writers and directors at television stations had already earned a good deal of attention from both the media and society. They were only awaiting the right opportunity to enter the Hong Kong film industry. The first to do so were Yim Ho and Dennis Yu of HK-TVB. In 1978, they allied with Philip Chan to establish their New Force Company. The founding New Wave work, *The Extra*, a comedy, was produced. The narrative centred around an actor of bit parts, from the lower class, and his struggle for survival. Under a façade of lightness, the film had a bitter edge. It was also full of human feeling, sharp images and rich details.

The closure of CTV in 1979 also sped up Tsui Hark's entry to the film industry. His debut feature, *The Butterfly Murders*, earned rave reviews for its tremendous creativity and sophisticated imagery. That same year, Ann Hui left RTHK and finished her earliest picture, *The Secret*. Alex Cheung also made a similar move, and the crime thriller *Cops and Robbers* was his first work. The list goes on: Patrick Tam's *The Sword*, Dennis Yu's *See Bar* and *The Beast*, Clifford Choi's *Encore* and Lau Shing-hon's *The House of Lute*. In the 1980s, Tsui Hark, Ann Hui and Yim Ho each released their second films, which were, respectively, *Dangerous Encounter – 1st Kind*, *The Spooky Bunch* and *The Happening*. All demonstrated a great deal of creativity.

The next year, Allen Fong left RTHK and completed his debut assignment, *Father and Son*. Kirk Wong, who had left HK-TVB, made *The Club*. The film-making projects continued: Pak Tong Cheuk's *The Securities*, Rachel Zen's *Cream Milk and Soda*, Lee Pui-kuen's *Ghost Story*, Wong Chi's *The Crazy Corp*, Patrick Tam's second feature, *The Love Massacre*, Yim Ho's third picture, *Wedding Bells*, Tsui Hark's third film, *All the Wrong Clues (for the Right Solution...)*, Alex Cheung's second movie, *Man on the Brink*, Ann Hui's third picture, *The Story of Woo Viet*, Dennis Yu's second feature, *The Imp*, and Clifford Choi's second movie, *No U-Turn*.

In 1982, the New Wave productions included Patrick Tam's third film *Nomad*, Ann Hui's fourth picture, *The Boat People*, Yim Ho's *Buddha's Lock and Latch*, Clifford Choi's *Teenage Dreamers*, Pak Tong Cheuk's second feature, *Marianna*, Ng Siu-wan's debut work, *Once Upon A Rainbow*, and Lau Shing-hon's second movie, *Head Hunter*.

The New Wave films that were released in 1983 were Allen Fong's second picture, *Ah Ying*, Kirk Wong's second movie, *Health Warning*, Alex Cheung's third film, *Twinkle Twinkle Little Star*, Clifford Choi's fourth picture, *Hong Kong, Hong Kong*, and Tsui Hark's fourth feature, *Zu, Warriors of the Magic Mountain*. All are evidence of the beginning of the emergence in the late 1970s of phenomenal variety and competition in Hong Kong cinema. In the history of Hong Kong cinema, it was unprecedented for so many directors to move from television to the film industry and to produce such a large body of work in a diverse range of styles and genres.

In fact, at about this time, Hong Kong kung fu films were in decline; and Michael Hui's comedies, although popular enough, alone could hardly invigorate the industry. The subgenre of kung fu comedies was in its infancy; the big studios were fading away; and independent film-making required a tremendous infusion of new blood. In other words, the rise of independent film-making showed that there was an appetite for Hong Kong movies in Southeast Asia, Europe and America. As Hong Kong society became increasingly sophisticated and pluralistic, there was a demand for different kinds of information, entertainment and culture; and the existing movies simply could not satisfy the audience. Those young directors, working in television, felt the pulse of society and divined the needs of the audience. During their many years in television, they had gained a full mastery of cinematic language and other skills and were well prepared to enter film-making. In 1978, led by Yim Ho, they signalled to the world the birth of Hong Kong's New Wave cinema.

Notes

1. Ko Tim-keung, (ed.) *Hong Kong Today and Yesterday*. 3rd edition. Hong Kong: Joint Publishing House, 1995, p. 16.
2. *Eleven Years of Hong Kong's Leap and Bounds – Wah Kiu Daily's Witnesses of History*. Hong Kong: South China Morning Post Publishing House. August 1995, p. 88.
3. *Hong Kong Annual Report 1987*. Hong Kong: Hong Kong Information Bureau, 1986, p. 253.

4. Kam Cheung-kau. *Lectures on Hong Kong's Economy*. 1st edition. Guangzhou: Zhongshan University Press, April 1989, p. 445.
5. *Hong Kong Annual Report*. Hong Kong: Hong Kong Information Bureau. 1960–1972.
6. *Eleven Years of Hong Kong's Leap and Bounds – Wah Kiu Daily's Witnesses of History*. Hong Kong: South China Morning Post Publishing House. August 1995, p. 78.
7. Zhu Ke. *Behind the Screen*. Hong Kong: Cosmos Books, 1985.
8. Ibid., p. 18.
9. *Hong Kong Television Weekly 241*. Hong Kong: Television Broadcasts Ltd. Press, 20 June 1970, pp. 17–18.
10. Ibid., p. 14.
11. Informed by a survey conducted by SRHK in August 1970, *Enjoy Yourself Tonight* had an audienceship sized over 1 million people.
12. The drama series that Rediffusion adapted included *The Lost Ring, A Life with Hate* and *Yianshuihan.** Those made by HK-TVB were *The Story of Ching Palace, To Live Like Hell, Yianyu mengmeng** and *The Boat*.
13. Weekend Theatre, released every Saturday, had half-an-hour or one-hour episodes. The first long drama series was *Mengduan qiantian.* Sunday Theatre* was shown on Sundays, and *Jade Theatre* was aired during peak hours from Monday to Friday.
14. Rediffusion Television, HK-TVB, RTHK, Commercial Radio and CTV were dubbed 'Five Stations Hill'.
15. HK-TVB continued to release martial arts series namely *Luk Siu Fung, Legend of the Flying Swordsman* and *Chao Lau Hong*.
16. The two dramas, *CID* and *Wonderful*, were produced by Lau Fong-kong's film unit, whereas *Seven Women* was made by Patrick Tam.
17. Leong Suk-yi dealt a severe blow to HK-TVB by bringing with her about 200 executives and artists, particularly Yip Kit-hing, Sek Siu-ming and Lo Kwok-dzim. Thus, began the battle of 'Five Stations Hill'.
18. See the front page (full page) of *Ming Pao Daily*, 30–31 June, 2–3 and 6 July 1978.
19. See the front page of *Ming Pao Daily*, 1–2, 6, 16 July 1978.
20. *Hong Kong Television* 494. Hong Kong: Television Broadcasts Ltd. Press, April 1977, p. 23.
21. An international market survey conducted in November 1977 by Nga Tat Soon Company indicated that the top five television programmes were, respectively, 1. *A House is Not a House* (2,400,000); 2. *Luk Siu Fung* (2,308,000); 3. *Two for Three* (2,083,000); 4. *K100* (1,992,000); and 5. *When We Were Young* (1,096,000).
22. *Colourful Youth* was directed by Chan Wan, *Girls are Flowers* by Wong Yiu and *Waste Not Our Youth* by Ng Dan.
23. Pak Tong Cheuk. 'The Characteristics of Sixties Youth Movies,' *The Restless Breed: Cantonese Stars of the Sixties*. 20th Hong Kong International Film Festival (HKIFF). Law Kar, ed. Hong Kong: Urban Council, 1996, pp. 69–70.
24. I. C. Jarvie, *Window on Hong Kong: A Sociological Study of Hong Kong Film Industry and Its Audience*. Hong Kong Center of Asian Studies, Hong Kong University, 1977, p. 129.
25. The following table is from *Hong Kong Television* 495. Hong Kong: Television Broadcasts Ltd. Press, April 1977, p. 91.

Year	Total number of television subscribers	Percentage of TV subscribers among Hong Kong families	Date of survey
1968	97,000	12.4	September 1968
1969	216,000	27.3	May 1969
1970	336,000	41.2	January 1970
1971	504,000	60.0	July 1971
1972	609,000	72.0	July 1972
1973	671,000	77.8	July 1973
1974	748,000	84.7	January 1974
1975	785,000	87.8	January 1975
1976	860,000	90.0	March 1976

26. Mo Kai. *The Structural Changes and Economic Development of Hong Kong*. Hong Kong: Joint Publishing, 1993, p. 55.
27. *Hong Kong Annual Report*. Hong Kong: Hong Kong Information Bureau, 1981, p. 25.
28. Ibid., 1979, p. 35.
29. *Hong Kong Television 202*. Hong Kong: Television Broadcasts Ltd. Press, 21 September 1971, p. 41.
30. *Hong Kong Annual Report*. Hong Kong: Hong Kong Information Bureau, 1969–1977.
31. The Hong Kong films in which Bruce Lee starred included *Golden Gate Girl* (1945), *Wealth is Like a Dream* (1948), *The Kid* (1950), *Infancy* (1951), *Thunderstorm* (1957) and *The Orphan* (1960). He later moved to the United States to study at the University of Washington, majoring in philosophy and psychology. After this, he acted in some movies in Hollywood. Unable to fulfil his aspirations there, he returned to Hong Kong in 1970 to pursue greater opportunities.
32. Cheng Yu. 'Anatomy of a Legend.' *A Study of Hong Kong Cinema in the Seventies*. 8th HKIFF. Li Cheuk-to, Michael Lam and Leong Mo-ling, eds. Hong Kong: Urban Council, 1984, p. 19.
33. Law Kar. 'A Decade of Sword Grinding.' *A Study of Hong Kong Cinema in the Seventies*. 8th HKIFF. Li Cheuk-to, Michael Lam, and Leong Mo-ling, eds. Hong Kong: Urban Council, 1984, p. 62.
34. Kung, James and Zhang Yueai. 'Hon Kong Cinema and Television in the 1970s: A Perspective.' *A Study of Hong Kong Cinema in the Seventies*. 8th HKIFF. Li Cheuk-to, Michael Lam and Leong Mo-ling, eds. Hong Kong: Urban Council, 1984, p. 11.
35. *Hong Kong Annual Report*. Hong Kong: Hong Kong Information Bureau, 1978, p. 45.
36. Kung, James and Zhang Yueai. 'Hon Kong Cinema and Television in the 1970s: A Perspective.' *A Study of Hong Kong Cinema in the Seventies*. 8th HKIFF. Li Cheuk-to, Michael Lam and Leong Mo-ling, eds. Hong Kong: Urban Council, 1984, p. 11.

3

Ann Hui

Hui On-wah, Ann, was born in Anshan, in the province of Liaoning in 1947. She spent her childhood in Macau and moved to Hong Kong to attend high school and university. She earned her master's degree from the University of Hong Kong, with a major in English and comparative literature. She continued her studies in the London Film School, graduating in 1975. This was followed by a stint in King Hu's film production business in Hong Kong. She then began working for TVB as a scriptwriter-director and produced documentaries such as *Wonderful*, four episodes of the *CID* series, two of the *Social Worker* series and one of the *Dragon, Tiger, Panther* series.[1] In March 1977 she directed six dramas for the Independent Commission Against Corruption (ICAC).[2] In 1978, she joined RTHK and produced three episodes of *Below the Lion Rock*.[3] In the same year, she moved into the film industry and, in 1979, directed *The Secret,* which launched her in a feature film-making career that is now into its 23rd year. To date, Hui has directed a total of seventeen pictures and produced three.[4] Amongst the New Wave directors, Hui has been the most prolific in terms of the number of television productions she has worked on and, in terms of the number of films she has directed, she is second only to Tsui Hark. During her career she has worked in various genres, including those of the detective thriller, ghost film, martial-art epic, romance, family-ethics melodrama, the semi-autobiographical film and the documentary film. With regard to the diversity of the films directed she is at the forefront of her New Wave contemporaries.

In Hui's films an intimate relationship between television and cinema authorship is unveiled. This is apparent in the subject matter, and even in the modes of narration employed in her works. Many parallels can be found between her film and television work. For example, between her *The Boy from Vietnam* (1978) and the *Story of Woo Viet* (1981) and between *Murder* (1977) and *The Secret* (1979). One of the most remarkable features of the Hong Kong New Wave in general is that its film-makers have worked in both film and television. The new directors moved into film from television, and the experience gained in television acted as a platform for their later film-making careers. This characteristic also marks a key difference between them and both the later Taiwan New Cinema and Chinese New Cinema (Fifth Generation) groups. The latter two made a clear distinction between film and television, rather than emphasizing the complementarity of the two forms. Hui's films are amongst the best illustrations of this particular characteristic of the Hong Kong New Wave group of film-makers.

If localization was one of the prominent achievements of the New Wave films, then Hui's works also stand out in this regard. As early as the time during which she was working in television, Hui's works were steeped in the social problems of Hong Kong. For example, *The Bridge* (1978) investigated the issue of bureaucratic government institutions turning a blind eye to the kinds of living environments that were hazardous to people's health. Other examples include *ICAC,* which exposed corruption within the police force, and *The Boy from Vietnam,* which examined the issue of Vietnamese boat refugees. These films display a concern with issues surrounding the realistic representation of social problems and society. For example, *The Secret* (1980) presents images from the gloomy and dreary old Western District, with its worn-out mansions, shadowy alleys, fallen leaves and religious rituals, such as the ceremonial rite of releasing the soul from purgatory by burning paper money and cutting off the head of a chicken. *The Secret* also presents indigenous and traditional images, such as the desolate island of Cheung Chau, village opera groups, haunting ghosts, spirit possession, magical amulets and altar rituals. However, Hui's films are not solely concerned with social problems and traditions and also focus on the question of identity. Examples are the *Song of the Exile* (1990) and *As Time Goes By* (1997). She extended this concern with identity to embrace questions of individual and national identity in *The Romance of Book and Sword Parts I and II* (1987) and *Ordinary Heroes* (1999), and conflicts between different nations and cultures in *An American Grandson* (1991). She also made *The Boat People* (1982), a film that covers all of these issues with a tolerant and humanist sensibility. More recently, Hui has made films in a similar vein, including *Summer Snow* (1995), *As Time Goes By* (1997) and *Ordinary Heroes* (1999).

Cinematic Language and Genres

Hui's tendency to experiment with an array of subjects and unusual modes of narration dates back to her days working in television. *Dragon, Tiger, Panther* (1976) was the first drama she worked on after leaving the television industry.[5] In it, the protagonist Wong Yuen-sun commissions an attorney, Ho Sau-shun, to handle his divorce from his wife, Lee Yan-yee, on the grounds of adultery. Apparently unable to withstand the resulting pressure from the media, Lee commits suicide. However, it is later discovered that the case is not a simple one and that the victim is not Lee, who has actually fled to Switzerland, but someone else. The mystery of the real identity of the dead woman remains unresolved. Various people express various points of view, and arcane plots and moods are created through the use of multi-narrative voices. This kind of narration is also used again in Hui's later films, such as *The Secret* (1979), *The Spooky Bunch* (1980), *Eighteen Springs* (1997) and others.

In addition to the specific mode of narration, Hui also uses voice-over as a device to link scenes and shots. This is a hallmark of Hui's films. In Hui's features, voice-over functions not solely to (1) narrate the plot and (2) bring to the surface the interior thoughts and feelings of the characters, but also (3) to catalyze the connection between shots. In most cases, voice-over is employed to give oral expression to the interior thoughts and feelings of the characters. Here, Hui sometimes uses the technique of having someone read out a letter; at other times, she makes use of dialogues. Regardless of the form taken, however, voice-over tends to have the above three functions. This aural device usually provides possibilities for changing the film's structure with regard to time and space, thus also making it convenient to use multi-perspective narration and creating opportunities to do so. Furthermore, it also enriches the narrative function of the film. In *Dragon, Tiger, Panther,* examples can be found of the alternation of time and space using voice-over. Details of this will be discussed later. In addition to the 'Trilogy of Grieving Ghosts'[6] discussed earlier, Hui's later works, *Song of the Exile, Eighteen Springs* and *Ordinary Heroes,* have narrative structures that evolve from multiple points of view to multiple layers of time and space intertwining with each other.

Both *Social Work - Boy* (1977) and *Social Work - Ah Sze* (1977) were made for TVB. *Social Work - Boy* tells a story of a family that takes the calculated risk of faking a car accident in order to bring a measure of ease to their difficult lives. The mother attempts to slam against the vehicle to induce the owner of the car to pay her a sum for medical fees. This episode shows some similarity to the *Cruel Story of Youth,* a film by the Japanese director Nagisa Oshima. What is impressive is that a scene, in which the mother Miu Kam-feng is seriously knocked down by the car, is put in parallel editing with another scene - of the son's head being hit by a ball as he watches a football game. This is then followed by the image of a flashing red light, coupled with an image that arises from the mother's imagination - an image of the father bringing along her two sons shouting, 'Ma—'.

Social Work - Ah Sze centres around a lady called Ah Sze, played by Wong Hang-sau. Stranded, Ah Sze migrates illegally from mainland China to Macau and then to Hong Kong. In Macau, she is sold into prostitution to earn money for the trip to Hong Kong. In Hong Kong, she participates in the same 'business' under triad control. She then meets a drug addict, played by Ng Wai-kwok, and bears his baby. But the baby is given to someone else to raise, as Ah Sze chooses the lonely path of struggle and survival. The narrative illustrates Ah Sze's helplessness and weariness as she deals with her surroundings and with life, and this is conveyed through a series of lamentations and sighs. It is also an expression of the director's feelings of concern and sympathy for women. The message revealed in this movie is that an individual can find no home in such a big, complicated world, and shall suffer from destitution and exile. This became the chief motif of many of Hui's subsequent films. For example, *Below the Lion Rock – The Road* (1978), another tale about women, depicts a mother and a daughter, played respectively by Wong Man-lei and Dodo Cheng, who, as a result of the harsh environment they find themselves within, turn to drugs and become addicted. However, their relationship then changes from one characterized by quarrels and recriminations, to one characterized by consoling support. The strength of the women upon having survived is noted.

Another drama, *CID: Murder* (1977), is a reference to a real case. The male protagonist, James Wong, is a man living in poverty. After divorcing his wife, he lives with his daughter, Ah Hung, and his mother in a squatter hut. Planning to contract a new marriage with Wong Man-wai, James finds his fiancée and daughter at odds with each other. Under accumulated pressure from his fiancée, daughter and the environment, James becomes psychotic and kills Ah Hung. Two episodes of the ICAC series,[7] *The Investigation* and *The Real Man* (both 1977), were similarly based on real events. They were censored after completion, however, and were not released until the 1990s. The former is about the corruption case against the chief superintendent of the Hong Kong Police, Peter Godber. The beginning of the episode shows Godber noticing that an investigation into his activities is taking place and escaping to his home in England. The ICAC can only begin taking action against his subordinate, Wah Tak, and then arrest Officer Lau Dan. After three years, Godber is sent back to Hong Kong for trial and is taken into custody. Through sophisticated handling in the narrative of the various pieces of evidence, Hui gave a clear and well-organized presentation. *The Real Man* is about a police superintendent, Wai Lit, who is transferred to the station in Cheung Chau. He discovers that most of the staff at that station, senior and junior, are involved in corrupt activities. Acting according to his conscience, he submits a report to the ICAC. However, he is accused of doing so too late. Confronting pressure from all sides: threats from the villagers, obstacles intentionally put in his path by his seniors and ostracized by his colleagues, he goes through a series of internal struggles. After discussing the matter with his girlfriend, played by Dodo Cheng, he opts to take the path of uprightness and helps to arrest his corrupt superior and colleagues. Set in a fishing village on the island, the streets and alleys were shot to appear dark and mysterious, and the mood is as eerie as that in *The Secret*.

The three dramas shot for the ICAC, *Three Women* (1977), *Steak Expense* (1978) and *Black and White* (1978), are all propaganda vehicles for the ICAC. Nonetheless, Hui's camera shows no ICAC investigators as omnipotent heroes. Rather, they are shown as more likely than not to encounter misunderstanding and ridicule. As in *Black and White*, Dodo Cheng, who has just been accepted to work in the ICAC, is at times ridiculed by her former classmates. Even Kam Kwok-leung, who initially shows interest in her, immediately turns away from her after realizing that she works for the ICAC. The accusation is that if an ICAC staff member appears at the front door of a place, there will surely be somebody fleeing to the back and throwing himself/herself from the building. This exemplified the confrontation between the public and ICAC at that time. The investigators in *Steak Expense*, Lau Chong-yan and Kwan Chong, often fail to find evidence when investigating defective buildings that had been constructed by cement mixed using salt water rather than fresh water. At times, it was not possible for them to resist over-exercising their authority, a mistake that many people would commit, in order to complete tasks. In *Three Women*, policeman Tin Ching is being investigated by the ICAC, who are suspicious of how he is managing to support three families on a salary of three thousand Hong Kong dollars a month. The three women in his life have chosen their own way of surviving in life. The chief wife, Lee Shi-kee, merely cares about looking after the family, which includes her infant daughter and her mother-in-law. The second wife, Tse Yuet-mei, has only married for money. In contrast, the concubine, Cheung Ma-li, has married for love. As the investigation into Tin Ching begins, each of the women has her way of handling the situation, however, each also has her own weakness. The chief wife continues to immerse herself in hard work. The second wife, for her part, enters into negotiations with the ICAC staff to provide information for money. The concubine, on the other hand, lends her yacht to her lover to allow him to flee. The man himself suffers from tremendous fear as he is abandoned, communicating to viewers a sense of desolation and loneliness. The portrayal of women in this film is particularly impressive, demonstrated through a classic scene in which the three appear simultaneously in a washroom in the ICAC office and see but do not recognize each other.

Both *The Bridge* and *The Boy from Vietnam* (both 1978), belonging to the series *Below the Lion Rock*, are Hui's most audacious responses to social issues current in Hong Kong at the time. In *The Bridge*, the government's demolition of a bridge, without sufficient justification, provokes a strong reaction from residents. Conflicts between the people and the police are expressed via demonstrations. A foreign broadcast journalist reveals that the bureaucratic system functions in such a way as to neglect the opinions of the public and even put people's lives in danger. In the end, the journalist resigns from his job in anger and is forced to leave Hong Kong when the government refuses to renew his residence permit. Moreover, the evil intentions of the residents lead to disunity and to their exploitation without their being conscious of it. The film closes with the government succumbing to popular pressure to rebuilding the bridge. Another episode, *The Boy from Vietnam*, depicts several Vietnamese-Chinese refugees escaping for their lives from Vietnam to Hong Kong. Some of them hope to work in Hong Kong to earn money enough to transfer their family overseas, while others hope to visit places like the United States. This film is similar to two subsequent works of Hui, *Story of Woo Viet* (1981) and *Boat People* (1982). Collectively, the three have been named the 'Trilogy of Vietnam', as they all focus on problems involving Vietnam. They are about the tragic destinies of displaced individuals seeking a place to which they can belong and who are struggling in a period of changes, leading in the end to failure.

Materials Selected from the People and from Real Life, and a Modern Mode of Narration

After moving into film, Ann Hui's first picture was *The Secret* from the 'Trilogy of Grieving Ghosts'. This was followed the next year by *The Spooky Bunch*. Both films contain materials taken from tradition, using folk legends as blueprints. *The Secret* narrates a murder involving a triangular relationship and two deaths. Streets and alleys were shown as being supernatural and ghostly, arousing fear in human hearts and causing people to feel that mysterious shadows may be the haunted spirits of the dead. During the investigation, Miss Lin (Sylvia Chiang) discovers that the case is more complicated than it first appears. The dead person was not, as everybody expects, Lee Wun (Chiu Ngar-chi), who is still alive, but someone else. This sort of mysterious mood seems familiar. As in *Murder*, James Wong kills his daughter under various kinds of pressure. Under a hallucination, he is terrified and shocked when his girlfriend comes to him to inform him of the arrival of his boss. Psychosis is also evoked when he meets the brother of his dead wife, who is a cop (Ho Pik-kin). Imagining himself to be the object of Ho's suspicion, Wong attempts an attack on Ho in the back stairs with a knife, but fails. A note of suspense is also present in *Dragon, Tiger, Panther*. The case of Lee Yan-yee's death is as mysterious as that in *The Secret*, in that the dead person is later discovered not to be Lee but somebody else. What makes the circumstance more confusing is that the blood taken from the body and from the suspect are of the blood types B and AB, respectively. In the end, from the rituals of worship he practises at the location of incident, the murderer in *The Murder*, James Wong, is uncovered by Ho. In *Dragon, Tiger, Panther*, the suicide case of Lee, which had been faked, is investigated by lawyers and reporters. With regard to the real victim, the film offers an unresolved ending. The parallel between *the Secret* and *Dragon, Tiger, Panther* is that the murder is first presented as a mystery and is investigated step by step. Together with the haunting of spirits, an atmosphere suffused with suspense is created.

In fact, the haunting in the film was not by real spirits but by imagined ones. The narrative of *The Secret* proceeds as Lin systematically investigates the murder. As part of her investigation, she develops some photographs and discovers that the victim, Yuen Shi-cheuk (Man Chi-leung), has an unknown girlfriend, Mui Siu-kee. Mui is a prostitute who suffers from tuberculosis. Lin discovers a record of Lee's pregnancy in the pocket of Lee's red coat. The murder remains vague until Lee's re-appearance. Within the story is the eyewitness account of the idiot Tsui Siu-keung – thus, a multi-perspective narration is established. The whole case then is resolved. With a tone that is grotesque, frightening and terrifying, the film is considered more of a horror film or a thriller than a 'drama about humanity':

> In the beginning, I saw this story not as an adventure but as a drama about humanity. This was because the personality of the female protagonist is quite similar to that of Electra in the Greek tragedy: People thought the female protagonist, Lee Wun, had already died but in fact she was still alive. Nonetheless, Sylvia Chiang could not decide whether or not to report her criminal act. It is this aspect that I was interested in.[8]

Under commercial considerations, it is never an easy task for a director, especially one new to film-making, as Hui was at that time to achieve a balance between suspense and the psyche/humanity: 'Because we sometimes focus so much on achieving suspense, the result is flat characterization. At other times, we devote too much attention to depicting the personality of a character, leading to no sense of suspense at all....'[9] *The Secret* is also a unique film by Hui, and this uniqueness lies in the mode of narration employed. Chiang's memory was triggered by photographs, and the application of voice-over in a letter-reading scene (of letters written by Lee to Mui), interlacing past and present or even multiple layers of time and space, results in a narrative structure that is made up of manifold perspectives. This kind of technique is by no means commonplace for Hong Kong films of that period, and this film was regarded as one that 'breaks a simplified mode of pattern and displays the narrative at a complex level. Thus it can be said to be extraordinary'.[10] The achievement of *The Secret* is not due to the fact that it is a 'typical' genre film. Rather, it is said to lie in the film's strong sensitivity.[11] Furthermore, Hui certainly presents relatively new ideas when exploring images (cinematic language).[12] These also give her narrative style a solid foundation.

The Spooky Bunch is a ghost film that employs humour. This film also draws from folklore and traditions: souls, possession, female shamans, magical amulets, altar rituals and so forth. As with *Dragon, Tiger, Panther*, the story is set in an outlying island, Cheung Chau. However, *The Spooky Bunch* is a genuine ghost story, unlike *The Secret* in which the ghosts were imaginary. What is notable in this film is that the ghosts do not simply appear at night, but also in the daytime. A village opera troupe stays in Cheung Chau to perform. The spirits of a troop of soldiers of a previous generation who died because they had taken the wrong medication are searching for substitutes to poison the offspring of their enemies, the troupe members, to death. These ghosts have taken human form in order to carry out their plan to kill and throw the troupe into disarray. Among the members, Ah Chi (Josephine Siao), who is the only one not superstitious, intrepidly challenges the ghosts. The film closes with the defeat of the ghosts, who are then imprisoned in a bottle gourd by a Master. Again, this movie is one in which Hui consciously experiments with narrative form. In particular, she adopts light comedy to present an interchange of points of view between humans, between humans and ghosts and between ghosts. Although there are confusing points of intersection at times, this is quickly clarified, thanks to the smooth and organic development of the plot. The film also achieves a balance between the grotesque and the comic, exuding vitality. It opens up a new path, blending the supernatural, superstitions, Chinese folklore and the dynamic interpersonal relationships of common people. Under Hui's insightful organization, these elements create a colourful and inventive film.[13]

Peripatetic Spirits and Personal Helplessness in an Era of Change

Following the 'Trilogy of Grieving Ghosts', Ann Hui demonstrated a shift in concern from exploring film form to exploring the wider realm of the human spirit, specifically focusing on the life of the individual person. Following her *The Boy from Vietnam*, she shot the *Story of Woo Viet* (1981) and *Boat People* (1982), together dubbed the 'Trilogy of Vietnam'. *The Boy from Vietnam*, produced in the period during which Hui worked in television, opens with a horrifying scene, in which the Viet Cong invade a house to attack people. This is followed by a scene of frightened people clambering onto a boat to make their escape. This constitutes an introduction to the film. After this the camera cuts to Hong Kong, where the male protagonist, Ah Man, a young Vietnamese-Chinese boy, drifts to Hong Kong, looks for a place to live and hopes to work extremely hard and make money in order to bring his mother over. The escape, exile and displacement of Vietnamese Chinese was a particular tragedy of the period, and also a further example of the fate of all diasporic Chinese. Like Ah Man, another Chinese, Lee Kwok-chong, possesses no identity card and risks being arrested and sent back to Vietnam. Therefore, he is forced to tolerate exploitation from his boss. The cousin of Ah Man, Yau Hing-feng, is no exception. Because of war, he loses the chance to study. The fact that it is never easy to find a job in Hong Kong leads him to engage in prostitution. Yau is reluctant to work as a male prostitute. It is exactly as Lee said to Ah Man, 'Just like your cousin, I have no choice.' Having "no choice" is a full expression of their misery, as, under such a situation, individuals, in fact, have no choice.

Later, Yau is murdered by a john while Lee is sent back to Vietnam after an identification spot check by the police. The lives of both characters are proof of their miserable destiny of having "no choice". Ah Man's life is no better. She endures disdain and grievances in Hong Kong in the hope of being able to bring her mother here. Likewise, the protagonist Woo Viet (Chow Yun-fat) in the *Story of Woo Viet* experiences the 'choice' under conditions of no choice when moving from Vietnam to Hong Kong, then from Hong Kong to the Philippines. Consider the life of Woo. He was a soldier under the old government of Vietnam, who is forced to leave the country for Hong Kong after the country is taken over by the new government. Arriving in Hong Kong, he is targeted for assassination by a Vietnamese agent. Woo fights back, killing the agent, and has to leave again. He initially plans to go to the United States, but eventually flees to the Philippines. This twist is partially due to the control of the triads, who issue a fake passport for Woo, and partially because of a woman, Sum Ching (Cherie Chung), whom Woo befriends and then comes to love. The two buy forged passports; however, Sum is sold to prostitution in a Chinatown in the Philippines. Woo then endangers himself in order to save her, by committing himself to serve as an assassination for a godfather in Chinatown, Mr Chong. But Woo is betrayed by Chong and has no option but to murder him. At this moment, Sum also dies and we see Woo slowly lower her dead body into the sea. He escapes alone on a boat, to an uncertain future, and the close of the film marks the beginning of another lonely, nomadic journey for Woo.

After this film, portraying Vietnam-Chinese expatriates away from home no longer satisfied Ann Hui, and, in *Boat People*, she goes a step further and depicts the

Vietnamese and Chinese living in Vietnam. But interestingly, the Vietnam that we see through the lens of Hui is easily mistaken for mainland China, in part because the people and the government officials of the two nations bear a startling resemblance to each other. It is not clear whether this is a result of coincidence or whether the similarity arises from the choice of shooting location, in Hainan Island in China. A Japanese photojournalist named Akutagawa (George Lam), on the basis of his status as a foreign friend, visits Vietnam after Liberation. The more he sees, the more he realizes that the façade of bliss and happiness of the so-called New Economics Region touted by Vietnamese Communist officials is in fact a fake. The true conditions behind the façade are poverty and food shortages. People are forced to engage in prostitution, to dig up landmines and to rob from the dead. The New Economics Region is actually a place of deception, where people are brainwashed and tortured. The soldiers can shoot people at will. Ah Ming (Andy Lau) gives all of his money to a cadre, to purchase passage on a boat to escape; however, every single person on the boat is shot dead. 'I was deceived' Akutagawa asserts, when he finally sees the truth. The film closes with the photographer sacrificing his life to help Cam Nuong and her younger brother flee Vietnam – a hell on earth.

Social Worker – Ah Sze is also about showing compassion and concern for the weak. Ah Sze (Wong Hang-sau) leaves mainland China alone and comes to Macau. She is unable to locate her relatives and, in order to raise money to get to Hong Kong, she engages in prostitution, but is exploited by her pimp. Ah Sze finally makes it to Hong Kong but becomes a money-making instrument for a gangster who also becomes her first lover. Not only does he take most of the money she makes, she actually ends up owing him some money. To avoid being sold to the triads, she escapes. Her second lover, Ng Wai-kwok, is a drug addict who is unable to break his addiction. The film ends with Ah Sze's decision to pursue a new life, abandoning the past. Via Hui's lens, the heroine, despite hardships and adversity, retains the traditional virtues of Chinese women – perseverance and kindness.

Song of the Exile (1990) is a semi-autobiographical film. In the film, Hui's mother turns out to have been Japanese. When she was young, she emigrated with her older brother to China's northeast region. In the closing years of the Sino-Japanese War she falls in love with a translator (Waise Lee) with the Chinese army. She forsakes her family to marry Lee. This couple from different nations then migrates to Macau to live with Lee's parents. She cannot speak Chinese. Because of work, her husband later leaves for Hong Kong, where he lives alone, while she and their daughter, A Hong (symbolizing Ann Hui), remain in Macau. Because she is Japanese, and because prior to her marriage Lee's parents had not known this, they have never treated her in a particularly friendly manner. This has also influenced her young daughter's attitude towards her. The mother-daughter relationship has always been distant and even, at times, conflicting. After her grandparents move to Guangzhou, A Hong comes to Hong Kong to live with her mother, who has moved there earlier to rejoin her husband.

The relationship between the two is still tense until A Hong returns after completing her master's degree studies in England, and makes a journey to Japan, her mother's native home, together with her. Not until that moment can A Hong understand the depression her mother feels as an expatriate. After this, the tension in their relationship eases, and mother and daughter are reconciled. In fact, the grievances of the mother, who had abandoned her nation to follow her husband and live as an expatriate in Macau and Hong Kong, principally arose from the complicated relationship between the two nations. Added to this was her family's lack of understanding. Her father-in-law also experiences this kind of melancholy. He moves to Guangzhou to serve his country and people, but his long-cherished hopes are frustrated. In fact, when he mails a book of prose from the Song dynasty to his granddaughter, he is held for a day's interrogation by the Red Guard. His disillusionment can well be imagined. It is just like the lines in Bai Hua's *The Bitter Love* (*Kulian*), 'You love your motherland, but does your motherland love you?' However, the grandfather never loses hope for his motherland as this wish, after all, is what has sustained him for decades. Near the end of the film, A Hong visits her bedridden grandfather in Guangzhou, whose last words to her are, 'Don't lose hope in your motherland, as the hope is in you. You are China.' The June 4th Incident in Beijing took place as this film was being shot. This scene is a response from Ann Hui, Ng Nienzhen and others to serve as encouragement after disillusionment.[14]

Hui's subsequent film, *Zodiac Killers* (1991), falls under the subgenre of *qiqing pian* (literally, a film with an unusual or odd plot) and is purely fictitious. The characters in the film, namely Ah Ben (Andy Lau), Hong Gu (Cherie Chung), Ah Ming and Ah Chung, are all young people from Hong Kong and mainland China who go to Japan in search of adventure. If truth be told, they are all marginalized even at home. Consider, for example, the character of Ah Ben. He earns the lowest score in Hong Kong in the public examinations. As a member of a group that has been abandoned by society, nobody, except his mother, loves him. In Japan, these four young people study the Japanese language and work part-time, the men as tour guides and the women as bar girls. Hong Gu, as a bar girl, only drinks with customers but does not provide sexual services. However, in order to be able to stay in Japan, they are forced to submit to bullying on the part of their guarantors. Hong Gu is nearly raped and Ah Ming is forced to marry the sister of a Japanese crime boss. He is there to satisfy her sexual desire in exchange for material pleasures such as a car and even an airplane. Later, Hong Gu finds herself falling in love with another one of her guarantors, an escape artist of a gang. She even helps him to deliver to the Ying Mun Club a videotape showing evidence of a godfather raking off money earned from drug trafficking. But she is killed by being pushed into the subway tracks and struck by a train. Ah Ming, who hopes to save her, is also murdered by the gang. Hong Gu's former roommate, Meimei, commits suicide after killing her greedy boyfriend. In the end, Ah Ben, who wishes to help Hong Gu, sneaks back alone to Hong Kong by sea. This film is an affirmation of these Chinese youngsters, who struggle to survive, go to foreign lands in pursuit of their dreams and never live in remorse but with courage and integrity in the lower class of society. Moreover, they are chivalrous and righteous in that they would rather sacrifice themselves to preserve the dignity of others. Their acts are, therefore, worthy of sympathy.

Death is a motif that Hui's films usually address. Her early works in particular dwell on this motif in an unsettling manner. In *Dragon, Tiger, Panther*, the female protagonist, unable to bear the pressures of media reports on the scandal of her divorce, suddenly commits suicide. Although it is later revealed that the victim is not the divorced woman but someone else, a shadow falls over those surrounding her. In *Murder*, James Wong, driven by family and marriage pressures, kills his own daughter. For the remainder of his days, he is unstable and prone to hallucinations. Another episode of the *CID* series, *Professor, Wife and Student*, shows the murder of the professor's wife, carried out by Kam Kwok-leung. To atone for her death, he takes to lying in a coffin. In *Below the Lion Rock – The Bridge*, Wong Sun steals electricity to sell to the villagers. His son is then killed in a car accident, in what appears to be an act of deserved fate for Wong's criminal act. In *Below the Lion Rock – The Boy from Vietnam*, the cousin of Ah Man, a Vietnamese Chinese, works as a male prostitute to earn money in Hong Kong and is finally killed by a pimp. The motif of death is also found in Hui's feature films. *The Secret* involves a dual murder in which the prostitute Mui stabs to death the doctor, Yuen, and then is killed by Lee. An atmosphere of terror pervades the entire movie. In *The Spooky Bunch*, a group of ghosts snatch people and kill them. The *Story of Woo Viet* shows Woo's girlfriend being sold to a brothel in a Chinatown in the Philippines. In the end, Woo is knocked down and killed by a car when trying to rescue his lover. The film is a lamentation for the doomed fate of displaced Chinese. In *The Boat People*, Can Nuong's mother sells her body to earn money to survive. When she is arrested, she chooses suicide by stabbing her neck with a hook. And, in the end, Akutagawa sets fire to himself in order to protect Cam Nuong and her brother. The second part of *The Romance of Book and Sword*: *Princess Fragrance* is about the hero Chen Jialuo who, out of feelings of brotherhood and revolt against the Manchu Qing dynasty, offers the woman he loves, Princess Fragrance, to the Emperor Qian Long, who has destroyed the princess's entire family and tribe. Rather than submit, the princess prefers to commit suicide, both for love and for her tribe – (the Weijiang) in order to preserve her chastity and honour. Reminiscent of the *Story of Woo Viet*, *Zodiac Killers* is another elegy for diasporic Chinese; in this case those in Japan, who in the struggle to survive, to find love, or out of chivalry, die in a foreign land.

Marriage, Struggle and the Fate of Women

In *ICAC: A Real Man*: Superintendent Wai Lit, no longer able to bear the corruption found at every level of the police, chooses to make a report to ICAC. Initially, his girlfriend, Dodo Cheng, perceives his act as being too risky, as it pits him against the entire police force. However, after thinking the matter over thoroughly, she supports Wai's choice without regrets, acting as his witness and even resigning from her job. In her letter of resignation she writes, 'Nothing is stable in this world. What is right can be become wrong; and vice versa. It is the same with integrity.' This sequence is not only an accusation against an unjust society, but also a reflection of the persistence and righteousness of women. Likewise, women's fine qualities are featured in *Below the Lion Rock - The Road*. Here, a mother and a daughter, both drug addicts, finally succeed in breaking themselves of addiction by encouraging and supporting each other. There is also another female character, who has become involved in prostitution in order to pay off her gambler father's debts and, in the process, become addicted to drugs. These women have been harmed both physically and psychologically by being suppressed by men, but have never given up their struggle to survive. The films show understanding and sympathy for them and their troubles.

Adapted from a Zhang Ailing's novel of the same title, *Love in A Fallen City* (1984) is a film that is highly faithful to the original work. Ann Hui made this story into a film chiefly because of her fondness for the author. 'I was so surprised. How could an author write about Hong Kong in just the same way as I feel about it? ...... The feeling of resonance is very special.'[15] The female protagonist, Bai Liusu (Miu Hin-yan) marries a prodigal son but later divorces him and returns to her home. There, she discovers that her elder brother has spent all of her savings, and even wants to expel her from the family. She runs into Fan Liuyuan (Chow Yun-fat), who was originally meant to be a match for Bai's younger sister. Fan is from a wealthy Malaysian Chinese family who is interested in women and gambling and in everything except establishing a decent family. The film treats Bai's divorce and mockery from her brothers and sisters-in-law as matters not to be taken too seriously. As the housemaid tells her, 'Your elder brother has used up all of your money. But he will be supporting you for your entire life, so this is justified.' Bai later comes to know and to learn to deal with the worldly, sophisticated Fan. She is happy, but also depicted as being having a woman's endurance. This definitely mirrors the standpoint of the director, as a woman, toward love.

Within the film, there are a number of problematic moments due to over-fidelity to the original work. Examples are dialogues such as 'Separation and death are big issues in life over which we have no control. Compared to the forces outside, we are tiny, so tiny...', and 'This explosion has bombed away the ending of too many stories. If you are bombed to death, my story will end. If I am bombed to death, your story will persist for a long time'. These expressions, which are interesting and unique in the novel, do not come across the same way in the film. As cinematic dialogue, they are too literary. There are also two other shortcomings to the film. It is a great pity that the first occasion in which Bai and Fan encounter each other is not described directly, but is only told through a few sentences uttered by some minor characters. Similarly, in the war sequence, there is insufficient depiction of Bai's helplessness and Fan's dedication in return to his lover. The film would surely be more impressive if more elaboration could have been made on these points in the plot.[16] More focus could also have been given to the relationship between the hero and the heroine. The love between the two grows deeper with Bai's arrival in Hong Kong. However, when Bai sees Fan acting intimately with an Indian girl, she inevitably feels doubt and distrust. The irony is that the relationship between Bai and Fan does not bear fruit until the moment of the

Japanese occupation of Hong Kong. Only in a time of battle does Fan, returning from England, become serious about love. Finally, the lovers announce their marriage in the newspaper. The romance in this film is among the happiest of Hui's stories, as most of her other romances have involved love triangles that have ended in an unsatisfactory manner or involved the death of one party. For example, in *The Secret* the corpses of both Yuen and Lee are found on the eve of their wedding. A third person, Miu, had intruded on their relationship, which led to Lee murdering Yuen and then committing suicide. Similarly, the device of a triangular relationship is replicated in *Dragon, Tiger, Panther*. The couple Wong and Lee separated because each of them had taken up lovers. The film closes with Lee faking a scene of suicide and then transferring her property, setting the stage for her departure. In *Murder*, the love between James Wong and Wong Man-wai has about to reach the stage of marriage when a third person enters the picture. This person is James Wong's daughter, Ah Hung. Ah Hung is a burden to the couple and is eventually killed. In the end, the lovers are both punished in accordance with the law.

The Romance of Book and Sword, the second part of which is known as *Princess Fragrance* (1987), was adapted from Louis Cha's classic work. As the leader of the Red Flower Society, Chen Jialuo retrieves a classic book of the Uighur people, with the assistance of the daughter of the leader of the Mulun people, Qing Tong. Qing Tong admires Chen and sends him a sword as a gift before leaving the Wei people. However, Chen later falls in love with the sister of Qing Tong, Princess Fragrance. Subsequently, Emperor Qian Long attacks the Wei and utterly defeats them. Princess Fragrance is taken by Qian Long as a concubine. Chen accepts this, as he believes that the emperor will overthrow the Manchu Qing dynasty and restore the Han Chinese Ming dynasty. However, Fragrance does not turn away from her true love and chooses to commit suicide as a demonstration of her faithfulness. In the end, Chen loses not only Fragrance but also the lives of the Red Flower brothers, who are assassinated by Qian Long by trickery. In other words, the love between Chan and Fragrance is aborted with the emergence of a third person, Emperor Qian Long. No doubt Chen's attitude toward love is, to a large extent, problematic, in that he transfers his affections from Qing Tong to Fragrance because of the latter's beauty. It is nonetheless confusing that such a hero as Chen would exhort Fragrance to devote herself to Qian Long, who has extinguished her whole family and people. Does he really love her or not?

The film contains certain neglected or underwritten scenes. For instance, there is a scene in which Chen sends Fragrance a piece of jade presented by Emperor Qian Long. This is immediately followed by a scene of Fragrance already in Qian Long's palace. The film neglects details about the Qing soldiers' attack on the Wei people and the enslavement of Fragrance. The omission is similar to the one in *Love in a Fallen City*, of the first encounter of the hero and the heroine. Furthermore, the scene of the great battle between the Qing troops and the Uighurs is not reminiscent enough of a battle in that no battle carriages are shown at all. Another scene of the 'mysterious city' is, again, not "mysterious" enough. However, as a compact, historical film, *Princess Fragrance* is worthy of praise.

Starry is the Night (1988) is a love story involving social changes in Hong Kong, told from a woman's perspective. The romance in question is a triangular one. In the late 1960s, the heroine, Bridgette Lin, who is a university student, falls in love with a married lecturer, George Lam. He has a sort of revolutionary flair, yet is also impractical, indecisive and cowardly. Lin becomes pregnant by him, but he turns his back on her and flees to England. Lin's second love story takes place twenty years later. Aged about forty, she falls in love with David Ng, Lam's son. Ng acts as the third person in the relationship, as Lin still pines after her first love. Hui's shift in emphasis from the wanderings of Chinese émigrés (see the *Story of Woo Viet*), romance in the cities of Shanghai and Hong Kong in the 1930s and 40s (see *Love in A Fallen City*) and conflicts between individuals and nations during the Qing dynasty (see *Romance of Book and Sword* Parts I & II) back to the people and events of Hong Kong and Macau with which she is familiar, is a laudable one. *Starry is the Night* spans twenty years, covering a series of social and political occurrences such as the riots in 1967 that developed from labour disputes, students' movements, the movement to protect the Diaoyutai Islands from foreign claimants, the evolution of a democratic political system, the issue of popular votes, the District Board elections and so forth. Lin, as a woman, goes from being a university student to a social worker to an assistant of a councillor and, lastly, becomes the lover of a young man. In the past, she expected Lam to bring her to visit the Great Wall. Today, as the film closes, she can pay the visit there on her own. If Ann Hui has been transformed by the social changes that have taken place over those twenty years to become more mature, then the character of Lin mirrors this process of maturation. That Hui has chosen a love story in which to play out the social changes that have taken place over time is also significant. As a result of the failure of her first love, Lin matures. However, her second romance also comes under pressure from various sources, including from herself and society. Set in a realistic sociality, Lin's two loves are placed in the dual spatial framework of Macau and Hong Kong, and that duality is expressed using a highly complicated structure of temporality and space, which employs the technique of shifting the camera back and forth and makes use of flashbacks. Such a technique is appropriate to the core dualistic themes of the film.[17]

The romance between Cherie Chung and the Japanese gangster in *Zodiac Killers* evolves from a relationship in which each makes use of the other to find genuine love. This relationship between people from two countries is however doomed to be a tragic one. The male, a triad member, is destined to die, while the woman displays persistence and affection. After he dies, Chung is killed by the triads when she is pushed onto the path of a train when attempting to deliver a message for her Japanese lover. Andy Lau, who secretly loves Chung, has done his best to protect her despite the risk to his own life. He is nearly assassinated, yet escaped injury with Ah Ming's help. In *Ah Kam* (1996), Michelle Yeoh is a stuntwoman whose extraordinary choreography attracts the attention and approval of Sammo Hung. Love could have developed between them, but the entrance of a wealthy man into the picture ruins the opportunity. In the belief that this wealthy man would be a good partner for her, Ah Kam moves to Shenzhen to manage his karaoke enterprise. She is heartbroken to discover that he is involved in affairs with other women. This causes her to return to Hong Kong to take up her old career. The film expresses the uncertainty, hardship and helplessness in the profession of stuntmen. It also portrays the many reverses in Ah Kam's love life, although the film ends in a positive note, as she manages to pull herself together emotionally and proceed on her journey. *Eighteen Springs* (1997) also involves a turbulent, doomed romance. Shen Shijun (Leon Lai) and Gu Manzhen (Wu Chien-lien) meet, fall in love, and are on the point of marrying when Shen's father falls ill and Shen is forced to return to Nanjing to care for him. Shen's father disapproves of the relationship, as he is prejudiced against Manzhen's elder sister, Manlu (Anita Mui). Furthermore, Manzhen is raped by her brother-in-law when she comes to look after her sister. Shen searches for Manzhen but does not meet with her, in the mistaken belief that Manzhen has married someone else. He therefore marries Cuizhi (Wu Chenjun) who, just like Shen, comes from a rich family. The two former lovers meet again fourteen years later. Manzhen, following Manlu, lived with her brother-in-law for a while, then left, taking her son. Shen and Cuizhi, on the other hand, have two sons and live a contented life. The film plays upon the theme of the desperate, tragic fate of women in the 1930s and 40s: the heroine Manzhen is manipulated by both her family and the times, losing herself and any chance for real happiness.

In *Ordinary Heroes*, a 1999 feature film, Hui turns the focus of her camera back on Hong Kong. Serving as an expression of Hui's concerns and feelings toward the place and its people, the film chronicles a series of social movements and incidents that occurred in the 1980s. For Hui, 'it was hard to concisely describe those feelings, consisting as they did of a mixture of excitement, fear, disappointment, disillusionment and helplessness'. But the attempt had to be made.[18] The heroine So Feng (Loretta Lee Lai-chun) falls in love twice: once with a now-married man, Yau Ming-foon (Tse Kwan-ho); and the second time with a young man, Ah Dong (Lee Kangsheng), for whom she is his first love. So, the daughter of a fisherman had been attracted by Yau, a social activist who was fighting for the rights of fishing families. Later, Yau ran for election and So worked as his assistant. An intimate relationship developed between them, and So became pregnant. However, Yau marries someone else. So and Yau continue seeing each other secretly, however. Then So breaks down under the strain, suffers from amnesia and has an abortion. She is cared for by Ah Dong who genuinely loves So. In helping So regain her memory, Ah Dong stays with her until her condition improves, then leaves. Of the heroine's two romances, one leads to physical and psychological wounds, while the other ends, though without pain.

Ann Hui's *Summer Snow* returns to Hong Kong scenes and deals mostly with such issues as aging, women, the family and so forth. Employing a realistic style, the film takes the mundane matters of everyday life, presenting them in an unadorned way.

The narrative centres on May Sun (Josephine Siao). She is a practical woman, devoted to both her family and her work. Besides looking after her husband and son, she has to care for her father-in-law, who is suffering from Alzheimer's disease. She manages to juggle her multiple tasks well and modestly. The story is a homage to the virtues of women – to their diligence, persistence and tolerance. Facing life with an attitude of love is the central message of the narrative. *Summer Snow* earned Siao an international award for her sophisticated yet humorous acting, and the film received popular recognition from the public.[19]

Conflicts between the Individual and Society or the Nation

Hui's explorations of personal identity began as early as the time she was making shows for television. *Below the Lion Rock – The Boy from Vietnam* depicts three young men – Ah Man, Lee Kwok-chung and Yau Hing-feng – who flee to Hong Kong from the Vietnam War and the unification of North and South Vietnam. The three are ethnically Chinese and nationally Vietnamese. With no identity cards in their new refuge, they are 'the other', and exist at the margins of society. They barely manage to tolerate ridicule and humiliation in order to satisfy the most fundamental needs of having enough to eat and being able to live in safety. In fact, the film does not only portray the condition of Vietnamese-Chinese refugees, but that of most Chinese émigrés in the past century. The situation of these expatriates that the film depicts – that 'those who leave home are the lowest of the low' – has, therefore, a more general reality. Such people can neither return home nor enjoy basic respect and recognition, as perhaps most Hong Kong people can. They feel frustrated and helpless. Their condition resembles that of the character played by Chow Yun-fat in the *Story of Woo Viet*. As a Vietnamese Chinese and a former Vietnamese soldier, Chow is forced into exile in Hong Kong and is harassed by a Vietnamese assassin. Later, he flees to the Philippines, where his girlfriend, Cherie Chung, is, and makes his way to Chinatown. In order to rescue her, Chow once again acts alone. What supports him is a simple belief that 'Sum Ching will certainly be able stay in the United States permanently, and design her own house.... She will also be able to bring over and adopt the child in the refugee camp in Hong Kong. With these hopes, we will finish our journey.'[20] His life is, therefore, supported by an unrealistic hope, a fantasy.

Song of the Exile is a story about a film-maker. Two characters, a mother and a grandfather, have a problem with complex issues of identity at both the personal and national levels. A Hong's mother made the most important choice of her life when she, a Japanese woman, married a Chinese soldier, Waise Lee; then went with him from northeast China, Macau, Hong Kong, Japan and, finally, back to Hong Kong, which she finally decided was to be her home. The film spans three decades, from the1940s to 1960s. Due to linguistic and national differences, the Japanese woman is unable to live in harmony with her parents-in-law. In the husband's absence, A Hong, influenced by her grandparents, often has disagreements with her mother. It is always hard to clearly explain the grievances and suffering that A Hong's mother experiences. It is not until after the death of her husband, when her daughter is in university, that she returns to

Japan on a trip with her daughter, and mother and daughter are reconciled. The grandfather, on the other hand, stays in the colony of Macau but misses his motherland. He longs to return to his homeland and his dream is fulfilled. However, what can be more ironic than the fact that, after returning to China, he dies of depression in the end? Trapped between grandfather and mother, A Hong refuses to take sides but shows understanding for both as she gradually identifies with their problems. In the wider political context, A Hong is not actively involved in, but only a spectator of, events such as the Cultural Revolution, anti-corruption activities, demonstrations and protests, the June 4th Incident and so forth. Like A Hong, Ann Hui is also more of a spectator than an agent, but one is able to comment on the changing historical context in films such as *Starry is the Night, Ordinary Heroes, As Time Goes By* and *Song of the Exile*.

With regard to the relationship between personal identity and national identity, there is no better example than the *Romance of Book and Sword*. The movie depicts Emperor Qian Long as a Han Chinese. Less than a month after his birth, he is taken into the royal family and thus becomes a candidate to succeed the emperor. Later his brother, the leader of the Red Flower Society, Chen Jialuo, tries to persuade him to overthrow the Qing dynasty and to restore the Han dynasty. However, the Qing/Han emperor sees no point in doing this. He prefers to maintain a peaceful reign for his people with the justification that war will take the lives of numerous innocent people. Such questions as the following go round and round in his mind: 'How can I hardheartedly destroy the prosperity and peace of the country? Can I do this solely because I am a Han Chinese? Isn't it true that the ethnicity of an emperor does not matter but rather the quality of his rule? Is the society stable and are the people happy? To him, therefore, there was no reason to overthrow the Qing dynasty, as under his reign the country was flourishing. Chen agrees with this point and does not force Qian Long to rebel. As Chen explains to the members of Red Flower Society, he holds an attitude similar to that of Qian Long, 'If the purpose of subverting the Qing dynasty is simply to restore the name of Han and not for the betterment of people's lives, I would rather not rebel.' As Chen says to Qian Long, 'If you are killed, the person who succeeds you as emperor may be worse than you.' If this is the case, the status quo is preferable.

In fact, there is no ambiguity in the standpoint of the anti-Qing Red Flower Society, and thus no room for bargaining. What leads to Chen's decision is that he meets Qian Long, who is his biological elder brother, in front of the tomb of their dead mother. He hails Qian Long three times but the emperor does not respond even once. Clearly, Qian Long is not about to reveal his thoughts. Struggling between feelings of brotherhood and racial hatred of the Manchus, Chan finally decides: 'He (Qian Long) is my real brother, I will not kill him.' Therefore, after Qian Long releases fourth brother Wen and gives his word to be a good ruler, this pair of real brothers makes a vow to never hurt each other. Immediately following this is a scene in which Qian Long is enticed to Liuhe Tower by Chan and is forced to revolt against the Qing.

Chen and Qian Long then make a blood vow in Liuhe Tower to collaborate in the restoration of the Han dynasty. However, this vow does not guarantee that Qian Long will not annihilate the Red Flower Society and the Wei people. In the end, the emperor killed all of the members of these two communities and maintained his rule. The film then turns to join the trajectory of real history. Qian Long's subsequent decision to confer amnesty on Chen is due to his adherence to the principle of never letting national affairs cause one to hurt a brother tied by blood, and the plot of the whole film revolves around the conflicts between brotherhood and nation.

Ordinary Heroes is Ann Hui's investigation of social movements in Hong Kong in the 1980s. The narrative centres on several characters, namely Father Franco Mella, So Feng, Little Dong and others, who are to a greater or lesser degree based on real people. This film again shows the social movements that were significant at the time, showing the sentiments of those involved and the hidden implications of their participation. Some people are devoted to righteous deeds and help the weak regardless of clearly anticipated difficulties. Others do so without thinking, and sustain physical or psychological wounds as a result, whereas still others only take advantage of the movements. The realistic style of *Ordinary Heroes* was also employed in by Hui in her next documentary, *As Time Goes By*. The similarity in approach between the two works is palpable. In the documentary, the form is adopted of conversations between the director and several of her friends about their childhood, the conditions under which they grew up, their education and the social movements they experienced (specifically, the 1967 riots). It is also a record of their viewpoints toward the past, present and future. Likewise, the film is an unadorned retrospective and reflection of a certain period in Hong Kong's history.

The contradictions and conflicts arising from differences between two cultures are addressed in *An American Grandson* (1991). Wu Ma, a retired primary school teacher in Shanghai, one day receives a telephone call from his son in the United States, who tells Wu Ma that his grandson will be arriving because the young father does not have the time to take care of him. The cultural differences between the grandfather and the grandson first surface when they meet at the airport. The child expects to ride in a car, while the old man has only a bicycle. The disparity in expectations then extends to aspects of daily life. There are no washrooms at home, only a commode. The grandfather then takes the child to use a public washroom, which is inconvenient. In order for his grandson to take a shower, the grandfather even books him into a hotel. Cultural differences are also manifested in Gu Ming's school life. The teacher lectures on a 'typical' story of a Chinese hero who sacrifices his life to protect national property by using his body to put out a fire. However, Gu Ming considers this 'heroic' act stupid. He provides a more intelligent alternative of calling up the police and firemen for help, thus avoiding a pointless sacrifice. In response to what he considers the unintelligent content of the instruction, Gu Ming chooses not to pay attention in class but, instead, to read comic books. As punishment, he is told to copy sections from a textbook three times; however, he hits upon the trick of using carbon paper. The ideas of making use of technology, pursuing efficiency and professionalism, of making no senseless sacrifices, of respecting the individual and of employing strong reasoning are treated as outrageous by the mainland China teachers.

Here, two different countries/societies/systems possess different cultures, ways of living, and material standards. The different values lead to different or even opposing perspectives. Chinese values celebrate placing the interests of the nation over those of individuals, while the Americans place more weight on individuals and their lives. These differences emerge throughout the course of the film. However, the film closes on a note of harmony. Gu Ming is slapped by his grandfather and runs away from home. He faints on the road and is rescued by a peasant family. Under their tender care, Gu Ming sees and is moved by the love, warmth and happiness of a traditional Chinese family. When Gu Ming returns to his grandfather, he is greeted with love. The two embrace and weep. The conflicts between the two seem to melt away, and that between the two cultures finds some degree of reconciliation.

Mode of Narration: Montage and Multi-Perspective Narration

Ann Hui had already begun to experiment with cinematic form when working in television. Consider a scene from *Social Worker – Boy*. Two brothers are watching a basketball game, peering through the wire fence that surrounds the court. The ball is thrown towards the elder brother, who is shown using a close-up shot. Hui then cuts to a medium shot of their mother being knocked down by a car. This is followed by a close-up of the traffic lights turning red. The camera then cuts back to an extreme close-up of the elder brother, who has a terrified expression on his face. The scene shifts back to a medium shot of the mother falling down in slow motion. Using an extreme close-up of the expressionless face of the elder brother, the director cuts to a long shot of the father running forward with the two brothers. The younger brother is also simultaneously crying, 'Mom...Mom....' The aforementioned groups of shots are combined to juxtapose three groups of actions – the brothers watching a ball game, the mother having a car accident, and the father and the brothers running – all of which are happening in different places and at different times. Making use of the characters' responses, the director creates a situation in which the elder brother can see or sense the mother's accident and then, without delay, attract the attention of his father. Father and son then rush to the scene of the accident. In this way, the three spaces are connected together, producing an effect of pseudo-simultaneity of the actions. The power of 'montage' is clearly evident here. This technique is also manifested in another work, *CID: Murder*. Here, James Wong sits in the living room while the daughter, Siu Hung, sleeps on the bed and the mother chops meat on a table. The pace of her chopping accelerates, with the image being reflected from the lens of James Wong's glasses. The camera cuts to a scene of Siu Hung running up the stairs carrying a bowl of noodles, then to another showing a close-up of the mother's fast, chopping hands. This is followed by a scene of Siu Hung dropping her bowl. She immediately wakes from her dream and runs to Wong, saying, 'Father, I see much blood.' Wong is terrified, but still consoles her, 'It is only a dream.' A subsequent shot shows Siu Hung holding on tightly to her father and refusing to let go. This montage series displays three lines of actions that occur concurrently and closely connect the daughter's dream with reality. Wong feels a tremendous amount of tension, which prefigures his action of the next day, of killing his daughter. These two sequences of 'montage' are the most self-conscious and spectacular to be found in Hui's television career.

The Secret opens with a group of montages - fragmented shots - portraying the setting and imagery: 7x7 rituals, red flames, burning paper dolls, the saying of prayers, the burning of incense, statues of idols, bleak alleys covered with fallen leaves. Then, the camera shifts to Lee wearing a wedding costume and serving tea to her grandmother. Suddenly the telephone rings. Startled, Lee drops the tea cup; at the same time, Hui cuts to a scene in a hospital of a nurse picking up a child from the ground. Here the cross-cut between the dropping of the cup and the falling/picking up of the child is used. Then Lee is shown once again offering tea to her grandmother and receiving a red packet of money from her. What comes next is a prolonged series of montages revealing scenes related to the four main characters: Lee answering a phone call from Yuen, Yuen leaving from work, the nurse Lin Ching-ming helping a child to walk, Lee taking a call from Mui to confirm the arrival of her letter, Yuen getting off a bus and walking towards home, Tsui walking towards Dragon Tiger Hill, Lin saying goodbye to the child as she leaves work, Lee giving no reply to Yuen about where she is going to but walking out of the door, Yuen going in pursuit, the two of them coming across Lin who invites Yuen to home, Yuen giving no response, Lee walking uphill and picking up a red packet that has been dropped, Yuen walking, Lee walking, Lee walking upstairs, Lin enjoying tea at home, two students making a report in a police station about having discovered two dead bodies. What we see here is a quite unconventional mode of narration at the opening of the film. Moreover, the intention of the film is to confuse the audience in sight and mind about the causal relationship between the occurrences and to create a complicated, interwoven web of space and time. In addition to the later constant changes of points of view, from the objective to the subjective, of certain characters such as Lee, Lin and Tsui, a multi-perspective narration is thus employed.

In fact, almost the entire film is told from an objective point of view (the omnipotent viewpoint of the director). Sequences such as the 7x7 rituals for the dead, Lee serving tea to her grandmother, and Lin supporting the falling child adopt this technique. Apparently, Lin's subjective point of view is also embodied in two sequences: on the boat she finds Doctor Yuen inspecting the prostitute Mui, who has fainted; and she discovers Lee dressing up and wearing Mui's high-heeled shoes. In the case of Lee's two memories, which are constructed from a subjective point of view, she tenderly embraces Yuen and finds herself in the presence of Yuen and Mui in a nightclub. Another sequence shows Lee looking down at the street from the window of her home and witnessing Yuen's encounter with Lin. The last manifestation of Lee's subjective perspective is the scene in which she sees the digging up of a dead body to be re-examined in an autopsy. There is also a subjective viewpoint related to Tsui Siu-keung in the closing sequence of the film. Here, he arrives at the murder scene and sees Lin and Lee quarrelling. Next, Hui cuts to a scene from the past, when the murder occurred: Lee invites Mui for a talk and demands that she leave Yuen. Yuen then appears and wants to leave with Lee, but is eventually killed by both Mui and Lee. There then follows a scene set in the present, of a fight that has broken out between Lin and Lee, and which can only be stopped by Tsui. It can be concluded that this film adopts a multiple-perspective narration ranging from the objective to the subjective, from past to present. The intersection of time and space, and memory within memory, is complicated, the progression of the plot is not easily followed, and the audience may easily confuse the time-space frameworks of different people and events. Approaching the end, the previous sequences are re-arranged and re-organized so that the relationships among characters are made clear. Finally, the causes and consequences of the entire murder, and of the truth, are revealed. Undoubtedly, montage is used here as part of an exploration of multi-perspective, complicated narration that breaks with the traditional single-perspective mode. Ann Hui has been successful in employing the technique to play a pioneering role in Hong Kong cinema. Furthermore, this film also has other merits, such as displaying the keen sensitivity of female directors, presenting delicate, rich and realistic details and telling its story with a 'great deal of sensitivity'.[21]

Reminiscent of *The Secret*, *The Spooky Bunch* also uses multi-perspective modes of narration. Both films incorporate traditional, ritualistic elements, such as the 7x7 rituals for the dead, female shamans, ghosts who have taken human form and so forth. But the stories differ in that the former is about humans harassing humans, while the latter is about ghosts harassing humans. The multiple perspectives of *The Spooky Bunch* cover those of humans, ghosts and part humans-part ghosts. They may seem to be more complicated than in *The Secret*, but this may not really be the case. Unlike its antecedent, *The Spooky Bunch* does not employ multiple layers of time-space intersections or series of fragmented montage. Thus, *The Spooky Bunch* seems much clearer in terms of the narrative mode adopted. For example, no frameworks have been constructed of recollections of past times and spaces, and even the sequence that recalls a past event in which the soldiers were given the wrong medication is only given verbally. According to the narrative of *The Spooky Bunch*, Uncle Dan (Lau Hak-shuen) is granted the supernatural power of being able to see, apart from the material world, the metaphysical world. In a certain sense, Uncle Dan's field of vision is equal to that of ghosts, because when they appear, he is the only one able to see them. Uncle Dan's supernatural sight first manifests itself in the sequence showing Wan Gong-fat and a mysterious girl. Wan is beaten up for stealing Ah Chi's food and he falls down in front of a girl, who smiles at him. Wan puts his hand out to touch her and invites her to his performance in a play. Uncle Dan immediately shouts out to him to stop, and the girl disappears in mid-air, frightening Wan. Here, only Uncle Dan has identified the girl as a ghost in human form; to everyone else she seems to be a normal human being.

That Uncle Dan can really see ghosts with his special vision where others see only people is also illustrated in a scene in which a woman in the troop who is a Catholic is burning incense and praying. Uncle Dan discovers that a 'woman' in black is standing between the Catholic woman and Ah Chi (Josephine Siao). Another sequence is when Ah Chi accompanies a female ghost named Cat Shit black. Uncle Dan walks with them to the seashore and sees the head of another female ghost floating in front of them. In addition to Uncle Dan's semi-human/ghost perspective, there is a scene incorporating a ghost's point of view. Master Ma is killed by ghosts, who hang his body from the ceiling. Uncle Dan enters the room and the scene is presented from an overhead shot – that of the perspective of the ghost at the roof. When Uncle Dan looks up from the bottom, with a semi-ghost point of view, to see Master Ma, he is fatally shot by the ghost (a dead soldier). Another scene is of a performance where both the performers and the spectators are ghosts. Double layers of spectatorship, both diegetic and extra-diegetic, are revealed here: the ghosts (seeing the performers on the stage) and the real audience (seeing the performers both on stage and off the stage). To a certain extent, the perspective of humans and that of ghosts are unified, and clarity is eventually provided. This is a remarkable play of perspectives. After all, the fundamental and initial source of perspectives, of both human and ghost, is the director. Only she can possess the omniscient perspective that allows the audience to have an equally omniscient view of events.

Changes in the Use of Voice-over and Narrative Structure

From the 'Trilogy of Grieving Ghosts' to the *Boat People*, Ann Hui moves from the exploration of 'montage' to more realistic types of storytelling. In terms of subject matter and content, she also stops drawing from folklore and legend and shifts back to using more realistic stories about society. Montage may be one form of cinematic aesthetic, and the long take another. It is not a question of which is 'better' but of what kind of subject matter, content, style and effect the director intends to achieve through the use of these approaches. In the one hundred years of the history of film-making, both forms of aesthetics have been used alongside each other, and this is also the case in Ann Hui's films. Sometimes she tends to use 'montage' more frequently, such as in the 'Trilogy of Grieving Ghosts'; at other times, she prefers to employ long takes, plus a large number of camera movements and long shots, for example, in the *Boat People* (the opening shot is worth particular mention here). In addition to the aesthetics created from 'montage' and the multi-perspective narration, the voice-over is a common technique employed by Hui. In *Dragon, Tiger, Panther*, Hui was already experimenting with the form and functions of voice-over. For example, in the scene in which Shek Shau is involved in investigating a case of adultery, he finds the third party to the marriage, Lee's driver, Wong Wan-choi, and a conversation begins. Wong reveals that he was fired by Lee. The dialogue here changes into a voice-over: 'She always exhibits her superiority by demanding that I open the door for her...' (the image is that of Wong driving her home). The voice-over continues, 'She is a total hypocrite....' (a swimming scene of Wong and Lee is seen). Then, 'I know that she is looking at me...' (the scene is of Wong driving Lee and her husband, and the husband getting off at work). The swimming scene is shown again, then the camera cuts to the present – Driver Wong is cleaning a car.

This sequence is composed of a series of images: 1. the present scene of the car being cleaned; 2. Wong driving Lee somewhere; 3. a swimming scene; 4. Wong driving Lee's husband to work; 5. Wong and Lee swimming at a beach; 6. back to the present scene of the car being cleaned. Among these six scenes, 2, 3, 4 and 5 are the memory sequences of the driver. The time and space involved are not the same. Moreover, scenes 1 and 6 are actually the same. The director only split it up for the purpose of inserting the flashback. Under normal conditions, the occurrences in scenes 2, 3, 4 and 5 would bear no sequential correlation. If they have merely been inserted in the narrative in the form of visual 'memory', they could not be thoroughly understood. As a result, the use of voice-over is prominent here. In fact, the voice-over, presented in the absence of the speaker's face, should be extended from the conversation between Wong and Shek Shau to the memory and point of view of Wong as a narrator, synchronized with the corresponding images.

The attempt to turn dialogue into voice-over is also found in *CID: Murder*, where different characters and scenes are placed in conjunction. For instance, three lines of action, 1. James Wong and his fiancée having a date in Lei Yu Mun, 2. Ho and his wife bringing Wong's daughter, Ah Hung, to the playground and 3. Wong and Ho talking in a restaurant, are connected by a voice-over of a conversation between the Ho couple. Two *ICAC* episodes, *A Real Man* and *Black and White*, also adopt voice-over renderings of letters: Dodo Cheng's resignation letter in *A Real Man* and the letter written by the man who commits suicide to his girlfriend in *Black and White*. This device is not uncommon because it does not involve problems such as changes of time, space and perspective. Likewise, in *A Boy From Vietnam*, Ah Man's letter to his mother in Vietnam is read by him in a voice-over. The audio presents ideas such as how good his life is, how well his cousin is treating him, and how he plans to bring his family over to Hong Kong. However, the visuals show another story. The frame reveals that his condition is far from satisfactory. Put another way, there is an ironic disjuncture between the audio and the visual. The closing sequence is of Ah Man bidding farewell to Lee, who is being sent back to Vietnam. At that moment, a voice-over of Ah Man is heard, introducing himself: He was born in Vietnam and lives in Saigon. His father died before he was born. His brother works as an interpreter in the American army. Via the voice-over, audience is allowed to gain a deeper understanding of Ah Man, whose character thus becomes more concrete.

There are three voice-over renderings of letters in the *Story of Woo Viet* that Woo writes to his pen friend, Lee Lap Quan, in Hong Kong. The reading of his first letter which also serves as the opening of the film, shows the arrival of Woo, as a fugitive, by boat. In the boat shown in the frame, he is soothing a baby to sleep when a noise of hailing is heard and the vessel stops. He hopes that he will be able to recognize Lee. This letter was sent when Woo was in Vietnam and is received at the moment of

Woo's arrival. The letter is thus in the past tense as a 'memory', whereas the image is of the present. The reading of the letter happens here first to contract cinematic time and, second, to place the focus on Woo, to deepen the audience's understanding of him. His second letter was written when Woo and Sum Ching were staying in the Philippines. It embodies the synchrony between the voice (letter reading) and the diegesis (images), both of which are in present tense. The image is of Woo writing the letter, and this is alternated with a scene of Woo and Ah Sam (Law Lit) drinking, and with fragments of a scene showing Woo and Sum Ching. Then the director cuts to Lap Quan's reading of the letter, and this functions in linking the two people, who are in different time-space frameworks. The third letter forms the closure of the film when, following the death of Sam, Woo once again goes on a journey into exile. As the letter is being read, the image is of the itinerant Woo. Here, the letter seems to be in future tense, and to foretell the life that he is about to lead. However, there is also a possibility that the letter was written in the past, since it contains the following sentence: 'Sum Ching and I will leave the Philippines tomorrow'. This implies that they are now leaving on the boat, indicating that the letter was perhaps written the day before. But the tense is no longer significant because it carries no implications for Woo's fate of exile. The three voice-over renderings of letters can, on the one hand, shorten the psychological distance between the two people in two places and, on the other, enrich the quality of representations in the film.

In *Love in a Fallen City*, Bai writes to Fan, who is in England, and the letter is again read through voice-over. Accompanied by Bai's narration, the frame shows her taking a rickshaw alone at night to go home, and then lying exhausted in bed. What is different about *Song of the Exile* is that it is a self-narrative of the heroine. As the film is an autobiography, the narrator or the speaker encompasses the double identities of both the heroine and the auteur. In other words, the heroine is the auteur (director) and the film presents the auteur's point of view in looking at herself (the heroine). When we hear that A Hong/Hui graduated in England in 1973, the image shows A Hong walking in a relaxed manner along the streets of London with several friends, and then the young women taking different paths of their own. The second voice-over of self-narration is of A Hong's childhood memories in Macau. Her grandfather, with his old partner, returns to Guangzhou, China, a place that he can never forget. A Hong herself is sent to Hong Kong, a completely unfamiliar environment, and experiences a sense of abandonment for the first time. The image at that time is of A Hong alone on a ship. Here, the voice-over is an interpretation of the heroine's interior subjectivity: indescribable loneliness and helplessness as her grandparents, who adore her, die. These sentiments are not easy to represent using images, and their impact will be heightened with the adoption of voice-over. Therefore, the voice of the heroine is more powerful than her image. Originally a supportive device, it has a capacity for broader and deeper expressions than can be achieved by images alone.

Another film which will serve this discussion of the use of voice-over is *Ordinary Heroes*. The two major characters here, Father Franco Mella (Anthony Wong) and Ah

Dong, are committed to protesting against the government's plan to send 'water brides' (mothers without the proper papers) back to the mainland. In the midst of Father Mella's hunger strike, we hear his voice-over expressing feelings of determination and persistence. Ah Dong also makes a self-narration to reveal his feelings of helplessness arising from Father Mella's 'fruitless' strike and his feelings about the death of his mother. In this film, the deployment of voice-over centres on the character's interiority and supplements the representation of the plot. On the boat, Ah Dong's nostalgic voice-over reveals that, before she lost her memory, So was surrounded by people, in contrast to the present situation, where there is nobody around her. Another scene shows So grabbing Ah Dong's wallet as he waits for her on shore, implying that he is 'waiting for her to come ashore', expressed through voice-over. Voice-over is used sixteen times in *Eighteen Springs*, a record for Hui, and contributes to the film's narrative complexity. These voice-overs emerge sometimes in the reading of letters, but principally as narrations or monologues of the hero, Shen (Leon Lai) and the heroine, Manzhen (Wu Chien-lien). This is the case in the first half of the film. To be specific, Shen once expresses the view that 'When you find that you have never thought of loving somebody, in fact, you have already fallen in love with her', in which the 'her' ostensibly refers to Manzhen. Manzhen also utters the thought that 'Although Shen seems to be happy when my sister's wedding is mentioned, I know that he is offended by her occupation. He has accompanied me home for many times but has never asked to enter. Perhaps my sister is the cause.' The image is of Shen going downstairs from Manzhen's home and of his shadow disappearing in the darkness. The narration unveils the inner thoughts of Manzhen – revealing his uncertainty and lack of confidence regarding Shen. Later, for a variety of reasons (such as misunderstandings), Shen marries Chui-chi, a girl he does not love. Shen's monologue is heard, 'When you find that the one you truly love does not return your love, you may also discover that the one you hate is actually not so hateful.' The corresponding image is of a wedding scene. Given a situation over which he has no control, he 'chooses' a secondary option. Furthermore, Manzhen's rape by her brother-in-law and her subsequent pregnancy causes her to live with her brother-in-law. Manzhen's monologue emerges, 'It is equally difficult to love and to hate a person for one's whole life.... In the old days, I thought I was not the same as my sister. However, after having lived for half of my life, I find that I have actually been following behind her.' Here it is articulated that although Manzhen is stubborn, she cannot escape the physical and psychological bondage of her sad destiny.

'Monologue' or 'narration' or 'voice-over'[22] functions in the final part of this film in the way that editing or montage does: it is used to change or adjust time, space and the narrative structure. Also, the effects of sound and speech are maximized. In the film, there is a monologue from Shen, describing that, while Shuhui has been abroad for ten years, it feels like several days only. The director cuts to a welcome scene where Shen's whole family has come to meet Shuhui at the pier. They gather for dinner that night. While Shen is on his way to pick Shuhui up, he reads a letter Manzhen sent some time ago. Here, Manzhen's voice-over is heard, 'Shijun, yesterday I visited Shuhui although

I knew that he was not in...(the image shows a view of Shuhui's home). Shuhui's mother told me many interesting things about your school days. I felt contented when I heard them...(the camera shows Shen walking alone towards Shuhui's home). As you have left for a number of days, I began to have anxiety attacks, for no reason.' The reading of the letter ends as Shen arrives at Shuhui's home. Prior to Shen, Manzhen had come to visit Shuhui, but he was not there. Then the two former lovers go to a restaurant and the scene ends with them embracing. This image is followed by a scene at Shen's home, where Shuhui and Chui-chi are waiting for Shen. The camera then cuts back to the restaurant scene. The two lovers recall things that happened more than ten years ago. At that time Manzhen had been discharged from the hospital and had received no letter from Shen. She felt that this meant that Shen did not want to see her. In fact, Shen also had no news from Manzhen. As the past can never be changed, they consoled themselves with the thought that they have been fortunate enough to be able to meet again in the present. The next scene shows Shen finding a red glove that Manzhen had brought during his walk on the street at night. The closure, led by a voice-over, starts with a present-day sequence (a scene welcoming Shuhui). Then the voice-over rendering of the letter begins, narrating events of the past ten years (for instance, Shuhui's mother recalling Shen, and Manzhen's panic subsequent to Shen's return to Nanjing that foreshadowing the impending misfortune). In between these events, there are scenes set in the present (of both Shen and Manzhen coincidentally visiting Shuhui's home). Put another way, the shift between present and past is initiated by the voice-over reading of the letter. Voice-over even plays the crucial role of leading the shift, which is utterly seamless. Remember that the letters contain the two attributes of time and space: present (at the moment of reading) and past (at the moment of writing). Nevertheless, the restaurant conversation (present) between Shen and Manzhen addresses events that happened fourteen years ago (past). In fact, the closure involves a cross-cut of multiple strands of time and space. It is thanks to Ann Hui's orderly treatment here that the audience is able to connect the sequences, and Hui exercises a bold and successful experiment on the integration of sound, including speech, monologue, voice-over and narrative structure.

In *Starry is the Night* and *Song of the Exile*, the strategies of voice-over and monologue employed are not taken as modes of narration in the senses just referred to. Rather, Hui adopts a more complicated pattern of intersection in temporal and spatial dimensions. She employs the device of parallel editing to insert memory or correspondence. Different times (past and present) and spaces (two places or more) are thus put together to create a new type of narration. *Starry is the Night*, spanning more than twenty years, begins in 1966 with George Lam discussing the incident of the Chinese Communist Party's Long March in a tutorial session in The University of Hong Kong. The next sequence is already of a moment 21 years later. A former university student, Brigitte Lin, has already become a social worker. She lives with David Wu in Macau (another place). This is followed by Lin's memory (place: Hong Kong), dating back to 21 years ago, of her days spent in Lam's company. Then the director cuts back to the present in Macau with Wu's appearance (the space shifts again). The plot continues with Lin's memory of her dance with Lam 21 years ago (Hong Kong), then switches to her present life in Macau with Wu. The entire film revolves around these four points in time and space: the past and present, Hong Kong and Macau. The ending involves a convergence of time and space in that Lin, Lam and Wu appear in Hong Kong at the same time.

In the case of the *Song of the Exile*, the film begins in 1973 in a street in London (space). The heroine, A Hong, has just graduated and returns to Hong Kong (space). Then the plot shows her childhood memory (past) in Macau (space). It jumps back to the present and exhibits the conflicts she has with her mother. This leads to her recalling the distant relationship she had with her mother during her early days (past) in Macau. After a short while, mother and daughter visit Japan. Then, A Hong travels to Guangzhou to meet her grandfather before his death. The film ends here. This film covers an even longer period of about 20 to 30 years. There are five places involved: London, Hong Kong, Macau, Japan and Guangzhou. Hui similarly uses the device of parallel editing to present a more complicated web of time and space, as the mode of narration employed becomes part of the content of the film.

Ann Hui is extremely conscious of the form and content of her films. However, as she stated after completing her 'Trilogy of Vietnam', 'I have not yet found a suitable balance between fantasy and reality'.[23] She also judges her cinematic sensibility and sense of rhythm as not being particularly strong.[24] The difficulty in creating a successful sense of rhythm in *Love in a Fallen City* is one instance that can be noted in this respect. Clearly concerned about her cinematic language, she expressed the wish that her technique could be brought up-to-date, although she claims to have no ambition to achieve breakthroughs in style and skill.[25] Nevertheless, she constantly carries out self-appraisals of her work with regard to skill, style and so forth, in order to improve. Film art, just like other kinds of art, demands innovation and creativity in both content and form. To a certain extent, form also carries more weight than content. Ann Hui demonstrates this by showing tremendous interest in cinematic formal exploration and aesthetics. If she develops new visions, she will be very contented.[26] That is why she is proud of her experiments with temporal-spatial cross-cuts in *Eighteen Springs*.[27] Hui has made a number of contributions in narrative mode and structure. *The Secret*, *Eighteen Springs* and *Ordinary Heroes* are the best evidence of this. In her cinematic practice, she has gradually come to understand the form of the medium of film – film language itself is inherently a type of art form.[28] The pursuit of a perfect synthesis of form and content has obviously become the mission of her film-making career.

Notes

1. The four episodes of the *CID* series include *Dragon, Tiger, Panther* (1976, scriptwriter: Chan Wan-man), *Murder* (scriptwriter: Yim Ho, 1976) and *CID: Professor, Wife and Student* (1976); *Social Worker – Ah Sze* (scriptwriter: Chan Wan-man, 1977) and *Social Worker – Boy* (scriptwriter: Moyung Kit, 1977).

2. The six dramas are respectively *Three Women* (scriptwriter: Chan Wan-man, 1977), *A Real Man* (scriptwriter: Yim Ho, 1977), *The Investigation* (scriptwriter: Chan Wan-man, 1977), *The Ninth Clause* (scriptwriter: Yim Ho, 1977), *Black and White* (scriptwriter: Kam Kwok-leong, 1978) and *Steak Expenses* (scriptwriter: Ni Kuang, 1978).
3. *Below the Lion Rock* series: *The Boy from Vietnam* (scriptwriter: Wong Chi, 1978), *The Bridge* (scriptwriter: Chan Wan-man, 1978) and *The Road* (scriptwriter: Lam Tak-luk, 1978).
4. A separate list of the 17 films that Ann Hui directed is provided. The three films that she produced are: Fong Sak-yuk (Corey Yuen, 1993), *The Day the Sun Turned Cold* (Yim Ho, 1994), *A Little Life - Opera* (Allen Fong, 1997) and *The Opium War* (Xie Jin, 1997).
5. *Dragon, Tiger, Panther* is a TVB anthology series produced by Lau Fong-kong. The series consists of 13 episodes, which were released at a frequency of once per week. Ann Hui was asked to produce one episode on an impromptu basis in the midst of making *Wonderful*. Film stock was used through the whole production of the episode.
6. The phrase 'Trilogy of Grieving Ghosts' was first coined by Shek Kei (Ming Pao, 9 November 1987).
7. The Independent Commission Against Corruption (ICAC) was established in April 1974. It was under the direct supervision of the Governor of Hong Kong. Fighting corruption was the ICAC's main duty.
8. Chan, Yin-ching, 'Interviewing Ann Hui'. *City Entertainment*. No. 20. 1978, p. 180.
9. Ibid.
10. Shek Kei, 'Cuozhong mili de Fengjie' (The Complicated and Mysterious *The Secret*). *Shiqi yinghuaji* (The Collection of Film Reviews by Shek Kei). Hong Kong: Subculture, 1999, p. 35.
11. Shuqi. 'The Secret: Sense and Sensibility'. *City Entertainment*. No. 95. 23 September 1982, p. 33.
12. Ngou Long. 'Dangdai zhongguo dianying daoyan qunxianglu' (The Album of Chinese Contemporary Directors). *Zhongwai yinghua* (Chinese and Foreign Motion Pictures). No. 82. 5 October 1982, p. 79.
13. Jiao Xiongping, ed. *Xianggang dianying fengmao, 1975-1986* (A View of Hong Kong Cinema, 1975-1986). Taipei Times Press. 1 May 1987, p. 61.
14. Kwong Po-wai. *Ann Hui on Ann Hui*. Hong Kong: Kwong Po-wai. December 1998, p. 42.
15. Ibid., p. 29.
16. Yang Zigang. 'Xi "Qingchengzhilian de cangbei"' (Analysing 'The Whiteness of Love in a Fallen City'). *Nanbeiji* (North and South Poles). No. 72. Hong Kong. 16 September 1984, p. 81.
17. Yang Nian. 'Interview with Ann Hui on "Starry is the Night"'. *Dayinghua* (Big Motion Picture). 1 October 1998, p. 10.
18. Ann Hui, 'Words of the Director'. *Special Issue of 23rd Hong Kong International Film Festival*. Hong Kong Temporary Urban Council. 31 March, 1999, p. 15.
19. This film's female lead, Josephine Siao, won the Best Actress award in the Berlin Film Festival in 1995. The film earned up to 20 million Hong Kong dollars?] at the box office, which was a big shot in the arm for the ailing Hong Kong film industry.
20. In the film, the technique of the 'flash-forward' voice-over is employed in the reading of the letter that Woo Viet writes to his pen friend in Hong Kong, Lap Quan.

21. Shuqi. 'The Secret: Sense and Sensibility'. *City Entertainment*. No. 95. 23 September 1982, p. 33.
22. Narration is usually employed for interpretation. In most cases, the content of the narration shows no relationship with the characters, although sometimes it appears as the speech narration of some of the characters. Monologue refers to the interior thoughts of the characters, which are not spoken. Voice-over, in contrast, can be generally regarded as all sounds that are out of the scenes. It can be presented as the continuation of the speech of certain characters who appeared in the previous shot but are not seen in this shot. In Ann Hui's pictures, most narrations, monologues and voice-overs are used as the speech and interiority of the characters. However, there are still cases in which they are deployed as tools to help interpret the plot and to lead the mood. An example is the voice-over in the opening of *The Spooky Bunch*.
23. Arranged by Li Chuek-to, 'Tsui Hark Interviewing Ann Hui.' *City Entertainment*. No. 58. 1981, p. 9.
24. Tao Bing. 'Huaguo piaoling de chouxu – Xuanhua de "yuenan sanbuqu" (The Desolate Melancholy – Ann Hui's "Trilogy of Vietnam")'. *Dayinghua* (Big Motion Picture. No. 30. 19 September 1989, p. 20.
25. Zhang Liang. 'Ann Hui's Summer Snow and As Time Goes By'. Huang Wulan ed. *Dangdai zhongguo dianying 1995–1997* (Contemporary Chinese Cinema 1995–1997). Taipei: Times Press. 17 March 1998, p. 161.
26. Ibid., p. 20
27. Lai, Linda. 'Interviewing Ann Hui – the Worldview of The Eighteen Springs'. *Hong Kong Panorama 97–98*. 21st Hong Kong International Film Festival. Hong Kong Temporary Urban Council, 1998. p. 50.
28. Ibid., p. 46.

4

Tsui Hark

Tsui Hark, born Tsui Man-kwong, is undoubtedly one of the most energetic and creative of the New Wave directors. He has a distinctive personality and is full of the anger and edginess of youth. This is reflected in works such as *The Butterfly Murders*, *We're Going to Eat You*, *Dangerous Encounter – 1st Kind* and others, which juxtapose the ideas of innovation and devastation. The images are sharp, and the style bizarre and unique. Tsui joined Cinema City in 1981 and produced two films, namely, *All The Wrong Clues (For the Right Solution)* and *Aces Go Places III: Our Man from Bond Street*. He was very quickly embraced by mainstream cinema, becoming the main stream among the mainstream. In somewhat more than twenty years, he has been involved in over thirty films as a director or co-director, and in over ten as a producer. In terms of quantity, he is the king among the New Wave talents.

His entry into the film industry was no different from that of other New Wave film-makers. In 1977, after returning from studying broadcasting, television and cinema at the University of Texas (Austin), Tsui was snapped up by Hong Kong – Television Broadcast Limited (TVB). Unknown at the time, he joined the production work for several dramas such as *A House is Not a Home*, *The Underdogs* and *Tycoon**. In the television wars of 1978, Selina Leong Suk-yi migrated from TVB to its rival Commercial Television (CTV), taking with her a group of artists, Tsui among them. In the new station, Tsui directed the martial arts drama *Golden Blade Sentimental Swordsman*. His commitment and innovations in the production were rewarded when the drama received good reviews. Although CTV launched a strong publicity campaign, it was forced to close after one month. However, CTV's one million Hong Kong dollar publicity campaign was not a total loss, since it at least built up Tsui Hark's credentials. Tsui was immediately employed by Ng Sze-yuen to make his first feature, *The Butterfly Murders*, which was a futuristic martial arts movie.[1] This marked the beginning of Tsui's film-making career.

Tsui's personal experiences fostered his distinctiveness from his New Wave counterparts. Born in 1951 in Vietnam, Tsui experienced hardships during the Vietnam War. He moved to Hong Kong and there received a middle school education. An overseas Chinese with war experience, Tsui obviously possessed particularly deep national feelings, or a national 'complex'. Furthermore, during the time he studied in the United States, he was struck by certain events that were taking place at the time; for instance, the anti-Vietnam War movement, the civil rights movement and the movement to defend the Diaoyu Islands for the Chinese. These events caused him to think even more deeply about the nation's past, present and future. This is exemplified in some of his films, such as *Shanghai Blues, A Better Tomorrow III, Swordsman* and the series *Once Upon a Time in China*. In particular, the series *Once Upon a Time in China* integrates the themes of the future of the nation and feelings about the impending handover of sovereignty over Hong Kong in 1997. The characters in the film show dignity, heroism, strength and confidence. In addition, the film is suffused with romance.

Furthermore, Tsui pioneered the trends of 'hero films' (as the producer of *A Better Tomorrow I* and *II* and the director of *III*) and 'films with special effects' (as the producer of the series *A Chinese Ghost Story* and the director of *Zu – Warrior of Magic Mountain*). He was also innovative enough to adopt traditions and legends in his works, such as in *The Lovers* and *Green Snake*. He recreated the classics from his point of view. Neither a conformist nor a coward, he 'gallantly renews traditional tales, offering vitality and delight, to make them neo-classics, distinctive and magical.'[2] Unquestionably, Tsui Hark, who has been a presence in Hong Kong cinema for two decades, has already become the most prolific and influential New Wave director.

Breaking Away from Convention and Striving for Change

As early as during his days in television, Tsui Hark was already searching for innovations. When he worked for CTV, he directed *Golden Blade Sentimental Swordsman* – a drama adapted from a martial arts legend popularized by the contemporary writer Gu Long. He noted that Gu Long's stories were characterized by mood and suspense, and that they particularly emphasized the personality of the characters through their outlook and the rationality of the plot. Therefore, the director retained the atmosphere of the original. Every incident in the narrative is not revealed until the proper time. Consider, for example, a plot of a romance. Ye Kai (You Tianlong) was once saved by Shangguan Xiaoxian (Yu Anan), while Ding Ningning (Dodo Cheng), whom Ye admires, is rescued by Guo Ding. The news of Ding and Guo's marriage is announced. Later, unexpectedly, Shangguan is revealed to be one of the 'Four Kings' of a cult, 'Lonely Mountain' (Gu Feng). She was the one who initiated cruel events such as the murder of Guo and the disfigurement of Ding. Eventually, Ye kills her in a final confrontation. The story closes with Ye and Ding embracing. This is an instance in which the plot takes an unexpected twist.

Tsui consciously breaks the tradition in martial arts dramas of fights dominating the picture. Instead, he places the focus on mood and romance. Continuing the discussion on the abovementioned sequence, when Ding is rescued by Guo she believes that Ye is already dead. Because Guo rescued her and stayed by her side for three days and three nights until she regained consciousness, she is intensely grateful to him and commits herself to him. She sleeps with Guo, but the person she thinks about in her heart is Ye, and tears well up in her eyes. Another episode involves a romance between Ye and a Taoist nun (Wei Qiuhua). Ye is wounded by Ding, who is made unconscious by the 'Jade Flute' Taoist's witchcraft. Ye is then rescued by a Taoist nun. She brews him some medicine and serves it to him. Seeing that Ye is seized by chill, she ignores the norm that a distance should be kept between a man and a woman and takes off her clothes in order to warm Ye with her body. She overcomes her shyness in order to save Ye from cold. Such a realistic yet subtle depiction of love is rarely, if ever, found in current martial arts dramas as well as in Tsui's subsequent films. It was not until *The Lovers* that this kind of portrayal re-appeared.

In another bold breakthrough, Tsui made use of on-location shooting. Even in a studio, he employs cinematic practices that are unusual in studio production. For example, shots are taken one after another with a single camera, instead of with three shooting simultaneously.[3] In other words, he employs a method used in on-site shooting, which allows him to re-set the lights for every single shot. In this way, the atmosphere of the scene can be better controlled. In the studio, he prefers a panorama set. As in on-site shooting, he does not place the camera on one side, but in the centre, enabling him to achieve total control over lighting and mood.

> I hope that every frame contains meaning and that the theme can be highlighted. Sources of illumination can be designed in a three-dimensional manner. But these arrangements demand time – the actors need to rehearse their positions in relation to the cameras because both the actors and the cameras are restricted by the lighting. Only in this way can the peculiar mood of Gu Long's classics be created.[4]

In fact, on-location shooting and single-camera cinematography were practiced by certain New Wave directors in the same period who worked in the film unit of Hong Kong Television. Tsui put effort into controlling lighting in order to reveal the personality of the characters. For instance, front lighting is used when Ye first appears, to communicate a sense of hardness and strength. In contrast, lateral lighting is employed when Ding, Shangguan and the Taoist nun appear.[5] Camera shots are unambiguous and concise. With the aid of quick 'montage', illusion, past, present and flash-forwards are all combined. This technique is to be found repeatedly in Tsui's subsequent films such as the series *Once Upon a Time in China*, *The Blade*, *King of Chess* and *The Lovers*. It has become an important part of Tsui's works and is also his signature.

In addition, Tsui's fighting scenes differ from the customary ones. He makes use of sound effects and close-ups. When people and objects flash in front of the camera, Tsui immediately cuts to the final moment of the fight. This treatment is new and saves time because long descriptions are unnecessary. The opening of *Golden Blade Sentimental Swordsman* is an example. The scene is of the final confrontation between Guo Ding and Nangong Yan. There is a medium shot of Guo holding a blade and twirling it. We hear the sound of stabbing but see no image of the blade. What comes next is a close-up of the blade, dropped on the snow. This is followed by a shot of a falling Nangong. This ends the battle. Nothing could be more plain and direct. Such fighting scenes have the flavour of Japanese warrior (*bushido*) sagas. Tsui's handling of the drama subverted the practice of most contemporary martial arts dramas, which overemphasized the fighting process. As Tsui said, 'I somewhat dislike "the process", because I believe that so much description is boring. Therefore, most of the time, I do not show the process but directly go to the things that need to be delivered.'[6] This characteristic is found in his later works including *The Butterfly Murders, We're Going to Eat You, Dangerous Encounter – 1st Kind* and *All the Wrong Clues.*

Against Tradition, Against the System, Against Society

After *Golden Blade Sentimental Swordsman,* Tsui joined the film industry. His debut work was *The Butterfly Murders* (1979). Set in Shen's castle, the plot focuses on an investigation of the 'butterfly killers', who have committed a string of murders. Valiant men from various places have also been killing each other. A writer-reporter, Fang Hongye, is writing about all of these incidents to anthologize them in a book entitled *Diary of Hongye.* In the process, Fang discovers that all of the killings have been initiated by the master of the castle, as part of his plan to become the king of *wulin* (the martial arts world). Other people, one by one, are murdered and the sole survivor is Fang. This movie marked the beginning of the director's trial use of sci-fi special effects as a substitute for the special effects seen in traditional martial arts movies. The intention behind this work was to blend the dichotomies of tradition and modernity, myth and science, and the Orient and the Occident (including Japan). These oppositions, however, are mixed not in an organic but in a connotative manner, ultimately subverting myths through science. The narrative eschews magic devices of the traditional martial arts world, such as flashes of light, flying swords, thunder coming from the palm of a hand, flying through the air and digging through the ground. It makes use of certain substitutes, for instance, a slingshot arrow and string-and-hook instead of *qinggong* [the ability to move lightly and swiftly], gunpowder instead of secret weapons, tin and lead amour instead of a golden bell cover/iron-cloth garment. Unfortunately, this approach of trying to find scientific explanations greatly neglects the unlimited potential of the human imagination. This neglect is a big fault, particularly in the cinematic world where imagination is a source of creativity and is a criterion. In addition, the metaphysical arts and extraordinary powers of the Orient contain their own spectacular attributes, which are well suited to the exercising of the imagination.

The martial arts genre with special effects has an illustrious history. It is the successor of a Shanghai feature, *Torching the Red Lotus Temple,*[7] which already incorporated the technology to show light and force emanating from swords, palm thunder, people flying through the air and so forth. This movie was so well received that a total of eighteen episodes were produced. At the peak of its popularity in 1931, the drama was suddenly banned by the Film Inspection Committee of the National Government.[8] This prohibition also put to an end the making of martial arts films in mainland China. However, the Japanese occupation and the civil war led a number of pioneers of the martial arts movies, such as Wang Yuanlong, Hong Zhonghao, Ren Pengnian, Wu Lizhu (actress), Lu Jiping (set designer), to migrate to Hong Kong, thus allowing the genre to live on.

The 1950s and 1960s were the golden decades of Hong Kong martial arts movies. Films such as *Marvelous Gallants of the Jianghu* and *Temple of the Red Lotus I* and *II* were made in 1956 and *Torching the Red Lotus Temple I* and *II* were made in 1963. In the 1960s, over thirty such films were made,[9] of which *The Secret Book* (1960), *Buddha's Palm* (1964) and *Holy Flame of the Martial World** were the most memorable. In that period, the technology that was adopted in the martial arts movies of that decade bears reference to certain foreign pictures such as *Godzilla, King Kong* and others. More complex animation, optical effects and archetypes came into use. Added to this the locally created *yinbogong* (sound-wave martial arts) and other technologies, these films were so spectacular that the audience was amazed. The final episode of *The Secret Book* even earned 280,000 Hong Kong dollars in box office revenues, which broke the record for local and foreign films in the past ten years.[10]

The 1970s were basically dominated by the kung fu genre, in which practical fights and moves were emphasized. However, King Hu's *Dragon Gate Inn, A Touch of Zen* and some other movies made use of optical effects and animation.[11] Tsui took these traditional special effects and updated them into modern, sci-fi type effects. Besides being a pioneer, Tsui has also taken on the role of advocate, which has bolstered his reputation as one of the most prominent auteur of 'special effects' movies.

Without doubt, Tsui's *The Butterfly Murders* is a breathtaking work that contains extraordinary characters, spectacular images and peculiar moods. However, he was overambitious and tried to raise too many questions in this film. The content was confusing and appeared to beyond the director's control. Moreover, this film incorporates too many pastiches from other movies, namely *Yatsuhaka Mura* from Japan, *The Birds* by Hitchcock and robot figures from *Star Wars*. In the process of appropriation, the director did not sufficiently digest the elements and make them part of his own. The result was a film with a disorganized structure and confusing logic. Little wonder that the editor of the French periodical *Cahier de Cinema* wrote, 'The plot is so disorganized that, soon after the beginning, I was already unable to follow the movie.'[12] If even a film professional was bewildered, it is not surprising if the general audience was as well. However, this work certainly tried to challenge traditional myths and attempted to be 'different'. While the movie may perhaps be overly exaggerated or perhaps 'be stuck at the stage of handicraft techniques,'[13] the film-maker did indeed take a significant step in the direction of reforming martial arts movies.

We're Going to Eat You (1980) was Tsui's second feature. The box office failure of *The Butterfly Murders* put tremendous pressure on Tsui. It added to the unease surrounding his second production, which dealt with a closed society. The plot was as follows: In the early years of the Chinese Republic an undercover policeman with the number 999 (Tsui Siu-keung) of the central special police enters a cannibal village named 'Tai Ka Heung' (the word "Heung", which literally means village, has a phonic resemblance in Cantonese with another character that denotes the idea of 'death') in order to arrest a wanted criminal. This village has a rule that anybody who enters the village is doomed to be killed and eaten by the inhabitants. Fortunately, Tsui's extraordinarily good physique and skills save himself from such a catastrophe. He not only succeeds in saving his own life, but also rescues a beautiful woman from danger. Horror and black humour (or 'absurd comedy') are the constituents of the narrative. The plot describes a cannibalistic, wild society in which no distinction between right and wrong and between good and evil is found. It fully exhibits mankind's selfishness, cruelty and fatuousness. As the film opens, we see a villager beating up a passer-by to death. The victim's companion is also killed and the body is chopped up. The entire community beats gongs and drums, announcing that there is human meat and distributing a share to each villager. The cannibals, in their turn, may be eaten up. The captain of the guards in the village is eventually hanged, and his limbs torn off as food for the dwellers.

This film conveys a shocked disappointment towards society (the cannibal village) and pessimism towards life. Most of the time, one cannot alter reality, just as the vice captain of the village could not convert to the right path because of the restrictions placed upon him by his superior. As for the undercover policeman 999, he has no intention of changing the community ('Tai Ka Heung'). What he ends up choosing to do is to escape. In other words, an individual has too little power to battle against society or existing systems. At the close of the film, the undercover policemen, Tsui and Long, and the beautiful lady, Cheung Mo-lin, leave 'Tai Ka Heung'. They run to the seashore and escape in a wooden boat. When an enemy emerges, Cheung stabs him to death. Then Cheung holds the heart of the enemy, which is bloody and pumping, and says to her two companions (and also to the audience), 'You see his heart.' The two policemen are so frightened they fall into the water. Cheung's act indicates that she, too, has not been able to escape her fate of becoming a cannibal – this is Tsui Hark's philosophy of fatalism.

Comic elements are also injected in the plot. In the scene in which the human flesh is to be divided, the inhabitants gather in a temple and celebrate with firecrackers. There are scenes of satire and mockery. They play with the ancestral tablet. The explosion of the firecrackers, in a humorous way, blackens the face of a villager named Tam Tin-nam with scraps of paper and dust. Imitating a Chinese deity, Master Guan, the captain, carrying a big blade, demonstrates playfully with policeman 999. The cop says, 'Your face is so expressionless that you resemble Master Guan.' The captain replies, 'Then let me act like Master Guan.' The cop adds, 'You look like nobody but

Lincoln.' The captain answers, 'Huh, Lincoln?' The fight then continues. Tsui's ridicule of famous figures in ancient and contemporary times from China and the West creates a sense of relaxation and dilutes the feeling of brutality and horror. 'Perhaps it is a matter of personality. The films I make are never serious. *The Butterfly Murders* is probably my most somber work – not an ounce of humour, and everybody in the film has a cheerless face.'[14] Contrary to what Tsui had hoped for, the combination of the two elements of black humour and horror did not surprise and delight the audience. As with his first feature, *We're Going to Eat You* failed at the box office. There were four mean reasons for the failure: 1. The film was too terrifying. For example, the scenes of human bodies being divided and limbs being severed were difficult to tolerate. 2. The black humour arising from bloodiness was unconvincing. 3. The impossibility of achieving a balance between horror and black humour lay at the core of the problem. 4. None of the characters (including the hero) was amiable. In other words, the audience failed to warm to any of the characters. The film was full of absurd behaviour, such as ceaseless and purposeless pursuits, fights, killings and the eating of human flesh, making it a film without much substance.

Disillusionment with Mankind and Society, Leading to Violent Devastation

Tsui Hark's third feature, *Dangerous Encounter – 1st Kind*, originally named *The Gang of Four*, was banned by the Film Censorship Unit for its penetrating subject matter, audacious style and apparently political elements.[15] There were three reasons for the prohibition:

1. In the film, three students in uniform (with school logos) intentionally set off a bomb in a theatre, triggering a series of violent incidents. The film was deemed to have an 'unhealthy consciousness'. The concern was raised that high-school students might imitate the acts in the film.
2. The Film Censorship Unit argued that middle-school students would probably not be able to produce bombs, whereas if college students had been depicted, that would have been acceptable.
3. The conflicts between the retired American soldiers and the Chinese in the film might encourage xenophobia.[16] Later, the director made certain alterations to the film: cutting out overly violent shots, re-shooting some scenes and re-naming the movie. He then re-submitted the new version for inspection. The film was passed by the censors. The ban provoked a series of debates,[17] becoming the focus of media attention at the time.

In fact, it is not rare to see films from both East and West that contain violence. Take Zhang Che's and Luo Wei's films made in the 1960s and 1970s as examples. In their films, the depiction of violence is unrealistic, with aesthetic images of masculine men. Their works, among them, *Golden Swallow* (1967) and *The One-Armed Swordsman* (1968, directed by Zhang Che), are essentially films about romantic heroes. Generally speaking, the violence in 'violent movies' can be categorized into three types:

1. Aestheticized violence – *Bonnie and Clyde* and *The Wild Bunch* are representative works. The films' broad vision raises the violence in the scenes to the level of romance, with its mix of myth and reality, romantic and tragic.
2. Critical violence – best illustrated by *A Clockwork Orange*. The narrative describes a hero from the future, 'Alex', who is a member of a villainous group. The repressive apparatus of the state takes away his ability to make moral choices. He thus becomes a clockwork orange – he retains some humanity but is virtually a machine.
3. Mere violence (with no purpose) – as exemplified by *Dirty Harry*.[18] The hero of the film has the nature of a beast and a talent for destruction. He uses violence as a solution for all problems. As for *Dangerous Encounter – 1st Kind*, the widespread media attention that it aroused was, to a great extent, related to the fact that two equally brutal, bloody films, *Lost Soul* (Mou Tun Fei) and *The Beasts* (Dennis Yu), were released at about the same time.

Dangerous Encounter – 1st Kind depicts four youngsters who get into trouble and become acquainted with one another. By chance, they come across a pile of cheques issued by a Japanese military bank. They are then pursued by the police and by retired American soldiers. The story ends in a frenzy of killing, with the gang murdering each other. The only survivor is Ah Go. The third of Tsui's works, this film had the most complete narrative, the clearest structure and was the most coherent of his films up to then. All of the characters act unscrupulously, with no concern for consequences and norms. They regard everything and everybody with disdain. Their intention is to destroy society, even though they rely on it to survive and even at a price of their lives. Their attitude bears some relation to their environment and society. The retired American soldiers and the Hong Kong youngsters share similar experiences and situations: The former endured an irrational, flawed war in Vietnam that caused them to become unbalanced; the latter, likewise, had to endure an extremely repressive upbringing in uncomfortable circumstances. For example, Lam Chun-kee lives in a broken family. She is often beaten up by her brother, Law Lit. She herself is so violent that she frequently lashes out at others. Of the parallels between the American soldiers and the Hong Kong youths, Tsui said, 'I stress this similarity because I hope to raise the dramatic conflict to the level of urban warfare.'[19] In this approach, both groups of characters have the inclination to kill and a general tendency to be violent. For no reason, the American soldiers killed prostitutes, the homosexual, the gang boss (by drowning) and Lam Chun-kee (by throwing her into the street). A group of Hong Kong youngsters, led by Lam, are equally cruel. They engage in such acts as jabbing needles into rats, throwing a cat into the street, pouring gasoline on three other teenagers, putting a cigarette butt into the pants of a gang leader, robbing a tourist coach, bombing the shopkeeper and the guard of a currency exchange shop and so forth. The final scene is a fierce massacre between the soldiers and the youngsters over a pile of Japanese cheques. It can be claimed that, here, Tsui Hark has applied a political metaphor.

Careful consideration was given to the structure of the film. In addition to the parallel between the two groups of characters, the plot unfolds in a manner that emphasizes causality and coherence. For example, the beginning and the ending of the film echo one another. The film opens with a scene of a bag of blood being thrown from the roof of a building. It closes with a similar scene, with the addition of a lady passer-by holding an umbrella. She shouts at the unknown person for committing the act. The impression that is given is that the whole city is in crisis. Another scene, showing Lam tossing a cat out of the window, is the scene in which 'montage' is used most skilfully. This scene later finds an echo in the scene where Lam is heaved on to the street by an American soldier and killed by being pierced by a pointed pole. It cannot be denied that the film reflected the current social situation of the time, when young people were suppressed and could see no way out of their predicament. Furthermore, this movie bears a very close relation to Tsui Hark's own inner feelings. The unsatisfactory box office response to his first two films was certainly a blow to him – a director who thirsts for recognition from the audience. He was eager to have 'his works be accepted by the public', and for his works to be viewed by the audience as 'a part of the audience themselves'.[20] He made *We're Going to Eat You* when he was in a dark mood and *Dangerous Encounter – 1st Kind* in a furious mood. 'Perhaps because I shared the same feelings with certain characters in the film, my emotions were trapped and could be released. Thus the sentiments in the film come across as frustrated and explosive.'[21] In other words, Tsui transferred his discontent, accumulated over many years, to the images of this movie, producing scenes of blind, cruel massacres. The film is an intense, unrestrained expression of the film-maker.

From the Negation to the Affirmation of Life

All the Wrong Clues is the first detective comedy that Tsui Hark directed for Cinema City. In contrast to his previous three productions, this film is not pessimistic and violent but easy, fluid, relaxing, cheerful and humorous. It bore some relation to his work done in collaboration with Karl Maka, Raymond Wong and Dean Shek. However, what is more significant is that in a situation in which he was not under pressure but was given support, Tsui was able to demonstrate his potential in comedy.[22] His long-held wish for acknowledgement from the audience was finally fulfilled, as indicated by the office return of seven million Hong Kong dollars. He also earned the Best Director award in the Golden Horse Awards that year.

The relationship between Tsui Hark and Cinema City was one of mutual assistance. In 1980, when Cinema City was established, it produced comedies such as *Laughing Times* (dir. John Woo) and *Beware of Pickpockets* (dir. Ng Ma), which depicted the lower classes of society. These were 'hoodlum comedies' or so-called 'shabby' melodramas. The plot usually focused on stories about struggling through difficult times and optimism in suffering. Dean Shek performed a very well-received imitation of Charlie Chaplin. With Tsui Hark, the company shifted direction and began to produce modern comedies. The style of the productions changed to one of elegance and neatness. The focus was on the urban and the modern, and the protagonists were no longer rogues but people who considered fantasies of love to be of prime importance. Subsequent to *All the Wrong Clues*, Cinema City put out several big productions with big stars, specifically, *Chasing Girls* (1981, dir. Karl Maka), *Aces Go Places* (1982, dir. Eric Tsang), *Aces Go Places II* (1983), and *Aces Go Places III – Our Man from Bond Street* (1984, dir. Tsui Hark). All were box office winners. These successes earned acclaim for Cinema City.[23]

All the Wrong Clues is about a gang boss, Capone (Karl Maka), who covets the property of a former cheat, Tang Kee-chen. Capone tries everything to lay his hands on this property. He intimidates a private detective, George Lam, and the fraud's wife, Yiu Wai, to kidnap Tang's daughter. With the aid of a smart policeman, Teddy Robin, Capone is defeated. The plot is simple and has no theme, only a series of actions and comic-like gags. What is attractive are the avant-garde shooting style and the creativity. For instance, the film opens with a scene of an arrest for gambling. The cop, Teddy Robin, accompanied by other colleagues, is on assignment. Three people are shown in an overlapping pattern, the other two hidden behind the first. Not until the first moves away is the second revealed. Also, in another sequence, Lam brings the fraud's daughter home. Four women appear successively, in different rooms. Again, the sequence is impressive. The entire film is linked by actions, with gags in between. Every single character is likeable, including the 'antagonist', Karl Maka. Therefore, this film is fast-paced and made up of a series of actions and a great deal of humour. Through it all it is still possible to get a glimpse of Tsui Hark's vitality, creativity and distinctive style.

With no blood and no deaths, *All the Wrong Clues* marked a 180-degree turn from Tsui's three previous movies. 'Perhaps I was too pessimistic before. Now I have tried to change my perspective to view life in a more optimistic manner.'[24] Therefore, the message conveyed by this film is that the world has hope. But, it has to be said that it is precisely because of such an affirmation about people, that the film loses its power to reflect, protest and criticize. It displays Tsui's mode of narration, which is one dominated by events. Such a mode has the advantage of being lively, having a cinematic feel and being easy for the audience to accept. Certainly, the issue here is one of choice of perspective and mode of narration, not of good or bad. Tsui, however, evaluates himself as being weak at storytelling. In fact, this seems untrue if we observe his *Dangerous Encounter – 1st Kind*. Although he understands the technique of telling a story, he refuses to be restricted by norms, for fear of becoming 'too typical'.[25]

Because of this, Tsui's *Zu – Warriors from the Magic Mountain* (1983, abbreviated as *Zu*) centres on the characters rather than the story. Even the events are narrated from the points of view of the characters. Naturally, the main characters represent Tsui himself. Their perspectives, narrated in first-person, are actually Tsui's. In this way, Tsui undoubtedly can freely express his opinions and insights. In this movie, as early as in the stage of constructing the plot, Tsui already put himself into the protagonist, Yuan

Biao. He inserted some of his experiences from childhood, namely of the Vietnam War. At the time, he did not understand why the war was being fought and why his family had to escape. Thus, at the beginning of the film, set in ancient Sichuan, two sets of troops from the same village do battle with one another. Here, Tsui draws on the past to satirize the present: if even two armies from the same village are unable to live in harmony, how much more difficult must it be for those who from different regions / ethnicities / faiths to do so? The three protagonists, Yuen Biao, Little Monk Meng Hai and the disciple of Icy-Cloud Palace, Moon Lee, are the objects of a sacrifice who die in an ice cave because of the battles involving the older generation. They sigh for the selfishness of each School in the martial arts world, 'The righteous people not only fail to unite, they also come across numerous difficulties in their mission. We have not yet acquired the swords (two swords, Purple and Green), and our Masters have already died. They are only concerned about their own school, not the entire martial arts world. They claim that they share the same duty, that of fighting against the devils and maintaining justice for the purpose of saving the world. But – in fact they are simply too disunited. If we follow them, we will not only be unable to save them, but also ourselves.' Later, the trio obtain the two swords with the help of Taoist Master Xiangmei and Taoist Mistress Lee Yik-king (Judy Ong). The two swords turn out to be all-powerful ones that integrate all the essences from the cosmos and the forces from nature and human beings. However, under normal circumstances, the swords, possessing opposite natures, *yin* and *yang*, cannot be used simultaneously. Otherwise, a calamity would result – if minor, the death of the sword players; if major, the destruction of heaven and earth. Yet, if the two sword players are wholly united, in mind and in speech, the two swords will also become one and the reverse would occur – heaven and the earth would be united. With the dual swords, Yuan and Meng win the duel with the head devil and thereby save Xiangmei. Here, Tsui explains that the presence of devils can be eliminated by honesty and unity; there is still hope for mankind.

Narrating through characters allows the director to speak directly. However, if sufficient caution is not exercised, it is easy to stray into verbosity and didacticism; the plot may suffer and the tone of the film may be dull. Fortunately, *Zu* is not flawed in this manner. Although the emphasis in this film is on the characters, action has not been neglected. Event follows event, such as Yuan falling from a cliff, the devils attacking the Taoists and the monk, and the hero (Adam Cheng) helping to resist the devils. The monk is poisoned and Cheng brings him to the ice cave to be treated by the cave mistress (Brigitte Lin). Actions are frequent. Moreover, magic (technology) is at play, which enables the characters to perform acrobatics including flying, landing, climbing mountains and diving in water. The actions penetrate spaces of various dimensions, and the illusions are boundless. All of these are realized by the creative Tsui Hark, to the astonishment of the audience.

In fact, the most remarkable accomplishment of *Zu* is Tsui Hark's complete adoption of modern sci-fi technology. Prior to this film, Hollywood had already produced certain sci-fi pictures – notably *Star Wars* and *Close Encounters of the Third Kind* – that broke ground in the use of technology in film-making. Tsui, known for his quick wits, invited a Hollywood professional on optical effects, Tom Savini, to help him with the Golden Harvest production. Tsui even established a group to oversee the special effects for the entire film.[26] Later, this group became a central part of the series of *A Chinese Ghost Story* (1986), for which Tsui was the producer.

Pioneering Cinematic Technology to Hail the Martial Arts Fantasy World

At around the same time, another New Wave director, Alex Cheung, also began shooting a sci-fi film, *Twinkle Twinkle Little Star* (1983), for Shaw. A Japanese cinematic technology expert was invited to assist with those aspects of the film related to optical effects. One of the scenes in the movie involved a UFO landing on Earth. The film-maker first finished shooting a model of a UFO landing. Then, the method of 'front projection' was used, where the image was projected as the background and the heroine, Cherie Chung, was in the foreground, discovering the flying object. Another fighting scene between Yi Lui and the extra-terrestrials included animation; sparks and light beams were added as emanating from the clashing swords. Unfortunately, because of a flawed script and other problems, the production was not up to standard.

In one of Tsui Hark's early works, *The Butterfly Killers*, an attempt is made to use 'science' rather than 'technology' to explain the mysterious martial arts world. The film thus fails to represent a martial arts world of imagination that is fantastic, marvelous, changeful and unexpected. Tsui then came to realize the limitations of science as means of finding evidence and making interpretations. Hence, he made a radical turn and began to employ advanced sci-fi technology as a tool for film-making. And, indeed, he created a traditional martial arts world with a supernatural dimension. The results were spectacular. For example, in the scene where the devils attack the hero (Adam Cheng) and the monk, globes of fire in the sky turn into countless UFOs that split a mountain. The spirit of the old man with the long eyebrows is separated from his body in a red halo, which then turns into a triangular one, protecting the two protagonists and making it possible for them to take the purple and green swords. Another scene shows the hero bringing the seriously wounded monk to the mistress of the Icy-Cloud Palace, Brigitte Lin, to seek help. The palace ends up exploding. Light beams and fire beams intersect. The beams are then transformed into ice – and the scene becomes cool, silent and solitary. All, except for the three protagonists, die in the ice. The sequence closes with a freeze shot. With technologies related to models, optical effects and explosions, Tsui produced a rich, ever-changing fantasy world that had never before been seen in a locally made production. It was an amalgamation of the traditional and the modern (technology), local and western. The cinematic language of the film was enriched, and its substance was enhanced.

Aces Go Places III – Our Man from Bond Street was the first comedy that Tsui Hark made at Cinema City. The plot focuses on a super-thief, Sam Hui, who is called back to Hong Kong to retrieve the diamond stolen from the crown of the British Queen. He gets into a series of fights with the Hong Kong police. Later, he discovers the tricks of the international criminals and collaborates with the police to arrest them. This film makes use of a great deal of action technology as well as computing technology. For example, the scene in which the false Queen comes forward from the portrait hanging on the wall to shake hands with Sam Hui was produced with computing technology. This kind of device was replicated in another Hong Kong movie of the same period, *Till Death Do We Scare* (1982). The heroine's three dead husbands each emerge from their photographs and discuss ways of protecting their wife from dying.

In *Aces Go Places III*, there is a scene in which the bold policeman, Karl Maka, consults the computer on the identity of the person who has stolen the Queen's diamond, 'The Lucky Star'. The screen of the computer suddenly displays the picture of Sam Hui – a humorous effect produced by technology. In another scene, Sam Hui masquerades as a Santa Clause to sneak into a jewelry exhibition. Right after stealing the huge diamond 'Star of the King', he learns that there are many Santa Clauses flying to the roof of the New World Building. Hui himself flies towards a submarine and then to a railway station. This series of flying actions was put together using computing technology. Although this sort of technology had already been used in the western movie, *Superman*, *Aces Go Places III* shows the hero flying horizontally as well as vertically, while Superman only flies horizontally. *Aces Go Places III* was the first Hong Kong movie to use modern technology to such a large extent and in such a precise manner. Added to this the comic elements characterizing Cinema City productions, *Aces Go Places III* stirred up a massive amount of attention when it was released and topped the box office that year.

A Chinese Ghost Story (1987, dir. Ching Siu-tung) and its sequels, *A Chinese Ghost Story II: The Story Continues* (1990, dir. also Ching) and *A Chinese Ghost Story III* (1991, dir. also Ching), all with Tsui Hark as the producer, attained a high level of sophistication in the use of technology. The narrative of *A Chinese Ghost Story*, adapted from *Liao Zhai's Collection of Ghost Stories*, centres on the love between a female ghost, Nie Xiaoqian, and a scholar, Ning Caichen. The film shows the tremendous potential of computer technology as applied to models and optical effects. For example, the fight between Laolao's huge tongue and Xiaoqian's cloth, the fights that took place in the air and on the ground, secret weapons, blazing fires, flying arrows, explosions and so forth. There were countless scenes of incredible power showing the horror of the ghost regime and the unfathomable depths of the mysterious forces. The two sequels basically employ similar special effects as the original film and tell a similar story. The huge tongue and cloth continue to intimidate. Laolao's martial arts supremacy still prevails. There are other fantastic scenes – sea water flows skyward; the Taoist's amour and blade are unveiled; one wooden pillar multiplies into many and then turns into golden garments; in the last scene Xiaoqian (Wang Zuxian) rescues Tony Leung Chiu-wai and sends his golden garment in the air to absorb the essence of sunlight. Then, with extraordinary power, she blasts Laolao into ash.

Beginning in the 1990s, Hong Kong high-tech movies were already moving towards the digital era. Digital technology was employed in scenes in *Happy Ghost IV* (1990) and *Fai and Chi: Kings of Kung Fu* (1990): the animated image of a tiger, and the simultaneous appearance of a turtle and a human being. *Umbrella Story* (1995) imitated *Forrest Gump* by having real historical figures such as Chiang Kai-shek, Zhou Xuan, Ng Chor-fan, Linda Ching (Lam Doi) and Bruce Lee appear at the same time as characters in the film. This was the first local film to make use of digital images. The most successful integration of digital images and drama is undoubtedly *Storm Riders* (1998, dir. Andrew Lau). The duel between Hong Ba and Nip Yan King at the Big Buddha at Le Shan shows multiple shadows moving along the figures, fostering the atmosphere of 'the real in fantastic and the fantastic in the real'. Furthermore, digital imagery allows world-famous sights, such as the Big Buddha at Le Shan and the Statue of Liberty,[27] to be 'transferred' to the studio for shooting. The actors could even perform in front of nothing – the images can be added using digital technology,[28] with the virtual images and the real images being merged into one frame. *Storm Riders* is a typical example of a film that is a combination of different elements such as digital images, popular comics and traditional martial arts. The success of these films opened a new path toward globalization for Hong Kong movies. This, directly or indirectly, is connected to Tsui's fervent advocacy of sci-fi technology of many years.

From the high-tech films that Tsui Hark either directed or produced, one can see the transformation of cinematic language and aesthetic form brought about by technology. The two series of *A Chinese Ghost Story* and *Zu* are the best evidence of this. Aided by modern special effects, these works were novel in style and aesthetic form. These new styles then become pivotal to the content of the films. Tsui Hark, therefore, should be credited for creating a 'new wave' of modern technology films in Hong Kong.

Using the Past as an Allegory for the Present – Giving Voice to Discontent with Politics

In *A Chinese Ghost Story*, the Taoist monk laments that in the human world, there is no distinction between right and wrong; between good and evil. He is disappointed with society. He would rather live in the world of ghosts, where black and white are clearly demarcated. Later, the Taoist monk (Wu Ma), together with Xiaoqian (Joey Wang) and Ning Caichen (Leslie Cheung), win the surrender of Laolao. Furthermore, Xiaoqian's ashes are brought home for burial, foreshadowing the fulfillment of her final wish to be reincarnated. *A Chinese Ghost Story II* closes with the departure of Wang and Cheung on horseback, signifying a happy ending for the lovers. In *A Chinese Ghost Story III*, Wang rescues Cheung at the price of her life. All of these sequences show that if everybody, whether human or ghost, works together, anything be achieved. For example, in *Zu*, two people united in will and heart succeeded in eradicating the devils. *Zu* also addresses certain political issues in contemporary China; for instance, the opposition between leftists and rightists, the divisions in the nation and other problems.

A number of films namely *Shanghai Blues* (1984), *Peking Opera Blues* (1986), *A Better Tomorrow III* and *Swordsman* more or less reflect the anxiety and frustration that Hong Kong people felt about their future: should they emigrate or should they stay? This uncertainty had enveloped the peninsula for years until the signing of the Joint Declaration in 1984. Many people had compared the handover of Hong Kong to Shanghai in the 1930s.[29] This was the inspiration for the making of *Shanghai Blues*. The story is set in 1937 in Japanese-occupied Shanghai. When fleeing Shanghai, Kenny Bee Chung becomes acquainted with Sylvia Chiang. The two pledge to meet again under a bridge after the country is victorious. Ten years later, they meet again without recognizing each other. Finally, on the train to Hong Kong, they do recognize each other. The romance involving separation, reunion and the lovers' departure from Shanghai is deeply touching. Is it not an exact reflection of the relationship between Hong Kong and mainland China? In the film, Chiang stands for Hong Kong. She leaves during wartime and returns after the victory. Then, she becomes a nightclub girl (a product of capitalism). But what is praiseworthy about her is that in order to help a young girl of the song-and-dance troupe, she was willing to relinquish Chung to a village girl, Sally Yeh. Chung once again finds himself struggling to make a living, as a street musician (a typical proletariat), at the grass-root level of society. He is so eager to find his lost lover, Chiang, that he is even willing to leave mainland China. In the end, the couple are reunited, having undergone various twists and turns in their lives. Their embarrassment, discomfort and contradictory feelings at the time can be understood without any need for words.

The occupation of Shanghai by the Japanese military caused many people to flee, and led to feelings of hatred for the loss of nation and home. Following the victory against Japan, a civil war broke out, the currency depreciated and inflation escalated. Some people were selling blood for money; yet there continued to be displays of indulgence and decadence in the city. Some people continued to emigrate. This kind of *fin de siecle* atmosphere gives a certain silhouette to Hong Kong at the time, although Tsui Hark's did not go overboard in portraying the atmosphere of the 1940s. 'I merely view the past from a subjective perspective; I am not seeking to replicate the past. Just as with a costume drama, it is definitely not a bad thing to employ a realistic style. However, I see no point in being too realistic. I can romanticize and modify certain parts.'[30] Only in this way could Tsui break through norms and constraints to develop himself in a larger imaginative space. In fact, of the New Wave talents, Tsui is a creative director who changes the most and is the least willing to work under restrictions. If he copies the ideas of previous directors in his films such as *A Chinese Ghost Story*, *Zu* and *Shanghai Blues*, he would be nothing more than a puppet.

Peking Opera Blues is one of the few movies of Tsui Hark set in a particular time and place. The story is set in 1913, two years after the 1911 Revolution, which led to the establishment of the Republic of China. China has fallen to military dictators, who have divided the country into fiefdoms. Their selfishness imperils the nation and brings suffering to the people. The daughter of superintendent Duan, Brigitte Lin, secretly joins the Revolutionary Party and is responsible for stealing documents about the complicity between the military dictators and foreign powers. Unfortunately, she fails in this task. Later, aided by Sally Yeh, the daughter of the master of an opera troupe, and an opera singer, Cherie Chung, the documents are successfully acquired and delivered to the parliament in the south. The parliament then send a force to attack Yuan Shikai, the provisional president of the Republic of China and most powerful military figure in China. Using a story set in a definite time and place, Tsui said what he wanted to say, that the splitting up of a nation, its weaknesses and its colonization are all due to the selfishness and disunity of its people. Although his material may be humorous and action-filled, Tsui is still concerned about the affairs of the nation, or, more accurately, he satirizes these events, balancing the solemn and the amusing. To explore with great seriousness is not consistent with his personality,[31] nor his style.

A Better Tomorrow III is set around the period of the fall of Vietnam to the communists. Chow Yun-fat travels from Hong Kong to Saigon in order to bring his uncle, Shek Kin, who owns a medicine shop, and cousin, Tony Leung Ka-fai, back to Hong Kong. Intersecting the major plot is the triangular relationship between Chow, Anita Mui and Saburo Tokito (Mui's former lover). Although the film is historically and geographically specific – 1974 Vietnam (and the director's childhood is reflected in Shek's Chinese medicine shop, as his family ran a similar business in Vietnam when he was young), the characters do not have a sense of roots. They could have been placed anywhere. Even their appearance is no different from that of Hong Kong heroes. The film depicts a change in era with a change in sovereignty, and individuals who appear small and powerless because they lack the right to choose. It is as Chou said, 'Fate is a bet. A greater hope is usually exchanged with a greater disappointment.... You presumably have options, but actually you have none.' Was this not exactly the predicament in which Hong Kong people found themselves? Hong Kong people had no say in the negotiations between China and Britain over Hong Kong's future. The only thing that they could do was 'leave' or 'stay', just as was depicted in the film.

Are the scenes in *A Better Tomorrow III: Love and Death in Saigon* of the demonstration by Vietnamese students and their suppression by gun-toting troops not mirror images of the June 4th Incident?[32] Under the powerful ruling apparatus of the Vietnamese government and the suppression by its military policemen, individuals are completely powerless. At the end of the film, when North Vietnam overruns the south, Chow and Leung carry the wounded Mui to try to break into a military airport and get on a helicopter. However, with the arrival of the Vietnamese Communist army, the trio are shot. When the helicopter gradually rises, a song called 'The Song of Sunset' is heard, lamenting the misery of life. Apart from such themes as the persistence of the heroes and the uncertainty of fate, Tsui draws a parallel between the story in the film and the situation in Hong Kong.

Swordsman is likewise set in a specific time and place – in the Wanli reign of the Ming Dynasty. According to historians, in that period, the palace stressed ritual over administration. It was an era of prosperity, and the Wanli reign was the longest reign of that dynasty.[33] At the same time, it was also a time when the government was terrorized by two spy organizations, the East Factory and the West Factory. In the movie 'Sunflower Bible', a top-secret martial arts book is suddenly stolen from the palace. A variety of people (including the eunuchs of the East Factory) then contend with each other, all attempting to get their hands on the book. The competition for the book reveals the dark side of the human character – despair, deception, a willingness to sell one's body and a lust for power. The eunuch of the East Factory, Lau Shun, signifies the dominant power, whereas Jacky Cheung and Yuen Wah are people who bend with the wind and who flatter whoever is in authority. Cheung and Yuen are willing to serve Lau and to help him carry out his evil, cold-blooded murders. Lau once cautioned Cheung, 'You are quick and sharp, and could go beyond me if I am not cautious. Young man, do not overreach yourself or you will be killed.' That is, caution is vital or one will die. Furthermore, the leader of Huashan, Yue Buqun, is a hypocrite, speaking of justice and care for Huashan but in fact betraying his disciples and surrendering to the eunuch for the sake of personal interest. Here, the movie satirizes real-life politics.

A similar story, *Working Class* (1985), set in contemporary Hong Kong focuses on the relationship between the working class and the capitalists. The theme is one that is taken from *Zu* and *Shanghai Blues*, which is that unity can change fate and bring peace to the world. In the film, a poor man, Sam Hui, falls in love with the daughter of a factory boss, Joey Wang. In order not to injure Hui's self-esteem, Wang conceals her real identity. The boss is mean and makes things difficult for the employees (Hui, Teddy Robin, Tsui Hark). One day, the factory catches fire and all of the machines are ruined. Hui rescues Wang from the fire and repairs the machines, enabling production to continue normally. The boss is overjoyed and gives Hui and his colleagues half of the holdings of the business. The movie closes with a happy ending. The message of the film is: Unity can resolve problems. Even employers and employees can live in harmony; their relationship does not necessarily have to be characterized by conflict and confrontation. Perhaps the movie has simplified the issues and made light of them. But thinking it over, aren't the resolution of conflicts and the fulfillment of objectives achieved in a light-hearted manner exactly Tsui Hark's goals?

Tsui Hark's National Sentiments – The Myths of Wong Fei-hung

Since 1991, Tsui Hark has directed a total of four films about Wong Fei-hung: *Once Upon a Time in China* (1991) and its sequels II, III and IV (1992, 1993, 1994, respectively). Moreover, Tsui was the producer of *Once Upon a Time in China IV* (1993, dir. Yuen Bun) and *Once Upon a Time in China VI* (1997, dir. Sammo Hung). It can be claimed that the series *Once Upon a Time in China* contains the largest number of works directed by Tsui about the same figure or under the same title, followed by the series *A Chinese Ghost Story*. Wong Fei-hung is a legend familiar to everyone in Hong Kong; it is also a legend in Hong Kong cinema. Since the earliest Wong Fei-hung movie, *The True Story of Wong Fei-hung Part I* (dir. Hu Peng), appeared in 1949, there have been more than a hundred films (excluding TV dramas) on this figure.[34] This is a record in Hong Kong as well as the world and has been mentioned in the Guinness Book of Records.[35]

There is a very big difference between Tsui's Wong Fei-hung series and the films that preceded it. In the older films, the key figure is solely a symbol of righteousness. He has both martial arts skills and virtue and is willing to help the weak against the strong. In addition, his skill for healing enables him to help ordinary people when they fall sick. Although he is provoked by villains, his belief in harmony and tolerance always causes him to postpone the fight to the last moment. He always wins over the villains by teaching them lessons. This is the 'generic pattern', which develops from the opposition between good and evil, chivalry and villainy. Generally speaking, Tsui Hark's films follow this kind of narrative. Still the embodiment of heroism, Wong Fei-hung is situated in the intersection between two epochs – the Qing Dynasty is in decline; at the same time, imperialist powers are invading the territory. The first stirrings of revolution are beginning to be felt. Wong struggles between the imperialists and the republicans, Chinese tradition and western culture. His mind is filled with contradictions, confusion and change. Through Wong's predicament, Tsui expresses his concern and opinions about the nation's crises and its future. There is a strong sense of mission to the film. As a result, Wong's image was elevated to loftier heights than ever before.

Conflicts between East and West

The opening of *Once Upon a Time in China* highlights, in the most obvious way, that in a recent era China's territory was divided up by a number of powers: the United Kingdom took Hong Kong; Portugal, Macau; and Russia, the province of Heilongjiang (in northeast China). Wong Fei-hung is given a paper fan by the minister in charge of waterworks, Liu Yongfu, on which the words 'unequal treaty' are written. It serves as a sign calling for people to unite to protect their country and to remember the insults to the nation. The director cuts to a scene of Wong at the seashore, leading members of civil organizations in undergoing training. They are strong and vigorous, and the scene is spectacular and heroic, filled with the spirit of true manhood. The allegory is clear.

In another scene, in the city of Foshan in China, an orchestra is playing the tune 'Xiqi Yangyang' (literally, euphoria) in a tea house. A group of western missionaries then enters and sings 'Hallelujah' (in praise of the Virgin Mary). The Chinese orchestra steps up its playing, while, not to be outdone, the missionaries chant in louder voices. In the midst of this competition, a thunderous noise is suddenly heard. It is the whistle from a big boat from the West, and it drowns out the melodic sounds of both parties. Both the musicians and the missionaries have not yet identified the nature of the noise, which signifies the coming of imperialism to the land.

The winds from the West have arrived in the East; the times are changing. Everything before one's eyes is in flux and all is confusion. Wong Fei-hung, who has had a

Confucian upbringing and respects tradition, finds the changes difficult to deal with and accept. Aunt Yee (a heroine representing western culture) brings Wong a western-style suit and says, 'Western people invented the steam engine and are scientifically advanced. We are lagging behind and will lag behind even more if we do not learn from others.' Wong responds, 'Chinese people wear Western-style suits? Is the West really so good that we must learn everything from them?' Aunt Yee replies, 'Railways and telegraph stations have just opened here. Everything will change.' Wong argued, 'Yes, everything is changing. Not until every other Chinese person dresses in a Western-style suit will I wear one.' As a symbol of the Confucian moral system, it was natural for Wong to initially show defiance against foreign fashions. Others, out of ignorance and a feeling of inferiority, might blindly reject or resist the challenge from the West. In *Once Upon a Time in China II*, adherents of the White Lotus religion, under the slogan of 'Help the Qing, eliminate the West', blindly burn western imports including clocks, paintings, dogs and other items. There is a corresponding scene in sequel IV (1993, dir. Yuen Bun, produced by Tsui Hark) of antagonism toward westerners. Followers of the White Lotus religion stir up chaos in the streets, set fire to a building, attack foreign consulates and commit assault and murder (including of primary school students). Aunt Yee and Wong Fei-hung rush over and send the victims to the magistrate's office, and then, when the magistrate is unable to protect them, to the consulates. Later, the White Lotus followers burn the consulates, the telegraph station and anything related to the West.

Aunt Yee, who has returned from abroad, carries a camera and wears western clothing. She attracts the attention of people in the street as something bizarre. Once, she wants to take a picture of a little girl, but the girl pours water on her, throws things at her and curses her for being a 'false foreign devil'. She hurries over to take a photograph of the alter that the followers of the White Lotus religion have set up in front of the telegraph station (a symbol of the West). The disciples of the White Lotus religion, taking her for an evil woman, capture her. Fortunately, she is saved by Wong. The followers of the White Lotus religion hate foreigners, and their motto is 'Kill all Westerners and achieve ultimate peace'. Such thinking arises purely from naivety and ignorance. Their claim to possess an extraordinary power that is resistant against blades and bombs is mere trickery. Their deception is uncovered in a couple of scenes. Luk Hao-dong accidentally shoots a White Lotus girl to death. Later, Wong batters the leader of the White Lotus sect, while Lu tries to shoot him without success. Finally, Wong kills him with his fists and a tin plate slips off from the body of the leader – he has been wearing a shield against bullets. When Wong unveils the White Lotus' deceptions, the nation turns against the White Lotus sect. In addition to despising evil, Wong is also sympathetic to the cause of the revolutionaries (Sun Yat-sen and Luk Hao-dong). In the final scene, Wong guards Sun as the latter makes his departure, guarding a list of the names of the revolutionists that had been carried by Luk, and also hands Sun the flag of the Nationalist Party.

A Blending of the Cultures of East and West

Wong Fei-hung is a stubborn hero who insists on traditional virtues and abhors evil. He is forced to confront the crisis of the country being divided up by foreign powers. A martial arts practitioner, Wong undergoes a transformation in his attitude toward the rapid westernization that is nearly subverting the country: from complete rejection, to a measure of tolerance, and finally to acceptance. Such metamorphosis was due to his forbearing and subtle temperament, and also to the influence of Aunt Yee. Thus, in the series *Once Upon a Time in China*, Aunt Yee plays the key role of facilitating Wong's connection with and contemplation of western culture (including modern technology; for example, in episode III, the significance of steam engines to the Industrial Revolution is introduced).

The figure of Aunt Yee is included because she is a representative of western culture. She returns from studying in England, wearing western clothing, bringing a camera, a movie camera and projectors, which all are signs of western culture. She even acts as a pioneer in introducing the western media – a symbol of freedom of speech – to China. In the second sequel, while riding in a train, Aunt Yee discourses to passengers around her on the invention of the train, as well as on western cuisine and table manners. Wong, in the third sequel, demands to go to Beijing to learn English, because some western people understand the Chinese language. Aunt Yee, seeing that Wong has started to want to understand western culture, begins to teach him English. The language class is somewhat humorous, in that Wong, amusingly, articulates the English words with a Cantonese accent. For example, he pronounces the word 'woman' as '*wumeng*', 'man' as '*mei*', 'I love you too' as '*ao lup fu yu to*' and so forth. Furthermore, Wong's medical business, 'Po Chi Lam', switches to brewing herbal tea using a steam engine, again Aunt Yee's idea. This adoption of western knowledge is extended in a scene in *Once Upon a Time in China II*, showing Wong behaving confidently in a medical conference. Discoursing on the meridian system and the 'five elements', he provides a clear explanation of Chinese medicine. He also confidently performs a demonstration, using acupuncture, on how the nervous system operates, formulating a comparison with 'reflex theory' (knocking on the knee) in western medicine. In the last scene, in the embassy of the United Kingdom, Wong and Sun Yat-sen respectively use Chinese and western medicine to save the life of a foreigner – Wong feeling his pulse and employing acupuncture, and Sun using a stethoscope and giving the patient injections. The two streams of medicine and two cultures show strengths of their own and supplement each other. The film has a happy ending.

In *Once Upon a Time in China IV*, Wong's hostility towards the West, which was a dominant idea in the series, has dissipated. Wong Fei-hung, in a duel, uses rifles rather than his fists to kill Cheung Po Chai's son-in-law. Tsui Hark's allusion is obvious: under the impact of western culture, China has no choice but to modernize (i.e., westernize) if the country is to achieve power and prosperity. However, not all conflicts can end in reconciliation, harmony and resolution. The character of Buck Teeth (Jackie Cheung) in *Once Upon a Time in China* is one example. He returns from the United States speaking fluent English, but halting Chinese. This makes it difficult for him to communicate with others, and he sometimes selects the wrong medicine, as the labels are written in Chinese. He is so discouraged by the many setbacks he encounters that, eventually, he leaves for the United States in distress. He is an example of the problems and obstacles encountered in the exchange of the two cultures.

The Internal and External Misfortunes of the Nation

Living in an era of unrest, both internal and external misfortunes led to Wong Fei-hung's transformation. The dramatic conflicts in the series also revolve around these misfortunes. In the series of *Once Upon a Time in China*, the nation is challenged both internally and externally, but it is the domestic conflict that is especially severe. A gang, the Sha Ho Gang, tyrannizes the locality. It demands 'protection fees' from the residents. It also sets Po Chi Lam on fire, during which the 'unequal treaties' paper fan is partially spoiled: the 'un-' is burned away. Here, Tsui makes an inference to reality. The gang colludes with some westerners to bring harm to local people. And a skilled martial arts fighter, Yim Chun-dong, comes far from the North to join the Sha Ho Gang. He kidnaps Aunt Yee, who is eventually rescued by Wong. The mob is also defeated in the end. In the sequel, it is the White Lotus sect that incites chaos, killing the innocents and blindly attacking anything that smacked of western civilization and westerners under the banner of 'Help the Qing and annihilate the West'. An antagonist, Yuan Shu, a high-ranking minister of the Qing government, has been secretly protecting the White Lotus sect. He orders the arrest of advocates of democracy and republicanism, such as Sun Yat-sen and Luk Hao-dong, and attacks against Wong and his followers. In *Once Upon a Time in China III*, in order to manipulate the Lion King contest organized by the Governor's office, Chiu Tin-ba attacks the Guangdong Assembly Hall. This results in the members of other big martial arts schools, such as Choy Li-fat and White Eyebrows, to begin fighting and killing each other. They are driven by the desire to win the championship in the Lion King contest, but such attacks not only sap the strength of the members, but are also contrary to the goal of engaging in martial arts – to strengthen the body. Little wonder that, after Wong has won the championship and meets the Chief Dean, he boldly tells him,

> Who was the winner and who the loser? In fact that this Lion King contest has led to the deaths of so many martial arts experts that everybody has lost. The brave feel no fear and the virtuous have no enemies. The practice of martial arts is to strengthen the body. It also requires the unification of wisdom and acrobatics. If the practitioners fail to keep their minds open to the wisdom of the people, but solely emphasize their physiques, how can martial arts help to fortify the nation and the people? What, in the end, was the cost of mere medal of the Lion King? I beg Your Excellency's to give the matter some thought. Here, I give this gold medal to you as a remembrance! (Wong immediately tosses the medal up to the Chief Dean, who is sitting in the gallery.) Goodbye.

He then makes a dashing departure. Tsui takes this opportunity to satirize that rulers' lack of understanding of the predicament of their people, which is again an allegory for the present.

The fourth episode of the series is about the difficulty of distinguishing between cops and robbers. On the one hand, pirates uphold the social order on behalf of the dynasty and are suddenly appointed government officials. On the other, soldiers suffering from hunger are forced to rob to survive. Later, Cheung Po Chai's descendants revert to piracy, and Wong and his disciples have to fight against them to maintain the security of the country. In times of chaos, furthermore, money-minded merchants deliberately mark up the price of rice to obtain more profits. 'The more chaotic the society is, the more money can be earned. Times of mayhem produce heroes. This is what can be regarded as prosperity.' Unethical businessmen show their true colours when they make money from turmoil. As for external perils, they are also a major theme in the series of *Once Upon a Time in China*. The opening scene of the first film already began to directly depict the occupation of China by various powers. Such a situation marked the beginning of a nightmarish century of weakness for the Chinese people. An American, Chik Sin (literally, 'accumulating goodness'), sells Chinese workers to San Francisco. The workers endure torture and exploitation. The American also conspires with the Sha Ho Gang to attempt to kill Wong Fei-hung. When Chik Sin's conspiracy is smashed by Master Wong, Chik Sin arrogantly says, 'Chink, even if I kill you, there will be no consequences for me to bear after I return to America.' This demonstrates the depth of the westerners' lack of shame. In the third episode, Russians send To Man-kee, a classmate of Aunt Yee's in England, to assassinate a Chief Dean during the Lion King contest. The aim is to prevent him from signing a contract with the Japanese. This plot is uncovered by Aunt Yee. Aunt Yee, Wong Fei-hung and others intervene and rescue Chief Dean. To is eventually killed by his colleagues.

In *Once Upon a Time in China IV*, the eight powers, representing the idea of imperialism, put together the 'monster brigade' to surround and attack Wong Fei-hung's South-Lion team (Guangdong). They vow to defeat Wong. Not surprisingly, in the end they are unable to do so. On the contrary, Wong wins a big victory that brings glory to his country. Not all westerners, however, are villains. For example, in *Once Upon a Time in China* there is a western missionary who witnessed the fire and slaughter at Po Chi Lam. He steps out and acts as a witness for Wong Fei-hung. In the sequel, there is also a westerner from the British consulate who protected Chinese primary students who were studying English, and also the revolutionaries, such as Sun and Luk, from being arrested by the Qing government. However, westerners who perform good deeds are not often shown in this film series.

A Marginal Culture Challenging the Central Culture

From its establishment to the 1970s, the People's Republic of China was closed to the world for nearly thirty years. A planned economy was practiced. In addition, there were numerous political movements, which stifled the development of culture and art. By contrast, Hong Kong, as a colony, all along had a capitalist free market economy, and the society prospered. In the 1970s, the city had already become one of the four 'economic dragons' of Asia. In what was a pluralistic society, people's minds were active, and artistic creations, particularly in the areas of film, television and music, flourished. The productions were excellent, of high quality and gorgeously packaged. They were warmly received by mainland audiences and rapidly gained a position in the mainland market. Their influence was not small. This was the start of the challenge to the culture of the centre posed by a marginal culture. In Tsui's *Once Upon a Time in China* series, Wong migrates to Beijing, making a name for himself and accomplishing a great deal. This is an example of the kind of development described above and is an instance of Tsui's use of the past to allegorize the present.

In the first picture of the series, Wong Fei-hung is in Foshan (the location of Po Chi Lam) defeating the Sha Ho Gang, liberating the Chinese labourers and solving the problem of the selling of labourers by westerners (Americans). In the second feature, Wong moves to Guangzhou. He obliterates the White Lotus sect; encounters certain revolutionists, namely Sun Yat-sen; becomes acquainted with western culture (medicine); and defeats the Qing General, Yuan Shu, who has been shielding the White Lotus sect. In the third movie, the hero has gone on a long journey to Beijing – the heart of Central culture. Wong, representing the Guangdong Assembly Hall, wins the championship in a nation-wide competition. He also exposes the conspiracy of the Russians and saves the life of Li Hongzhang. The next sequel shows Wong on a greater mission, one that relates to the security of the city of Beijing and the dignity of the country. As expected, Wong demolishes the trap set by the alliance of Eight Powers, deflating their pride and bolstering the authority of the Qing court. In the early Wong Fei-hung movies, Wong's activities were limited to the southern province of Guangdong; he had never set foot in Beijing. Yet now, Tsui has Wong exhibiting his power in Beijing, earning fame not only for the Guangdong Assembly Hall, but also for the entire country. In other words, Tsui's vision in the making of Wong Fei-hung movies was vastly broader than his predecessors. Furthermore, the new series is closely tied to the fate of the nation and the future of the people. It is not only about the challenge posed by a marginal culture to the central one, but also about the ultimate victory of the former over the latter.[36]

Tsui's movies are an expression of his personal feelings about the nation – the misery of China – and the world. Thus, we will not upbraid Tsui for his great inaccuracies with regard to historical times, places and figures. After all, a film is a work of creativity, in which the imagination may run wild. Moreover, Tsui has never claimed to make realistic movies. 'I do not feel that films have to be too realistic. I can romanticize and modify certain points.' Modification is also creation. Hence, the following plots: In *Once Upon a Time in China*, Wong receives a command from Qinghai General Liu Yongfu to help organize a civil defense force. In its sequel, Wong together with Sun Yat-sen are present at a medical conference. In the third feature, Wong wins the championship in the Lion King competition. He also, afterwards, lectures Li Hongzhang on the flaws of the contest. In the next picture, Wong in Beijing defeats the alliance of Eight Powers, which raises China's prestige. The real Wong, who had never left Guangdong, is now represented as journeying to Beijing and later even to the United States (in *Once Upon a Time in China V*, 1997, directed by Sammo Hung and produced by Tsui Hark). Wong visits America for the one-year anniversary of Buck Teeth's Po Chi Lam's business in San Francisco. In the foreign land, Wong is involved in a battle with Indians, which makes him famous in North America. To conclude, Tsui Hark takes ancient legends of historical figures and transforms them by romanticizing them and adding new perspectives. This mode of narration strengthens the tone of irony and didacticism that prevails throughout his films.

Borrowing the tongue of Wong Fei-hung, Tsui presents his insights into the past and into reality, and links the past with the present. Consider the ending of *Once Upon a Time in China*. Wong sighs at the fact that so many Chinese would risk their lives to go to San Francisco (the 'Gold Mountain') to work as labourers. 'Is there a real Gold Mountain? Why then do Western ships travel to our shores? Perhaps the place we are standing on is a 'Gold Mountain''. What happened a hundred years ago, sounds familiar today. Is it not true that more and more westerners (including second- and third-generation Chinese) are coming to the East? How do you define 'Gold Mountain'? It can be anywhere depending on how you construct it in your imagination. Wong, in the midst of the collision of East and West, while somewhat confused, has the confidence of a hero.

Restructuring Classical Legends with New Perspectives

In adapting traditional tales, Tsui Hark pursues change and innovation, and his creativity is boundless. Based on the success of the two series, *A Chinese Ghost Story* and *Once Upon a Time in China*, Tsui produced *Green Snake* (1993), *The Lovers* (1994) and the animation *A Chinese Ghost Story* (1997, Tsui Hark as producer and Chan Wai-man as director). Tsui's imaginative power continued to develop, which made his work different from those that had come before. *Green Snake* was adapted from *The Tale of the White Snake*, a novel written by Lillian Lee. The story is told from the point of view of the Green Snake (Maggie Cheung). From the romance between her older sister, White Snake (Joey Wang), and Hui Sin (Ng Hing-kwok), and the later attempts by the Monk Fat-hoi to break it up, Green Snake gradually comes to understand what real love is. She sheds tears when she learns that an old monk has had Hui Sin's five *skandhas* blocked and caused him to lose his sense of hearing. In addition, Monk Fat-hoi claims that his mission is to eradicate devils and love his people, but he cannot tolerate White Snake, who tames the waters and saves people from floods. Still less is he able to accept the idea of a romance between a human and a demon. He drowns the monks of Jinshan Temple and once again attempts to murder Green Snake. Green Snake reproaches him, 'There is love in the human world, but what is love? It is ironic that even you humans are not clear about this. When you are clear about this point, I will return.' Expressionless, emotionless, rigid in thought and stubborn, Monk Fat-hoi resembles the senior monk Baiyun in *A Chinese Ghost Story*. He prohibits ghosts who have been wrongly judged from being reincarnated as humans. Here, Tsui Hark is criticizing those individuals who stand for orthodox thinking.

In Tsui Hark's film adaptation, *The Lovers*, the operatic elements are replaced with modern ideas in narrating an ancient love story, said to have taken place one thousand and six hundred years ago. In this film, Zhu Yingtai is not a talented lady, but an unruly girl who is spoiled by her family and has no interest in her studies. She becomes acquainted with Liang Shanbo in the classroom. They used to play together and cheat in examinations (a modern version of school scenes). As their relationship develops, they become intimate. Such behaviour, which violates traditional moral codes, conforms to the way present-day teenagers view love. The first half of the movie is full of jokes, liveliness and laughter. The second half is just the opposite. Liang learns that Zhu is going to be forced to marry into the Ma family. Zhu is imprisoned by her parents. An ailing Liang writes his pledge in blood. Zhu is married and cries as Liang's tomb collapses. She commits suicide by burying herself in the tomb. Numerous scenes make up the poignant and tragic love story. The contrast between the two halves of the film makes the second half seem particularly tragic. This movie can be considered Tsui's most heart-rending literary-artistic love story. However, as a director who is eager to convey aspirations and truths, Tsui Hark would never have been contented with merely telling a love story. Therefore, part of the plot shows Zhu's parents sending her to school disguised as a boy, not for only the sake of propriety, but also to use her to associate with the wealthy and powerful. Zhu Yingtai is thus later forced to become the wife of the power official Ma, so as to secure the status of the Zhu family in the political arena. That is to say, under the façade of a love story we find hidden political messages, which are communicated verbally – the usual means adopted by Tsui Hark.

The Psyche of a Superman – I am in Control of Everything

Tsui Hark's shadow is seen in almost every single one of his films. He enjoys this kind of self-narration and shows no signs of being tired of it. For this reason, action scenes (which he has a taste for) and dialogue or narration (the didactic side of him) are often juxtaposed. This is evident in his works ranging from *The Butterfly Murders* to *Zu*, to the three series *A Chinese Ghost Story*, *Swordsman* and *Once Upon a Time in China*. In a certain sense, *The Chinese Feast* (1995), *The Blade* (1995) and *Tri-star* (1996) manifest his continued dissatisfaction with reality and his attempts to save the world on his own, reflecting the psyche of a superman.

In *Tri-star*, a chef, Kenny Bee Chung, abandons his career because he has lost both his wife and daughter. He leads a desperate life as a wanderer in the city of Guangzhou. Later, Leslie Cheung and Anita Yuen find and rescue him. They invite him to participate in a cooking contest on behalf of Mun Hon Lou, to compete with Extraordinary Corporation's Hung Yan-yan for the title of the 'God of Cookery'. In *The Blade*, Vincent Zhao leaves the blade manufacturer, 'Lin Feng Ho', to search for his real identity and for the truth behind the murder of his father. In the process of rescuing his junior classmate, Siu Ling-chi, he is trapped by the thief Ma and loses an arm. He wanders around, destitute, and ends up living in a village. Certain similarities can be observed in the heroes of both films. Chung loses his wife, while Chiu loses his father plus one of his arms. Both men are destitute, enduring physical and psychological pain. Later, Chung trains his senses of taste, smell and sight and restores them to normal, just as he would train himself in the martial arts. Similarly, Chiu, to avenge his father's death, trains himself assiduously based on instructions contained in a secret book. He uses a rope to hang himself up to acquire the skill of twirling a sword using one arm. As for the priest (Leslie Cheung) in *Tri-star*, noticing the various problems that beset society, he suddenly conceives a desire to save all of mankind from going to hell. He enters society and lives with a group of prostitutes. He even serves them, for instance, preparing breakfast for them, organizing a band for them and helping them to find jobs. He hopes the women will reform themselves and live a new life. When one of the prostitutes, Anita Yuen, falls in love with him, he responds by retreating to the church.

In *Tri-star*, Chung adjusts his ingredients from monkey brains to bean curd in the 'Mun Hon Feast' cooking contest. In the end, he wins over Hung and regains his status in the food-and-beverage world. In fact, his prestige is enhanced by having been awarded the title of 'God of Cookery'. Likewise, Chiu, in *The Blade*, acquires the skill of twirling a blade with one arm. In a duel, Chiu kills Flying Dragon Hung yan-yan in revenge for his father's death. Both Chung and Chiu show themselves to be extraordinary. Although they have fallen low in life, in the end they had the courage to lift themselves up. The decision made by the priest in Tri-star, on the other hand, to live among prostitutes, was made out of a desire to understand their lives. In other words, his action was a rather impulsive one and did not arise out of a strong feeling of determination. Thus, when he was approached by Anita Yuen, he had no idea of how to handle the situation and simply retreated to the church. It was not until Yuen was caught by her creditor that Cheung re-appeared. Cheung's indecisiveness may reflect Tsui's psyche at the time. This character is not the only example; Chui in *The Blade* bears a certain resemblance to Tsui. Chui is impetuous, furious and hysterically violent. His hyperactivity and intense anger drive him to destroy everything. This recalls the emotions involved in *Dangerous Encounter – 1st Kind*. At the time, Tsui was an angry young man. Now, he is an angry middle-aged man. In *Time and Tide* (2000), Wu Bai plays the role of a mercenary soldier who resigns because of his family. However, he is pursued by other soldiers. He, therefore, asks Nicholas Tse to take care of his pregnant wife. In the end, he manages to kill his enemies and survive. This time, the voice-over is Tsui's voice, 'The world is actually not controlled by us. We are not allowed to do anything we like.' He places his hopes on the next generation. It seems that the middle-aged Tsui has awakened to the realization that a man is only a man and not an omnipotent god.

Tsui's next two movies, *Double Team* (1997) and *Knock Off* (1998), are Hollywood productions. *Double Team* is about a retired secret agent, Jack Quinn (Jean-Claude van

Damme), who is called up by the police to pursue a criminal, Stavros (Mickey Rourke). After a series of fights, gunplay and explosions, struggles in the sea and air, and even a bout with tigers in an ancient Roman arena, Quinn finally conquers Stavros and rescues his kidnapped son. *Knock Off* is set in Hong Kong on the eve of the handover. The Russian mafia is smuggling a tiny high-tech product to the terrorists via Hong Kong. The Hong Kong police are therefore collaborating with the CIA to capture the criminals. Apart from the impressive action in these two movies, they are full of clichés. The scenes in *Double Team* are excessive in number and fragmented, whereas *Knock Off* is like a film shot by a foreigner of scenes deemed to be typical of Hong Kong. Naturally, such scenes as rickshaw contests and Lyndhurst Terrance are featured, to satisfy the foreign view of Asia as 'exotic'. The characters and plots in this film are the most incoherent of Tsui's films. Only chases and fights are to be seen; there is little in the way of plot, to say nothing of any attempts at didacticism. On the one hand, Tsui avoids confrontation with the system of commercial film-making; on the other, he still hopes to articulate discontent (his signature), 'intending to prove himself as a filmmaker with a conscience'. Tsui's attitude in facing such a dilemma has been criticized as 'doggie cowardice'.[37] As a matter of fact, this exactly exemplifies the core contradiction between commercial cinema and individual film-makers. Perhaps it is because of Tsui's amiable character that he is courageous enough to exhibit this kind of contradictory attitude of being a 'doggie coward'.

The Use of 'Montage' to Compose Past, Present and Fantasy

As early as during his days in television, Tsui had already shown an interest in the device of 'montage'. He made frequent use of it in *The Gold Dagger Romance I* and *II*. Part of the plot describes Ding Ningning as being manipulated by the magic of Taoist Jade Flute and unconsciously stabbing Ye Kai. She is then rescued by Guo Ding. The next day Ding tries to avenge herself on the Taoist, but is harassed by him. Fortunately, Guo arrives at the most critical moment and puts a stop to the harassment. The Taoist then uses his magic to cause Guo to lose consciousness. The camera cuts to the shots: Guo, presented in eight images, is running on the hill, and Ding is struggling. Then Guo awakes, his consciousness restored. Without intending to, he stabs the Taoist. The rapid cross-cutting of illusion and reality is brilliantly executed. Another instance of the use of montage is the marriage scene of Guo and Ding. A human head is sent as a gift, to the astonishment of all those present. In this sequence, within 24 seconds there are a total of 28 shots, chiefly close-ups of people's faces. On average, each shot was for no longer than 1 second. Yet in this short space of time each person's emotional response is shown. The following sequence is of Ding rushing out to look for Ye. When she returns, she learns that Guo is wounded and lying on the ground, and that all of the others are dead. With the wedding music continuing to play in the background, the director takes 50 shots within 22 seconds to compose this scene. There is parallel editing of the close-ups of Ding, Guo, the statue of the deity and of other guests in the scene. On the one hand, Ding's shock and grievance are revealed; on the other, the chaos at the scene is shown. In the end, Ding cannot endure the strain and faints.

In *The Butterfly Murders,* butterflies appear and kill people. Master Shen is bitten to death. People are fleeing and some are collapsing. The land is covered with the murderous insects. This is a 30-second scene filled with mystery and horror. The butterflies here are a source of fear, demonstrating a similarity to Hitchcock's *The Birds.* In *Dangerous Encounter – 1st Kind,* too, a cat falls on a pointed iron pole and dies; this can be regarded as Tsui's most creative 'montage'. It involves an array of images exhibited via a range of shots: a rat runs into a cage; a cat passes by and tries to catch it; Lam Chun-kee discovers this and grabs the cat and throws it out of the window; the cat falls; a pointed iron pole; the cat continues to fall; a close-up of its paw, a close-up of its head; a full shot showing the cat pierced by the pole; a close-up of Lam. This juxtaposition of the shots, predominantly close-ups, was achieved by parallel editing. A sense of dread is communicated. Together with the abovementioned sequence in *The Butterfly Murders,* these examples are the classics of 'montage' in Tsui's films. The editing structure – the juxtaposition of shots – in Tsui's movies is well known for its speed. Usually, as one shot ends another begins. Shots are so intimately connected that not a single second is left blank. Even before one is aware that one shot has ended, a new shot or message would have already 'jumped out', leading one to rush along with the current message. In particular, when two shots are composed with actions that are of similar speed and intensity, it is hardly possible to distinguish between the two shots in a temporal sense. By and large, the general audience is not able to differentiate between the two shots, implying that they have lost the ability to discern the difference. In other words, they are manipulated by the pace of the editing and overwhelmed by the actions of the characters. This editing pattern repeats. Sometimes, if the actions are not fast enough or are flawed, the director will remove certain frames from the film. This is a characteristic of Tsui Hark's films and part of his style.

Examples of a combination of illusion, past and reality are common in Tsui Hark's films. In *Swordsman,* a girl from the Miao people, Sharla Zhang Min, sees the *qin* (a Chinese musical instrument) that had belonged to the dead Wu Ma. The camera cuts to the scene of a dying Wu singing the song 'Xiaoao Jianghu' (the same as the Chinese title of the film) on a boat that is ablaze. In a later scene, people are fighting to gain possession of the 'Sunflower Bible'. Jacky Cheung points a gun at the eunuch of East Factory. This scene comes immediately after the one showing the eunuch lecturing Cheung, '...Young man, do not reveal too much. Be careful or you will lose your life.' Cheung responds, 'Yes.' Here the director highlights the betrayals and false submissiveness in the political arena. In *Once Upon a Time in China II,* Club Foot, who was originally a subordinate of Wong Tin-ba's, is injured in the leg during a lion-dance contest. As a cripple, he is mocked by his superior and turned out of doors. He is crawling through the streets in a heavy downpour, when Aunt Yee comes forth and offers him an umbrella. The camera cuts to his recollection of being bullied and humiliated by Wong Tin-ba. He is finally touched by Wong Fei-hung's sincerity and sheds tears. In *The Lovers,* Liang Shanbo is assaulted by the servants of the Zhu family. At home, his mother gives him some medicine. This is then followed by Liang's memory of scenes of him and Zhu at school. These scenes reappear when Liang writes a 'blood letter' to Zhu. Memory scenes are even more frequent in *The Blade*. As Ding On (Vincent Zhao) is being told about the death of his father, shots of his memory of his father being hanged are inserted. Later, the film demonstrates a cross-cutting of present and past, narrating, through images, the fight between Ding On's father and Thief Ma that took place when the hero was still young. Ding On's life, but not his father's, is spared. His father is eventually hanged by the villain. The tactic of using fragmented shots has the following functions:

1. The shots can be inserted whenever necessary to help the narration.
2. The narration process is simplified, as only the most significant and impressive parts need to be included.
3. The characters can become more rounded as their past and insights are presented. Shots of fantasies can also be incorporated in this manner.

Consider, for example, the kung fu class in *Once Upon a Time in China II*. Wong Fei-hung teaches Aunt Yee a martial arts tactic of 'the Grabbing Hands':

> 'The first skill involves seizing the head - binding the hands - twisting the waist'; and the second involves 'grabbing the throat - bowing down - robbing the chariot'. At this moment, Aunt Yee raises her head and sees an imaginary scene of Wong and her dancing projected on the wall. Returning to reality, Wong is holding her hands, instructing her in martial arts moves. Not a second later, she daydreams again. Wong drops her hands and calls to her. The camera instantaneously cuts to a scene of a silhouette on the wall of two people dancing. This is followed by a shot of Aunt Yee staring up at the wall; then the camera once again shifts to the dancing scene. Back to the present again, she is still staring. Wong grasps her hands, then drops them; he sees that she is frozen in a dance position. He calls to her again. We see her dancing shadow on the wall collapse; simultaneously, she herself falls. Wong immediately pulls on her hands and tells her to be careful and to pay attention. She excuses herself, telling him that she has been reciting to herself the skills he has taught her. In this sequence, a correspondence between reality and illusion is created. A romantic interlude is inserted in the kung fu lesson, which is an innovative and organic combination.

Cross-Cutting and Correspondence

To juxtapose two or more events that are occurring at the same time but in different places is coined parallel editing or cross-cutting. In fact, not long after the invention of film, E. Porter already began to use this technique in his 1903 production *The Great Train Robbery*. In *The Birth of a Nation* (1915), D. W. Griffith also adopted cross-cutting in the scene in which Lincoln is assassinated. Since then, the control of temporality in film has been affirmed, and such control has shifted from the acts of the performers to the hands of the director. Tsui already made use of parallel editing in his pioneering work *The Golden Dagger of Romance*. For example, the Taoist nun saves the wounded

Ye Kai by warming up the chilled hero with her body. The camera moves to a scene of Guo Ding and Ding Ningning, and then cuts back to the nun and Ye. These two couples are alternately shown. *Dangerous Encounter - 1st Kind* also demonstrates the use of parallel editing. For example, Lam Chun-kee is tied up at home, three youngsters hurry to the graveyard; the American soldiers drown Uncle Dark by pushing his head into a bucket; the soldiers break in when Lam is struggling; Lam's brother (Law Lit) returns home; Lam is pushed out of the window by the soldiers and is punctured to death by a tin pole; Law Lit witnesses the scene of Lam dying. This film is complicated in that a number of events are juxtaposed. This section reveals the brutality of the American soldiers. Furthermore, the echo between the death of Lam and that of the rat has the function of establishing an inherent connection between the two.

Although the *King of Chess* (1991) is a co-production of Yim Ho and Tsui Hark, it would appear from viewing the film that the first half, on the Cultural Revolution in mainland China, was directed by Yim; while the second half, displaying cross-cut scenes of Taipei and the mainland, was the work of Tsui. There is parallel editing of scenes of a televised contest in Taipei between a child and a professor, and a Chinese chess competition in mainland between Red Guards. The cross-cutting sequence occupies more than a half of the entire film, which is rare in Hong Kong movies. Most interestingly, the film uses Cheng Ling (John Chen) who has visited the mainland as a child and a cross to link up the two games taking place in two venues. In the end, the King of Chess from the mainland meets with the little genius from Taipei. Their encounter completes the unity of the two events happening at different times and places that were linked via cross-cutting.

In the co-directed film *Twin Dragons* (1991), cross-cutting constituted the main narrative structure. The twin brothers, 'Boomer' and John (both played by Jackie Chan), are raised from birth to adulthood in different environments. The film opens with Sylvia Chiang giving birth to this pair of twins. However, for various reasons, she is forced to separate the siblings. The tool of parallel editing is adopted to show the brothers growing up: Boomer's family is poor and he gets a job repairing cars. By contrast, John grows up in a wealthy neighbourhood and becomes a famous conductor. Once, John visits Hong Kong for a performance and encounters his older brother. The same editing technique is employed to show the girlfriends of the twins mistaking each brother for the other. Moreover, the identical reactions displayed by the twins are presented as jokes. Later, John is captured by a gang and forced to drive a car and, thus, becomes involved in a gang slaughter. 'Boomer', on the other hand, is dragged off to conduct a concert in a large hall. The film is principally made up of gags. The theme, if there is one, is the eradication of class differences, extended from his *Working Class*. Cross-cutting is also employed in *The Lovers*, particularly in the second half of the film. When Zhu's mother brings along the letter written in blood by Liang to Zhu, a Buddhist Master (the ex-boyfriend of Zhu's mother) appears and gives her some advice, 'It would be a matter of boundless virtue to set them free.' The director cuts to a scene of the Master consoling Liang. This is followed by a scene of

Zhu writing a letter. The camera alternately shows Liang and Zhu, until the moment that Zhu gets married. The technique of cross-cutting draws the two characters closer. Near the end, when Liang dies and Zhu cries over the tomb, the sentiment of tragedy is heightened and extended. Parallel editing functions here to show how closely interlocked the two characters are in affection, thus heightening the sense of tragedy.

From parallel editing to cross-cutting, Tsui went to complicate the narrative through reversals of time and space, not just once, but two or three times. *Love in the Time of Twilight* is the best example of this approach. The film portrays a bank worker, Nicky Wu, and the female lead of an opera troupe, Charlie Yeung. The two are destined to be lovers but are always fighting. Wu is tricked into robbing the bank and is strangled to death. In order to find justice, his spirit returns to the human world and asks Yeung for help. He intends to revisit the moment of his death to prevent the tragedy. Wu journeys back to several incidents prior to his death: the encounter between him and Yeung, the moment the opera group begins its performance, his falling into the river, the bank robbery, the moment just prior to his murder. Many characters are involved: Yeung, Yeung's father, the villains and others. When an individual goes back to the past, he must encounter at least three times every person involved in that period of his past. With the large number of people involved, the narrative becomes confusing. The result is a reversal of the reversal of the reversal, a repetition of the repetition of the repetition. Here, Tsui focused on the narrative structure, with multiple reversals and subversions of time and space. He did what other people dared not do and challenged the limits.

Tsui Hark's Distinctive Use of Language

Tsui Hark's movies do not just tell a story, but usually also include some personal pronouncements. Furthermore, these pronouncements do not necessarily follow the veins of the plot or the development of the characters. They are often impulsive flows of words, uttered whenever Tsui intuitively considers there to be a need. The words emanate from the mouths of the characters, in order to fulfill his aspiration to communicate truth and irony. Sometimes they come naturally and sometimes abruptly. As with his images, the words are often delivered at top speed, despite the possibility that the audience might not be able to catch the utterance. The characters give the impression of being in a rush, of not waiting for you and not wanting to allow you to catch up. This is the language of Tsui Hark. Look at a segment of a dialogue in *We're Going to Eat You*.

> To save someone, then to be saved by someone, and to save someone in return – when will the cycle end? When you are caught, I save you. When I am caught, the vice team leader saves me. When you are caught again, I save you again. Later, when we are caught, he saves us. Now he goes to save you. If we are all caught, someone else has to save us. When will this end?...

In *Zu*, the hero, Adam Cheng, says to the wounded monk, 'This world always turns out to be more complicated than I expected. Initially, I begged you to rescue ordinary people. Now we are confused about who should rescue whom.' The speeches cited above illustrate that Tsui's perceives the realistic world as being more positive than negative. Thus, it is not surprising to find the Taoist, Wu Ma, in *A Chinese Ghost Story*, arguing that the human world shows 'no distinction between right and wrong. Things grow to be too complicated. By contrast, ghosts are extremely clear about light and darkness'. The hint here is that humans are not superior to ghosts. A human being is no bigger than most animals even. As the Green Snake in *Green Snake* tells the monk, 'There is love in the human world. However, it is ironic that you humans are not clear about what true love is...'

It is not uncommon to find criticism of intellectuals and the literati in Tsui's films. In *The Butterfly Murders*, the master of the castle speaks with contempt, 'The weak literati have few achievements and a surplus of failures.' 'The literati only speak and do not act.' In *We're Going to Eat You*, the criticism is that 'Intellectuals like to exaggerate – to appear to know more than they actually do'. In *Shanghai Blues*, the opinion is expressed that 'A youth who is concerned about theory is not practical, and disappoints me every time'. Is the director mocking himself or satirizing others? The answer is clear. In *The Lovers*, Zhu's mother lectures Liang, 'You two think that you can change the world. But the reality is people are all hypocritical, corrupt, and money-minded. You believe that all by yourselves, you can change other people and thus this world.' Tsui Hark expresses his disappointment of the world and his criticism of Zhu's mother. The immense pressure from the external environment forces the pair of lovers to commit suicide, as they are given no choice. Tsui's films also contain statements that are consistent and even contradictory. For example, in *Zu*, Adam Cheng bids farewell to Brigitte Lin, 'Fate will not allow us to meet again. See you.' Lin asks, 'If it doesn't, how will you see me in the future?' This is similar to the conversation in *Shanghai Blues* between Hu Feng and Sylvia Chiang before Hu migrates to Hong Kong. Not waiting for Hu's engagement ring, Chiang says, 'Manager Lam, our match is not made.' Hu replies, 'I am clear about my past.... Do I not even have a little hope?' But then he says, 'I only have one chance of hope. If it is given to you, then don't I lose it?' Chiang eventually rejects Hu. This film contains long speeches that are articulated quickly and rhythmically. For instance, the boss introduces a number of 'Queens of the Calendar' to Sally Yeh: the Queen of Chickens, Queen of Matches, Queen of Soaps, Queen of Toilet Paper, Queen of Milk Powders, Queen of Toothpicks, Queen of Light Bulbs, etc. Another scene shows Tin Ching scolding Kenny Bee Chung, calling him various sorts of 'eggs': 'stupid egg', 'salty duck egg', '*wong bat*' egg (literally, bastard) and so on. This demonstrates, on the one hand, the director's short temper and, on the other, his attitude that 'an event must be told in full and a scene acted in full'. When watching Tsui Hark's films, attention should be paid to the dialogues, and hidden meanings will be discovered.

Notes

1. What is 'futurism'? Tsui Hark himself does not have an adequate understanding of it. He only makes something extreme out of the ordinary, usual and everyday. See Ko Mun-kai and Tang Chi-kit. 'Words from the Director.' *City Entertainment*. No. 13. 25 July 1979, p. 14.
2. Shek Kei. 'The Lovers: Innovating from Cliché, Impressing with Tears and Laughter.' *Ming Pao*. 16 August 1994.
3. Triple shooting is a characteristic of studio production. Lighting is set once – that is, the so-called 'world lighting', deviating from the practice of on-location shooting where specific lighting arrangements are set for every single shot. In addition, the sets are not set in panorama, rather, at three sides, with the fourth side being reserved for the placement of the three cameras. The simultaneous shooting of three cameras is a time-saving measure. However, it is hard to foster any sort of mood, and a relatively dull effect is created.
4. Yan Zunli. 'Wutaishan "qingxia" – Xuke fangwen ji.' (The sentimental swordsman in 'Five Stations Hill'). *Datexie* (Close-Up). No. 62. 4 August 1978, p. 28.
5. Ibid.
6. Li Cheuk-to arranged. Liu Wing-leung and Li Cheuk-to interviewed. 'Tsui Hark Longs to be the Property of the Audience.' *City Entertainment*. No. 68. 3 September 1981, p. 24.
7. *Marvelous Gallants of the Jianghu*, adapted from Pingjiang Buxiaosheng's seminal novel of the same title, was directed by Zhang Shichuan and written by Zheng Zhengqiu. It is a production of Mingxing (Bright Star) Film Company. From 1928–1931 a total of 18 episodes were made in the series. See Du Yunzhi. *Zhongguo dianying qishinian* (Seventy Years of Chinese Cinema). Taipei: Film Fund of Republic of China. 1986, p. 100.
8. Li Yunsu, Hu Jubin. Zhongguo wusheng dianyingshi (History of the Silent Era of Chinese Cinema). Beijing: Zhongguo dianying chubanshe. 1966, p. 242.
9. Yu Mo-wan. 'A Preliminary Study of Cantonese Swordplay Films.' *A Study of the Hong Kong Swordplay Films 1945–1980*. 5th Hong Kong International Film Festival. 1981, p. 97.
10. Ibid.
11. Pak Tong Cheuk. 'From Digital Effects to Cross Border Co-Productions.' *Border Crossings in Hong Kong Cinema*. 24th Hong Kong International Film Festival. HK: The Leisure and Cultural Services Department. April 2000, p. 92.
12. Par Serge Daney. Kam Wah trans. 'The Chief Editor of *Cahiers du Cinema* sees Hong Kong New Cinema.' *City Entertainment*. No. 63. 25 June 1981, p. 20.
13. Shek Kei. 'The Development of *Wuda* in Hong Kong Cinema.' A Study of the Hong Kong Martial Arts Films. HKIFF. April 1980, p. 25.
14. Nie Da, You Chongsheng. 'The First Step to Sexy Logic – Interview with Tsui Hark'. *City Entertainment*. No. 147. 11 October 1984, p. 26.
15. This film was originally named *The Gang of Four*. Tsui explained the reason for adopting this title, '"The Four Gang is a tragic incident. In the 1970s, the mythology surrounding Chinese politics was exposed and the reality was found to be desperate. What stimulated me to make *Dangerous* was also a sense of loss – the loss of the root of life, dreams, and everything."' Refer to Liu Wing-leung and Li Cheuk-to. 'Tsui Hark Longs to be the Property of the Audience.' *City Entertainment*. No. 68. 3 September 1981, p. 41.
16. The banning of the film by the Film Censorship Unit provoked the following responses from the media: (1) The periodical *City Entertainment*, issue No. 43 published on 11 September

1980, had a headline in red on its cover, reading '*Dangerous Encounter – 1st Kind* BANNED'. This was an indication of the industry's concern on the issue. In the magazine, an article written by An Po entitled '*Dangerous Encounter – 1st Kind*'s Dangerous Encounter' refuted the statements made by the Film Censorship Unit, point by point: That there was no hint of praise for this group of young people in the film is proven by the fact that each of them met a miserable end. It is unclear on what grounds the film can be accused of having an 'unhealthy' consciousness. Furthermore, why should there have been a problem with portraying the retired American soldiers as brutal, particularly it was a requirement of the plot? Chinese are usually depicted as stupid and cunning in American movies. Why shouldn't the reverse be acceptable? (2) Two seminars on 'Violent Movies of Hong Kong' were organized at Hong Kong Film Culture Centre on 21 December 1980. In the seminars, the original version of *Dangerous Encounter – 1st Kind* was screened. Moreover, the director Tsui Hark, the producer John Shum and the co-coordinator Chan Ka-suen were invited to speak. Quite a number of film workers were also present. All of the participants, without an exception, objected to the banning of the film. For details, refer to To Wai-yin. 'Tsui Hark's *Dangerous Encounter – 1st Kind* and others'. Chinese-Western Motion Pictures. No. 11, January 1981, p. 42.

17. For the opinions of those who opposed the ban, refer to item 16. The main objection was that the Film Censorship Unit's standards of assessment were full of ambiguity and that double standards were applied in assessing foreign and local productions. In particular, the argument that the portrayal of middle-school students making bombs was problematic, whereas it would have been acceptable if the subjects were changed to college students, was laughable. On the other hand, those who supported the banning of the film pointed out that *Dangerous* overemphasized violence, depicted brutal killings in detail and glorified illegal behaviour. This would cause harm to society and should not be permitted. It should be dealt with according to the law. Refer to Yu Mo-wan. 'About *Dangerous Encounter – 1st Kind.*' *City Entertainment*. No. 55. January 1981. 39. In addition, several articles were included in *City Entertainment* No. 50, in the December 1981 issue, discussing the problem of violence in films. Both positive and negative comments were presented.
18. *Bonnie and Clyde* (dir. Arthur Penn, 1968). *The Wild Bunch* (dir. Sam Peckinpah, 1969). *A Clockwork Orange* (dir. Stanley Kubrick, 1971). *Dirty Harry* (dir. Don Siegel, 1971).
19. Roger Garcia, Liu Wing-leung and Li Cheuk-to. 'Reviewing Tsui Hark with Tsui Hark.' *City Entertainment*. No. 68. 3 September 1981, p. 26.
20. Liu Wing-leung and Li Cheuk-to. 'Tsui Hark Longs to be the Property of the Audience.' *City Entertainment*. No. 68. 3 September 1981, p. 26.
21. Ibid., item 14, pp. 26–27.
22. Ibid., item 20, p. 26.
23. The box office receipts were, respectively (in millions of Hong Kong dollars), 9, 26, 23 and 19. Each film topped the box office. Cinema City was successful in establishing its brand for several reasons: (1) collective creation and coordination, (2) a self-owned theatrical circuit enabling the company to monopolize of the 'golden period' of the release of its films, (3) an emphasis on promotion, packaging and marketing.
24. Ibid., item 19, p. 28.

25. Wong Ho-wan. 'Tsui Hark – a Man who is Ordinary, but a Glutton for Work.' *City Entertainment*. No. 400. 11 August 1994, p. 34–36.
26. The team that was responsible for special effects in *Zu* later became the main pillar of Tsui's upcoming hi-tech films. In the mid-1980s, the group then re-formed as the 'New Visual Effects Workshop' and the 'Wuji Teshi'. They have contributed much to special effects in Hong Kong films. See Wai Hin, 'A Brief Description of the technology industry in Hong Kong Cinema.' *City Entertainment*. 20 August 1990, pp. 8, 20, 49.
27. In the production of *Storm Riders*, the director first shot the real scenes of the Big Buddha at Le Shan, a famous spot in mainland China. The images were then processed by computer to eliminate the inappropriate parts of the scene; a prototype was then created for the background. The performers acted in front of the background for the duel sequence. The duel scene at the Statue of Liberty in *A Man Called Hero* (1999) was relatively complicated to arrange. First, a model of the statue was made. Then stuntmen demonstrated the actions that Ekin Cheng and Francis Ng were to perform. The two actors performed the actions, with facial expressions, according to the stuntmen's demonstration. Later, with the use of computing technology, the faces of Cheng and Ng were integrated with the bodies of the stuntmen. Finally, the programme was converted into film.
28. In *Storm Riders*, Ekin Cheng, alone, waves a sword in the air. An image of a fire kylin is created, in computer, from a bone frame, the skin and the fire are then added, layer by layer. The completed image of the monster is merged with the shots of Cheng waving the sword.
29. In the 1930s, Shanghai was the most prosperous city in China and was ranked with London, Paris and Tokyo as among the great cities of the world. It was known as the New York of the East.
30. Ibid., item 14, p. 25.
31. Once, in an interview, Tsui Hark commented, 'Perhaps driven by my personality, my films are never serious. The only exception may be *The Butterfly Murders* – all of the characters have expressionless faces.' Refer to Nie Da, You Chongsheng. 'The First Step to Sexy Logic – Interview with Tsui Hark', p. 26.
32. *A Better Tomorrow III: Love and Death in Saigon* was shot on location in Saigon, Vietnam. The production of this film coincided with the outbreak of the June 4th Tiananmen Incident.
33. Huang Renyu. *Wanli shiwunian* (The Fifteenth Year of the Wanli Reign). Taiwan shihuo chubanshe, 11 April 2000, pp. 45–47.
34. Hu Peng. *Wong Fei-hung and I*. Hong Kong: Sanhe maoyi gongsi. December 1995, pp. 239–249.
35. Monographs of Hong Kong Film Veterans 1 – Hong Kong Here I Come. Hong Kong Film Archive. 2000, p. 101.
36. Lie Fu. 'Xuke "Huang Feihong" xilie yanjiu.' (A Study of Tsui Hark's series of Wong Fei-hung films). *Dangdai dianying* (Contemporary Films). No. 3. Beijing. 1997, p. 101.
37. Ngok Wan. 'Auteur Theory in Hong Kong Cinema – Both Tsui Hark's Progress and His Doggie Cowardice'. *Hong Kong Economic Journal*. 23 July 1987.

5

PATRICK TAM

Among Hong Kong's New Wave directors, Patrick Tam certainly occupies the role of a pioneer. He established himself in the 1970s during his time with TVB. He came to the attention of the public principally because of his very experimental works, reflecting a strong individualism. His first effort as director, of *A Spectrum of Multiple Stars: Wang Chuanru** (1975), earned him international fame.[1] Since then, he has become a focus of the media and critics. He has been interested in film from a young age. While in middle school, he made some attempts at writing criticisms of films and submitted his works to *Zhongguo Xuesheng Zhoubao* and *Haibao*.[2] After graduating from middle school, he joined TVB, starting his career as a general assistant. He was then promoted to cinematographer. In 1971, he rose to the position of director of on-site shooting.[3] Partial outdoor scenes of *The Hui Brothers Show* (Michael Hui's situation comedy) and *73* were those for which Patrick Tam was responsible. *A Spectrum of Multiple Stars** was his maiden effort at directing. It was a project that consisted of three and a half episodes. In 1975, he was sent by his employer to the Academy of Half Moon Bay in San Francisco to receive advanced training in film. Seven months later, the shooting of the 16mm film *CID* (1976) began, and Tam was called back to participate in the project. Other films followed, including *Seven Women* (1976), *Social Worker* (1976), *Thirteen* (1977), *Mingliuqingshi** (1978) and others.[4]

Without exception, each of the dramas that Tam made for local television stations was an experiment in terms of narrative and cinematic language, including the use of montage, *mise-en-scène*, colour and so forth. Innovations and changes earned him attention and the reputation of being the most creative young director in Hong Kong. As he had made his reputation when young, he took the opportunity afforded by the 'Mutiny at Five Stations Hill' to make his exit from television industry in late 1977.[5] He was promptly absorbed by the film industry. His first feature, *The Sword,* was produced in 1980. His subsequent films included *Love Massacre* (1981), *Nomad* (1982), *Cherie* (1984), *Final Victory* (1987), *Burning Snow* (1988) and *My Heart is that Eternal Rose*

(1988). Although Tam was not a prolific film-maker and was under a great deal of commercial pressure, he still persisted in attempting various experiments and innovations. In particular, he concentrated on the form of a film. The fruits of his painstaking studies include ideas of 'decomposition' and 'positioning' in the colour spectrum. Employing film as a vehicle to express his insights about life, the capitalist classes and commodity consumption, Tam's films exhibited his personality and unique style to the fullest.

A Closed World and the Captive Souls of Modern People

Tam's characters mostly are subjects living in total isolation in an enclosed world. The problem of mental imprisonment is a defect that is innate or acquired. Although external forces sometimes try to break through, such isolation endures. The sixth episode of the series, *Seven Women*, shows a typical example of someone suffering from such a condition. The protagonist, Victoria Lam, is a secretary employed by an author whom she never sees. Her only job is to make a written record of the author's story, which is orally recorded on tape. Lam works in the evenings at her employer's home. She is alone except for the occasional arrival of a cleaning woman. Lam falls under the control of the tape recorder and the author, to the point where, gradually, her every action, thought and desire seem to be completely in the author's hands. In the process of recording, Lam starts to confuse her identity with the heroine in the story, Yuen-kwan. When the author articulates his admiration for Lam through the machine, she is trapped between her own desires and his. Added to this the fear generated from the environment, and she becomes lost, falling into the web constructed by the author like a spider horror-stricken, Lam tries to physically leave the room and psychologically abandon her desires, escaping from the imprisonment of the web she or he has constructed. In darkness, she finds no way out, and her fear reaches an extreme point. At this moment, gathering together her strength, Lam runs forward, approaching the camera, which is pulled backward, until she is barred by a glass door from moving any further ahead. The camera continues the backward movement, becoming farther and farther away from the character, who gradually diminishes in size. An array of elements including an enclosed space, a performer, a genuine display of an individual's psyche, a depiction of a confrontation of desires and a terrifying journey constitute a successful representation.

In the seventh episode of *Seven Women*, Lisa Wang's love for her brother causes her to become mad. After her brother's suicide, she becomes seriously depressed. Her parents send her to a mental hospital for treatment, and to a hospice. A doctor, Yu Yeung, is hired to take care of Wang. As time passes, they come to have feelings for each other. They become confused with their emotions, and it becomes unclear who is ill, who needs whom and who is unable to leave whom. The two of them are entangled in each other. The film closes with the reemergence of Wang's mental illness. In an uncontrollable fit of emotion, she cuts herself with fragments of glass. She then runs to her room – a secure place to her – and locks up herself, once again, in a solitary and enclosed space.

The second episode of *Seven Women* is, in a sense, a story about modern people living in a rich, materialistic culture, who are in the thrall of commodity-capitalism without being conscious of it. The film opens with a monologue of the heroine (Miu Kam-fung), about the ambiguity about her identity as a housewife and an actress. Although she enjoys material things such as clothing and advertised products, she feels empty. She does not know that her husband is having an affair. However, even when she is informed about this, she chooses to silently accept it. Towards the end of the story, her husband brings his second girlfriend home and introduces her to Miu. Her heart filled with turbulence, Miu does not know how to respond. She retreats to the kitchen and mechanically places the groceries, item by item, into the fringe. She hopes, in this way, to be able to conceal her frustration and anxiety. Her actions are a portrayal of the long-term psychological imprisonment of modern women.

Love Massacre was Tam's second feature film. The male protagonist, Cheung Kwok-chu, is a married mental patient. While in the United States, he fell in love with Brigitte Lin, who was pursuing her studies there. Similar to Lisa Wang of the seventh episode of *Seven Women*, Cheung's younger sister, Tina Lau, is obsessed with her brother. Disapproving of the love between her brother and Lin, Lau crashes her car and dies. In the funeral parlour, Cheung lies in a white coffin; an allusion to his tendency for self-destruction. In order to marry Lin, Cheung murders his wife in Hong Kong and then revisits the United States. His behaviour, already abnormal, becomes even more so, to the extent that Cheung becomes out of control. In Lin's apartment – a completely isolated space, Cheung frenziedly murders Lin's flatmates one by one, turning the apartment into a killing field.

Because of the poverty of her family, the female protagonist of *Burning Snow*, Ah Suet (Yip Chuen-chun) from the Peng Hu Islands, is sold into marriage on the main island of Taiwan. Her husband is a vulgar old man who often treats her with violence. He takes her whenever he wishes, regardless of whether she is willing. In a traditional male-dominated society and family, she is powerless to protect herself and is reduced to being a toy and a sex slave for men. By coincidence, she comes across an escaped prisoner, Simon Yam. They fall in love with each other and plan to flee secretly together. Unfortunately, this plan is dashed when Ah Suet's husband makes a report to the police, who shoot Yam to death. Ah Suet murders her husband and is arrested. She is hence transferred from one closed space, her family, to another, the jail.

Tam's characters often use a narrow, enclosed space as a temporary asylum, which even becomes a permanent destination. Victoria Lam's workroom and the sanatorium where Lisa Wang stays are two examples, and Ivy Ho's broadcast room, in the second episode of *Seven Women*, is another. When Ivy Ho narrates the story of her life from an area not larger than one hundred square feet, the audience is invited to view her inner life. Viewed from a different perspective, Ho's inability to share her thoughts and desires with her parents, friends and classmates is part of the sorrow of modern man. In other words, only in a closed room – a secret space – can all her words can be articulated or expressed and her imagination exercised without any constraints. Such a room indisputably becomes a place for expression and a safe port for one who is oppressed by the real world.

The World Goes Round – The End is the Beginning

It is not uncommon for Patrick Tam's dramas, both those made for TV and the silver screen, to focus on such themes as the unpredictability of life and the ubiquity of change. To transform reality is never easy in that an enormous amount of effort may simply result in fruitlessness or the status quo. In the seventh episode of *Seven Women*, when the recovering Lisa Wang discovers that the young doctor Yu Yeung, with whom she has struck up a romance, was sent by her parents on purpose, her fragile esteem is hurt, and she relapses to a state of mental disorder. She locks herself up in a room and builds a wall between herself and the outside world. She returns to a state of autism, rejecting all communication with other people, including her parents.

In the second episode of *Seven Women*, the heroine Lee Yan-yee is the hostess of a television programme providing advice about romance and love affairs. She encourages a female listener who has fallen in love with a married man to throw caution to the winds and take the initiative to advance the relationship, including discussing the matter with the man's wife. Following this advice, the female listener approaches the hostess, who turns out to be the man's wife, but who is still unaware of the truth. The woman asks the television hostess, 'It was you who advised me to talk to the wife.' 'Did you do so?' asked the hostess. 'Am I not here?' was the reply. Only now does the shocked hostess realize the truth. A consultant on romance, she herself is facing problems with her marital relationship. This fully demonstrates the unpredictability of life.

In the last episode, 'Night', in *CID: Four Moments of Life*, a policeman, Wong Yuen-sun, is in charge of investigating a car accident involving a pedestrian victim. The victim is another policeman's (Yu Yeung) wife. When handling this case, Wong is also under investigation by the ICAC (Independent Commission Against Corruption), which is causing him a great deal of strain and worry. In an interrogation scene, Wong sits across from a witness of the car accident, the boss of a *tai pai dong* (food stall), Ma Kim-tong. This is a simple scene, involving only two characters. Employing a track shot, the camera moves from the back shoulder of one character to a front shot of the other character. This is followed by another front shot of the other character, with the camera moving at the same pace as before. The two shots are connected in a jerky, odd manner, to indicate that the interrogation has been fruitless.

The four episodes in *CID: Four Moments of Life*, 'Morning', 'Afternoon', 'Evening' and 'Night', are put together in the sequential order of time of day. The characters in the four stories are of four different age ranges. The series begins with 'Morning' and ends with 'Night'. In the last episode, when Wong achieves no results in the interrogation of Ma, he leaves the room looking helpless. When he walks out of the police station, it is morning, which can be connected to the beginning of the first episode 'Morning', completing a temporal cycle.

In the eleventh episode of *Social Worker*, the parents of a delinquent, Liu Wing-sheung, divorce, and Liu therefore leaves home. Social Worker Wai Yee-yan, who is responsible for Liu's case, discovers that the girl is living with a married man, Wong Chik-sum. Their romance is then discovered by Wong's wife, who demands that Liu leave her husband. One day, Liu is attacked by two youngsters, who splash her with toxic liquid, and is sent to a hospital. The social worker comes to the realization that things change frequently and suddenly, and that it is often not possible to help people. This echoes the advice given by Wai's supervisor, 'Doctors cannot guarantee that their patients will achieve a full recovery. What matters is to try one's best.' To put it another way, the experience instead of the result is what matters most.

In *My Heart is that Eternal Rose*, Kenny Bee Chung offers to help Kwan Hoi-shan deliver by car the kidnapped son (Cheung Tat-ming) of a triad boss, Brother Shing, to the urban area of Hong Kong. During the drive, the policeman Ng Man-tat expresses his discontent over the excessively small ransom. In the resulting dispute, he accidentally kills Cheung. Chung then also kills Ng with a bullet. Chung is left with no choice but to flee to the Philippines. Moreover, his lover (Kwan's daughter), Joey Wang, is forced to become the concubine of another gangster, the Grandfather of God (Chan Wai-man), in order to save her father, who has been seized by Brother Shing. Wang's glamorous appearance cannot conceal her grief and bitterness. Her father observes it all and grieves. As a result, he becomes an alcoholic and later loses his life in a car accident. All of these events have occurred too suddenly for the traumatized Chung, Wang and Kwan to assimilate. They can do nothing to change the tragic events of separation, death and wounds (physical and psychological) and are left feeling helpless and bewildered.

Is it a question of environment or fate? Tam's characters are placed in an endless swirl of unpredictability. In *My Heart is that Eternal Rose*, Chung revisits the place – a small store – where he killed a policeman six years ago. Hired by the Grandfather of God, he re-encounters Joey Wang. They again make a pledge to escape together. However, their plan is disrupted by the Grandfather of God. After a series of killings, Chung is hurt and returns to that store to hide and to seek treatment. This can be called fate. Both of the lovers die when the subordinates of Grandfather of God ambush them and kill them. Ah Cheung (Tony Leung Chiu-wai), who loves Wang, is the only survivor. He vanquishes his enemies and starts his lonely life of exile. His solitary journey is a repetition of Chung's fate of six years ago.

Another film, *The Sword*, involves similar events. Lee Mo-yin (Adam Cheng) is wounded by the subordinates of Lin Wan (Tsui Siu-keung). Lying on the bank of the river, he is saved by Yuen Kei. At the same time, Fa Chin-shu, who is a friend of Yuen Kei's, seeks help from her as his daughter, Fa Ying-chi, has been caught. Lee nominates himself to save Ying-chi in order to repay Yuen Kei for having saved his life. Before Lee sets to rescue Fa Ying-chi, Yuen Kei sends him a gift – a sword that is a treasure of the Qi Empire. This sword originally belonged to Fa Chin-shu; he had given it to Yuen Kei as a token of gratitude some years ago when she had saved his life. As this sword can bring both good and bad luck, Fa believed that giving the sword to Yuen Kei would free him from misfortune. Who would have imagined that, today, Lee would be using this sword to fight Fa in a duel. As Yuen Kei said to Fa, 'I should not have given your gift to somebody else.' Fa responded, 'It is not your fault. The sword is inherently unlucky to me. It all depends on fate.' Fa well understands the game of fate; thus he confronts the duel with honesty and courage. The ailing Fa is eventually defeated by Lee's sword. In another plot line, Lee's childhood lover, Yin Siu-yu (Chan Kee-kee), marries Lin Wan, as for ten years she had received no news of Lee, who had departed to receive training in the use of the sword. Coincidentally enough, as an opponent of Lee, Lin Wan fights with Lee for the sword. In the end, Lin kills Siu-yu and is, in return, murdered by Lee with the sword.

Likewise, in *Nomad*, Cecilia Yip is torn between two men. She is filled with ambiguity as to who her real love is and is unable to control the situation. Mr A, for whom she has no affection, harasses her by telephoning her all day, while Mr B, in whom she is interested, does not answer her telephone calls. She visits Mr B and he throws her things one by one out of the window as a sign of separation. Yip cries, heartbroken. The message is that we can control nothing, including love.

In *Final Victory*, before he is sent to jail, the triad boss, Tsui Hark, gives a neophyte, Eric Tsang, a dressing down, because the latter's girlfriend is having an affair with a Filipino man. The admonition is of little use, as Tsang is not able to keep the woman. Tsui entrusts his two women, Margaret Lee and Loretta Lee, to the care of Tsang. Unexpectedly, Tsang and Loretta Lee fall in love with each other. Is it not fate that the one to whom the boss had dealt a lesson should steal his girlfriend? Released from jail, Tsui intends to kill Tsang as a betrayer but in the end, he softens and spares Tsang and even sanctions Tsang's love with Loretta Lee. This is the only one of Patrick Tam's films in which problems are not resolved by killing and which has a happy ending.

Lethargy and Death of the Capitalist Class

Patrick Tam's television dramas and films show the influence of European directors, particularly Godard,[6] Antonioni and Bresson. These men opposed the anti-capitalist class and the commodity culture and had an unruffled visual style, all of which can be seen in Tam's works. Of course, his personality, characterized by remoteness from people and from the world in general, is also apparent.[7] The best example is the second episode of *Seven Women*, which, of all his works, is also the one that shows the most social consciousness. Both performer and housewife, the heroine, Miu Kam-fung, is confused about her identity. She indulges in a sea of material commodities. Her husband, Lo Yuen, a car salesman, is interested in cars, enjoying himself and in pursing love affairs, all pleasures of a material sort. Even his lovemaking has become affectionless and mechanical. The film opens with a scene of Miu washing her hair, which is actually the shooting of a TV commercial for a shampoo. The penetration of advertising in life is also shown in a restaurant scene, where a huge Coca-Cola poster can be seen. Moreover, Miu is more concerned about material things than she is about her husband. This is evident in a ball sequence, where Miu spends the whole evening calling the agent to repair her washing machine, paying no notice to her husband, who is dancing with a girlfriend.

Lo's interest in Beethoven's Fifth Symphony and even in The Internationale is also a reflection of his love for popular material culture. With marketing, all products including cultural and artistic ones have become commodified. Lo knows virtually nothing about these two pieces of music and is only aware of their strong rhythms and beautiful melodies. Under the large-scale promotion of capitalism, classical music, popular magazines and newspapers are essential parts of his daily life. This undoubtedly illustrates the exploitation of the power of media by the capitalistic consumer market. In addition, the characters in the film engage in no spiritual or mental communication. When Lo takes his girlfriend, Ng Yuen-ching, home, two women are shown wandering in front of the camera, discussing fashion and popular items. By contrast, Lo alone reads aloud from a newspaper. Each character focuses on doing his/her own thing; they have nothing in common to talk about, and there is no point of intersection. Consider, furthermore, the dinner sequence of the couple. Lo learns of the accidental death of his girlfriend from a friend's phone call. He shows no response but only praises the fine food. In fact, his reaction hints that he will soon take up with another girl. The message is that love in the modern context is characterized by convenience and speed. Relationships between men and women have become frighteningly detached.

Detached relationships and a lack of mutual understanding are repeatedly found in *CID: Four Moments of Life*. In the episode 'Morning', Man's mother shows no concern for her daughter and knows nothing about her daily life or even that she has been injured and hospitalized. In the episode 'Evening', two elderly men get into a fight using knives over a struggle to view pornographic photographs. One of them is chopped, and the episode has a bloody ending. In the last episode of *Seven Women*, Lisa Wang is discharged from a mental hospital, and her real need is for care and attention from her parents when she is discharged from the mental hospital. However, her parents arrange for her to live alone, believing that their responsibility to her is discharged by providing materially for her and hiring servants. Her parents only visit her on an unplanned, infrequent basis. Then, a doctor is hired to take care of Wang, and a romance springs up between the two. In the process, the patient gradually recovers, while it is the doctor who almost becomes sick. In fact, in modern times, the line between so-called normality and abnormality is a thin one. The relationship between the two people blossoms because of the emergence of Wang's illness and dies because of its re-emergence.

Tam's only comedy, *Cherie*, depicts the enjoyments of the minor capitalist class. In the film, Cherie Chung is a dance teacher, fresh-faced and pretty. She is pursued by a millionaire, Cho Yuen, who sends her flowers and clothes and invites her to dinners. However, Chung is unmoved and rejects all of his offers. In fact, she is interested in a photographer, Tony Leung Ka-fai, whose desire is to makes films of his own. Noticing this, Cho offers Leung a blank cheque and invites him to direct a film, on the condition that Leung leave Chung on the pretext that he has contracted a terminal illness. Surprisingly, Leung accepts the millionaire's condition to deceive Chung. In a capitalist society, wealthy men (represented in the narrative by Cho) perceive that money is all-powerful, while artists (exemplified by Leung) may surrender their dignity for money. Such unethical behaviour on the part of the wealthy to 'buy' the life and love of others is not uncommon in Hong Kong. Thus, this movie is a realistic one. However, it remains unclear whether the work is a self-satire on the part of the director. As expected, neither Cho nor Leung are finally able to obtain what they desire: Leung gains no money and Cho fails to win Chung.

Quest of Women: From Awakening to Autonomy

Among the New Wave directors, Patrick Tam is well known for his portrayal of women; in particular, for his explorations of the interior life of women. This may be partly due to the women scriptwriters Chan Wen-man and Ivy Ho, who have collaborated with him for quite some time. In Tam's films, from his early ones such as *A Spectrum of Multiple Stars** and *Seven Women*, to recent ones such as *Final Victory* and *Burning Snow*, the women mostly have their own points of view – regardless of maturity, after trials and tribulations they are finally able to control their own fate and marriage. In *A Spectrum of Multiple Stars: Wang Chuanru**, Wang's businessman husband places money over love, spending more time outside than at home. Instigated by her sister, Wang goes on dates with strangers, with whom she nearly has affairs. Fortunately, after a series of mental struggles, she regains control over her emotions. In the first episode of *Seven Women*, a middle-school girl, played by Liu Wing-sheung, experiences the first awakenings of love. Being audacious and emotionally aggressive, she has an open mind on the subject of sex. Together with some schoolmates, she reads 'Playgirl' while in school uniform and on public transport, while those around them look on askance. She takes the initiative to befriend the school librarian, Wong Wen-choi, and a relationship of intimacy develops. Later, she comes to know an advertising photographer, Chow Yun-fat, with whom she also develops an intimate relationship. Juggling the two men, she is more than capable of dealing with the situation. In the final scene, held in a café, she chats cheerfully and naturally with Wong and Chow. The attitude of women subverting traditional male roles was shocking at the time. The courage of Patrick Tam as director and Lillian Lee as scriptwriter is admirable.

The film contains controversial scenes of middle-school students kissing and even having sex. Although not given in detail, the depictions were certainly enough for the film to provoke debate and concern. Besides viewers calling in to complain and the

Film Censorship Unit issuing warnings, some columnists criticized the film for 'showing obscenities, bringing them into the household, and defaming female students'.[8] Furthermore, they questioned the director failing to take a stand,

> Since she (Liu) is represented as a depraved student, why does the film still hold an objective stance and not take either an affirmative or a negative position?...It is true that there is evilness and iniquity in reality, but there are also beautiful things. Why must we choose to expose the dark side of things?[9]

From this, one can sense the fieriness of the debate. In facing the accusations of the media, Patrick Tam had no choice but to stand up and defend himself. He denied that *Seven Women* was a pornographic drama. 'Those sex scenes were necessary to the plot. I disclosed the loose behaviour of what, in our minds, was a pure, innocent female student, of whom a critical judgement has already been made.'[10] The debates that occurred 25 years ago can shed light on the extent to which society accepted the contents of the movie and film-making style.

The second episode of *Seven Women* is one of Tam's relatively conservative or, perhaps, realistic works about women. In the film, Miu is a typical middle-class urban housewife who enjoys a materialistic life. She does not complain about her husband's affairs and the fact that he has brought several of his girlfriends home. On the contrary, in her silent acceptance, she embodies the weakness of traditional, domestic females. Most of the time, she works hard or concentrates on doing household chores and employs the satisfaction obtained from popular commodities to suppress her emotions and desires. In the final scene, her husband introduces a new girlfriend to her. Rattled, she enters the kitchen and places the things she has bought from the supermarket in the refrigerator. This act of retreating to the kitchen – a place dominated by traditional women – is undoubtedly a kind of spiritual 'imprisonment of the self'.

The next film for discussion is the second episode of *Seven Women*, which consists of three parts. The first part, 'Ivy Ho', shows Ivy Ho growing up. She has the ability to think independently, which causes her to realize that adults (her parents) have adult problems and that she is not able to intrude into this world. Similarly, she develops her own troubles and thoughts, which are not comprehensible to the older generation. She realizes that one day she will leave her parents and take her own path. When listening to the monologue about her inner world, it is possible to detect a female member of the new generation awakening to a sense of confidence about controlling one's fate. The third part, 'Yeung Sze-ti', tells the story of a divorced woman. She owns a design company and devotes her energy to her work, enabling her to live a happy life. One day, she dines out with her ex-husband, Siu Leong, who has returned from abroad. Later, when she is in Siu's hotel room, she answers a telephone call from a lady while Siu is taking a shower. After hanging up, she reflects for a while and then leaves, realizing the inappropriateness of this one-night date. It was better to make her departure at an early stage. The theme of this film, which is clearly expressed, is the right to control one's actions and the need to take responsibility for them.

The eleventh episode of *Social Worker* portrays two women - Wai Yee-yan, a social worker, and Liu Wing-sheung, a delinquent - who have two kinds of experiences. The similarity between the two lies in their family backgrounds - both come from broken families. However, the two have taken different paths in life: Wai helps other people, while Liu has left her family and is living with her boyfriend. Wai often tries to offer assistance and consolation to Liu; with little result, however. Later, Liu injured by toxic chemicals is hospitalized. She later goes abroad. Wai feels frustrated at not having been competent enough to help Liu. However, Wai continues to work faithfully at her job helping female delinquents. The film pays homage to Wai's positive philosophy of life - persistence and complete devotion - holding her up as a most praiseworthy example of womankind.

Cherie Chung in the film *Cherie* is no weak woman. On the contrary, she has a job from which she makes her own living. Pursued ardently by the wealthy Cho Yuen, she accepts only one of his invitations - an evening banquet on a cruise ship. She pretends to be drunk and unveils Cho's treachery in having added a hallucinogenic drug to her drink. She gives Cho a slap on the face and then, without any hurry, takes her leave by jumping into the water. The film closes with a scene that is Patrick Tam's favorite. Cherie arrives on a beach and exposes the deceit of Cho and Leung who have accepted the rich man's money. The two men start to fight for a cheque and both are injured. Having seen through these hypocrites, Cherie feels that there is nothing for her to remain attached to. Wearing a smile on her face, she leaves alone on a boat, moving toward the sea that symbolizes tranquility and purification.[11] This scene illustrates that she, at the moment, has freed herself of all emotional bonds and worries.

Most of the romances depicted in Patrick Tam's movies do not have a happy ending. In the abovementioned seventh episode of *Seven Women*, Lisa Wang's obsession with her brother causes her to develop a mental disorder. Later, her love for the doctor, Yu Yeung, is aborted as she discovers his real identity and, as a result, relapses. In *The Sword*, the hero, Adam Cheng, leaves his childhood love, Chan Kee-kee, to become an apprentice in sword playing. This results in Chan's marriage to Lin Wan (Tsui Siu-keung) and, in the end, to her death under Lin's hands. Something similar is evident with the couple, Brigitte Lin and Cheung Kwok-chong, in *Love Massacre*. In order to possess the wife, the schizophrenic Cheung attempts to stab Lin as well as her flatmates to death. Lastly, Cheung even asks his wife to murder him. Ah Suet (Yip Chuen-chun) in *Burning Snow* is forced to marry a vulgar old man, Lau Chung, because of her family's poverty. Her lover - an escaped prisoner, Simon Yam - is shot dead after her husband secretly reports him to the police. Unable to tolerate his violent ill-treatment, Ah Suet stabs Lau to death. In *My Heart is that Eternal Rose*, due to a careless murder of a policeman, Chung flees to another country. His lover, Joey Wang, commits her life to a gangster boss. Although the couple is later reunited and makes plans to escape together, in the end they are killed by the triads. The only survivor is the exile Cheung (Tony Leung Chiu-wai), a follower of the gang who had fallen in love with Wang and helped her during a time of crisis.

Nomad is a film that portrays women taking an active role in love and gives a relatively natural description of love. In the film, Patricia Ha, together with other female friends, takes the initiative to flirt with the lifeguard Ken Tong, pushing him into the water and removing his swimming trunks. Later one night, Ha and Tong even make love in a moving tram when nobody is around. The film's open attitude toward sexuality and the intrepid filming style provoked a massive response from society at the time. Some people wrote letters demanding that the film undergo another inspection from the authorities, while others objected to the re-editing of the film.[12] 'This film advocates new, open concepts toward sexuality.... What the film embodies is ridicule towards, and a negation of, the institution of marriage.'[13] The opponents of the film even hoped to raise the criticism to a higher level: 'It can be claimed that such a phenomenon is the prelude to the third clean-out of Hong Kong cinema.'[14] There was a series of debates. Despite the arguments that were stirred up, fortunately this third 'cleaning-up' did not take place. This shows the importance of freedom of speech in a society.

The controversy over *Nomad* focused on two points: first, the lovemaking scene on the tram and in the street; second, the plot in which Ha is intimate with both Tong and a Japanese soldier, as well as the sex scene involving Leslie Cheung and Cecilia Yip. As a matter of fact, these scenes are not obscene or completely unrealistic (lovemaking on trams also occurs in real life). Nevertheless, there seems to be no intention in the film to highlight such actions. Instead, those scenes, particularly the one involving Cheung and Yip, are natural to the plot. They are developed logically and fit the mood feel. Observe the encounter of Cheung and Yip in a restaurant. Cheung sees Yip switch between two telephone calls: one is made by the man in whom she has no interest but who threatens her with death; the other consists of a conversation in which Yips begs Andy not to leave her. In despair, Cheung gives Yip a lift to Andy's home. Discovering that Andy has tossed out her belongings, Yip cries. Cheung comes to carry Yip's luggage, then they spend a night in an inn. Their affection grows from compassion to love, manifested first by embraces and then lovemaking. This transformation is in accordance with the development of the plot and is the most natural outcome.

Of Patrick Tam's movies, the most romantic is *Final Victory*. One sequence describes the ways in which Eric Tsang and Loretta Lee's affections toward each other grow. However, the development of such feelings is hindered by Lee's identity as the lover of a triad boss. Tsang is not courageous enough to express his love. One day, Margaret Lee is nearly caught by triad members when she is playing mahjong. She has accompanied Tsang, and Loretta Lee immediately escapes. Margaret and Tsang first jump on to a red sedan, while Loretta keeps running and is caught by their opponents.

Tsang orders Margaret, who drives, to take a U-turn to save his lover. Reluctantly, Margaret returns, but a truck moving toward them blocks her car. In a second, Margaret makes up her mind to keep the vehicle moving and finally lifts up the roof. Margaret and Tsang succeed in reaching Loretta – she jumps into the car, joining her friends in making an escape.

Of Patrick Tam's films, *Final Victory* is the one in which the female character appears most courageous, and relations between men and women are described in the most natural manner. In the narrative, Tsang is commissioned to take care of the two women of his boss, Margaret and Loretta. In fact, under a façade of strength, Tsang is a coward. This is shown when he dares not discipline his boss's disloyal girlfriend and her new boyfriend. Another instance is the bank robbery sequence. Tsang passes by three banks without even entering them, giving the excuse that the banks are either too crowded or too deserted. In the end, their plan to commit robbery plan fails. By contrast, the two heroines are tough and brave. They are armed and succeed in robbing a bank, although Loretta is injured. Later, both are arrested by the police. At the moment that Loretta is taken to the police car, Tsang shouts to her from outside, 'Wait for me. I will register for a marriage with you. Our Big Brother knows somebody in jail. Remember, I will wait for you.' Loretta is touched and the film ends with a close-up of her face, which has an expression of contentment.

The film demonstrates a complete reversal of the conventional status of the two genders. Women, who have been long considered weak, are now depicted as genuinely strong. The change in the status of women can be charted in many of Patrick Tam's films. To begin with, there is Miu Kam-fung, in the second episode of *Seven Women*, in the role of the traditional housewife. Then, there is Ivy Ho in the third episode of *Seven Women*, who is developing a sense of self. Next is a responsible, dedicated social worker, Wai Yee-yan, in the eleventh episode of *Social Worker*. Then, there is the confident Cherie Chung in *Cherie*, who comes to the realization that, in love, she is no longer willing to serve as a man's plaything. The next female role to be depicted is the bold and strong-minded Patricia Ha in *Nomad*. Yip Chuen-chun in *Burning Snow* shows resistance against the violence of men, although the possible price of doing so is the loss of her life. Then, there is the image of a real heroine – Loretta Lee in *Final Victory* – who has learned to control her life. With only a few exceptional cases, in particular, Liu Wing-sheung in *Seven Women* who breaks taboos in a male-dominated society, the women portrayed by Tam are characters who are positive, aggressive, anti-traditional, anti-restrictive, independent or striving for autonomy. The emergence in the 1970s and 1980s of these images of women had a certain impact on Hong Kong society. If Patrick Tam's films are understood in the context of the social development of Hong Kong, they indisputably contain a certain amount of realistic significance.

An Emphasis on Detail over Dramatic Structure

As Patrick Tam is a director who concentrates primarily on innovations of film form, it is easy to understand that dramatic or narrative structure is not the focus of his movies. This explains the lack of background to support the actions of most of his characters. The character of Cheung Kwok-chu in *Love Massacre* is one example. Cheung's image is an extremely violent one, with his sudden turn to madness and murder (of his wife and Brigitte Lin's flatmates). How had his schizophrenic behaviour come into being? The film does not provide a single response. There is inconsistency and contradiction between the two halves of the narrative. The first half fosters a mood of desolation and coldness, while the second half is extremely violent, bloody and sensational. This sort of disharmony between content and form creates a vast incongruity. Here, we may only claim that this is the consequence of Tam's attention to form (such as the use of colour) instead of plot or narrative. This point will be elaborated upon later. Therefore, some critics have declared that Tam is 'a thorough formalist. His reference is primarily the film; reality is barely a footnote'.[15] This criticism has a certain amount of truth.

Consider the character of Patricia Ha in *Nomad*. The film reveals absolutely nothing about her background. She has a strong sensual relationship with one man early in the film. Then, she abruptly falls in love with a Japanese Red soldier, who is the epitome of the Japanese culture and who has aspirations and insights. The differences between the two men are so great that it is hard to reconcile Ha's two choices. The film does not offer any explanation of how such a tremendous chasm has been bridged. The only interpretation for the heroine's simultaneous love of these two men is that the choices exemplify her dual personalities – one relationship is on the physical/sensual level, while another is on the spiritual/mental level. This corresponds to the situation of the characters in the films having no past, only a present; hence, the stories behind all their deeds can hardly be traced. The same situation applies to another character, Cecilia Yip. As a Hong Konger, there is no indication that she would have any ability to speak Japanese; thus, it is surprising to see her speaking Japanese fluently when in the company of Japanese. She is represented all along as a pure and innocent young girl. Yet, this is belied in the final scene, which takes place on a beach. A female Japanese Red soldier, Chiyo, forces the traitor Takeda Shinsuke to commit suicide. At this critical moment, Yip is somehow able to lift up a wooden boat, under which she hides. She even kills Chiyo with arrows. Astonishingly, Yip has somehow become a skilled archer. In fact, this massacre on the beach seems to be a fragment tacked on to the ending of the film, perhaps, for commercial considerations. Shek Kei has argued that this scene 'has taken a movie about youth and shattered it into fragments; it does not work as a coherent movie'.[16]

A similar problem is found with *Burning Snow*. The heroine, Yip Chuen-chun, who originated from the Peng Hu Islands, is sold as a wife to the main island of Taiwan due to her family's poverty. To find a means for her to become acquainted with an escaped prisoner, Simon Yam, the film depicts her as capable of driving, which (given her poverty) is not logical. In *My Heart is that Eternal Rose*, Kenny Bee Chung carelessly commits a murder, which forces him to exile in the Philippines. The film does not provide any clues about his émigré situation. After six years, he returns to Hong Kong and suddenly becomes a professional killer. Such a change occurs abruptly, with no attempt made to trace its cause. The director's handling of the plot must unavoidably be considered overly impetuous.

Narrative and plot structure are not Patrick Tam's concerns. However, his films still rely on stories – although the dramatic structure is not tightly organized – to say what he wants to say and to test his exploration of film in terms of style, cinematic language (including *mise-en-scène*, montage, colours, etc.). This is all due to the great influence that the previously mentioned European directors have had on him, such as Godard, Antonioni and others. Therefore, he has neglected the importance that the audience places on a complete story. He also ignores the vast functions and meanings arising from an integration of content and form. The reasons for his extreme fondness for form in film can perhaps be found in these words of his: 'The world is chaotic, and our perceptions and impressions of things are also fragmented. A system or an orderly mode of narration is not my intension. This is why my films are split apart, presented in pieces.'[17] In fact, some of his works prove that he is capable of telling a complete story, but this is just not his desire. To conclude, he prefers film form to narrative structure.

Trials of Narrative Mode

Even in his days working in television, Tam had explored visual media, particularly narrative/storytelling. Unrestricted by tradition, Tam demonstrated courage and adventurousness in trying new things. For example, he used 16mm film to make *CID: Four Moments of Life*, which consists of four different stories. Each of the four episodes appears to be independent, but this turns out not to be the case. Every story does not have a closure, but ends in the middle of the plot. The audience has to see the next episode in order to comprehend the narrative. The fact is that the ending of each story is connected to the beginning of the next episode. The four stories, in this way, are put together to constitute an entirety. Each story tells about a criminal case: 'Morning' depicts an investigation carried out by a policeman, Simon Yam, of a case of a child injured because of lack of care from his parents. Another investigation, by policeman Cheung Lui, is presented in 'Afternoon', in which a rooftop voyeur tricks and sexually harasses a young girl. The subject of the examination in 'Evening' is different: senior citizens. A policeman, Ho Pik, looks into a case involving injuries caused by a quarrel that broke out in an old-age home. This case sheds light on the fear and crises that people face in old age. And in 'Night', the policeman, Wong Yuen-sun, investigates the injury of his colleague's wife in a car accident.

The main characters involved in these four episodes, in sequential order, are a child, a young girl, elderly people and people of middle age. The ages function to illuminate the themes of the episodes. Oddly, none of the investigations is resolved, revealing the fact that many cases that the police handle are unresolved. This idea is repeated in the eleventh episode of *Social Worker*. In the narrative, not only is the social worker, Wai

Yee-yan, unable to help the delinquent girl, Liu Wing-sheung, but also her mother, who commits suicide. This echoes the last episode, 'Night'. In that episode, Wong Yuen-sun interrogates a witness to an accident, Ma Kim-tong, with no results, making the policeman feel helpless. The mood is bleak and miserable. When Wong gets out of the police station, it is already sunrise of the next day. The narrative revolves back to the beginning of the first episode, 'Morning'.

This device, of the ending echoing the beginning, is not rare in Tam's films. The third episode of *Seven Women* is one instance of the use of this device. This drama is composed by three stories: 1. Ivy Ho acts as a DJ. In front of the microphone and the camera, she narrates stories about her life, friends, parents, family as well as her world-view and values. 2. Yeung Sze-ti, a working lady, meets her ex-husband in a hotel. While her ex-husband is taking a bath, she answers a call from a lady for him. Then she decides to leave silently. 3. An expert in heterosexual relationships, Lee Yan-yee, provides consultations in a radio show. She advises a female listener to win her lover, who it turns out is the husband of Lee herself. The end of the film revolves back to the beginning – with Ivy Ho sharing her inner feelings in front of the camera.

The Underdogs: The Story of Ah Soon (1977) tells a real-life story. The film opens with the protagonist in front of the camera, narrating stories about the community in which he lives, Sau Mau Ping, and his family. The middle part of the film shows a medium shot of him, directly addressing the audience, telling them that his relationship with his girlfriend, Chan Yuk-lin, has ended; about his participation in the public examinations; and about his job. The final scene is a close-up of Ah Soon (bareheaded) alone. He is addressing the audience:

> The film just shown is about my real-life experiences; it is not a drama.... Hong Kong is such a big place where I can definitely earn money if I am ready to work hard. I will not fool around.... When I was small, my lips split, which was very painful. That is why I am called Ah Soon (in Cantonese, literally meaning 'lips').

Tam uses a person from real life to present his story about being in elementary school, in middle school, about dating, work and joblessness. There are documentary-like interviews inserted throughout the film, which directly address the audience in first-person narrative. They is also evidence of the innovative mode of narration that characterizes Tam's works.

In terms of mode of narration, the most is definitely found in the aforementioned film's sixth episode of *Seven Women*. The entire 50 minutes of the film is dominated by a voice, coming literally from a cassette player, but the connotation is of a closed, isolated space. Disturbingly provocative, it is this audio thread that arouses the emotional responses of the secretary, Victoria Lam, who is working on transcription. Slowly, she falls into an emotional trap. She becomes unable to control her feelings and to escape from the trap. This film demonstrates the director's competence in manipulating the emotions of both the performers and the audience.

In his days in television, Tam made relatively more experiments with the narrative mode. *Seven Women No. 7* is an example. Certainly, during this period Tam enjoyed more freedom and space to be creative. Thus, his works during this period show a higher degree of achievement than his later works. Indeed, when he entered the film industry, such narrative experiments stop. Instead, he only poured his efforts into exploring the use of colour and cinematic language through a conventional narrative structure. This probably reflects pressure from the market and box office.

The Audacious Use of Colour

Colour carries considerable significance in Patrick Tam's works, particularly his cinematic ones. It is also the most vital element in his strong visual style. In the chromatic world, such colour as red, white and blue are the most primary, and also the most eye-catching. Tam is very fond of these three colours and often employs them in his films to express the relationship between the plot and personality of the characters, the transformation of their psyches or the environment. As early as during his television days, Tam's sensitivity toward colour began to be evident. For example, in *A Spectrum of Multiple Stars: Wang Chuanru**, Wang, under the abetment and arrangement of her sister, dates a stranger. In the period between which she makes a telephone call and leaves her room, she changes clothes three times. 'That connotes Wang's indecisiveness and nervousness.'[18] Here, the director uses the number of times the character changed her clothes and the colours of her costumes to indicate her emotional state. In the second episode of *Seven Women*, the telephone in Miu's family 'shows three different changes in colour, which changes in her psyche. I do not agree that this manner of representation is unnatural'.[19] Perhaps Tam's play of colours is too deliberate and can be subjected to criticism.[20] In any case, Tam's attempts to indicate the psyche of his characters using colour had already begun in the mid-1970s. In the last episode of *Seven Women*, the female protagonist Lisa Wang is discharged from a mental hospital and meets a young doctor, Yu Yeung. As their relationship develops, they fall in love with each other. But then her discovery of Yu's true identity leads to heated quarrels between them. This causes Wang to feel turbulent and unable to control herself. In one scene she dresses in red and walks to the seashore; the red colour serves as a sign that Wang has again become emotionally unstable.

Tam is not satisfied with the kind of deployment of colour found in most movies, which is consistent with 'reality'. In his cinematic world, colours are employed as a way of producing and preserving 'realistic imagination'. He does this in two steps: (1) decomposition, and (2) positioning to re-acknowledge the significance of colour in films.

1. Decomposition refers to the liberation of colours from their attached subjects/objects in order to restore their independence and autonomy.... As a means of representation, colours are at their most powerful when they appear as most 'singular'...because they become a completely independent vehicle of representation, sharing a status equivalent to other cinematic elements. Together, these elements

contribute to the 'incarnation' of the film's text according to the creativity of the author.

2. Positioning – Colours, as a means of cinematic representation, should retain its 'independence' but not in a state of 'isolation'.... The positioning of colours is a constituent of 'an entire performance' and is a strategy of the framing/composition of colours.... When the strategy of positioning is applied to a scene in the film, this refers to the distribution, composition, and deployment of colours.... When it is applied to the narrative structure, this refers to the positioning of people, events, objects, scenes, and movements of psyche with regard to the level of colour.[21]

In Tam's mind, individual colours can function independently to freely convey any meanings intended by the creators. Take the abovementioned example in the last episode of *Seven Women*. Lisa Wang is unable to control her emotions. She walks by the seashore, dressed in red. The red colour signifies the character's state of mind, which is restless and frustrated; whereas the blue colour of the sea suggests tranquility. In terms of chromatic perspective, the two colours are in conflict. Yet even in the tranquil sea, there are waves, which imply instability. This highlights the situation in which the characters find themselves: Wang and Yu are confronting the dilemma of staying together or leaving, while the restlessness of the heroine is highlighted. Wang has gone to the seashore in search of tranquility but cannot find it. The opposing elements in the conflict cannot be harmonized; rather, they become even shaper. Here the director's intention could not have been made clearer.

The film *Love Massacre* became a site where Tam exhibited colours and, in particular, where he explored the 'decomposition' and 'positioning' of chromatic elements. He expounded the role of colours in the mutually influential and ongoing relationship between the distribution, composition and movement in the frame and constituents in narrative structure, such as events, people, scenes and psyche. In the film, Tina Lau (Cheung Kwok-chu's younger sister), who has incestuous tendencies, is dressed in white and lying on a green pasture. Meanwhile, Brigitte Lin is driving a red sports car to the airport to welcome Cheung. They then drive on a grey highway, which shows no end. In these two lines of action, two sets of order are indicated: one is the order of colours and another is the order of the environment (objects). Put in another way, the sequences reveal the correlation not only between white/red and green/grey but also between Tina Lau/sports car and pasture/highway. The highlighting of white and red is about getting rid of the constraints of objects; of course, there are the other constraints of colours. Lying on the meadow, Lau is almost frighteningly motionless and quiet. By contrast, the scene of Lin and Cheung, in the moving vehicle, conveys happiness and a sense of freedom.

Many scenes in the film involve the three primary colours of red, white and blue. The colours of the characters' clothes change according to shifts in the plot and in their inner feelings. For example, the character of Brigitte Lin wears pink and violet at the beginning of the film, changes to red in the middle and appears in white in the end.

Cheung mainly wears blue and near the end he changes into white. The art director of the film, William Chang, stated, 'The images in *Love Massacre* are similar to those of the painter Piet Mondrian. Based on graphic design, quite a number of horizontal and vertical lines are used in the composition.'[22] The use of the three primary colours is what makes the film distinctive. In a sequence, Cheung murders a member of his family and then is met by Lin. There is a blue wall in the background, and Cheung is wearing white. Lin, in red, runs to him, bypassing the blue wall. Such an action, repeated twice, shows the colour contrast in a particularly impressive way. In another sequence, set in Hong Kong, Cheung, dressed in white, is drawing blue and red on a blank sheet of paper. He is also smearing blue colour on the face of his little boy, which makes the child cry and leave. Furthermore, he marks both of his palms with red and blue. Eerie enough his deeds are, these two colours that he uses sketch the silhouette of the narrative structure of the film. This also signifies the return of Cheung's mental illness. His psyche is distorted to the level of irrationality. It can be stated that he exploits the colours of red and blue to 'position' himself. The strategic deployment of colour arrangement and the narrative structure have a mutual influence, circular and dramatic. Now, the colours have finished generating their inherent meanings (given by the author) and return to their independent status.

Consider the closing scene on the roof. Lin, in a white bathing robe, walks through the drying frames on which long strips of cloth of the colours blue, white and red are hanging. The three colours compose a three-dimensional space, with blue as the foreground, white as the middle ground (with Lin in white passing through the cloths) and red as the background. Then Lin returns, followed by the camera. At that moment, Cheung, whose white clothing is stained with red blood, emerges. He asks Lin, 'Do you love me?' He gradually approaches Lin as Lin simultaneously backs away. He wields his blade and both of them stop in between two rows of blue cloth. He hands over the blade to Lin, and Lin stabs him straight in the body. He collapses and dies. Lin wraps Cheung's dead body and holds him. The sequence closes with the embrace. It can be claimed that the 'tension' in this sequence comes wholly from the bursting forth of colour. Colour comes prior to plot. The plot and narrative are influenced or even stirred up by the strategy of colour arrangement. To paraphrase, the bright colours are not reliant on the plot. Rather they have a kind of independent and specific existence and are a key constituent of the plot (narrative). It can be said that the use of colour in this film is a sort of style, or form, and even part of the content.

Looking at the various New Wave directors from the late 1970s to the early 1980s, Patrick Tam is the one who most cherishes colour aesthetics. At times, Tam uses colours merely for their own sake. An example is the lobby scene in *Love Massacre*. Brigritte Lin encounters Chun Cheung-lam in the lobby of a mansion. Wearing white, Lin walks by a couch with a pattern of big red circles and stops in front of it. An image of a woman in white standing in a patch of red is displayed. One more example is the roof scene. There is a wooden chest, which is completely red. The two frames on top and at the bottom of the door are painted red and blue and are extremely eye-catching. Colours, thus, become an essential element in a frame. They are used in a way that goes beyond reality and approaches formalism.

Meticulous *Mise-en-scène*

Tam's cinematic aesthetics show the heavy imprint of European cinema, in which *mise-en-scène* is a key feature. Of course, in the exploration of 'montage' he has his own personality. This will be discussed in the next section. According to André Bazin's theory, Patrick Tam would be classified as a director who 'believes in images'. He uses everything – lighting, colour, sets, composition, and editing to enhance the depiction of subjects.[23] If the two classifications of 'The Auteur Theory' are referred to: one advocates substance, meaning and, thus, themes; while the other stresses style and *mise-en-scène*,[24] Patrick Tam undeniably falls under the latter.

It is considered that *mise-en-scène* reveals the details of the frame through the movement of the camera. Such details include characters, costumes, make-up, accessories, sets and so forth. Of course, *mise-en-scène* demands coordination with long takes. In the history of film, a well-known example is Visconti's *Death in Venice*. Think of the scene in which the male protagonist, Humphrey Bogart, first encounters a handsome young boy in the hotel. Another example is found in Antonioni's *Passenger*. The hero is killed in an inn. The camera shoots from the room through the window, displaying several scenes of people and automobiles passing by. Finally, the police's car arrives. The police enter the inn and visit the venue of the murder. The camera is not cut throughout this 10-minute sequence, which is noted as a classical instance of the exercise of *mise-en-scène*. A classic of the long take is a scene in J. Flaherty's *Nanook of the North*. Nanook is waiting outside a snow cave for seals to emerge. A shot of deep focal length in Orson Welles' *Citizen Kane* should also be on the list.[25] Both sequences take the premise that the wholeness and consistency of the time and space of events should be respected, and nothing is added to or deleted from the scenes. Ambiguity, ambivalence and obscurity in reality are unveiled in a complete way. This makes it possible to uncover an even more deeply realistic framework.

In the third episode of *Seven Women*, made during Tam's days working in television, a case of *mise-en-scène* represented by a long take is found in the first episode 'Ivy Ho'. The sequence opens with a long shot, showing Ivy Ho sitting in front of a microphone narrating her thoughts. The camera then slowly moves to the right to capture a 'close-up' of the heroine. She stops narrating as the music comes on. The camera gradually moves backward to take a full shot. She signals for the music to stop and resumes talking about her insights on life, friends and love. Near the end, the music is heard again. She does not continue talking, but puts on headphones and hums a melody. Now the camera moves towards her to show another 'close-up'. The whole shot is a continuous one of lasting ten minutes.

The fourth episode of the drama is actually an extension of the first, with an insertion of the two episodes of Yeung Sze-ti and Lee Yan-yee. This is because this fourth episode revolves back to the studio, displaying Ivy Ho sitting by the microphone and narrating her worries about her family, particularly her parents. Her father is having an affair, which is making her feel anxious. This part is also filmed in a single shot. At this moment, she stops speaking and the music starts up. The close-up is altered to a long shot with the camera moving backward. The lights fade and the scene goes black, replicating the same scene as in the beginning of the first episode. The duration of this shot is seven minutes. Tam's unconventional technique demonstrates a certain degree of inheritance of the style of some European directors, chiefly Godard, to whom Tam even offers homage at the end of the second episode of *Seven Women*.

In the episode 'Evening' in *CID: Four Moments of Life*, the scene of two elderly mean fighting over pictures of beautiful women is worth considering. Old man A exhibits a range of pictures of beautiful women that he has been collecting for a long time along the window of the kitchen. He then leaves the room and the camera follows him. At the same time, we are shown old man B in the background, sitting by a desk writing a letter. He glances at A's pictures. A has already reached the corridor and then goes outside, feeling good. The camera then shifts back to the house, showing B walking toward the kitchen. He looks at the pictures that A has displayed. A unexpectedly returns at that moment and discovers B enjoying his pictures. A immediately rushes forward and a fight breaks out. This scene is captured with one shot. Careful calculation and clever design have gone into the movements of the characters and of the camera. The entrances and exits of the two men have been perfectly timed to a single second. Because of a few pictures, the two men attack each other with blades. This sheds light on the isolation, coldness, mistrust and violence in the world. The old-age home has become a strange, frightening place.

A father-daughter scene in the eleventh episode of *Social Worker* is also a fine example of *mise-en-scène*. Using a medium shot, the female protagonist, Wai Yee-yan, is shown sitting at her desk working on her notes. The camera then moves horizontally to capture her father, Ng Tung, on the couch smoking and reading a newspaper. Ng asks, 'How is your job?' Wai answers, 'Not bad. But I need to work hard.' Ng responds, 'This is always true whatever job you take.' Wai continues, 'Today I talked to Mom.' Ng glances at Wai, who is at the rear, and conceals any thoughts and emotions he might have. He then asks, 'Is she fine?' Wai replies, 'Yes. But she doesn't approve of me changing my job. She prefers the occupation of a teacher.' At that moment the telephone rings. Wai goes to answer it, and the camera follows him, then takes a close-up. The voice on the other side of the line is Little Kwong's (the younger brother of Wai's client). Little Kwong tells Wai that his older sister, Liu Wing-sheung, has returned home and that he hopes to invite Wai over for dinner. After their conversation, this long take ends. This sequence is indicative of the divorce and the subsequent relationship between Wai's parents, about which Ng pretends to be unconcerned. The arrival of Little Kwong's telephone call, delivering the news of the homecoming of a delinquent girl, undeniably dilutes the suppressive, bleak atmosphere of Wai's family.

The film cuts to a dinner scene with Wai, Little Kwong, Liu and her boyfriend, Wong Chit-sum. During their conversation, we learn that Wong runs a business in Taiwan. This sequence also contains a long take, shot from a high angle, which lasts for approximately three minutes. What immediately appears is a long take of a *mise-en-scène* – a medium shot of Liu resting in a couch in the sitting room. After a short while, the bell rings. She walks past the front door and goes upstairs, pursued by the camera, which fails to follow closely and thus stops at the front door that Liu has just walked past, exactly capturing the entrance of Lui's father. He then hears the noise of steps upstairs and, just as naturally, he looks upwards. Here, the director cuts to the next sequence. Also a long take, it shows the father meeting his daughter, Liu. He mistakenly believes that giving her money is a way of showing care and fulfilling his responsibility as a father. He has no idea that the real reason why Liu left home is that she feels no sense of genuine care and warmth. This long take is broken once (that is, there is one cut), implying that there is an obstacle in the relationship between the father and his daughter. This carries on the hint contained in the previous shot when the daughter went upstairs as her father entered the house, so that there was no point at which they met. This was the intention of the director – to illustrate the relationship via shots of the movements of the characters.

The inn scene in the film *The Sword*, involving the hero, Adam Cheng, is also an epitome of *mise-en-scène*. Coincidentally, Cheng meets his childhood lover, Chan Kee-kee, and when Cheng visits Chan in her room, the camera follows his entrance. Inside the room, there is a 360-degree reversal, with the past of the lovers being presented: Cheng leaves his home to take up an apprenticeship in sword playing. There is no news of him in ten years, and Chan then marries Tsui Siu-keung – who becomes Cheng's adversary. Chan and Cheng face each other without words, and this sequence closes with silence. Fate has indeed forced her to play an awkward role.

The most memorable sequence of *mise-en-scène* is in *My Heart is that Eternal Rose*. Ma Lit (Kenny Bee Chung) is forced to flee to the Philippines after the trouble he has created, leaving his lover, Cheung Lap (Joey Wang), behind. Six years pass, and Ma returns to Hong Kong as a professional killer hired by the Grandfather of God (Chan Wai-man) to eliminate a witness for the police, who threatens the gang leader. Ma revisits the bar run by Cheung's father. As he enjoys his drinks, there is a voice-over of Cheung reading a letter. She reveals that she failed to meet Ma in the Philippines as promised. She had made that decision as a sign of separation after careful consideration, because she felt that they are not well matched. The fact, however, is that Cheung had been forced to become the concubine of the Grandfather of God in order to save her father. She had indeed been reluctant to breaking her pledge to Ma. When the voice-over ends, Ma rises, looks back and leaves the frame from another side. Exactly at the moment that Ma leaves the pub, a private car arrives. Cheung and her guard, Tony Leung chiu-wai, get out of the automobile and enter the pub. They sit at the table where Ma had just been sitting. Then Cheung goes to the counter, and Ma returns. But just as Ma appears at the counter to retrieve the lighter that he had inadvertently left behind, Cheung returns to her table. The two lovers missed each other by only a second or two. In this sequence, Tam employed amazingly skilful moments of *mise-en-scène* to represent the fate-dominated sentiments, as some critics have coined them.[26] His skill certainly compels admiration.

Montage and Transition

In Tam's movies, 'montage' and *mise-en-scène* supplement each other. They can be employed together, without contradicting and repelling each other, reminiscent of the situation with the two major, extremely divergent theoretical systems of Eisenstein and Bazin.[27] Put another way, Tam holds the open attitude that his deployment of these two techniques – long takes and montages – are exercised based on dramatic and supplementary demands. He does not adhere to a single rule. Consider, for instance, the aforementioned sequence in the episode of 'Evening' in *CID: Four Moments of Life*. The parts before and after the long take of *mise-en-scène* involving the old men are composed of 'montage' (editing). The preceding part can be divided as:

1. A long shot – the tracking camera displays the environment in the old-age home of lines of beds.
2. Close-ups of the photographs of the sexy beauties.
3. A medium shot of old man [A] who holds these photographs and gazes at them.
4. A medium shot of old man [B] who sits at a desk writing a letter.
5. A medium shot of old man [A], who stands up and walks forward carrying the photographs – this is a long take of *mise-en-scène*, which has been discussed earlier. The part following the long take is presented now, starting from the sixth shot.
6. The previous take has already shown that old man [A] has forcibly taken back the photos from old man [B], and old man [B] has departed. Now old man [B] is shown returning to the kitchen with a magnifying glass. He also carelessly knocks down old man [A]'s chopper.
7. A close-up of the chopper on the floor.
8. A medium shot of old man [A] shouting to [B], 'Wanna die?'
9. A close-up of old man [B]'s magnifying glass, which has just been placed in front of old man [A].
10. A close-up of old man [A] holding the chopper and chopping twice consecutively at the camera (that is the position of old man [B]). The lens is immediately splattered with blood and shakes.
11. A long shot captures both old men. Old man [B] collapses as he is cut by the chopper. His hands are stained with blood, and he wipes the glass on the kitchen door. Now the camera moves towards the blood on old man [B]'s hands and shows a close-up. The mood becomes suffocating and frightening, with the flavour of Hitchcock's horror films. Such an amalgam of montage and *mise-en-scène*, making use of each of their advantages, creates cinematic perfection.

In the eleventh episode of *Social Worker*, the sequence in which Liu is attacked is an example of an outstanding use of montage. The wife of Liu's boyfriend learns of the affair between Liu and her husband. One day, as Liu is leaving her boyfriend's residence, she is splattered with toxic chemicals. The montage here shows:

1. A long shot capturing Liu leaving a mansion.
2. From the inside of an automobile along the street, the camera follows Liu, capturing her profile and then her back.
3. A bird's-eye view shot reveals a small yellow sedan emerging, and stopping next to Liu. Two men jump out of the car.
4. A medium shot shows the two men rushing toward her and pouring toxic chemicals over her.
5. A bird's-eye view, long shot with iron tubes in the foreground, and the two men who immediately leave in the background. Liu falls on the ground and the camera then follows the movements of the men.
6. A bird's-eye view shot shows Liu slowly raising the upper part of her body, covering her eyes with her hands and shouting. This sequence is composed of six shots showing Liu being attacked suddenly, with movements as quick as lightning that she has no time to fend off her attackers. This montage demonstrates the power of speed. Actions are represented without delay. The director then cuts to a scene of Liu in the hospital.

The prime example of a complicated or perhaps quick montage is the final sequence of *The Sword*, which exhibits the function of the technique. This is of a massacre carried out by Adam Cheng and Tsui Siu-keung, who are competing for the two treasure swords 'Cool Star' and 'Qi Treasure'. Here is a breakdown of the second half of the scene into the smallest unit of shots: After several rounds of fighting, both heroes are injured.

1. A long shot of Cheng, who is hit against the wall and then collapses.
2. A long shot of the emergence of Tsui in a manner similar to that of a horizontally projected bomb.
3. A medium shot of Cheng, who immediately stands up.
4. A long shot of Tsui holding a sword with both hands and flying horizontally toward Cheng.
5. The camera moves towards Cheng and shows a close-up of him standing straight with a sword in his hands welcoming the battle.
6. A shot similar to shot number 4.
7. A close-up of Cheng holding his sword tightly in readiness for battle.
8. A close-up of a reflection of Cheng at the blade of Tsui's sword.
9. A close-up of Cheng receding to avoid Tsui's attack.
10. A long shot of both men showing protecting himself with his sword from an attack by Tsui, who is flying horizontally toward him.
11. A close-up of Cheng receiving a sword thrust by Tsui and falling back towards a wall. Cheng disgorges blood.
12. A close-up of Tsui's continuous horizontal movements in attacking Cheng.

13. A close-up of Cheng protecting himself with his sword from Tsui's attacks, and Tsui's blade being hacked into two.
14. A close-up of Tsui crashing toward Cheng, who is still fighting with his sword.
15. A close-up of Cheng's sword splitting Tsui's face into two as Tsui charges towards Cheng.
16. A long shot of Cheng standing straight holding his sword, while both the face and body of Tsui are cut into two pieces.
17. A close-up of the motionless Cheng. Both his face and the wall are covered with blood. Cheng cries out.
18. A close-up of Cheng's wide-open eyes.
19. A long shot of a silent house. Then Cheng comes searching for Chan Kee-kee and finds her committing suicide. During the duel with Tsui, Cheng remained calm in the face of numerous rapid changes. In times of emergency, he used his sword to cut the flying Tsui into two. This amazing tactic was praised by a critic, as the one that 'reverses the destiny of the winner and the loser, and is astonishing enough to shock the audience'.[28] These nineteen shots last for a total of only twelve minutes – on average, about half a second per shot. The images have not yet been completely comprehended when the next shot is delivered. The editing is marvelous. It is no exaggeration to call this sequence the best montage among Tam's films.

Patrick Tam is not careless or perfunctory about the linkage and transition between scenes. To be specific, he does not lightly make use of such common optical effects such as fade-in, fade-out, superimposition and sweep.[29] On the contrary, he is always thoughtful about the connection between scenes, so that they appear seamless. He mostly borrows elements from the previous scene to lead the audience unconsciously to the next scene. In *CID: Four Moments of Life*, policeman Ho Pik-kin is watching television with his family after supper. The scene closes with a close-up of the television. It is immediately followed by another shot, which opens the next sequence, of Ho already sleeping in bed. Prior to this shot, it appears to the audience that Ho or his family is still watching television. This tactic of a seamless transition of scenes is what Patrick Tam is most skilled at. The next sequence shows Ho waking up in the middle of the night and taking a drink of water. His daughter, Wai Yee-yan, is sound asleep. He turns off the lights of her room for her and then returns to his room. This time the camera follows Ho, then moves upward to take a close-up of the wind chimes on his window. Here, the sequence closes.

In the first episode of *Seven Women*, a classmate of Liu Wing-sheung's believes she is pregnant. Liu accompanies her to an examination. The pregnancy is confirmed. The sequence ends with a close-up of a human skeleton in the laboratory. Then the camera shifts to the next scene, in which Liu lies to the librarian about being pregnant. Another scene of a car accident shows victims being transferred to an ambulance. Here, Tam ends the sequence with a close-up of the signal light on the roof of the vehicle. The next scene is in the operating room of a hospital. Policemen Wong Yuen-sun and Yu

Yeung are waiting outside the room. This tactic of using the objects (props) available in the scene as a way of effecting a transition is one of Tam's trademarks. Another is using close-ups of characters to transition between scenes. Consider, for example, the scene in the eleventh episode of *Social Worker* of Wai Yee-yan visiting her mother. Her mother's live-in boyfriend returns, and the mother at once serves him tea, only to receive a critical response. Seeing this, Wai makes an early departure and her mother feels embarrassed. The scene ends with a close-up of the mother looking shamefaced.

In *The Underdogs: The Story of Ah Soon*, Ah Soon (Tam Yuen-sun) is helping his boss' wife (Victoria Lam) to bring her things home. She even exploits him by asking him to clear away the dog dirt from the doorway. Furious, Ah Soon shouts at her, 'Bitch!' At this moment, the camera takes a close-up of the shocked face of the boss' wife. This is followed by an extreme close-up of Ah Soon, and the scene concludes. In *My Heart Is That Eternal Rose*, Joey Wang commits her life to the Grandfather of God in order to rescue her father. Seeing her escort Japanese clients in a nightclub in the company of the Grandfather, her father is heartbroken. In order to assuage his grief, he becomes drunk. Under the guard of Tony Leung Chiu-wai, a subordinate of the Grandfather, he leaves. But the drunken old man is then knocked down by a car. After Wang learns the bad news, told to her by Leung, she shivers. The scene concludes with a close-up of her face, suffused with strange expressions. Tam likes to use editing to transition to the next scene. This shows, on the one hand, his rejection of optical effects – a more mechanical form; and on the other, his mastery over cinematic language, especially editing (montage).

It is worth mentioning that Tam is very fond of the sea. Scenes of the sea can be found in the majority of his works, in most cases, at the end of the story. The first episode of *Seven Women*, an early work produced during his days in television, includes a sea scene: Chow Yun-fat acts as a photographer, taking photographs for models. In another drama, the seventh episode of *Seven Women*, Lisa Wang is once again attacked by mental illness. Dressed in red, she goes alone to the seashore. She lies on the sand and gazes the sea in order to try to calm herself. In *The Sword*, Adam Cheng desires to be the king of the world and thus pursues the two treasure swords 'Cool Star' and 'Qi Treasure'. This leads to his childhood lover, Chan Kee-kee, being lost to Tsui Siu-keung. Tsui is eventually murdered by Cheng, and Chan falls on Tsui's sword. Acquiring the two swords, Cheng also awakens to the realization that 'fame and wealth are illusory. Even if you acquire them, this does not mean much'. He goes to the seashore, faces the sea and throws the two swords into water. This act symbolizes a kind of liberation, which leads to inner tranquility.

Near the end of *Love Massacre*, Brigitte Lin stabs Cheung Kwok-chu to death. In this sequence, ocean scenes are likewise included. There are even white sails in the sea. The ending of *Cherie* is similarly set at the seaside. Two men, an artist and his adversary, start a fight over their own interests. Exposing the trickery of the two men, Cherie Chung leaves alone on a boat. With a smile on her face, Chung moves toward a borderless sea with a light heart. In *Final Victory*, it is also beside the sea that Tsui Hark, who has just been discharged from jail, strikes Eric Tsang, who has stolen his lover, Loretta Lee. In the end, Tsui Hark thinks things through and releases his 'brother', and even helps to bring about Tsang's marriage with Lee. Here, the sea appears as a catalyst for a change of mind. The gangster boss is willing to set his brother free instead of killing him. In *My Heart Is That Eternal Rose*, Kenny Bee Chung returns from years of exile. He wants to leave together with his lover, Joey Wang. However, both of them are killed by the Grandfather of God. Wang's guard, Tony Leung chiu-wai, alone, escapes by sailing away, and this concludes the film. Scenes of oceans and seashores also carry a certain weight in *Nomad*. The final sequence - a duel between a Japanese female Red soldier and her betrayer - is also set by the sea. In the most critical moment, Cecilia Yip suddenly emerges from the bottom of a boat and murders the soldier with arrows. In this way, Leslie Cheung is saved. There is a freeze shot of the lovers embracing, followed by a shot of a boat 'Nomad'[30] (symbolizing ceaseless motion and exploration) setting off in the ocean - signifying purification and eternality.

Notes

1. *Wang Chuanru** was entered in the American International Film Festival in 1975 and earned the Bronze award.
2. See Zhang Jinman. 'Qinüxing houmian de nanren' (The Men Behind the Seven Women). *Datexie* (Close-Up). No. 25, 23 December, 1976, p. 46.
3. In television stations in the early 1970s, scriptwriters-directors were divided into two kinds: on-location and studio. The so-called studio sets referred to those with three cameras that could be used to shoot simultaneously. Studio sets were principally used and became the mainstream mode of television production. Occasionally, scenes were shot outdoors, and the shooting, which was dominated by a single camera, had to be done by the on-location directors.
4. In late 1977, the head of the production unit of TVB, Selina Leong Suk-yi, moved to Commercial Television. Patrick Tam also left TVB at about the same time. Leong, as a new arrival, produced the television drama *Mingliuqingshi*.* Patrick Tam was put in charge of part of the on-location shooting in Hawaii.
5. 'Five Stations Hill' refers to the avenue on the hill on Broadcast Drive, where Hong Kong's five broadcast institutions including TVB, Rediffusion Television (the antecedent of Asia TV), Commercial Television, Radio Television Hong Kong and Commercial Radio were located. The 'mutiny' refers to the transfer in 1977 of TVB's Leong, together with a group of staff members, to Commercial Television. In the next year, Leong initiated the 'May Campaign', the intention of which was to counter-attack Commercial Television's rival, TVB, which, with its quality programmes, held a prominent share of the viewership. Unfortunately, Commercial Television met with failure and folded in the same year.
6. Refer to Zhang Jinman. 'Qinüxing houmian de nanren.' *Datexie*. No. 25, 23 December, 1976, p. 46. '...I like Goddard but that never means I agree with all his viewpoints.... To a greater or lesser degree, however, my shooting has been influenced by him.'
7. 'When I see a family having dinner at the side road from the window of my room (of an inn), I would rather stay in the room than to join them, to share their happiness. My

personality is like this: I prefer to enjoy something from a distance to throwing myself into it.' Yin Yuet, Chow Chun-sun, et al. 'A Record of the Conversation with Patrick Tam.' *City Entertainment*. No. 40. 30 July, 1980.

8. Zhang Jinman. 'Qinuxing houmian de nanren.' *Datexie*. No. 25, 23 February 1976, p. 46.
9. Sun Boling. 'Ni pai dianshi wo bufangxin' (I Worry About Your Television Production). *Datexie*. No. 26, 6 November 1977, pp. 46–7.
10. Ibid., p. 46.
11. Interview of Patrick Tam. Conducted by Sam Ho, Stephen Teo etc. Format: Cassette. On 9 April, 1999, evening, at the Hong Kong International Film Festival, Level 7, Administrative Building, Hong Kong Cultural Centre.
12. Yu Mo-wan. 'Dianying *Liehuo Qingchun* fengbo mianmianguan' (A Panorama of the Controversy aroused by *Nomad*). *Nanbeiji* (North-South Poles). 16 January 1983, p. 61.
13. Ibid., p. 60.
14. Ibid., p. 62. In the history of Hong Kong cinema, there were two 'cinematic clean-outs': the first was in 1935 and was initiated by education workers; second was in 1949, by Leftist film workers.
15. Evans Chan. 'Things are Settled: Re-evaluating *Nomad*.' *City Entertainment*. No. 105, 1983, p. 32.
16. Shek Kei, *Shek Kei's Anthology of Film Reviews: The Raging Approach of the New Wave.** Hong Kong Subculture Press, 1999, p. 19.
17. Suet Hang. 'Things are Settled: Re-evaluating *Nomad*.' *City Entertainment*. No. 105, 1983, p. 32.
18. Words from Yip Kit-hing. Yip was Tam's wife at the time. See Li Mo. 'Qunxingpu Wang Chuanru teji' (A Special Issue on *A Spectrum of Multiple Stars: Wang Chuanru*).* *Datexie*. 1975, p. 52.
19. Zhang Jinman. 'Qinüxing houmian de nanren.' *Datexie*. No. 25, 23 December 1976, p. 47.
20. Shu Kei. 'Cong dianshi jiaoyu tandao dianshi daoyan' (From television education to television directing). *Datexie*. No. 30, 25 March 1977, p. 47.
21. Patrick Tam. 'Secai yu yingxiang' (Colour and Image). *Dianguang huanying – dianying yanjiu wenji* (Electrical Light and Shadow – An Anthology of Articles about Film Studies). Jointly published by School of Continuing Studies, Chinese University of Hong Kong and Unit of TV production, RTHK. 1st ed. November 1985, pp. 171–72.
22. 'Zhang Shuping de meishu sheji fengge' (William Chang's Artistic Design Style). *Jinri Dianying* (Film Today). No. 125, Taipei: January 1982, p. 57.
23. Bazin, Andre, *What is Cinema?* Vol. I. Selected and translated by Gray H. Berkeley: University of California Press, 1970, p. 24.
24. Wollen, Peter. *Signs and Meaning in the Cinema*. Bloomington: Indiana University Press, 1972, p. 78.
25. Bazin, Andre, *What is Cinema?* Vol. I. Selected and translated by Gray H. Berkeley: University of California Press, 1970, pp. 26, 27, 33, 36, 37.
26. Leung Leung. 'A New Sphere of Hong-Kong-Produced Genre Films?' *Big Motion Picture*. Hong Kong. 28 February 1989, p. 33.
27. According to Eisenstein's 'montage theory', images that capture reality can only become art via editing. Shot A + Shot B = C (a new meaning). Therefore, shots should be juxtaposed

and in striking against each other, meaning is created. Otherwise, shots are merely primitive materials instead of art. But Bazin's realist theory argues that if a long shot represents reality – the wholeness of time and space, then a series of long shots is already an art. No procedures are demanded in the process. That shows the equivalence between reality and art.

28. Shek Kei, *Shek Kei's Anthology of Film Reviews: The Raging Approach of the New Wave.** Hong Kong Subculture Press, 1999, p. 14.
29. Fade-in, fade-out – where one shot gradually becomes dim and then dark; while the next shot goes from dark to light. Superimposition – the merging of two shots. When the first shot slowly fades out, the next shot fades in to dominate the screen. Sweep: where a shot disappears either leftward or upward, followed by another shot. All of these effects have to be processed by an optical printer.
30. Interview with Patrick Tam. Conducted by Sam Ho, Stephen Teo and others. Format: Cassette. On 9 April 1999, evening, at the Hong Kong International Film Festival, Level 7, Administrative Building, Hong Kong Cultural Centre.

6

Yim Ho

Born in Hong Kong in 1952, Yim Ho is the son of Yim Shu-hing, a famous writer and journalist.[1] From a young age, he was trained by his family to love literature and art. After graduating from Heung To Middle School, he worked in a bank. In 1973, he enrolled in the London Film School. Two years later, he returned to Hong Kong and started to work for TVB, first as a scriptwriter and then as a director in the film unit. His productions included *Wonderful* (1976–77), *CID* (1976–77), *Seventeen* (1977), *Social Worker* (1977) and one episode of the *ICAC* series (1978). In 1978, he launched his entertainment business, Film Force, in collaboration with Dennis Yu, Ronny Yu and Philip Chan. Their first project was *The Extra,* which was a pioneering work of the New Wave and of great significance.

In his days in television, Yim's works already stood out. They were distinctive in two ways:

1. They showed concern for young intellectuals. This motif is hardly found in the films of other New Wave directors. Only Ann Hui's *Below the Lion Rock – The Bridge* can compare to it. In this drama, a British journalist from Radio Television Hong Kong uses the incident of the tearing down of the bridge to uncover bureaucracy and corruption in the government, which has been turning a deaf ear to the voices of the people. However, here, the depiction of intellectual youth is bound up with the status of the journalist. Thus, the main point of the film is not to explore the inner thought processes of intellectual youth. Yim Ho's *Seventeen: Art Life*, on the other hand, depicts a group of university graduates who have ambitions to launch a magazine. They are, to name a few, Lee Wing, Tang Siu-yu, Ringo Lam and Chan Chuk-chiu. The title of the magazine is exactly the same as that of the film, *Art Life*. In *Seventeen: 1977*, the protagonist, Lee Wing, is no longer involved in the publication of the magazine but is working for a television station as a scriptwriter. He is later promoted to become a director. Like his comrade, Wong Chi-cheng,

who in the past had devoted all of his time to student movements in defence of the Diaoyu Islands, Lee has buried his past ideals. Now, all that they are involved in during their spare time is sharing their personal experiences in a discussion group organized by the young Clifton Ko. Ko appears to be the opposite of them in that he, together with his colleagues, is actively committed to understanding and working for society. They represent the ideals of the present and of the future. Hence, these two works of Yim Ho seriously explored the subject of young intellectuals, which was rather rare at that time.

2. Concern about social problems in Hong Kong. This is a manifestation of the New Wave's focus on the local. *Seventeen: 1977*, spanning the period 1967 to 1970, incorporates issues and a range of activities that young people are involved in, including the defence of the Diaoyu Islands, striving to win approval for Chinese as an official language, street interviews, surveys, life-enriching activities, demonstrations in support of and with villagers, and requests to establish government child-care centres and others. The young people face society with a positive attitude, and with concern for its welfare. As an indigenous Hong Kong director, Yim Ho has insights about his experiences and those of his generation, which he communicates through his films. When these two dramas were broadcast, they shook the intellectual world, because they were the first such works to depict young intellectuals. The film *Seventeen: 1977* portrays some characters as being active in student movements and social campaigns, which shows their commitment to the community; while others have sunk into depravity. Wong Chi-ching is an example of the latter. He gets married and works at a senior level, but cares little about his subordinates' efforts to get their salaries raised. In the end, he even burns the broken glasses, arm badge and newspaper cuttings, all of which he had been so proud of in the past. Turning these objects, which were symbols of his participation in the movements of the past, into ashes signifies the vanishing of his past aspirations. Naturally, in the end he is revealed to be a hypocrite who does little more than brag. By contrast, Clifton Ko is still so passionate that he does volunteer work and helps to conduct social surveys. He does not let himself be held back by other people, but continues to pursue his dream to make life more meaningful and society fairer and happier. Perhaps this film has various flaws, such as shallowness, over-simplification and an abstract, blunt dichotomous understanding/classification of young intellectual as either 'progressive' or 'negative'.[2] However, these are not important. What is key is the ground-breaking nature of the film. It has a certain historical significance. Besides focusing attention on intellectuals and engaging society, this film is a symbol of the localization of the New Wave.

Yim's later works contain fewer portrayals of intellectuals. With the exception of *Red Dust*, there is hardly any mention of this subject in his other films. By contrast, there has been a consistent focus on local topics and content. This focus began with his television productions such as *CID: Wrongly Accused* and *CID: Two Stories*. It continued in his films, most notably, *The Extra*, *The Happening* (1980) and *Wedding*

Bell, Wedding Belles (1981). The plot of *Homecoming* (1984) involves Hong Kong, with descriptions of villages in mainland China. Yim' subsequent works, namely *Buddha's Lock* (1987), *King of Chess* (1988), *Red Dust* (1990), *The Day the Sun Turned Cold* (1995) and *The Sun Has Ears* (1996), all focus on mainland China. Of these films, only the *King of Chess* touches on Taiwan. It was not until his recent work *Kitchen* (1997) that Yim returned to setting a film wholly in Hong Kong. However, he, after all, misses the motherland, from which he is incapable of cutting himself off.

Environmental Constraints on People

Unable to free themselves from the control of situations, people's lives have gradually lost direction or even ended tragically – a motif that Yim Ho often explores. In *CID: Wrongly Accused*, a taxi driver Kwong Ngai, unaccountably has a pistol thrust into his hand in a place where policemen try to arrest criminals. The police then mistake him for a criminal. They open fire, and Kwong is shot in the leg and later sentenced to ten years of imprisonment. After he has completed his jail term, the true criminal appears and confesses to his deed. However, Kwong has lost both his wife, who is already engaged to another man, and his job. He is unable to find a job at first, but then works in a noodle stall. He thinks constantly about taking vengeance on the policeman who had arrested him, Wong Yuen-sun, but does not dare to put his plan into practice. After a short time, he finds work as a cleaner in an elementary school. Just then, the police find a pistol on him and arrest him again. The drama is a statement about Kwong's helplessness, as a member of the lower class. Although the evidence is circumstantial, Kwong has no way of defending himself. The law and the executors of the law do not fully practice their responsibility of protecting the powerless – those who have no money to hire lawyers. The equality of all before the law is nothing but a slogan. In the face of a powerful ruling apparatus, individuals become helpless, because they do not have the ability to control their life. Here, the director's concern for marginalized groups or individuals is clear. Likewise, the third episode of *Social Worker* tells the story of Ngai Chau-wah, who is a delinquent growing up in a typical public housing estate. Under the guidance of a social worker the young man slowly changes. However, when his girlfriend is teased and humiliated by hoodlums and he is unable to help her, he joins the triads. The police carry out a sweep and Ngai is sent to prison. The delinquent in the drama does not find it easy to stand alone in virtues. He goes astray once again. The film sheds light on how difficult it is for individuals, young people in particular, to not be influenced by their environment.

Yim's first feature after switching from television to the film industry was *The Extra*. In this film, the character, Yi Lui, is unconsciously restrained by the environment, specifically a film studio. A lover of the theatre, he felt stifled and therefore switched from the theater to film, acting as a freelance actor of bit parts. Starting from a low position, Yi suffers scorn and ridicule. Once, he was assigned the task of jumping from a height with wearing self-exploding bullets. Due to his extreme nervousness, the bullets exploded earlier than expected. He did not know what to do and simply stood still. The director swore at him, shouting that there are three curses in film-making:

animals, children and bit-part actors. In another incident, Yi, acting as a policeman, was bullied by another actor performing as a thief. The latter held Yi's head under the water, causing Yi to nearly faint and even drown. Yi was then called to play a gambler in a casino that had been set up by the real police, so that the police could be sure to have someone to arrest. However, the bogus casino was uncovered by ICAC staff. People on the scene, including Yi, were therefore detained. The agency that hired him was dissolved. Jobless, Yi saw a director in a restaurant. In order to attract the director's attention, he bribed the owner of the restaurant to keep making telephone calls and calling for him (using his screen name, 'Ti She', which the restaurant boss mockingly puns) to take the phone calls. The customers in the restaurant laugh contemptuously when they hear the pun. He then discovers that he has been cheated by the restaurant owner. Furthermore, in order to continue acting in movies, he agrees with Kenneth Tsang to be his substitute to deal with his girlfriend, who is a big star. However, at last, Yi can bear this no longer and reveals Tsang's despicable deeds of playing with girls. He is then assaulted by Tsang's gang, pushed out of a car and rolls downhill. The sequence foreshadows the criminal acts of a group of juvenile delinquents in *The Happenings*. Yi finds no way out of the film-making studio, which is an epitome of society. The conclusion of the film shows that he has married Chan Yuk-lin and has children. He is still acting; however, he appears to be much happier.

In *The Happening*, a group of teenagers, namely Cream, King Kong, Ah B, Ah Ying and Peter Pan, steal a car to go joyriding. This unexpectedly triggers off a series of troubles: they accidentally kill a gasoline station clerk and mow down a pedestrian. Their troubles snowball, and they are on a road from which there is no return. This group of delinquents is led by gangsters. However, these gangsters are unable to take care of themselves, let alone their followers. In fact, these gangsters are demanding help from the youngsters. Actually, the troubles that they come across are mostly coincidental. For example, they find that they have no money to buy gasoline. King Kong, who does not know this, negotiates with the clerk in the station. An argument turns into a fight, and the clerk is killed by King Kong. Frightened, the youngsters also kill the other employees there. At that time, the police are on patrol, and the youngsters immediately paint the station red in order to conceal the bloodstains. Using their quick wits, they manage to escape from the crisis. Put in another way, they are forced to react instantaneously. The result is that their troubles pile up, and they find themselves in deeper and deeper trouble. There is no turning back. Under a police cordon, some of the delinquents are killed, while others are injured; the survivors are all arrested by the police. A joyride evolved into a tragedy. The film tells a tale of the impossibility of transcending one's environment and fate.

This film contains action, fistfights, gunplay, violence, bloodiness, humour, compassion and suspense. Furthermore, it is fast-paced and exciting. Thus, it is an impressive, commercial movie. In this sense, the film-maker has a clear sense of self and is not hesitant or ambiguous.[3] In addition, Yim has all along stressed the dual characteristics of film: that it is artistic/technical and popular/entertaining. 'If I am asked which dimension is more fundamental, my answer would be that what lies at its foundation is sex. Just like survival is the foundation of human life; without survival, there is no point discussing a better or a more meaningful life.'[4] In other words, Yim's films pursue a balance or consistency between the artistic and the entertaining. *Wedding Bells, Wedding Belles*, similar to *The Extra*, belongs to the genre of comedy. But it is more dramatic and can be identified as a 'crazy comedy'. Both comedies take ordinary people as their subject, while *Wedding Bells, Wedding Belles* focuses specifically on boat people. A young boat resident, Ah Kiu (Yi Lui), falls in love with a girl with buck teeth, Tai Shui (Suet Lei). She, however, is interested in Ha (Kwan Chung), the assistant of the millionaire Chow Shi-wai (Lau Hac-suen). The plot develops in a web of relationships. Ha connives in Tai Shui's plot to marry Chow. He even invites Tai Shui to join the beauty pageant organized by Chow. The boat on which the pageant is held sinks. Tai Shui then jumps into the sea and drifts onto a desolate island. This incident enables her to understand Ah Kiu's love. In the end, she becomes engaged to him. The entire movie is tied to certain ideas such as boats, the sea and desolate islands, all of which refer to the living environment of fishermen. Even the characters' names carry a reference to water: Tai Shui (literally means 'carrying water'), Tai Chai (literally means 'carrying sons') and Ah Kiu (literally means 'cute'), etc. Falling in love with and being rejected by Ha implies that Tai Shui's hope to leave the life of the fishermen is not permitted by destiny. Not only Tai Shui, but even her parents want Ha to help them to move into public housing. But their hopes are not fulfilled. Thus, the film suggests a sense of fatalism. The fishermen are not able to leave the sea, which is their source of life. A similar situation applies to the millionaire, Chow. Hoping to acquire a young fisherwoman to produce offspring for him, Chow spends a large amount of money to gain the submission of the poor fishermen. However, his dream of obtaining a concubine is not fulfilled, mainly because he accidentally castrates himself in the end.

No Sun City (1991) is another TV drama by Yim Ho. The female protagonist, a police detective Yip Sun, spoils an undercover operation by revealing her identity too early. The result is that the police fail to round up the gang, and two of her colleagues lose their lives. She also comes under a curse from a cult religion and nearly dies. Her arm turns black and her illness cannot be cured for some time. Her senior officer suspects that she is affiliated with the criminals and, thus, transfers her to another position until the truth can be discovered. Yip's defense is rejected, and she has no way of making any complaints. She is no longer trusted by anyone in her workplace. Even her nephew, who was very close to her, has had his trust in her shaken by Yip's boss. Under attack both internally and externally, Yip is aggrieved by the unjust accusation. The film shows that people are often trapped, completely helpless, in circumstances that they have no way of anticipating and from which they cannot escape.

In 1987, Yim travelled a long way to shoot *Buddha's Lock* in Daliangshan (Huge Cool Mountain) in China. The film highlights the helplessness and despair of individuals trapped in circumstances over which they have no control. In the narrative, an American general hopes to make money in a region of China populated by minority ethnic groups by trading buttons for rings and earrings. Instead, he is captured by Yi clansmen and sold as a slave, dubbed 'a doll'. As a westerner, he becomes a 'western doll'. He is forced to engage in hard labour, tied up, treated unjustly and humiliated, just like an animal. He loses the basic dignity of being treated like a human being. Battles within the Yi clan are frequent, and he is often transferred from the loser to the winner. He serves various masters, but his status as a 'western doll' remains unchanged. The message that the environment or fate manipulates human beings could not be clearer. It is not until the entire nation is liberated that he is sent away from Liangshan by the People's Liberation Army and returns to the United States.

This story of an enslaved American soldier who visits Liangshan in China during the time of the War of Resistance has some reference to reality: He was most likely a member of General Claire Chennault's Flying Tigers, who helped the Nationalist Government of China during the war of resistance against the Japanese. Unluckily, he finds himself in a remote area and is enslaved. Being alone and isolated, it is never easy for him to flee. He is worked like an animal and exploited and barely manages to survive. During his enslavement, a female slave, Niu Niu, becomes interested in him. However, she is distressed when she sees him do the make-up for the master's daughter. He is accused of '*touji*' – literally, 'stealing chicken' – that is, of secretly having affairs with girls, specifically the daughter of the master. That is a violation of the clan's rules: '*touniu touyang, bukeyi touji*' (literally, 'it is all right to steal cows or sheep but never chickens'). He is thus punished by having his body hung up. Later, Niu Niu gets married and has children; not long afterwards her husband dies. She meets the man again, their affections are reignited, and they move in together. At this moment, he is discovered by the People's Liberation Army and released. The affection between the couple, which is based on empathy for their shared experience as slaves, is depicted in a subtle and sentimental manner.

Red Dust is a film that portrays the unstable epoch of the war of resistance against Japan and the civil war in China between the Nationalists and the Communists. Heedless of the advice of her friends and of social norms, the heroine, Shen Siu-wah (Brigitte Lin), falls in love with Cheung Nan-choi (Qin Han), a cultural official of the puppet regime under the Japanese. While knowing clearly that this love is hopeless, Lin nevertheless commits to the relationship without any regrets. After the surrender of the Japanese army, Qin escapes to a village. Lin arrives shortly afterwards and discovers that Qin has another lover. Devastated, Lin returns to Shanghai. She loses confidence in Qin who is self-centred, disloyal and without goals, but she finally helps him to flee the country. In the end, she perishes during the chaotic years of the new regime. It is as Qin said in a voice-over, when he returned to search for Lin, 'She exchanged her life for mine. In her time of greatest despair, she was alone. Perhaps the sole consolation is that the whole nation suffered together with her.'

It is said that Yim Ho and San Mao (the scriptwriter) got the idea for this film from the love story between the novelist Zhang Ailing and a Chinese traitor during the period of

Japanese occupation, Hu Lancheng.[5] This film can be considered Yim's largest-scale film. It integrates romance and the political issues of an epoch. It presents the conflicts between personal love and the nation's future, between personal will and collective will at a time of turbulence. Unlike Yue Feng and her boyfriend who resist the Japanese at the front line, the hero and the heroine pay no heed to the impending peril of the nation and the entire race. Rather, they hide in their world of fantasy, sympathizing with each other and begging for survival. An elegy of a heart-rending romance is created. The film has provoked a great deal of debate.[6] However, under Yim's directing, the plot runs in a natural and smooth manner. Yim uses rich visual language to affirm the true emotions of people in a turbulent era. Particularly remarkable is the depiction of women holding on to love as a remedy for internal conflict. The film also juxtaposes the two most significant periods in China's contemporary history, as expressed through a flamboyant romance. Moreover, it provides a stunning depiction of the youngest daughter's situation in such an important age.[7] In addition, the complicated interiority and a fact/fiction narrative enrich this epic love story.[8] This movie won eight awards in Taipei's Golden Horse Awards in 1990, which proves that it is a significant film in Chinese film history.

In a certain sense, the characters in the *King of Chess*, whether from mainland China or Taiwan, are at the mercy of the environment and the times. The part involving the mainland is set during the period of the riots by the Red Guards. At that time, everything related to capitalist class was denounced and prohibition. Even in a drawing class of art students, the naked human figure is condemned as being in opposition to the tide of history. Such an accusation incites the following bitter response from Yim Ho, the art student: 'From now on, the study of drawing can only take place in a mother's belly.' Young intellectuals are not provided with enough food, which forces them to catch rats to fill their stomachs. They mock themselves by saying that the food is 'swallow's nest stewed with baby pigeons' (an expensive dish) to fantasize about the flavour. They are even arrested when playing chess in their leisure time. In fact, similar things occur in Taipei, in slightly different form. A capitalist society is dominated by the economy. Advertising manipulates every single dimension of people's lives. All forms of consumer behaviour ultimately lead to earning money. Corrupt acts for the purpose of obtaining money are committed: a child who possesses extraordinary power is used to speculate on the stock market, a television station changes the hostess of a programme in order to gain the favour of advertisers, a woman provides sex for the rich man who buys the programme she is in charge of, so as to get the position of hostess. All of these are examples of individuals losing their right to choose and being manipulated and influenced by the situation. This theme is the very essence of these films.

Psychological Trauma and a Return to the Motherland

Homecoming marks a turning point from Yim Ho's *The Extra, The Happening* and *Wedding Bells, Wedding Belles*. There is a transformation from intense action and a fast pace to simplicity and tranquility; from ostentatious spectacles to interior reflection.

The change is a gratifying one. The film is about a Hong Kong lady, Shan-shan (Koo Mei-wah), who returns to her hometown to visit her childhood friends, Ah Chun (Siqin Gaowa) and Hao-chong (Tse Wai-hung), a married couple. The intense emotions stirred up by their reunion develop to an exploration of the discrepancy between two places, on both the mental and material levels. The story offers reflections on interpersonal relationships and on the perplexity of life. From the beginning of Shan-shan's journey, the differences in the material quality of life between Hong Kong and mainland China are made clear, as she is piled into a bus stuffed with chicken coops and other items. Her sudden arrival into the quiet life of Hao-chong and Ah Chun is clearly also the intrusion of an outsider. Even such things as a package of dried pork or a pair of waterproof boots are enough to arouse misunderstanding and jealousy between the couple. The couple's quarrels reach the point where Hao-chong utters the word 'divorce'. Around the big hotels in town, children squabble over the price of a drink. Even a brand-new camera that Shan-shan has brought unconsciously indicates the difference between the two systems in material standard of living. Furthermore, Shan-shan is heavily wounded psychologically. She is a loser in both romance and business. She worked hard to support her younger sister's overseas studies. Who would have imagined that she would one day be engaged in a lawsuit with her sister over the family inheritance? She had come to her home village in search of temporary mental relief. She was about to meet with her childhood companion, Ah Chun, and have a genuine heart-to-heart talk, without scruples and without the need to hide anything. This was something she could not have in Hong Kong. Also in the village was a pair of twins, Hong Gong and Tong Gong, who had returned from Australia. They enjoyed a happy, leisurely life, drinking tea and doing martial arts exercises. Truly, a picture of utopia. Shan-shan's encounters with these people and with events in the village were profitable. She became more at ease in her mind and more tolerant towards life. This could be seen in her farewell with Ah Chun.

This movie depicts ordinary people, everyday events and country scenes. Employing a very static mode of shooting, the film has an uncommon, subtle vitality. 'Under the influence of Yasujiro Ozu, I understand that aesthetics can be produced by motionlessness. Why couldn't we make the film more "Chinese", conveying a feeling similar to that of Chinese poetry or paintings?'[9] It can be said that *Homecoming* is a reflection of the director's changing attitude towards life, which came as a reaction to the death of his father. It is a mental journey about departing Hong Kong and returning to China.[10] Yim has claimed that Shan-shan is a reflection of himself, while Ah Chun represents the scriptwriter Hong Leung. Yim has adopted a prose style and has not emphasized dramatic structure as an entirety. Furthermore, he has taken a subtle, static approach to reveal the discrepancy between the material and the mental, the backward and the advanced, the rural and the urban. The images show the many facets of real life and allow the different life situations to tell their own story. The audience is allowed to come to their own conclusion. The director has shifted from, in his early days, the expression of the vigorous emotional rhythms of marginalized youth to, in the present day, quiet and peaceful representations of the philosophy of life and discernment of events in this world. This is a great leap in Yim's film-making journey.

Responsibility for One's Own Fate, the Mastery of the Self and a Desire for Transcendence

Since *Homecoming,* Yim Ho has addressed such themes as relationships and survival/death (the death of Shan-shan's mother-in-law). Subjects of a similar philosophical nature are found in *The Day the Sun Turned Cold* and *The Sun Has Ears,* which were filmed in China. The difference is that the two more recent films are no longer about losses in life but are about such optimistic sentiments as commitment and, thus, control over life. Set in a village in northern China, *The Day the Sun Turned Cold* was adapted from a literary report. It describes a son (Tou Chung-wah) who is accusing his mother of having murdered his father ten years ago. In the end, both his mother and her lover (now her second husband) were judged to be guilty and sentenced to death. The mother was actually a victim of arranged marriage. She was married to the principal of an elementary school, and the relationship was a loveless one. However, she gave birth to several children. It can be said that she was unable to escape from fate, and that she was destined to lead such life until her death. China's marriage law stipulates the freedom of divorce; but in practice, it is not that easy. Pressure from traditional morals and society, and the breakdown of the family, all need to be taken into consideration. Once, quite by chance, a lumberman saves the male protagonist (the son) and his mother, and develops feelings for the mother. In the end, the mother poisons her husband to death and then marries this lumberman.

Her act of poisoning her husband to death has far-reaching consequences. But in fact, this tragedy is largely due to the mother's role of victim under traditional moral codes, a closed culture and social imprisonment. Put another way, she finally stopped being an object of sacrifice and of fate and strove to be the master of her own fate and life. In the film, the mother says to the son, 'When I was small, the fortune-teller spoke of my bitter life. Bitterness can be produced even if it is absent.' This shows that her character was not one to be restricted by pressure and destiny. She eventually breaks through her constraints, even though the consequences were tragic – a death sentence.

As for the son's act in accusing his mother, it is not about a so-called clash between love and the law, but in fact an exemplification of the father-son blood relationship. The son's act is an inevitable consequence of a notion in Chinese traditional culture that is so orthodox as to be unbreakable. When considering whether or not to accuse his mother, the son is locked in the dilemma of knowing that he will betray either his father or his mother. His son's betrayal of his mother shows that he is influenced by the traditional culture, which holds patriarchy is an orthodox value. In the process of learning the present-day laws in order to accuse his mother and pursue the truth about his father's death, what he in fact protects is orthodoxy of traditional patriarchy.

The story is set in a poor, snow-covered village in northern China with a very realistic feel. The simple and conservative culture provides a convincing site for the happenings. The narration of events unfolds layer by layer, starting with the son's accusation of his mother. Then, the method of flashback is used to narrate his family's situation and the relationship between parents when he was a child, her mother's encounter with the adulterer, his mother's murder of his father and, lastly, the judgement. In fact, none of the characters, including the father, the mother, the lumberman and the male protagonist, is a villain. In a certain sense, each of them is a victim in particular circumstances. As ordinary people, when events occur, each one suffers. The mother and the adulterer are sentenced to death to take responsibility for their deed. The mother eventually can bravely accept it, whereas the son still suffers greatly. The causes leading to the murder could have been of many kinds: social, legal, moral, sensual.... This exactly demonstrates the ambivalent circumstances of the human world, filled as it is with the incomprehensible, unpredictable and complex. 'The perspective of humanity is always the starting point. To observe the complexity of humanity is our focus.'[11] This is the starting point of this film. It displays the original face of human beings in a real society in order to inspire the audience to think. This is the deeper meaning that this film hopes to convey.

Another film, *The Sun Has Ears* (1996), that gained acclaim in international film festivals but that had only two screenings in Hong Kong[12] has similar themes – people are manipulated by fate but can eventually break through the constraints of fatalism to regain the self. As with several of Yim's previous works, this film is set in mainland China. In this case, the setting is the 1920s, a period of military division. Of Yim's films, this is the one that deals most with legend. *The Sun Has Ears* is about a strong woman, Yau Yau (Cheung Yu). Married to an extremely ordinary man, Yau Yau lives an impoverished life, forced even to borrow food to survive. One day, a young military officer, who is also the bandit Poon Ho, shows up at her door. He has lent her food in the past and that night he rapes her. Later, Yau Yau's husband mortgages her to Poon for ten days. Unexpectedly, Yau Yau secretly falls in love with her creditor. Poon does not change his bandit ways. He participates in kidnappings, even killing a little girl who has been held hostage. Exactly on the day he is promoted to commander-in-chief, Yau Yau, driven by fury, kills him. Her fate is limited by her condition of poverty. Add to that a husband who is stupid and useless, Yau Yau is forced to commit her life to Poon, who has wealth and power. Interestingly, she develops feelings for Poon. There is a sentimental scene of Yau Yau making noodles for Poon. From then on, she is committed to Poon and becomes his concubine. This is the result of destiny. Yau Yau's husband reports Poon's iniquities. Surprisingly, he is recognized by Poon's senior, Captain Chan, and promoted by him to Vice Captain. Apart from the idea of human beings as the playthings of fate, the film also exposes corruption and malice in the military. In the second half of the movie, Yau Yau is already disillusioned with Poon's banditry and fierce ambitions. After Poon shoots a little girl to death, he takes Yau Yau and jumps on a horse, galloping away into the snowy woods. Poon expresses the desire to rear their future son as a 'wolf' – so that he would frighten everybody. Yau

Yau loses hope in him. Furious, she pushes Poon off the horse. Poon's head crashes against a tree trunk, and he bleeds to death. Yau Yau's deed prevents Poon from inflicting more troubles on the world. At the same time, she is able to turn the situation around, and to take control over her life.

Adapted from the novel *Kitchen*, a work by a Japanese popular writer, Yoshimoto Banana, the film version, under the same title, alters the narrator's point of view from a female one to a male (Jordan Chan Siu-chun) one. Through the eyes of Chan, the themes of life, death and uncertainty are examined, in the hope of attaining a kind of spiritual transcendence. Since *Wedding Bells, Wedding Belles*, Yim has made six films in mainland China. Now, he returns to Hong Kong. Such a cycle is reminiscent of the romance between the film's two main characters, Jordan Chan and Tomita Yasuko. After going halfway around the globe, they meet again in Hong Kong, which can be said to be the final shelter of their love.

At the start of the film, Yasuko's beloved grandmother dies. She is in utmost despair. Fortunately, she is taken care of by Chan, a friend of Yasuko's grandmother, as well as by Law Kar-ying, Chan's father who is disguised as a mother. She is then gradually able to recover. At the same time, Law Kar-ying suddenly commits suicide. This darkens Chan's world. He exiles himself to the mainland (Yim Ho's unbreakable connection with China). Yasuko also leaves for Europe to study cooking. Her desire to study cooking is related to her love of the kitchen since her childhood. The kitchen is the most ordinary, practical and warm of spaces, and is where life begins. Undeniably, it is a sign of the organic. Yasuko declared that she is able to detect the arrival of rain even before the observatory issues its forecast. The smell of rain emanates from clouds, soil, cement, the walls of buildings and the air. A person can sense it only if he/she has experienced the ups and downs of life, failures and the loss of someone very close. The film attempts to illuminate human existence on both the practical and spiritual levels. This is also seen in the return of the protagonists, their commitment to life, and their courage in facing the future. These messages are sufficient to make the film Yim Ho's most positive work.

Camera Movements and *Mise-en-scène*

There are many ways to practice camera movements. Yim Ho chooses to move the camera synchronously with the performers. Retaining the principle of smoothness, movements of this sort convey a sense of naturalness in motion. This can be seen in the opening sequence of *Seventeen:* 1977 at the Star Ferry Pier. The very first shots are about flagpoles, a poster on the wall of the magazine *Art Life*, the arrival of a ferry at the pier and the emergence of Clifton Ko.

1. A medium shot, by hand-held, of Ko doing a street survey.
2. A medium shot of another character, Lee Tong, walking and carrying a cassette player.
3. A medium shot of Ko continuing his survey with another interviewee.

4. A medium shot, with the camera following Lee, who comes forth to interview a passer-by.
5. A long shot of a ferry arriving at the pier.
6. A medium shot where the camera follows Ko passing by Lee, who is conducting a survey; at a farther point onward, somebody enters, his back to the camera, carrying a pile of *Playboy* magazines and walking toward the newspaper stand.
7. A close-up of Ko, moving from the right and across the lens, stopping Lee Wing, the man who is carrying the magazines, to ask for his opinion about the living environment in Hong Kong. These seven shots give a clear explanation of Yim Ho's movements with the camera and the characters. Ko and Lee, two individuals having no point of intersection, are both placed in the sixth shot. Then, in the seventh one, Ko happens to interview Lee – this is the first formal face-to-face interaction between them. More noteworthy, Lee is an intellectual but is carrying a stack of *Playboy* magazines. At the same time, he is full of discontent about the faults of the colonial government and certain unfair situations. He is an archetype of the inconsistency and lack of determination of the small intellectuals in the capitalist class. Often, they are easily frustrated by setbacks and thus give up their aspirations. Quite a few shots are used in this story. The characters introduced in a natural way and hints are given about their ways of thinking.

It is not uncommon in Yim's movies for characters to be introduced in this kind of natural, succinct manner. Take, for example, the scene of the encounter between Yau Yau and Poon Ho from *The Sun Has Ears*. The female protagonist, Yau Yau (Cheung Yu), collects water from a river. From the opposite side, the cries of a horse are heard. Yau Yau looks up and finds Poon arriving along the river on a horse. She gazes at him as he leaves at a gallop. The next shot shows Yau Yau carrying pails of water on the way back home and Poon, on his horse, following her. The faster she walks, the more closely he chases her, until they reach Yau Yau's home. With several shots, the film presents the encounter between the two characters, the mobster-like personality of the military official-bandit Poon and Yau Yau's mixed feelings of happiness and fear. Yim's earlier film, *Wedding Bells, Wedding Belles*, also adopted a natural and economical manner to show the encounter between the hero and the heroine. Chow and Ha drive to the boat shelter. The car knocks Tai Shui down. Ha carries Tai in his arms. Tai Shui recognizes him and faints. From this it can be seen that the buck-toothed Tai Shui is fascinated and captivated by the good-looking Ha.

The coupling of the two types of movements, the camera and the characters, and the interaction between the characters, are Yim's most skilful *mise-en-scène* techniques applied in one scene. Occasionally, Yim will stop using a combination of various shots and instead use one long take. In this way, a continued realistic mood can be captured, down to the smallest detail of emotional response. In *The Sun Has Ears*, Yau Yau was mortgaged by her husband to Poon, and she is making noodles for Poon at his place. At that moment, Poon approaches Yau Yau and stands behind her. After a medium shot of their faces, the director cuts to a close-up of Poon's hands covering Yau Yau's as, together, they feed the dough into the mill. Their hands slowly move the mill and press the shaft that turns the dough into noodles. This shot shows a strong symbol of the male and female sex organs. The camera only exhibits a close-up of their hands, but the shot is rich with implied meaning. A similar shot is found in *The Day the Sun Turned Cold*. After the judgement is announced, the son visits his mother in jail. Sitting opposite to each other, the son gives her a fruit, but she rejects it. He then offers her a cigarette, and she responds in the same way. From a close-up of the son lighting a tobacco pipe, the camera slides to rest on the mother's face, which has turned to the right. The camera follows the son's hand that is holding the pipe. Slowly, the son puts his hand down. Then, the camera reveals the bleeding, handcuffed hands of the mother, which are resting on her knees. With both of his hands, the son immediately presses on his mother's hands. The close-ups shift in perfect tempo as the actions change. The mother's sufferings are vividly shown through the lens. The son also suffers, as the comfort he has offered her is rejected. The disharmony of the relationship and the emotions of nervousness and frustration are appropriately manifested solely by this kind of highly sensitive arrangement. These sorts of shots are repeated in *No Sun City*. The female protagonist, Yip Sun, is an undercover cop. She is exchanging gunfire with the members of a gang. While pursuing the criminals, she comes across a crazy man who possesses black magic powers. Yip's hand that is holding a pistol is suddenly bent back so that she nearly shoots herself. She has no control over the hand holding the gun, which now turns to point at her stomach. The scene shows the power of the black magic, which triumphs over righteousness.

Narration, Subtitles, Intersection of Time and Space, and Complicated Narratives

In his mastery of montage, Yim has a style of his own (exemplified in, for instance, an eating scene on a train in *King of Chess*, where a character tries to remove a grain of rice that has fallen into a crack in the table). This style can be seen, in particular, in the capturing of people's responses, in the interaction between the camera and the characters and in the adjustments made within a scene. Since *Red Dust*, Yim Ho has changed from employing a direct, plain mode of narration based on a chronological sequence to a more complicated type of narration. For example, in the opening sequence, Cheung Nan-choi (Qin Han) is shown telling us that he has become acquainted with Siu-wah through her father. The fiction written by Siu-wah involves a character called Yuk-lan. Yuk-lan loses her parents when she is young and is sold to an old man as a servant. After being raped by the old man, Yuk-lan becomes pregnant. Later, she marries a young man, Chun-mong. The fictional portion, which appears six times, is merged with Siu-wah's own story and becomes part of the plot of the film. Such a mode of narration is rarely found in mainland Chinese films. Moreover, Cheung's narration is heard until the very last moment of the film. But in the middle of the movie Siu-wah's narration also breaks in. It is a conversation she has with Cheung while dancing with him on a balcony on the eve of Japan's surrender. Hence, the narrative style of this film is very complex. This unusual style is appropriate for use in large-scale epics. Since then, Yim has paid special attention on the establishment of a narrative style. Focusing on the dimensions of time and space, the director presents an intersecting occurrence of two events: the son going to court to accuse his mother, and the entire process of the mother poisoning her husband to death ten years ago. A total reversal of time and space is seen throughout the whole movie. A series of past events – the hostile relationship between the parents when the protagonist was young, how his mother and his stepfather met, the secret affair between them and its discovery by the son, as well as the report he made of it to his father, the father's punishment of his mother, the mother's poisoning of the soup, the father's death caused by the poison, the mother's marriage with her new lover – is cross-cut with events of the present – the accusation leveled against the mother, the arrival of the police in the village to conduct an investigation, the announcement of the mother's innocence, the transfer of the case to the provincial court, the exhumation of the dead body for examination, and, finally, the pronouncement of the death penalty for the mother and the stepfather. Such construction differs from the mere insertion of 'memory' in a particular part of the plot, which is common in other movies.

A combination of narration and subtitles is employed in *The Sun Has Ears*. The narration takes place at the close of the film. The murder of the bandit-soldier Poon Ho is immediately followed by the closing scene, showing a mud house from which the cries of an infant are emanating. Yau Yau's daughter begins a narration, explaining that the story in the film had been told to her by her mother and that the events are likely to have been fictional, as they are chaotic beyond belief. 'My mother hums a beautiful melody whenever she sees the sun. The melody is so fascinating that the sun is attracted to it....' There are reasons for having a narration at this point. First, to present the fact that Yau Yau has a daughter who is already living her own life; second, it is to explain the title of the film. Nonetheless, subtitles appear four times. The film opens with 'the chaotic battles of the 1920s', and an explanation is given of the background to the story. Then, after a medium close-up of the hero and the heroine, the following words appear: 'different insights will be earned after the digestion of certain occurrences'. These words are those of the director, apparently narrated by the female protagonist or her daughter. The ambivalence and plural possibilities of narrative are thus reinforced, constituting part of the structure. The style of the narration is also formulaic. In the film, the same images are repeated so that one part of the film echoes another part. For example, after the opening credits of *The Sun Has Ears*, there is a medium close-up of Yau Yau and Poon Ho. Poon stands behind Yau Yau, touching her tenderly. A similar image reappears in the noodle-making sequence in Poon's house. This sort of replication is also perceived in the opening of the *Kitchen*. Raindrops are falling in the sea and Jordan Chan's narration is heard, 'The granddaughter of my friend Aggie is strange. It is hard to tell whether the things she says are true or false....' Next comes a shot of a human head gradually coming to the surface of the sea. When the film ends, Chan is reunited with Yasuko. The scene is of a dim sky with rain. Raindrops fall on the surface of the water, and a human head is floating. This technique, called 're-represented montage', can be used to accentuate impressions and to echo the beginning of the film.

The narration in *Kitchen* is the first-person narration of Jordan Chan. Except for the beginning and the end, it is employed at various points throughout the film. In addition, after Chan's mother, Law Kar-ying, commits suicide, the letter she has left behind for her son is read out as her narration, '...If anything unfortunate happens to me, it will have been an accident. Do not be vexed by that. Life is about learning to handle many things: survival, old age, sickness, death, and being a man or a woman....' Apparently, the letter is about Law Kar-ying's thoughts on confronting oneself and loving others. The shot shifts from Yasuko to Law, who is writing the letter. As the narration is completed, the camera cuts back to Yasuko, who starts to smell and look about her, just as if she is sensing the return of Law. She picks up Law's letter and smells it and begins to shed tears. She then carefully puts the letter away and hugs herself. At at moment, Jordan Chan jumps and shouts, 'I am happy!' It is as if he has seen through life and death, and is now free from worry. The rest of the narration is about Chan swearing loyalty to his ex-girlfriend, about his feelings towards his dead mother, and his desire for a kind of spirituality that transcends the self and time/space. With the reunion of the two protagonists, the film projects feelings of optimism and hope.

Notes

1. Yim Hing-shu once worked as the editor-in chief of the leftist newspaper *Xinwanbao*. He was also a novelist. He became famous for his work *Jinling chunmeng*, written under a pseudonym.
2. Lui King-sheun. 'I see "Seventeen: 1977" and "My Glamour"',* *Hong Kong Cinema and Social Changes*. 12th Hong Kong International Film Festival. HK: Urban Council. 31 March – 15 April 1988, p. 36.
3. Shu Kei. 'The Last Declaration of "*The Happening*"'. *City Entertainment*. No. 32, 1980, p. 17.
4. Liu Fang, Chen Ziliang. 'Fangwen Yan Ho' (interviewing Yim Ho). *Zhongwai Yinghua* (Chinese-Western Motion Pictures). March 1986, p. 27.
5. During the period of Japanese occupation, Hu Lancheng served as the leader of the Cultural Department of the puppet regime. He fled to Japan after the war. He wrote a number of books, and *Jinsheng jinshi* (This Life) was one of them.
6. The film aroused controversy in Taiwan. The claim was that Chinese traitors were being eulogized and that the film was a hostile, false portrayal of the Nationalist Government.
7. Sam Ho. *Dangdai GangTai dianying 1988–1992* (Contemporary Hong Kong and Taiwan Cinema 1988–1992). Vol. I. Huang Wulan ed. Taipei renjian congshu. Taipei Times Press. 6 December 1992, p. 212.
8. Wong, Alvin. Ibid., p. 212.
9. Pak Tong Cheuk, Law Kar, Cheung Chi-shing. 'Interviews with 14 Film and Television Auteurs.' *Hong Kong New Wave Cinema – After Twenty Years.* 23rd Hong Kong International Film Festival. Hong Kong Temporary Urban Council. 31 March – 15 April 1999, p. 151.
10. Leung Nong-kong. 'Two self-reflections in Hong Kong Cinema as seen from the Chinese context in *China Behind* and *Homecoming*: In worrying in the melancholy of the past, is it possible to see Hong Kong in an idealized light?' *The Chinese Context in Hong Kong Cinema*. 14th Hong Kong International Film Festival. 6—21 April 1990, p. 70.

11. Lee Kin-wah. 'Interview with Yim Ho.' *Sing Tao Evening Post*. 16 October 1994, p. 25.
12. This film earned the Silver Bear Award for Best Director in the Berlin Film Festival in 1996. It was shown in Hong Kong just twice: 1. in a screening for film scholars from around the world, held on 17 September 1996 in the Academic Hall of the Hong Kong Baptist University for the First International Symposium on Chinese-language Films, organized by the university's Department of Cinema-Television; 2. in a screening at the Hong Kong Arts Centre on 27 December 1998.

7

Allen Fong

Allen Fong was born in Hong Kong in 1947. He attended the School of Communications of Baptist University (previously Baptist College). He continued his studies at the University of Georgia in the United States in 1971, majoring in broadcasting, television and film. He then earned his master's degree in Film Production (MFA) at the University of Southern California in 1975. After returning to Hong Kong, he joined the television unit of Radio Television Hong Kong (RTHK). He worked as an assistant director and was then promoted to a director. During this time, he participated in the projects *Below the Lion Rock*, the most notable episodes of which were *The Wild Child* and *The Story of Yuen Chau Chai* (both in 1977). The former episode won an international award.[1] In 1979, he switched to the film industry. He has directed six films, namely *Father and Son* (1981), *Ah Ying* (1982), *Just Like Weather* (1986), *Dancing Bull* (1990), *A Little Life – Opera* (1998) and *Tibetan Tao* (2000).

Realistic Style

Starting from his television days – or, rather, from the period when he studied film, Fong was particularly fond of documentaries and realistic subject matter in films. This was evident in his master's graduation project, which was a real record of a stilt walker's life. Containing no plot, it was a mere documentary that he shot with his camera in the streets of Los Angeles. This kind of documentary-like style was retained in his later works *The Wild Child* and *The Story of Yuen Chau Chai* that he produced for the television unit of RTHK. In these two dramas, he re-interpreted unjust incidents in society and caught the public's attention. These qualities are related to Fong's studies in the School of Communications at Baptist College, 'After all, I come from the fields of journalism and communications, and am thus persuaded by the idea that journalism is related to social conscience, which should involve the just, objective disclosure of social ills.'[2] This sheds light on his choice of realistic subject matter and the documentary form. Moreover, such influences even extended to the creative direction of his later works. He thus became an independent, distinctive artist in the Hong Kong film industry. A rarity among his mainstream counterparts, he has stuck to his principles, continuously come up with innovations and taken film-making as a way of experimenting and questioned the relationship between film and reality.

The Wild Child tells the story of a little boy, Ah Hoi. His father is always away piloting boats. His mother also needs to work, and therefore has no time to care for him. He is sent to his grandmother's home and spends all day playing with other children. With the exception of quite a few minor characters such as the grandmother and the mother, who are professional actors, the child actors are all amateurs. The settings are actual locations, such as the stone house, the hill, the graveyard and the rock pool. A handful of events are described from the point of view of Ah Hoi. For example, the children playing at war, earning some pocket money by helping visitors to the graveyard carry things and arranging and watering flowers for them, beating a snake, hitting a drug addict and the burial of the grandmother. The film is full of bleak images related to death: the graveyard, the death of animals such as a snake and a tortoise, as well as the death of human beings, including the grandmother and the drug addict, and the crows that fly in the sky. 'Since the beginning of their lives, those children have had the experience of burying the dead.'[3] A gloomy future for them is hinted at. The only hope in such bleakness is found in Ah Hoi's naivety. His innocent eyes dilute the gloomy atmosphere, illustrating the vitality of youth, which counteracts the misery of death. The film is heavily autobiographical, as is Fong's subsequent work, *Father and Son*.

Apart from the realistic style, *The Story of Yuen Chau Chai* opens our eyes to societal concerns, addressing as it does such issues as the survival of fishermen and the living environment. The film is set in Yuen Chau Chai in Tai Po, which has now been demolished, and was shot on location. The boat people there live in a vile environment. Snakes and rats appear, mud and dirty water spring up, insects breed, and there is no running water and toilet facilities. The old fishermen can barely survive by collecting seaweed. Living in a poor family, the son in the film, Ah Shing (Kwok Feng), uneducated and jobless, is keen on gambling. He loses the money that has been borrowed for domestic expenses on the betting table. With many children, food is scarce, and everything is devoured right after being served. There are no televisions, air conditioners or even electric fans at home. Every one sweats and is sleepless on hot nights. The unhygienic conditions make Yuen Chau Chai no place to live. However, the government is unconcerned about helping the fishermen improve their lives. The film exposed the face of poverty in society and drew the attention of the public. In doing so, it achieved the goal of changing the people's lives for the better.

In the closing sequence, Wong Sa-li tries to stop her husband, Kwok, from taking the housekeeping money to gamble, but is pushed to the ground. Later, she alone helps to bathe their son, who is covered in dirt and sweat. At that moment, two foreigners arrive, taking photographs. They are surrounded by children begging for money. They see Wong and immediately point their cameras at her. Amidst the continuous noise of the cameras clicking away is a close-up of Wong's helpless, frustrated face. The image freezes and the film ends. The foreigners regard Wong as a member of a backward nationality and as a subject to be photographed. The composition and inspiration (*fu er xing*) at the end of the narrative is full of political force.[4] Employing a plain style with nothing sensational, this drama reveals the desperate lives of the fishermen. No one cares about them or pays them any mind, with the exception of the curious foreigners. From what is displayed through the lens of his camera, the director's sincerity and social conscience are evident.

Personal Experience and the Father-Son Relationship

Allen Fong's first film, *Father and Son*, is about family ethics, focusing particularly on the father-son relationship. The film is strongly autobiographical. It is about a father who, hoping that his son will stand out among his peers, endures hardship and bitterness and even sacrifices the future of his two daughters. He sends his son to the United States to earn money, and thereby fulfils his lifelong wish. The film inherits the excellent tradition of realistic films about family ethics in Hong Kong in the 1950s and 1960s, such as Wu Hui's *Father and Son* (1954), which portrays a father who works as an ordinary employee, who also has high hopes for his son. He endures great hardship to send his son to an exclusive school; however, they are looked down upon and ridiculed by the wealthy children. Later, the father changes his mind and transfers his son to a school attended by ordinary children. There, among people of their own class, they are accepted and treated with kindness and consideration. Another 1950s film, Qin Jian's *Parents' Heart* (1955), depicts a poor father whose deepest desire is to have his son receive a good education and develop his talents so that he will one day be a useful member of society. The film communicates the greatness, tolerance and forgiving nature of the father. Apart from retaining a concern for society - depicting issues of ethics and problems with education - Fong's *Father and Son* depicts a generation that dares to express dissatisfaction with the older generation and to express their own opinions. This is where his films differ from those of the 1950s and 1960s. It is also shows a kind of progress for Fong.

Of course, this film is not against traditional ethical values, nor does it advocate a rupture from tradition. Breaking from convention has never been Fong's intention, nor, in a broad sense, that of the New Wave directors. They are not revolutionaries, but innovators. They have inherited the traditions of Hong Kong cinema, but have added their own insights, values and a fresh cinematic language. They have devoted their various talents to developing Hong Kong cinema. This is exactly the meaning and contribution of the New Wave. *Father and Son* focuses on the characters, supplemented with rich everyday details and fragments in order to highlight the father's concern for family, especially his son. Furthermore, the conflict between the father and the son is illustrated. Having no interest in studying, the son is transferred from one school to another, for a total of five times. The father patiently advises him to study hard, because even the younger sister who performs well academically has been forced to terminate her schooling and work as a nurse to earn money. She expresses her discontent by cutting her hair. The elder sister is asked to marry early, and to find a husband who will be able to support the son's studies in the United States. This indicates that the father has placed all of his hopes for himself and for the entire family solely onto his son. The naïve son, however, wants to quit school. He hopes to work in a theatre for two purposes: to watch movies and make money. He also dreams of being hired by a television station. There are some more incidents showing the son's aspirations. He puts on a rear-projected shadow show at a friend's home and sets the curtains on fire. Also, together with a companion, he steals the dollars collected from selling flags in order to buy movie tickets and to shoot experimental films. As the son is going completely against the hopes of his father, conflicts are inevitable, although the film closes with a scene of reconciliation. Informed by the school about the theft of money, the father fiercely cuffs his son on the way home, and the son's nose begins to bleed. The father does not stop hitting him until passers-by intercede. But the son at last runs to his father and holds his hand; they walk home together. The storms are over, and father and son are reconciled. Once, the father falls ill and is hospitalized. The son collects a bunch of wild flowers from the hill for him. Visiting his father who is asleep, the son makes him more comfortable by undoing the buttons of his shirt. Standing beside his father's bed, the son's love is clear. In another sequence, the son is unhappy that his father has publicly requested support for his oversea studies from the son-in-law. The son angrily leaves; at the same time, he receives a letter from the television station containing an offer of employment. It is raining; he fantasizes that he is commanding a troop of Japanese soldiers to execute his father, who is tied up. His father collapses. Then, he uses a revolver and personally shoots one bullet into his father's head. The son's dissatisfaction and hatred toward his father is discharged by means of the violence in his unconscious mind. It is a psychological venting of his rage. Returning to reality, he sees his father walking towards him. He tears up the offer of employment and goes back home with his father. This symbolizes a resolution of the father-son conflict. He has cast aside his dream of being an actor and is submitting to his father's will, to fulfill his father's wish to see his son achieve success.

The story is set in the 1960s and 1970s. More than a backdrop to the father-son conflict, the setting is also a very realistic depiction of the times. In the 1960s, the family of the main character lives in a squatter hut. The terrible living environment is a sign of the father's upbringing – he is poorly educated, unable to speak English and, therefore, can only find a mediocre job. In order to maintain a large family, it is necessary to practice frugality. He even takes toilet paper from his workplace – and he is not the only one in the company to do so. Furthermore, he cannot afford costly toys for his son. In the 1970s, the slum they are living in burns down. The family is moved to a temporary settlement, arranged by the government for low-income groups. There is a slight improvement in their living conditions in that their shelter is more resistant to storms and rain. However, their home is still extremely crowded, right up until the moment when the son returns from studying overseas. Although the film focuses on the conflict between father and son instead of on social issues, we are still able to make out the social conditions of Hong Kong in the 1960s and 1970s, and how they have directly or indirectly affected the relationships in a family and the family's future.

The Struggles of Women, Love and Family

To Allen Fong, every film is evidence of his feelings and of his urge to express them. The death of his father was a source of inspiration, and the friends around him were another. *Father and Son* triggered a desire to create a memoir of his father; likewise, the creation of *Ah Ying* was motivated by a similar impulse brought about by the death of a friend.[5] This friend's name is Go Mo. He had returned from the United States to Hong Kong to make a film. However, his employer placed various constraints on him. The film-making project failed and Go Mo fell ill and died. The narrative of *Ah Ying* centres on the protagonist Cheung Chong-pak (Wong Fong-ching playing the real-life Go Mo), who is teaching drama at the Centre of Film Culture during his stay in Hong Kong. The female main character, Ah Ying, is his student. She has a boyfriend, but he does not really love her. They later break up. She develops an affection for Cheung, and the understanding between them grows. In making this film, Fong also took the realistic route, basing it on an actual case. Where this film differs from *Father and Son* is that the latter is an autobiographical re-creation of the director. At certain times, a kind of impromptu filming technique is employed, which is a large step forward for Fong's narrative mode.

The focus of *Ah Ying* is on the life of the female protagonist, Ah Ying, and her family. Her parents run a fish stall in a market, and Ah Ying is the only child helping them in the business. One can say that Ah Ying is the epitome of a female lower-class worker, earning a mere 500 dollars each month. The working environment is not a pleasant one: it is damp, full of the stink of fish, crowded and noisy. All of this conjures up the picture of a disgusting, smelly street scene. Her home is similarly unpleasant. It is so crowded that only bunk beds can be used. She is not even able to find the space to enjoy music quietly. When she hopes to leave such repressive surroundings, her drama teacher Cheung intrudes in her life. From Cheung, she is introduced to another way of living. The wonders of film and drama help her to understand the close relationship between drama and life. As the friendship gradually grows, Cheung has to return to the United States, putting an end to the relationship. Yet Cheung's appearance is undeniably a force motivating her to go forward, and prompting her to recognize the value of life. Perhaps, as Allen Fong has said, 'Like yeast, he [Cheung] functions as a catalyst.'[6] He influences Ah Ying. And then he leaves.

Ah Ying's journey of love was also rough. She and her ex-boyfriend, Ah Hung, are emblematic of the present-day philosophy of the love of teenagers – to be daring and passionate. However, after the initial period of fervour, the relationship died down. Having no intention of shouldering responsibilities and being restricted, Ah Hung initiates a break-up. Although Ah Ying is fully committed to the relationship, she knows that this broken bond cannot be mended. Thus, she can only bravely confront the fact. Hers is a typical Chiu-chau family, where patriarchy holds sway. She is the only one among the siblings to help her elderly father with his fish stall, taking some of the burden from him. She longs to get away from this kind of life. However, in the end, she splits up with her boyfriend and Cheung returns to the US, and she returns to her life of selling fish. From her departure to her return, Ah Ying undergoes internal struggles. The ending shows Ah Ying at the fish stall, receiving a call from the television station to come in for a second interview. This is reminiscent of the ending of *Father and Son*, in which the son receives an offer of employment from the television station. The director, here, provides an open-ended closure, Ah Ying might attend the interview or she might remain in the fish stall. The film closes with a freeze shot of her smile.

Ah Ying had quite an impact on society, not just because of its realistic or heavily autographical narrative, but also because of the style that the director adopted. Many scenes were shot in a most genuine and natural fashion, without any pre-shooting arrangements. Except for the character of Cheung, all of the actors were amateurs playing themselves. This manner of handling characters was an avant-garde approach in Hong Kong cinema and will be elaborated upon in a later section.

Ah Ying does not contain so-called big meanings or particularly creative ideas or stories. Rather, the story is ordinary, even clichéd, with such themes as love, family ethics, the father-daughter relationship and so on. However, the film's value and meaning lie in the highly realistic ways in which everyday details are represented. The Chinese title of the film, literally 'Half of a Human', implies that everyone has many facets to them, and heartfelt desires that can never be completely fulfilled. If half of these desires are achieved, this would already be quite satisfactory.[7] Even if the film were to show only half of each person, as long as that half is a person's genuine self, the significance would already not be the same.

The transformation of the focus from the father in *Father and Son*, to friends in *Ah Ying*, and then to romance in *Just Like Weather*, shows Allen Fong's journey in film-making, which went from portrayals of the self, then of friends and, lastly, of other people. Although his films start with himself, they extend to other people who have undergone similar experiences. This is evidence of the broadening of Fong's vision. As an artist with a social conscience, Fong extends his feelers to the larger society, and his vision is also one of tolerance. Most importantly, he does not lose a sense of self and holds fast to his own standpoint. In Fong's film-making career of more than twenty years, he has maintained his confidence in the artistry of his films, continually pursuing innovations. Whether with regard to subject matter or to representational style, his hope is to find the way that best suits him of searching for the truth. He is forever questioning himself and correcting himself. Following the success of *Ah Ying, Just Like Weather* was a film made in this spirit of a continuous search for change.

Just Like Weather takes one great step forward from *Ah Ying* in that the male and female protagonists are real characters playing themselves and narrating their own stories. Both are not professional actors, but are only another couple among the millions in Hong Kong. The problems that they encounter in life, such as with work, relationships, family, migration and so forth, are the same as those faced by most other people. It was precisely because of their universality and typicality that the director selected them. Although not a documentary, this film is a reenactment of reality. Blending fact and fiction, Fong made an extremely creative experimental film that won him honours in three consecutive years, breaking the record for the Hong Kong Film Awards.[8]

Crises emerge in the marital relationship of the protagonists, Chan and Li. Dissatisfied with everything, Li hopes for an easier life. The need to make too many decisions is making her fatigued, physically and psychologically. Due to financial pressure, Li is forced to go to Shenzhen to get an abortion. Chan wants to be a driver, but because such an occupation is unstable Li advises him to work for a veterinarian, Mak. However, he is unwilling to do so and prefers to become a salesman in a company that deals in second-hand motors. He is used by his boss as a tool to cheat customers, leading him to be arrested by the police. One night, he sees Doctor Mak offering Li a lift home. Chan feels bitter. On the other hand, he does not want to drag Li into his unfortunate life and considers simply leaving. In order to redeem his increasingly distant relationship with his wife, Chan suggests that they migrate to the United States. But Li rejects the idea because she does not want to abandon her old parents in Hong Kong. As his wife refuses to leave, Chan also does not dare to leave, lest this precipitate a separation. The couple argue incessantly about everyday issues and their future. Later they come to a compromise: both of them will migrate to the United States. The film closes on a harmonious note, with their disputes temporarily settled and their relationship improved.

However, human beings are after all complex emotional beings. A short journey cannot reconcile the fissures in emotion and thought between the couple, particularly in times of despair and hopelessness. In real life, Chan and Li eventually terminated their marriage.[9]

Holding Fast to Dreams and the Bitterness of Love

Women feature prominently in most of Allen Fong's films, with *Father and Son* being the exception. Examples are Hui So-ying in *Ah Ying*, Li Yuk-kuen in *Just Like Weather*, Cora Miu Hin-yan in *Dancing Bull* and Yeung Kwai-mei (Ah Suet) in *A Little Life – Opera*, all of whom have strong personalities and their own points of view. Both of the protagonists in *Dancing Bull* and *A Little Life – Opera* are artists; the former is a dancer who runs a dance club, while the latter is the lead actor in a theatre troop. In *Dancing Bull*, Miu is competent, determined, tough and passionate about dancing. Originally a reporter, she joined a demonstration to oppose films that tarnish religion. When her uncle refused to repay the money he owed her, she took a placard and protested at the entrance to his home. She also debated with officials empowered to inspect and approve her dancing club, and went everywhere collecting money from donors to keep the club operating. This shows her passion for dancing. On the other hand, she is also capable of modifying an item in the programme at the request of a sponsor, which shows the accommodating side of her character. However, this act of hers sparked vehement protests from her live-in lover and dancing coach, Anthony Wong, who felt that a sponsor had no right to determine the direction of the club. This also shows the artist's determination. In the end, the lovers separate under various kinds of pressure and for various reasons. Wong returns to his childhood home, Tai O, to live and to work as a teacher. He marries Chan Ling-chi, another dancer. Miu manages the dance club alone and is later given the best artist award in recognition for her contributions to the art of dancing. The film presents the path each individual took to pursue their art, and their confusion and setbacks. In the end, each persisted in his/her own way and made his/her own choices.

In the final sequence of the film, while the filming was taking place, the June 4th Tiananmen Incident occurred. About four million people marched on the streets to oppose the Chinese government's unreasonable suppression of the students in Tiananmen Square. The demonstrators chanted slogans: 'Pay debts of blood with blood!', 'Long live democracy!', 'Democracy will never die, while a tyrannical government must fall!'. The members of the dance club also participated in the protests by performing street dramas satirizing the suppression of the students by the army. The director also appeared among the crowd, marching and shouting slogans. This incident is recorded as part of the film. The participation of the director and actors in the film reflects that, as part of society, they were unable to turn a blind eye to the event. Moreover, it showed that those who work in film and art are no longer hiding in ivory towers and pursuing art for art's sake. Rather, they are also concerned about society and have a social conscience.

Li Yuk-kuen in *Just Like Weather* chooses to get an abortion in Shenzhen due to a financial crisis, while Cora Miu in *Dancing Bull* also gets an abortion in order to develop her career in dance. Although their reasons are different, the choice they make is the same. Similarly, the son in *Father and Son* likes to go to the theater to watch movies. In *Ah Ying*, Cheung's passion for movies is also clear. Cheung is furious because the film *The Lin Family Shop* is stolen during the screening. He goes to the projection room and berates the staff for spoiling Chinese movies. This kind of sequence is repeatedly seen in Allen Fong's movies. Another motif, which is also not rare, is that of advanced studies. In *Father and Son*, the father demands that his son get a good education in the United States. In *Ah Ying*, the female protagonist attends a drama programme offered by the Centre of Film Culture, after finishing work at the fish stall - another form of further study. As for *A Little Life - Opera*, the situation is closer to the ideal in that the studies and the dream are not in opposition, as they are in *Father and Son*, but are one. The female protagonist expects her two daughters, both the biological and the adopted one, to enter university. However, both aspire to act. They get a place in the Beijing Art Academy instead of into a foreign languages programme in a mainstream university. Although the mother is not happy about this, she eventually gives in. When they return home after graduating, the daughters are hailed with a banner with the words 'Welcome the glorious return of the two new excellent graduates' held up by their mother and by members of their theatrical group. The two daughters have integrated their studies and their aspirations, fulfilling their lifelong objective. This is perhaps also a reconciliation of the two generations. That the next generation's determination and persistence are understood and even supported by the older generation is a great leap forward from the situation depicted in *Father and Son*. A group of artists in the film industry persists in pursuing their passion and respect for art without regretting the difficulties. At the same time, they wish to pass on their faith to the next generation. This, in fact, is Allen Fong's hope.

A Little Life – Opera is about a former leading actress in a Chinese opera group, Yeung Kwai-mei, who is getting no acting assignments. Usually, she works as an assistant in a food stall. Then, suddenly, she receives a letter of invitation from Tang Xi Village to put on a performance. She immediately resigns from her present job, organizes a troupe and sets off. Just before the opening of the opera, the host unit requires a change of programme – the insertion of a session of modern dance, but Yeung rejects the request. A parallel plot in which the person who provides the funds demands a change in the performance is also found in *Dancing Bull*. The sponsor asks Cora Miu to switch the programme from *Miyamoto Mukishi* to *Half of Man is Woman*. But the request is decisively turned down by Anthony Wong, who believes that the sponsor has no right to ask for such a change. In *A Little Life – Opera*, Yeung encounters a similar problem, and a deadlock ensues. Later, an actor turned businessman helps to resolve the impasse, and the performance begins. However, after the performance, the theatrical group faces the crisis of dissolving. In the climate of an open, capitalist market in which cost-effectiveness is emphasized, certain theatrical groups that introduce modern dances or popular dances can attract an audience, whereas the traditional opera groups can hardly achieve this. As a leading actress in the opera group, Yeung also blames herself for not creating more opportunities to put on performances. During periods of hardship, she is willing to take up a job in a food stall, but when it comes to art, she will not betray her conscience. She is like the character Winston Zhao, who had once played the *suona* (a Chinese woodwind instrument) in an opera troupe. Now, he is married, and his wife is a businesswoman. She believes there is no future in opera. At home, Zhao has no status. His only passions are the *suona* and his love for the theatre. When he comes across Yeung's theatrical group in the countryside, he acts in the show. On stage, he regains his identity and finds meaning in his existence. Later, his family business is inspected by the tax authorities, charged with tax evasion and forced to close. In fact, to him, this was a kind of release from bondage, as this allowed him to retreat from business. Since then, has he decided to stay with the opera group, singing opera every day with Yeung. He would rather live in material poverty, but in spiritual richness, to live a life with meaning. In fact, Yeung's opera troupe is struggling to survive. However, she has her companions from the stage, and the generation to succeed her in making her dream of art complete. Ironically, Zhao, a real lover of stage performance, seems rich but suffers an irresolvable pain in his heart. Eventually, he makes up his mind to return to the theatre to fulfill his vision on the stage. In addition, Cheung in *Ah Ying* and Cora Miu in *Dancing Bull* show their persistence in working in various art forms. They are representative of the director Allen Fong, who has committed his entire life to the art of film.

An Exploration of Film Form: Between Realistic Representation and Fiction

As a representation of personal experience, *Father and Son* is an autobiographical work that is constructed in the framework of memory. The introduction of the film shows the father receiving the son's graduation certificate from the United States, which brings him great joy. However, on his way home, he suffers a heart attack and falls down a staircase. This ends his hard life. But he has no regrets in the moment before death, as his hope that his son will become successful has been fulfilled. The son, Law Ka-hing, returns home following his graduation from university. At home, his eyes rest on a photograph of his elder and younger sisters, and memories come flooding back. They are shown in a flashback. The story is narrated by Law. He describes his experiences growing up, the father-son relationship, the ethics of a traditional family and the influence of patriarchy on the family. The father forces the son, who is not interested in school, to study. The son cannot do what he wants to do, but must bend to his father's will. At the father's request, his older sister marries a wealthy, middle-aged man who owns a business. His younger sister is required to terminate her studies and work as a nurse. Although she rebels by cutting her hair, nothing changes. As the master of the family, the father is obeyed by every member of the household. The son then goes to the United States to study. The film closes with a farewell scene at the airport and does not revert back to the opening scene of the present day, of the son looking at an old photograph. In this way, the entire film is treated as memory, with no reference made to the present.

In terms of narrative, *Ah Ying* is a great step ahead of its forerunner. Except for the character of Cheung, all of the characters, from the female protagonist Hui So-ying and her ex-boyfriend to her family, are people playing themselves, making it a bold and extremely experimental movie. The plot of this film was adjusted after an audition of performers for one of Fong's projects. Hui So-ying came in for the casting. When the director learned her story, he found that hers was even more interesting, more attractive and richer in terms of subject matter than his original one focusing on Cheung Chung-pak. Therefore, Fong at once revised his script to shift the focus of the narrative to Hui, making her the main line of the story. This was how the film *Ah Ying* came into being. Most remarkable of all was that Hui also brought her entire family, except for her pregnant sister-in-law and younger brother, to participate in the film.[10] Even the fish stall and the apartment are real. They are the underpinnings of the film's quality of genuineness.

There are two particularly impressive scenes. One shows Cheung in a Hong Kong-style restaurant being introduced to So-ying's boyfriend, Cheng Chi-hung. They eat and chat. Sitting opposite to the pair, Cheung asks Cheng why he loves So-ying. The lovers start to discuss about their relationship, which had gone from intimacy to estrangement. In the process, Cheng unveils his true feelings, and Hui unconsciously shows her reluctance to break up. Fong had given them no prior instructions about what answers they were to give to his questions; he had merely given them a rough idea about the contents of the conversation, not the details. The director did not intervene in the dialogue during shooting, and the speeches made by the lovers were thoroughly natural and genuine. Their inner feelings were revealed without any embellishments. There most genuine and awkward expressions are recorded on camera. This kind of impromptu technique enables the narrative to evolve naturally during the process of film-making. *Ah Ying* was the first time such a technique was used in Hong Kong, and it was a success. Another remarkable scene is of a family quarrel. Hui's father is slightly drunk when he returns home for dinner. The family quietly hide the knives in the house. After the meal, the younger sister goes next door and hides. Her mother then breaks the news of her pre-marital pregnancy to her father. Furious, the father rushes next door to look for the young girl, to give her a beating. All of the members of the family try to stop him, but to no avail. At this time, the mother kneels before the father, begging his forgiveness. The mood is one of despair. This scene is a replay of a real event – such a terrifying incident had indeed occurred in Hui's family. During the making of the film, Hui's father acted as realistically as if the film had been a pure documentary, which was very touching. 'That kneeling was completely unexpected, and even shocking.'[11] Had there been no basis in real experience, had the plot merely been fictional, such unembellished, realistic sensitivity would surely fail to be exhibited. Now the results were so astonishing that the audience was slow to respond.[12] Of course, not every detail of this film was transferred from real life. Many parts were not real; for instance, the drama within the drama. The play Cheung practices with his students was adapted from the novel *Tribe of Generals* written by a Taiwanese writer, Chen Yingzhen. The narrative is about an old soldier of the Nationalist Party and a poor woman. The old man uses his life savings to buy the woman out, rescuing her from her life of misery. When the two are reunited, they know that they cannot be together and therefore place their hopes in the afterlife. The idea, resembling the real situation of Cheung and Hui, is represented in the form of a play. This implies analogy (*bi*) and inspiration (*xing*).[13] Referring to the novel, the relationship between Cheung and Hui also ends in separation.

In order to reach a documentary-like standard, *Ah Ying* avoids post-production dubbing. Fong brought realistic filming techniques from his days in television to film, making it possible to capture the complexity and changeability of reality. In shooting *Ah Ying*, Fong took the approach of filming a little and then waiting for the narrative to evolve of itself. This device was employed in the 1920s by Flaherty to capture the spirit of realism.[14] Now, Fong applied it to real figures, which certainly differentiated his attempt from Flaherty's recreation of characters and events of the past. Going beyond surface reality, Flaherty made an in-depth exploration of reality possible. Fong's film was the opening of a brand new page in the investigation of truth and of the relationship between the representation of fact and fiction.

Based on his success with this film in representing real-life events, Fong unhesitatingly extended the approach to his next project, *Just Like Weather*. In addition, he took a more daring step forward in having all of the characters played by real people, letting them tell their own stories on screen. Furthermore, this time Allen Fong allows himself and his cinematography crew to intrude in the film, which is a pioneering step.

Intruding in the Film, Interfering with Life

The mode of narration of *Just Like Weather* is a distinctive one. The film opens with the main characters, Chan Hung-nin and Li Yuk-kuen, travelling in the United States. They drive from the western part of the country eastwards to New York City. At this time, it is raining and the weather is changeable; a hint that the couple's relationship is similarly unstable. Such a theme is also manifested through the English title of the film, *Just Like Weather*. This scene is followed by another, showing the couple walking hand-in-hand along the streets of Shenzhen. The director then cuts back to their journey in the United States, showing them resting in a motel. Here, Li asks Chan, 'Aren't you very much hoping to see Hong Kong? Why?' Chan replies, 'You are reluctant to stay in the United States.' Then they embrace and kiss. From the aforementioned dialogue, we get the rough idea that the couple is divided on the issue of whether or not to stay in America. Then the film shows the director's interview with Chan and Li. Questions such as when they got married, how they view marriage and what they expect from marriage, information on the divorce of Chan's parents and so forth. The couple is then shown at dinner, telephoning relatives on the East Coast of the US, informing them of their arrival. Afterwards, we see the director travelling with them from Hong Kong to the other side of the ocean. The director cuts back and forth in an a-chronological manner between images such as highways in America, Shenzhen, an inn in America, the family in Hong Kong, interview scenes, the Hong Kong airport and streets in San Francisco. In the beginning, they are presented in a rather confusing way, with the various places difficult to identify. Certain sequences, in particular, those of the streets in Shenzhen and those showing the director interviewing the couple, are scenes the audience would find it difficult to enter into. It is just because of such unclear elements that the emotional states and current situation of Chan and Li can be illustrated.

The film then goes on to narrate the couple's life in Hong Kong; for example, their different expectations of married life, their financial difficulties and the wife's abortion. Then the director cuts back and forth between the highway scenes in the United States and the scenes of their life in Hong Kong. In the America portion, it is raining and snowing, and the weather is very overcast; whereas in the Hong Kong portion, the couple are always arguing and holding different opinions. In particular, Chan's setbacks in his job and his departure from home exacerbate Li's discontent and complaints. The juxtaposition of the bad weather and the arguments of the couple form a strong correspondence. When they arrive in New York and meet their relatives, Li becomes much happier. She even rejects the use of condoms and resolves not to avoid becoming pregnant – which is in stark contrast to her abortion at the beginning of the film.

It was by chance that Fong discovered the female protagonist, Li Yuk-kuen, and was moved by her story. Fong made it the blueprint of his script. But in Fong's mind, Li's tale was not yet a complete one, thus the script was only a partial one. Fong started shooting while continuing to explore the narrative. It was in this way that the wedding sequence of Li's parents was discovered. On the other hand, Fong constructed fictional parts (only a few sequences) to supplement the loopholes and deficiencies in Li's story; for example, Chan is deceived when working in the second-hand motorcar company. However, this leads to a rupture in the plot – either the fictional parts are not well connected to the events in the real story or the points of nexus are more conspicuous than necessary. This problem could be attributed to the unavailability of a complete script and the adoption of an impromptu style. But, after all, the exploration of the character, Li, during the shooting of the film, appears as delicate, impressive and true, which would definitely have been difficult to achieve with a fictional plot and characters. Allen Fong's painstaking attempts in this film to achieve a truthful representation illustrate his views on the current situation in Hong Kong and on relationships between men and women. At the same time, this film is a technically and stylistically unique Hong Kong movie.[15]

The most avant-garde part of *Just Like Weather* is the director's intrusion into the characters' lives. He conducts face-to-face interviews, flies to the United States and travels through the continent with the couple. During the trip, Li is interviewed by the director about her perceptions of him. They also play with the snow, writing out the Chinese characters for 'congratulations'. After arriving in New York, Fong enjoys the 'union dinner' with the relatives of the couple. Fong even gives packets of money in a red envelope to the relatives as well as to his crew. All of these scenes are captured in the film. Film and life, fact and fiction are juxtaposed. The endless innovations and creativity of the director make this film Fong's most outstanding work and pioneering one in the history of Hong Kong cinema.

Fong's impromptu and direct intrusion into the characters' lives is replicated in *Dancing Bull* – this time what intrudes is a profound social and political event. The male protagonist, Anthony Wong, and Chan Ling-chi are highly agitated when they view the June 4th Incident on television. They want to respond to the event by doing something they are good at, because they do not want the children they may one day bear to have a life without hope. Therefore, they participate in the protest in the form of dancing. Fong, for his part, captures the demonstration with his camera to make it part of his film. Standing in the midst of the crowd, Fong cries out slogans together with the other protesters. The question of whether this section is coherent with the rest of the film is not a concern of the director. It can be said that what makes this film distinctive is that the director directly inserts the current social issue into the narrative in a high-profile manner when the event erupted during the time he was filming a movie. The director's participation in real life or in incidents that occur allows for a more comprehensive picture of reality and a more in-depth exploration of events. Fong's determination in his role as an artist and his social conscience has become his statement of commitment.

A documentary, *Tibetan Tao*, produced in 2000, is about a friend of Allen Fong, Ah Tao, who assists the shooting of Fong's film *A Little Life - Opera*. He is a businessman in the town of Shishi in the province of Fujian. *Tibetan Tao* shows the real-life situation Ah Tao's family, including his wife and two sons, as well as of his friends. Furthermore, Fong invites Ah Tao to go on a trip to Tibet. Ah Tao accepts. The film cross-cuts between scenes of Fujian and Tibet. The film opens with a Tibetan who bows down to worship as he walks (showing his religious devotion) and closes with the arrival of Ah Tao in Tibet. During the shooting, the director tries to keep the characters from becoming aware of the camera, in order to make the scenes natural and realistic. This is consistent with his commitment to reveal the truth. Although Allen Fong's films are not large in number, each of his works has surprises for the audience. From *A Wild Child*, which was produced during his days in televisions, and *Father and Son*, *Ah Ying* and *Just Like Weather* to the more recent *Dancing Bull*, *A Little Life - Opera* and *Tibetan Tao*, he began with the subject that was most familiar to him - himself, and then his friends, a couple and some artists. The subjects involved ranged from father-son relationships, family issues, love, confusion, the struggles of women, concern for society, persistence in art and so forth. Also, his films are permeated with rich personal experiences and challenges in life that are reflective of Fong's ideas and insights. Put in another way, every single one of his films communicates his existence; thus, he is a true film 'auteur'. Throughout his career of over twenty years, he has been loyal to himself, to truth, film, art and to aspirations. In terms of form and style, he constantly pursues innovations. He has gone from simple and plain narratives to an adventurous, unplanned way of capturing the truth; from casting no real-life characters in his films to a partial casting and then to a complete casting. In order to the reveal the truth and to explore the complexity, ambivalence and diversity of the world, Fong acts as a participant, instead of a spectator, in society and life. He tries to produce works that are true archetypes of the ideal. His works waver between fact and fiction, between life and drama, fulfilling his desire for creative experimentation. His persistence in exploring form in film had led him to deviate more and more from the mainstream of Hong Kong cinema. However, he does not care about this as long as he can participate in films. His creativity is enough to acclaim him the foremost director of non-mainstream Hong Kong films.

Notes

1. *The Wild Child* won the Best Young Director award from the Asian Broadcasting Association in 1977.
2. Pak Tong Cheuk, Law Kar and Cheung Chi-shing. 'Interview with Allen Fong'. *Hong Kong New Wave Cinema - After Twenty Years*. 23rd International Film Festival. Hong Kong Temporary Urban Council. 1999, p. 131.
3. Ma Qi. 'Fangwen "Shizi shanxia" daoyan Fang Yuping' (interview with the director of *Below the Lion Rock*). *Datexie* (Close-Up). No. 33, p. 37.
4. Lau Shing-hon. *The Poetic Characteristics of Film* (Dianying fubixing). HK: Cosmos Books. 1992, p. 36.

5. Lo Man-shing. 'Interview with Allen Fong.' Hong Kong Cinema in the 1980s. 15th Hong Kong International Film Festival. Hong Kong Government Urban Council, 28 March – 12 April 1991, p. 103.
6. Lee Cheuk-to and Cheung Shing-sheung. 'Interview with Ah Ying'. *City Entertainment*. No. 124, p. 5.
7. Ibid., p. 6.
8. *Father and Son* won awards for Best Picture and Best Director in the Hong Kong Film Awards in 1981. *Ah Ying* earned these two awards in 1983. *Just Like Weather* was given the Best Director award in 1986.
9. After returning from the United States to Hong Kong, Chan Hung-nin and Li Yuk-kuen divorced. This leads one to contemplate the relationship between real life and film.
10. Shu Kei. 'Rushes and Flashes.' *Haowei zazhi*. No. 81, May 1983, p. 54.
11. Ibid.
12. Yam Chi-keung. 'We are also "half of the human"/*Ah Ying*.' *Breakthrough Magazine*. No. 109, HK: Breakthrough. November 1983, p. 14.
13. Lau Shing-hon. *The Poetic Characteristics of Film* (Dianying fubixing). HK: Cosmos Books. 1992, pp. 26–33.
14. Robert Flaherty's *Nanook of the North* (1922) portrays such themes as the Eskimos' struggle for survival in nature, their control of fate and human dignity. The director lived with the family (the central characters) in the film. He established friendship and trust with them. He waited for the narrative to emerge and then started shooting. By describing and arranging the various details, Flaherty's intention was to portray the real face of the Eskimos of the past. This device of shaping reality is also an interpretation of reality.
15. Shek Kei. 'The Context of *Just Like Weather*'. *Baixing Yuekan* (People's Monthly). No. 131. 1 November 1986, 58.

8

ALEX CHEUNG

Cheung Kwok-ming, Alex, was born in Hong Kong on 22 December 1951. From a young age, he was obsessed by the world of images. In the early 1970s, he tried to make 8mm experimental films. His short film *Rings of the Telephone* won an award in 1973 in an experimental films contest organized by the Joint Association of Colleges in Hong Kong. In one of his short films, *Together*, named after a Beatles song, Cheung experimented with various film-making techniques, such as zooming in/out, fast motion, slow motion, flashback, freeze-frame, the editing of repetitive actions and so forth. These special visual effects, and the rhythm of the songs used, expressed such characteristics of youth as wildness, unruliness, a dislike of restrictions and a tendency to oppose the establishment. This film also illustrated the young Cheung's sensitivity to audio-visual language.

In 1974, Cheung joined Rediffusion Television. Using a 16mm camera and single-frame shots, a technique also used in animation, he directed a short promotional trailer that incorporated the company's logo. His work was acclaimed by the chief manager, Wong Shek-chiu, and Cheung went on to make other short promotional films. However, Cheung's real interest was in making dramas, and he had no opportunities to do this in Rediffusion Television. So, in 1976, he moved to the rival, TVB. He was soon transferred to the film group there, to direct a series of single drama episodes, namely *Huanxiang qiqing**, *Wonderful*, *CID*, *Seventeen*, *The Four-Eyed Cop*, *International Police*, *Taxi Driver*, *The First Step* and others. In 1979, Cheung made his entry into the film industry. His first feature was *Cops and Robbers*. Subsequent films included *Man on the Brink* (1981), *Twinkle, Twinkle Little Star* (1983), *The Royal Thief* (1985), *Imaginary Suspects Chatter Street Killer* (1988), *Framed* (1989), *Midnight Caller* (1995), *Made In Heaven* (1997) and others. He also directed an anthology series for RTHK and the ICAC in 1996 and 1997. In 1999, he began working for the ICAC and produced the series *ICAC Investigators*.

TV Dramas Weak in Plot but Strong in Rhythm

The third episode of *CID*, produced in 1977, was Alex Cheung's first attempt at filming a TV drama. In this episode, a lady over the age of sixty (Chan Lap-pun) one day receives a letter from her daughter-in-law in her home village in mainland China, informing her of the death of her son and the existence of her only grandson. Her daughter-in-law wants Chan to take the child to Hong Kong and look after him. Using all of her savings, Chan buys a child of a similar age as her grandson, with the intention of taking him to her village and exchanging him for her grandson, so as to be able to bring her grandson back with her to Hong Kong. However, she later discovers that the child she had bought had been kidnapped. They live together and become fond of one another. This makes it difficult for them to separate later. The dramatic contradictions in the movie start here.

Finally, the old woman decides to exchange the adopted boy with her grandson. At customs in Lo Wu, the policeman who was investigating the abduction case arrives and stops Chan. The old lady is reluctant to hand over the child. In the struggle over the child, Chan loses her temper and bites the policeman who is holding the boy. Perhaps the film is too sensational, but the narrative is clear, the plot evolves step by step, and the camera movements are lively. All of this proves that the director has mastered visual language as well as storytelling techniques.

Another of Cheung's TV dramas, *Seventeen: The Birdcage in the Air* (1977), portrays a girl deprived of family warmth who falls in love and has a sexual relationship with a friend of her father's. However, she later discovers that the man has been trifling with her all along. She is in despair and is on the road to self-destruction. As for the girl's family, her father spends his time in front of the television and her mother is addicted to gambling. The message is that children who lack care and attention can easily go astray. However, the film was criticized as biased, since it tended to place the blame for the girl's conduct solely on her parents or on the institution of the family, ignoring the responsibility of the girl herself.[1] In the ninth episode of *CID*, the younger sister of the male protagonist, the latter a martial arts coach, is raped by three mobsters. The protagonist goes to the police station to report the crime but is ignored. In a rage, he decides to take the law into his own hands. He goes in search of the criminals in order to settle accounts with them. Fortunately, the timely arrival of the police puts a stop to the massacre, and the criminals are arrested. The exploration of social issues in this film is not deep enough and merely provokes the emotions of the audience with its style. This caused the film to be criticized as being 'too sensational' and as 'condoning the personal enforcement of law'.[2] Certain critics have lauded Cheung. They point to his experimental films *Yishi zhisuo* and *Together*, which were breakthroughs, as well as to his primitive style, which was already evident in the very beginning of his film-making career; and to his establishment of character in *Birdcage in the Air* and *Fiancé Charlie*.[3] However, there are also deficiencies in Cheung's use of characterization. The main character in these latter films was a friend of his and the story was based on a true one;[4] yet this did not mean that the story has the quality of being representative.[5]

Furthermore, Cheung failed to show universality via specificity. This weakness led to criticism of Cheung's works as being 'weak in plot, but strong in rhythm'.[6] Cheung's 1997 production *Guohe zuzi* (1977) depicts a youngster who finds that Hong Kong does not live up to his expectations and decides to return to his hometown. The film does not discuss what he found disappointing about Hong Kong, for instance, the social system. Thus, the reasons for the main character's decision to return home are not fully set out in the film.

Dream, Rebellion and Compromise

Rather reminiscent of Tang Shuxun's *China Behind* (1974), *Seventeen: Guohe zuzi* explores ways of making a choice between reality and dream. The film focuses on four young people who illegally cross over from mainland China to Hong Kong One is eaten by a shark when attempting the crossing by sea. The second works hard, but is not ambitious. The third has difficulty adapting to life in Hong Kong. He comes to hate the world and is unhappy with his job in a fast-food restaurant, which he perceives as degrading and undignified. After a series of struggles, he chooses the wrong path. The last of the four loses his girlfriend and realizes that Hong Kong is not the place for him. He decides to participate in a robbery and then return home. Unfortunately, while doing so, he is shot dead. 'Going but not returning' is the implicit message in *Guohe zuzi*. Once a person leaves his hometown for an unfamiliar place, he has no option but to confront the situation and accept reality. Otherwise, he will go astray, behave in an extreme manner and, ultimately, die a tragic death.

This kind of attitude toward life is also noticeable in *Taxi Driver: The Trio*. In the film, Johnny (Teddy Robin) has an ardent love for music. When he returns from advanced studies of music in Europe, he expects to contribute to the development of the Hong Kong music scene. He has a vision that music should not be a passive art and actively invites the audience to participate, to feel the music first-hand. Unfortunately, in Hong Kong's commercialized society his artistic talents are not appreciated. Few tickets are sold for his avant-garde concert. Even when he gives out tickets for free, there is little response, and this makes him despondent. A friend then tells him about a job singing in a nightclub. He is unwilling to go at first, as he feels that this is not the kind of job for him. But, eventually, he chooses to compromise in order to make a living. Just before the close of the film, he says, 'Sometimes, a person's dream is not easily fulfilled. But it is true that if he works a bit harder toward the goal, he will get a bit closer to it.' Johnny does not give up on his dream, but adapts it to circumstances in order to realize it.

In *Taxi Driver: The Car Thief*, Apple (Kenny Bee Chung) is a coward and is submissive and obedient to his father. His father is well known in society as a philanthropist. He is exposed as having been involved in a corruption case involving the funds of a charity. But in order to keep his name clean, he places all of the blame on one member of his staff, who is then imprisoned. Apple disapproves of his father's deeds, but does not dare to reveal the truth. Instead, he chooses to rebel by stealing the taxi driven by Ah Tat (Kam Hing-yin) and driving around wildly. This brings Ah Tat no end of grief. In the end, after much persuasion from many people, Apple chooses to return home and report his action to the police, although such acts may ruin his father's good name. Here, there is both rebellion and compromise.

What is portrayed in *The Four-Eyed Cop* is also rebellion of a particularly odd type. Driven by dissatisfaction with the corrupt acts of certain officials, Chan Hou-shing (Ho Pik-kin), a munitions expert, deliberately designs time bombs in order to kill them one by one. The threatened policemen are exhausted by being constantly on the run. A super-cop, Lok Sum (Ken Cheng), investigates the case step by step. He confronts Chan and is tied up with a time bomb attached to him. At the critical moment, Lok succeeds in releasing himself and throws the bomb at Chan. It explodes. Chan's death seems to have been predestined.

Cherishing Kinship and Friendship, and Deep Fatalism

The themes of death and fatalism, kinship and friendship are frequently found in Alex Cheung's films. The abovementioned third episode of *CID* centres on the affection between a grandmother and her grandson and the insanity that develops after they are separated. The ninth episode in the same series describes the harmonious family of a karate coach (Kam Hing-yin), which includes his mother and younger sister. However, the younger sister is raped by hooligans. Kam is too impatient to wait for the police to resolve the case and goes in search of the criminals and punishes them himself. Both dramas are about people who go into mad frenzies when family relationships are broken. *Taxi Driver: The Trio* and *Taxi Driver: The Car Thief* both contain rich portrayals of love and friendship. The former is about the comradeship of three men, while the latter is about young people who are deprived of a father's love, their disillusionment with the patriarchal image and their consequent rebellion. In *Taxi Driver: The Car Thief*, the male comradeship between taxi drivers and the friendship/love between the male and female operators in the station are shown in a lively and touching manner. As for Cheung's films, *Cops and Robbers* (1979) and *Man on the Brink* (1981) communicate the deep, brotherly love between policemen.

Among Cheung's television dramas, *The First Step: Facing Death* (1979) can be regarded as the most sophisticated. The protagonist, Ah Kwong (Lee Kwok-lun), a movie lover, has a satisfactory job, a girlfriend that he gets along with and harmonious relationships with his colleagues. But after he learns that his closest colleague wants to take over his position and his girlfriend has fallen in love with his boss, he loses his reason. He gets on his motorbike and goes for a wild ride; eventually, he falls from a cliff. Injured and alone, he recalls the past and ponders on his experience of friendship, love and kinship. In despair he cries out. Finally, he is saved. Many people visit him in the hospital. However, brought back from the edge of death, everything seems unreal to him.

In *Taxi Driver, The Trio*, disputes and divergences of opinion arise among three close friends. For example, Johnny is at first reluctant to take up a job that he is not interested in. His friends are unable to understand him. They accuse him of being unrealistic, given that he has lost his job and has no income. This is how he came to quarrel with his friends. Later, he thinks things through and comes to the realization that a job should come first and dreams next. He sings in a nightclub and his friends show up to support him. Misunderstandings are cleared up and friendships are cherished. In *The Man on the Brink*, Ah Chiu's (Eddie) girlfriend complains about their unstable life, which causes her to worry constantly. Consequently, the lovers separate. Likewise, Ah Tai's (Kam Hing-yin) girlfriend dislikes his occupation as a policeman, as it gives her no sense of security. Their relationship also does not have a happy ending. In contrast, Ah Chiu and Ah Tai are buddies who help each other. In the end, Ah Tai even blames himself for not being able to save Ah Chiu's life. The value of friendship is thus highlighted.

In his earlier works, *The First Step: Facing Death*, *Cops and Robbers* and *The Man on the Brink*, there are no happy endings in love. Nearly all of the relationships end in separation. However, Cheung's more recent works are somewhat different. (*Midnight Caller* is excluded because, as Cheung explained, he was not the director of this work, he was only deputy director to Wong Pak-ming.) For example, the female protagonist in *Twinkle Twinkle Little Star*, Cherie Chung, who is beautiful and simple-minded, is violated by extraterrestrials and then abandoned by her rich boyfriend. She experiences many setbacks in life. In the end, she and a private investigator, who has suffered from the same illness as her and who therefore empathizes with her, become lovers. In *Cops and Robbers*, Cheung Kwok-keung, a policeman, gets to know a suspect, Kwan Yuk-ming, during the course of his investigation. In the end, the two fall in love and there is a happy ending. Ada Choi in *Made in Heaven* makes use of her extraordinary power to do good deeds. Her actions are rewarded in that the bad guy whom she loves changes to become a good man. Again, there is a happy ending.

Made in Heaven sheds light on such ideas as kinship, friendship, the fear of being betrayed, rebellion and abandonment. Perhaps it may be true that he is tremendously sensitive about the instability of friendships, the duality of good/evil in humanity, and fate and death in real life. This kind of sensitivity extends to his films.

Ambiguity of Good and Evil and the Conversion of Humanity

In 1979, Alex Cheung entered the film industry and directed two cop movies, *Cops and Robbers* and *Man on the Brink*, which sparked off a heated debate among the critics. The latter film also won three Golden Horse Awards in 1982, for Best Director, Best Scriptwriter and Best Lead Actor. Both films are about people who become twisted under the constraints of the social system. The robber in *Cops and Robbers*, Lee Biu, has wanted to be a policeman ever since he was small. Unfortunately, he has a congenital defect with his eyes. For this reason, he fails to pass the physical test to become a policeman. He loves playing with guns, however, he cannot become a cop and eventually becomes a robber. In contrast, another character, Ah Wing (Cheung Kwok-keung), seems to be too weak to be a policeman. Once while interrogating a suspect named So Ho, Cheung is instead himself questioned by So, nearly reversing the roles of cop and robber.

Once, the robber So Ho grabbed the girlfriend of Ah Wing's immediate superior, Superintendent Chow (Kam Hing-yin). Chow returns to his girlfriend's boutique and is unexpectedly shot by So. The criminal escapes and, in the course of fleeing, grabs a pedestrian to serve as a hostage. He keeps shooting at Ah Wing, who is eventually hit by a bullet. Ah Wing flees. So pursues him to kill him. Thus, this is a case of the robber chasing after the cop. This complete reversal is so well arranged that the effect is one of ridiculousness. With a fatalism that is almost metaphysical and conveying such a world-view with clarity, *Cops and Robbers* is probably the most successful cop movie made in Hong Kong.[7] Of course, the popularity of films in this genre at that time was based upon the way that they temporarily resolved the psychological conflicts that commonly exist in a real society.[8] This kind of unique artistic representational mode is not uncommon in Hong Kong cop movies. Specifically, *Cops and Robbers* certainly mirrors Hong Kong society and some of its values.

In *Man on the Brink*, the ambiguity between cops and robbers and between right and wrong is taken a step further. The male protagonist, Ah Chiu (Eddie), works for a short time at several jobs before finally joining the police. He thinks that as a 'real' man, he should not live an ordinary life but do something great and even die a grand and meaningful death. He is assigned an undercover job of penetrating a triad organization. In this way, he suddenly changes from a cop to a gangster, who spends entire days together with criminals. Gradually, he becomes neither a cop nor a gangster. Finally, even his girlfriend leaves him.

A robbery takes place in a clock and watch shop, and Ah Chiu is arrested. His supervisor, Superintendent Chan, knows that Ah Chiu holds a grudge against the owner of the shop and suspects that he was taking advantage of the situation to take revenge on the owner. Ah Chiu is expelled from the police force. With this, he suddenly loses his identity and is filled with a sense of helplessness and frustration. In the moment of his greatest despair, A Wah, a gangster who had fled, returns. He invites Ah Chiu to collaborate with him on a job. In a robbery, Ah Chiu intervenes to stop a criminal from raping a young lady. But, in the process, he is exposed as being one of the robbers and is assaulted by a crowd of neighbours who had come to the rescue. Although Ah Chiu's buddies, Chan and Ah Tai, come forward to help him, unfortunately, they are too late and Ah Chiu is severely beaten. Finally, he dies in Ah Tai's lap. That he would have been killed by a group of 'kind' neighbours could not have been predicted. Throughout the course of his undercover career, Ah Chiu had concealed his identity. However, he regretted this loss of identity as a cop and hoped to 'rejoin' the police force. However, he dies before his wish can come true.

This film demonstrates that people have no way of escaping from the restrictions of their environment and that they are the playthings of fate. On the other hand, it also affirms the importance of friendship. Ah Chiu and Ah Tai (Kam Hing-yin, who has been Alex Cheung's favorite actor since the director's television days), both undercover cops, appreciate each other. Ah Tai constantly looks out for Ah Chiu to prevent his real identity from being exposed to the gangsters. And, in the end, Ah Chiu dies in the lap of his comrade and achieves a kind of peace.

After the two films that made his name, Cheung stopped making cops-and-robbers flicks and switched to producing a sci-fi comedy, *Twinkle Twinkle Little Star* (1983). However, it was not a success, and the few additional films that had also been in the pipeline were aborted. In 1985, he again directed a cops-and-robbers movie, *The Royal Thief*. The film shows him questioning the good/evil sides of humanity and the uncertainty of comradeship. The protagonist (Fei Cheung) has always completely trusted his immediate superior (Chu Kong), perceiving him to be the only just person in the police force. Who could have imagined that the person who was planning to kill him was his boss, while it is the cruel killer who eventually saves his life?

In *Framed* (1989), the hero, Alex Man, is an impartial, righteous cop who repeatedly performs outstandingly. However, this attracts the envy of his boss. In a murder scene, Man is drunk and is accused by Simon Yam of committing a crime. This leads to his imprisonment. Man escapes from jail and investigates the case himself. With the aid of another cop, Lui Leung-wai, he succeeds in clearing his name. The two cops, who had previously been rivals, now become good friends. The film illustrates that the line between good and the evil can blur. It is unlike the cops-and-robbers movies of the past, which showed gangsters and cops in absolute and clear opposition. As society has evolved, people are becoming more and more complicated. By contrast, *Imaginary Suspects Chatter Street Killer* (1988) is a detective comedy. The cop, Cheung Kwok-keung, encounters a suspect, Kwan Yuk-ming, in the process of investigating a murder. Meanwhile, Cheung is wrongly identified as the criminal and is unjustly accused. Becoming a 'wanted man', he is chased in the streets. The film also echoes the reversal of the identities of cops and robbers, and the ambiguity between them, portrayed in *Cops and Robbers*.

Likewise, the comedy *Made In Heaven* (1997) is about the theme of karma – a good man will be rewarded – and the concept of transmigration. The female protagonist, Ada Choi, had been a male pickpocket in a previous life. Then, he is reincarnated as a woman. Choi has the supernatural ability to predict a person's future. She offers help to those in need but the more she helps people, the more trouble she finds herself falling into. She is unable to have a love affair, because whenever she gets close to a man, events take an unexpected turn. For instance, she falls in love with a triad gangster, but the gangster's girlfriend, Peng Dan, avenges herself by killing Choi. In a subsequent scene of a heavenly court, Choi is judged to be a good person who had not deserved to die. In the end, it is Peng who dies while Choi returns to life. This embodies the fatalistic view that 'good is repaid with good'.

Complicated Narrative Techniques and Natural *Mise-en-scène*

In fact, as early as during his days in television, Alex Cheung had already experimented with more complicated modes of narration, including a-chronological narration. A hint of this is seen in *Taxi Driver - The Trio*. The film opens with the male protagonist, Ah Tat, getting off work and taking a cab to a nightclub to listen to his old friend Johnny sing. Then, the camera shifts from Johnny to a scene of an airplane landing, accompanied by the sound of Ah Tat's voice beginning his narration. This is the start of the flashback. The audience is told that many years ago Johnny went to Europe to study music and returned to Hong Kong after graduation. At this point, the director cuts to a scene of Johnny at the airport, being welcomed by friends. Then, the narration continues, informing the audience about Johnny's concert, his difficulty in finding jobs and his reluctant decision to sing in a nightclub. As the film closes, we revolve back to the nightclub scene shown in the beginning, of Ah Tat listening to Johnny's performance.

The narrative of *The First Step: Facing Death* is more complex and daring. As the film starts, the protagonist, Ah Kwong, is at home feeling frustrated. He jumps on his motorbike and roars away. While he is on the road, using a 'dissolve lens', his recollections of his days in the workplace, the mutual support that existed among his colleagues and the kindness of his girlfriend are introduced. Afterwards, the camera cuts back to the present. He reaches a hill and joins a motor race. Then, he retreats alone to an open space on one side of the hill. It is extremely quiet, with not a person to be seen. The camera circles 360 degrees around him. Now, he is fantasizing that his colleagues have all come to this deserted area to have a barbeque. All around him are people and noise. Later, the camera again makes a 360-degree turn, the scene shifts back to one of silence. Ah Tat is alone. He starts the motor and begins to careen wildly down the slope. He is not careful and falls down the slope. He is seriously injured, and his body is covered with blood. A 'dissolve' sequence is introduced again, to show his memories of certain incidents: his friend gets a promotion and replaces him; his girlfriend transfers her affections to his boss; he blames his buddy for disloyalty; and he beats his girlfriend. Not until this moment is the audience clear about the reasons of his grievances. Then the director cuts back to the present, of Ah Tat lying on the hill. A series of juxtapositions of the past and present follow. Memory: the impending return from Europe to Hong Kong of Ah Tat's friend who makes experimental films. Present: Ah Tat lying on the hill. Memory: a scene of a barbecue with his workmates. Present: a bitter expression on his face. Memory: his mother visiting him in the hospital. Present: the hill scene. Then, he is shown lying in bed in a hospital. Ah Tat's mother, who is by his bedside, informs him that he had been saved by somebody. At the same time, Johnny and others are shown coming to the hospital to see him. Threads of the present, recollections of the past, time and space, are interwoven in the film. Although there is a lot of cutting back and forth, the story is presented with clarity. It is clear that Alex Chueng's experiment with a complex plot was a great success.

Localized Characteristics Communicated by Scenes

In addition to experimental narrative modes, since his television days Alex Cheung has also been fond of scenes of suspense, excitement and passion. He has shown particular skill in handling car chases, gunplay and explosions. This is evident in the third and ninth episodes of *CID* and in *Taxi Driver: The Car Thief*. In the later *Four-Eyed Cop: The Bomb Villain*, he even develops his techniques of suspense and excitement. For example, there is an explosion scene in which the assistant of the munitions expert is hurt when disabling a bomb. The explosion is extremely powerful; flames shoot straight up into the air, and the scene is spectacular. There is also the chase scene involving Ah Wing and So Ho in *Cops and Robbers*. In a corridor of a building, Ah Wing is holding a softball bat and rushes fiercely towards his adversary. This life-or-death battle, which is breathtaking, has tremendous tension. The cop-chasing-robber act is reversed, creating a sense of hyper-reality.[9] It has become the most memorable scene in cop movies in Hong Kong.

The closing scene in *Man on the Brink* shows Ah Chiu and other robbers being discovered and then beaten up by neighbours. Although Ah Chiu escapes to a staircase, he is found and beaten to death. The scene is a large-scale one, as a huge number of people are involved. Furthermore, events are closely connected, and thus the dramatic tension is highlighted. This is particularly the case with the scene of the neighbours beating up the robbers and the rising feelings of the crowd. Shortly afterwards, the police arrive and order is temporarily restored. However, when Ah Chiu is perceived too be one of the criminals, chaos again breaks out. The police are unable to help Ah Chiu, who finally dies. The crowd then quiets down. The mood, the emotions and the treatment of the plot make this a classic scene of cop movies of that period.

Most of the scenes in Alex Cheung's movies are set in squatter huts, temporary public housing estates, avenues and alleys, dim corners and so forth. These are the places frequented by low-income people. These images of destitute, run-down areas are the aesthetic hallmarks of the New Wave.[10] Apart from Alex Cheung's films, such settings are also found in, to mention a few, Ann Hui's *The Secret* and *The Spooky Bunch*; Yim Ho's *The Happening* and *Wedding Bell, Wedding Belles*; Tsui Hark's *Dangerous Encounter – 1st Kind*; Allen Fong's *Father and Son* and *Ah Ying*; and Terry Tong's *Collies Killer*. Under Cheung's lens, public housing estates are represented as a cradle of socially marginal people and delinquents. Other kinds of space that criminals often frequent are gymnasiums, billiard halls, inns, brothels, casinos and nightclubs. These places, portrayed as dim and dirty, are equated with crime. Shops such as banks, jewelry stores, watch and clock stores, as well as wealthy people, are the targets of criminals. The ritualistic signs of inauguration into the triads, including wine, a flag, the killing of a chicken and blood dripping, are essential visual elements. They heighten the realistic atmosphere and the colours, which makes the film more convincing. After all, compared to *Jumping Ash*,[11] Cheung's cop movies, specifically *Cops and Robbers*, conveys a sense of the ridiculous. Thus, despite the fast-paced shooting and an inability to escape from the genre form, Cheung's movie has a satirical feel to it, the philosophical sheen of fatalism.

Notes

1. Shu Kei. 'Ping Zhang Guoming de liangbu zuoping: *CID dijiuji* yu *kongzhe de niaolong*' (Critique of two works of Alex Cheung: *CID No. 9* and *An Empty Birdcage**). *Datexie* (Close-Up). No. 41. 9 September 1977, pp. 30–31.
2. Ibid.
3. Lu Li. 'Zhepian bushi Zhang Guoming de youdian he quedian dui *Datexie* de quedian he youdian' (About strengths and weaknesses not of Alex Cheung but of *Close-Up*). *Datexie*. No. 44, 21 October 1977, pp. 36–37.
4. Cheung Cheuk-cheung, To-to, Tang Siu-han. (Interview). 'How does Alex Cheung overcome death and challenges?' *City Entertainment*. No. 5, 15 March 1979, p. 34.
5. Li Tang. 'Zhang Guoming: wushizitong de tiancai?' (Alex Cheung: a genius who had no teacher, but learned on his own?) *Datexie*. No. 48. 23 December 1977, p. 52.
6. The same as endnote 3.
7. Lam Yu. 'Besides violence, what does *Cops and Robbers* have?' *City Entertainment*. No. 21, 25 October 1979, p. 6.
8. John Cawelti. *The Six-Gun Mystique*. Ohio: Bowling Green University Press, 1984, p. 12.
9. Shek Kei. *Shek Kei's Anthology of Film Reviews: The Raging Approach of the New Wave*. Hong Kong Subculture Press, 1999, p. 144.
10. Stephen Teo. *Hong Kong Cinema: The Extra Dimensions*. London: British Film Institute, 1997, p. 146.
11. *Jumping Ash* (dir. Leong Po-chih, 1976). The advertising style of shooting astonished audiences with its freshness. The film was, thus, a relatively experimental cop movie at that time.

9

Studies on Non-Core New Wave Directors

Kirk Wong and Clifford Choi

Kirk Wong

Wong Chi-keung, Kirk, was born in Hong Kong in 1949. In 1974, he went to England to study fashion design at the Jacob Kramer College in Leeds. After graduating, he continued studying stage design and film at Covert Art. He returned to Hong Kong in 1978, where he did a stint with TVB and directed dramas such as *Longtan qunying** *Nüren sanshi,**and entertainment programmes such as *Sounds Like Bang Bang** and *Enjoy Yourselves Tonight*. In the 1980s, he entered the film industry and made a handful of films, including *The Club* (1981), *Health Warning* (1983), *Life Line Express* (1985), *True Colours* (1986), *Gun Men* (1988), *Taking Manhattan* (1991), *Crime Story* (1993), *Organized Crime and Triad Bureau* (1993) and *The Big Hit* (1999). In recent years he has even been involved in acting.

During his days in television, Wong's potential had not yet been realized. His somewhat better works were *Longtan qunying** and *Sounds Like Bang Bang,** but these two dramas did not attract much public attention. It was not until the appearance of his first film, *The Club*, that his talent in shooting action movies was revealed, and he became considered a latter-day member of the New Wave. *The Club* is a story about triad battles over territory. The emphasis on manhood, masculinity and violence are elements inherited from Zhang Che. Wong's romantic and direct style strikes the audience with the force of his images and displays his special appeal. This has allowed him to carve out a place for himself in the film industry.

Sex, Violence and Death

The Club is in fact a film with a clichéd and empty story and formulaic characters. Chan Wai-man and Tsui Siu-keung's 'big brother', Brother Hon, jointly run the 'Princess Nightclub'. Its prosperity incites the jealousy of two gangs: Uncle Wah, who is in real estate; and Chow Kee who is also in the nightclub business. Chan and Hon are nearly murdered, but they bravely strike back and kill their adversaries. This film is actually nothing more than a combination of the 'pillow' and 'fists' approach; that is, the sex and violence formula. Except for the idea of righteousness and the male-dominated heroic myth, this film in fact contains no further meanings for contemplation. Perhaps it is a kind of emotional release for Kirk Wong. 'In the real world, I cannot wreak destruction, but in the film world I am permitted to do so', he said.[1] Therefore, *The Club* contains scene after scene of destruction, with gangs fighting over territories and interests. They are breathtaking and show the distinctive style of the director. The most remarkable scene is the one in which Chan Wai-man rejects Brother Hon's invitation to meet with Uncle Wah because he has an appointment with Lee Mei-po. Going to the meeting alone, Brother Hon is attacked as he sets foot in the building where Wah's office is located. This line of action is intercut with sex scenes between Chan and his lover. Brother Hon is chased by two big bodybuilders; he has been stabbed and is covered with blood. Just outside the building, road construction work is in process. The thundering noise of the machine motor accompanies the chase. When the two giants approach Brother Hon with an electric saw, the glass door of the building opens. As the noise of the machine motor fades, the sound of the electric saw rises. In the end, Brother Hon is killed with the saw. The camera immediately cuts to the street outside, whereupon the sounds from inside and outside the building merge and become indistinguishable. The design of this scene shows Kirk Wong's sensitivity in devising inner and outer and active and quiet atmospheres. The sounds from the machines blend together the drilling machine is used as a metaphor for the acts of making love and violent murder. The two lines of actions are shown using parallel editing. Progressing gradually, the climactic moment of the sex scene matches that of the murder. Though perhaps somewhat unsubtle and clichéd, the director has killed two birds with one stone. The conflicts in the film do not lie between the gangsters and the policemen, but between the gangsters themselves. 'This kind of internal conflict – between individual and society, between self interest and the public interest, between Chan's savageness and his morality – is projected onto the community.'[2]

In *The Club*, every sex scene is followed by a massacre. The love scene with Chan and Lee is linked to the murder of Brother Hon. Another one involving Chan and Miyai Lena is followed by the murder of Michiko by her opponent, a gangster. In the end, the protagonists and the antagonists massacre each other; with Chan and Tsui eliminating their foes, including Uncle Wah. Likewise, in *Health Warning*, Lui Leung-wai's injury incurred in the boxing ring is followed by a sex scene between him and a girl from the 'Cross Gang' who visits him. However, the girl burns him to death by spraying him with toxic chemicals. The master of Wong Lung-wai, Gao Hong, infiltrates the 'Cross Gang' to connect to a computer programme that will make it possible to rescue a little girl.

But he is killed by a female member of the 'Cross Gang'. Although his death does not come after a sex scene, it is caused by a woman. The film closes with the victory of Wong Lung-wai, a disciple of Justice House, who saves the small girl and defeats the 'Cross Gang', departing in glory. In *The Club*, women are merely sexual objects to men. The only role they play is that their death incites men to attack their enemies. In *Health Warning*, women are the opposite of men – such a binary opposition is a formula of genre films. Other instances of opposition are those between individuals and the community, between order and chaos and so forth.

Therefore, in *Health Warning*, women are the adversaries of men. In the plot, it is women who, active and aggressive, kill a male character, Lui Leung-wai, and show no sympathy. Compared to the characters in *Health Warning*, those in *The Club* are clearly categorized as good and evil, right or wrong. To rephrase this in negative terms, the representation of the characters is relatively superficial. But this sort of direct portrayal and narrative allows the audience to understand the plot and to become involved in it without much thought. *The Club* is similar to a costume martial arts film. The only difference is the modern visual element, modern packaging and strong rhythm of the editing. It is 'a martial arts film with a modern look'. The film's simple values have been dubbed 'comic heroism' by some critics.[3] In fact, the conflicts in both films are superficial; then turn into violence and are resolved via settling the threats hanging over individuals, groups or the entire society. This is the formula of genre films in general. Thus, this film became popular among midnight moviegoers and the public. With *Health Warning*, Wong shifted gears to making a film with something to say. The world portrayed in this film is one set in the future. The characters are wooden and unsympathetic, with expressionless faces and mechanical actions. Even the protagonists, including Gao Hong, Lui Leung-wai and Wong Lung-wai, who come from Justice House, hardly speak, and when they do their words are dull. As a result, the audience could not identify with them. In addition, the antagonists, such as the members of the 'Cross Gang', are all bizarre characters with demonic spirits. It is difficult to distinguish between the male and the female, and even between the good and the evil characters. For instance, the protagonist, played by Wong Lung-wai, is obsessed with porn magazines.

Is the intention to communicate the opposition between good and evil, tradition and technology or East and West? In fact, on this point the film is unclear and even contradictory. For example, Wong Lung-wai is wounded with a toxic needle by a female disciple of the 'Cross Gang'. His master, Gao Hung, heals him with indecent medical practices instead of orthodox Chinese medicine. Another scene shows Gao and Wong rescuing a little girl from the base of their opponents, the 'Cross Gang'. For a practitioner of Chinese traditional martial arts, Gao is surprisingly knowledgeable about advanced technology, such as how to smoothly operate a computer. This adds to the audience's confusion. An even greater contradiction is that the 'Cross Gang' is a high-tech gang that can even replicate human beings. In theory, it should possess advanced, high-tech weaponry. Strangely, when the master and student find themselves in a battle with the Gang, the gangsters have no weapons but their bare fists or, at most, toxic sprays. In the end, Gao and Wong win the fight. As a representative of high-end technology, the 'Cross Gang' fails to carry out its expected role and function. This enables Wong to rescue his mother and daughter and depart. In other words, *Health Warning* does have a message to communicate, but does not do this successfully, because it lacks a clear channel to deliver its message. That is to say, the film's portrayal of the world of the future is somewhat primitive. A concrete, workable mode of representation has not been achieved. The internal contradictions in this film are many and take place at various levels, for instance, in form and content. In the end, however, they cancel each other out as the plot develops.[4]

Despite the inconsistencies and even contradictions in characters and meanings of the film, what is evident is that Kirk Wong's unwillingness to repeat himself and his search for innovations are evident. Often, Wong operates in opposition to orthodoxy and tradition. In the boxing scene in *Health Warning*, for example, Wong uses long takes, whereas fight scenes are often constructed using fast-paced montages to produce excitement and impact. Wong, on the other hand, does just the opposite to show every single detail of the boxing, which allows the audience to witness the responses of the combatants in a complete time-and-space framework. This distinctive, strong style is the greatest strength of the film, while its most obvious flaw is that its representational mode fails to satisfy the expectations of the audiences in the way genre films are meant to do. Nevertheless, this film is full of imagination and is subversive of genres. It also employs an audacious representational style that it is made up of single shots. It can be called an avant-garde work in commercial mainstream cinema.[5]

Women as Subjects of Subordination and Sacrifice

In making a film, Kirk Wong's first concern is whether it is entertaining; vision is secondary. In other words, he tends to produce commercial films.[6] Wong relies on intuition when making his films. He wanders along the streets, goes to various places and visits various groups of people to feel the hidden vitality of the city of Hong Kong.

His later work, *Life Line Express*, is a black comedy that is about transformation of destiny by a supernatural power. Kent Cheng suspects that he will not live beyond his next birthday. He then consults a university professor, who teaches him how to perform certain ritualistic practices in front of an altar. In this way, he is able to change his fate. This film advocates superstition, conservative thinking and subversive actions. *True Colours* describes Raymond Wong and Ti Lung growing up in a newly developed district. They engage in delinquent behaviour of various kinds, even to the point of committing murder and 'jumping ash' (fleeing). The two friends separate and meet again after five years. Wong has become a priest, and Ti has come to him to seek help. By chance, Ti meets his ex-girlfriend, Brigitte Lin, who is already married to a gangster, Master Ku, but who is treated contemptuously by him. Ti bravely kills Ku and is sentenced to death. This film is an average production. The characters are not depicted in a persuasive manner; for example, Wong, who was formerly a criminal, suddenly becomes a saint – a priest. The process of his metamorphosis is not explained. The film is full of this sort of carelessness. *Taking Manhattan* is a story of a Hong Kong cop, Ah Chung, who goes to the United States and acts as an undercover agent to help the New York police force in an anti-drug action. The hero is entirely without a past. Although he is an undercover cop, his wife and son know his identity, which is completely opposite from what one would expect of an undercover agent. He would naturally need to communicate with the police of both Hong Kong and New York, but the film does not show this. What it does show is the sadness of a woman, Ah Chung's wife, who is reduced to pawning her scarf to buy food. This is the same sort of sorrow that Lee Mei-feng in *Gun Men* endures. What is different is the setting, with the latter living in Shanghai in the 1920s and 30s. This was a time of civil war, and society was chaotic. Lee had no choice but to live an impoverished life. This was the fate of so many Chinese women, and the Chinese people as a whole, in the decades of the 1920s, 30s, 40s and even earlier in the century. Facing no option but prostitution, Lee is humiliated and bullied. Then, she falls in love with a policeman, Tony Leung Ka-fai, who works in the foreign concessions. Leung's wife, Ng Ka-lai, later learns of the relationship between Leung and Lee and is heartbroken. In Kirk Wong's films, women are mostly portrayed as weak, living only for men, while men are disloyal in love. Relationships outside marriage are common; fortunately, the men do not abandon their wives. Women, including wives and lovers, can only silently accept the situation. They have no sense of self, let alone the courage to resist. They are doomed to being appendages of men. In this film, Lee even risks her life to help Leung, his wife and his daughter cross the bridge. Eventually, Lee is shot dead. Lee exchanges her life for the lives of Ng Ka-lai and her daughter, completing the wholeness of Leung's family. Lee's act is certainly a kind of compensation and redemption.

Triangular relationships and women sacrificing themselves for men are also important themes in *Organized Crime and Triad Bureau* and *Rock n' Roll Cop*. In fact, in Kirk Wong's films, the intensity of a woman's love merely serves to highlight the myth of men. In *Organized Crime and Triad Bureau*, a thief, Anthony Wong, and his lover, Cecilia Yip, escape from a police cordon. The lovers help each other and strive to stay together, manifesting the value of love. Their relationship, however, is never a smooth one. How Yip came to fall in love with a criminal like Wong arose from a horrible experience that she had. Yip was raped but, frightened by the rapist's threats, her parents did not dare report the case to the police. Wong happened to be driving past and knocked the rapist to death. From then on, out of gratitude, Yip stayed with Wong as his partner in crime. Wong, for his part, is disloyal and beds different women although he has a wife. In order to protect the relationship, Yip demonstrates tolerance and, finally, forgiveness toward Wong. Wong now repays, with his true love, Yip's total commitment to him. The cruelest killer still has compassion. Once Wong had a physical examination in the hospital and the police arrived. He intended to use a boy in the operating room as a hostage, to allow himself to escape. But the boy's mother begged to Wong to free her son. The gangster was moved and dropped his weapons, and surrendered to the police. In the end, the police mount a large-scale pursuit of them. Knowing that they have no way of getting away, Wong commits suicide by swallowing a gun in exchange for Yip's freedom. Although a brutal criminal, Wong not only has compassion, but even pays with his life so that his lover will be spared. The triangular relationship among the three policemen, Lee Sau-yin, Lee Mei-feng and Cheung Yiu-yeung, leads to leaking of information about a case of arrest. Cheung, a senior police, is actually a traitor, working in complicity with Anthony Wong. Making use of Mei-feng's weakness, he threatens her to get her to steal secret information from her boyfriend, Lee Sau-yin. This eventually leads to her capture by the police. In the film, Cheung epitomizes corruption in the police. Besides being in complicity with Anthony Wong, he also frequently made use of his position to interfere with Lee Sau-yin's movements, in order to enable Wong to escape. Most serious of all, he plans to release Wong, who is in detention awaiting trial.

Where the film is most ambivalent is in the misuse of authority by the police. The police look down on the complaints unit, and even use violence to oppose it. They have become an independent kingdom that cannot be controlled. The police treat suspects brutally, beating them, injecting water into their bodies and hitting their reproductive organs. As for the criminals, they are portrayed as both compassionate and righteous. For example, Wong sacrifices himself for Yip, and Cheung Yiu-yeung is loyal to his lover until death. This romanticizing of criminals definitely transforms villains into heroes. Kirk Wong is complex in that 'he at least admits that events are often both positive and negative intertwined.[7] Without doubt, human beings are complicated creatures, but a society should have standards of good and evil. Kirk Wong's films often 'only seek to thrill, but confuse good and evil'.[8] In addition to such ambivalence, a reversal of good and bad characters is repeatedly seen. This makes the film an oddity among works in the cop genre.

Ambiguity between Good and Evil, and the Reversal of the Roles of the Hong Kong Police and Mainland Cops

Rock 'n Roll Cop is a cop movie about crime and the investigation of cases of illegal migration. In fact, the border-crossing element was already present in the preceding movie, *Crime Story*, in which policemen Jackie Chan and Kent Cheng travel to Taiwan to inspect a kidnapping that took place in Hong Kong. In this movie, both Hong Kong and Shenzhen feature in the crimes. Anthony Wong, a policeman, goes to Shenzhen alone to pursue the gangsters (one of them is Yu Wing-kwong). Because of the different social systems and ideologies in the two places, Hong Kong and mainland police have distinct ways of capturing criminals. The result is both teamwork and bifurcation between the two groups of policemen. In the end, their misunderstandings and biases are cleared up and trust and solidarity established. Together, they arrest the criminals and send them to receive their lawful punishment.

The Chinese police (the military police) began appearing as main characters in Hong Kong movies as early as in 1990 in the *Her Fatal Ways* series. This was a reversal of the practice in Hong Kong cop movies of Hong Kong police taking the lead. Furthermore, in *Rock 'n Roll Cop* and *Body Guard from Beijing* (1994),[9] the hitherto leading role of the Hong Kong police became a supporting one. Furthermore, in these films the Hong Kong police are depicted as having few successes and many failures. They are no longer 'saints'. A gambler and cheat, Kent Cheng, the overweight cop in *Body Guard from Beijing*, is involved in gambling and treachery and leads a life without discipline. His colleagues are in cahoots with a triad gang, which involuntarily makes him a mobster. In *My Father is a Hero* (1995),[10] the Hong Kong policewoman Fong Yat-wah is very far from being the equal of the mainland policewoman Gong Wai, in terms of intelligence, courage, physique and endurance.[11] It is a fact that late in the transitional period leading to the handover of sovereignty over Hong Kong to China, the status of Hong Kong police has declined while that of mainland policemen has risen.

In this film, the Hong Kong cop, Anthony Wong, is assigned an investigation in Shenzhen. In the beginning, he is boastful, bragging about his quickness with a gun, the advanced computing system of Hong Kong police and so forth. Before long, he is continually finding himself in difficulties. Once, he is taken as a hostage by a criminal, then saved when a large number of mainland policemen are sent to help him. This nearly causes the captain of the mainland policemen, Ng Hing-kwok, to send Wong back to Hong Kong to prevent Wong from ruining the investigation. At first, Ng belittles Wong. Later, when Wong several times helps him solve problems, such as decoding the password of the criminals, his perception of Wong changes. In the film, the captain is portrayed as brave, intelligent and professional. He calmly instructs his outreach teams to follow Ng Ka-lai, who passes through customs using a fake passport. Ka-lai, an ex-girlfriend of the captain, is now a mistress of the chief gangster, Yu Wing-kwong. Furthermore, the mainland cops effortlessly disperse the paparazzi who cross the border to Shenzhen to seek information. This causes the Hong Kong police to lose face, while boosting the prestige of the mainland team. Captain Ng is portrayed as a man of compassion and righteousness. In the midst of pursuing Ng Ka-lai, he is discovered by the criminals. A shoot-out ensues, during which Ng Ka-lai is injured. The captain immediately holds his dying ex-girlfriend in his lap. He rushes out of the building, puts her in a wooden cart and sends her to the hospital. However, she has lost too much blood and dies on the way to the hospital. This sequence shows the captain's compassionate side. His righteousness is manifested in the final sequence, when the gangster boss is captured. Captain Ng transfers the criminal to Anthony Wong, who is at the border, to be escorted to Hong Kong. But looking through a pair of binoculars, he sees Wong being attacked by the gangster. At the most critical moment, Captain Ng, without delay, removes the golden badge of the mainland police and crosses the border to rescue Wong. This selfless spirit deserves respect. This film is a pioneer among Hong Kong films in depicting mainland policemen in a positive, even embellished light.

A subsequent film, *Body Guard from Beijing*, is about a mainland policeman sent by the Central Government, Jet Li. Li is given the assignment of guarding Miss Chung, a girlfriend of a merchant who has a close connection with mainland China. He is shown in his police uniform standing under the Chinese five-star red flag, then entering the colony of Hong Kong, a scene of intense significance. Li is sophisticated in martial arts skills, obeys commands and is decisive, serious, smart and good-looking. In a battle against criminals, he guards Miss Chung by shielding her with his body from bullets and nearly dies. Not merely a hero, this mainland policeman, who has been sent by the central government, becomes a 'superman'. In *My Father is a Hero*, a mainland policeman, Gong Wai, is given a secret mission by his superiors, which requires him to keep his identity a secret. Traveling to Hong Kong, he is compelled to ignore the security of his family. Even when his son is beaten up and nearly tortured to death, he can do nothing in order not to expose his real identity and thus spoil the plan. His life is an even smaller matter; he is ready to sacrifice it for his country at any time or place. This image of a mainland policeman is so elevated that it leaves the Hong Kong police far below in the dust. It can be said that the way in which mainland policemen were depicted in Hong Kong movies gradually changed as the handover approached. In the earlier works such as *Her Fatal Ways* I, II and III and the later *His Fatal Way*,[12] mainland policemen were pictured as being funny, humorous, old-fashioned and ignorant. Then, in *Her Fatal Ways* IV, they were shown as having an amiable side and as being responsible, courageous and persistent in finishing the tasks that had been assigned to them. In *The Trail*,[13] the mainland policeman, Lui Siu-po, is shown as being extremely disciplined, just and responsible. Hong Kong people, by contrast, are so profit-seeking that they will engage in libel or even arrange murders in exchange for money. Thus, the image of mainland cops has changed as communication and understanding between Hong Kong and mainland China have increased. However, their positive image was eventually elevated to that of a 'superman' or even a god, which is too far from reality. The intention of the film-maker was to turn what had been negative into something positive, but the result was overdone.

Hong Kong Glamour in Hollywood

Gun Men, a nostalgic film by Kirk Wong, is about a policeman, Tony Leung Ka-fai, in the foreign concessions who is battling the drug business. In the process, he becomes an implacable enemy of the leader of the drug traffickers, Adam Cheng. By coincidence, the story resembles that of the Hollywood production *The Untouchables*,[14] which is about an American finance official in the 1920s, Kevin Costner, who is combating the triad boss, Al Capone – the 'Mayor of the underground' – who is involved in bootlegging. The two films are similar in subject matter, but very different in scale of production. The former is a small production and the latter is a big-budget film. A film scholar, David Bordwell, compared the spaces in the scenes and the use of shots in these two works. He pointed out that in *The Untouchables*, extremely long shots have been taken in a wider space, which weakened the effects of the action. The pace appears too fast, but there are too many slow actions (especially those imitating the sequence of the Odessa Steps in *Battleship Potemkin*), which make the scenes appear uninteresting. By contrast, *Gun Men*, which was shot in narrow alleys, relies on close-ups and medium shots to give the film vigour.

With the use of artistic techniques, such as fast rhythm, appropriate *mise-en-scène* and economical use of montage, the scenes are spectacular.[15] With limited resources, Kirk Wong and his fellow workers in Hong Kong cinema directed films that are lively and accomplished. This gave them the qualifications to go to Hollywood[16] and for their films to become recognized globally.

The action comedy *The Big Hit* (1998)[17] was the first film Kirk Wong made in the United States. It is a comedy, with a strong comic-book flavour. Wong had the idea of making a comedy as early as the time when he was directing his first Hong Kong picture, *The Club*.[18] After seventeen years, his dream was fulfilled in Hollywood. This movie opens with a kidnapping scene. The four main characters, including Melvin and Cisco, kidnap Akiko, the daughter of a Japanese industrialist, unaware that she is the god-daughter of their boss. As a result, not only do they not obtain any money, they are in danger of getting killed. In *Organized Crime and Triad Bureau*, which he made before he moved to Hollywood, Wong shot scenes in the streets in Wan Chai (Hong Kong) to produce exciting gun battles. With a dynamic style and quick editing, Wong established a style of his own. In Hollywood, his production budgets and working conditions are better than in Hong Kong, which makes it possible for him to expand his skills. As in the opening scene of *The Big Hit*, there are gun battles and explosions. Roaring flames are reflected in the water, presenting a mesmerizing spectacle. The mood is adjusted appropriately and the excitement is interspersed with humour. A notable example is the scene in which Melvin sits at the same table as a man who intends to kill him and his future parents-in-law. Each killer is secretly aiming a gun at the other under the table. But when the tablecloth is removed, they hurry to hide their guns; those who fail to conceal them are forced to shoot. The sudden changes of action in such a short time have unexpected effects. For example, Akiko twice nearly encounters Melvin's girlfriend when she leaves the room. Another characteristic of this film is that the audience is first shown the consequence of certain events (similar to the technique of 'flash-forward') and later informed about the key parts of the process; the truth is then revealed. The effect that is created is that of a 'reversal', in that the result is different from the earlier impression. For example, Melvin is pursued by Cisco, who intends to murder him. The car hurtles down a hill toward Melvin, who immediately runs. The audience probably believes that Cisco has died in the car. But, unexpectedly, when Melvin leisurely goes to return a video tape, Cisco suddenly appears. At the moment, the audience is told that in the car crash sequence, Cisco merely escaped from the exploding car and jumped into a lake, unharmed. This technique is replicated in the closing part of the film. Akiko believes that Melvin has died in an explosion in the video shop. When she returns home, Melvin reappears and the two lovers embrace. To use the same device twice in one film is perhaps excessive. But it is remarkable that Kirk Wong has made use of the advantages of American capital and technology to produce distinctive films, with comic humour and a natural flow that is difficult to achieve.

Clifford Choi

Choi Kai-kwong, Clifford, was born in Hong Kong on 12 November 1946. He moved to Taiwan in 1965 to study at the National Taiwan Normal University, majoring in English. He then furthered his studies in English literature in the United States in 1968 at the University of California, Berkeley. Two years later, he enrolled in the Centre of Film Studies at the State University of San Francisco, earning his master's degree in 1972. In 1973, he began working in the city for KPIX Television on channel five as a news photographer. He also did a brief stint with the station KGO. In 1975, he returned to Hong Kong and joined TVB. As a scriptwriter-director, Choi made some dramas, including *Wonderful, Wong Fei Hung* (1976) and *The Water Margin* (1977). He moved to making feature films in 1978. He wrote the script for *Snake in the Eagle's Shadow* and, in the meantime, founded the Centre of Film Culture of Hong Kong with a group of young *cinephiles*. In 1979, he started teaching at the School of Communication of Hong Kong Baptist College. In the following decade, he made his first feature, *The Encore*. Several other films followed, namely *No U-turn* (1981), *Teenage Dreamers* (1982), *Hong Kong Hong Kong* (1983), *Grow Up In Anger* (1986), *Devil and Angel* (1987), *Big Brother* (1989), *Naughty Couple* (1994) and *Lai Man Wai* (2001). He is currently teaching in the School of Film and TV at the Hong Kong Academy for Performing Arts.

In Choi's days in television, his dramas, such as *Wong Fei Hung* and *The Water Margin*, already demonstrated a strong national consciousness and the anti-feudalist thinking. He re-interpreted folk legends or ancient novels in very innovative ways, using modern concepts and expressing his own ideas. Among his New Wave contemporaries who were still undergoing training in television stations, Choi was a director who was particularly imbued with national consciousness and a modern social consciousness. His television works were very well received.[19] This was not because they featured new narrative modes or experiments in cinematic language. Rather, Choi's success was because he put 'new wine into old bottles', expressed his own views and boldly changed old ways of looking at things. He re-created characters from traditional tales such as in his *The Water Margin No. 6* and combined figures in legends with prominent periods in Chinese, as in, for example, his *Wong Fei Hung* drama series. This is where Clifford Choi stands out.

Intense National and Social Consciousness

Wong Fei Hung was a figure in folk legends of Guangdong Province during the late Qing Dynasty and the early Republican period. This was a time of crisis, when the western powers were invading China, the Qing government was corrupt, the country was becoming weaker day by day and society was unstable. The Wong Fei Hung portrayed in the film is a national hero who, together with the people of Guangdong, resist the invasion of the foreign powers. In *Wong Fei Hung: Whipping the Dream of Gold Away**, a disciple of Wong Club Foot, returns slightly drunk to his lodgings. On the way there, he is shanghaied and placed on a boat with several dozen Chinese men who have been either forced or deceived into going to the 'Gold Mountain' (San

Francisco) in the United States. Some believed that upon arriving in America they would find gold lying about everywhere. They did not realize the trap they had fallen into. As soon as Wong heard about this, he led a group of disciples and forcibly boarded the boat just before it was about to leave. With long whips, they fought the westerners on board who had come to China to steal human labour. All of the captives were thus rescued. The 'golden dream' of the white villains was shattered. Another episode of the drama series was about the weak maritime defences of the Qing government. Japanese travelers and military men sometimes appear. Some of them are spies charged with the mission of appropriating information on China's maritime defences. They are disguised as merchants and are drawing maps of the coastline of Guangdong to bring back to Japan for use in invading China. The plot of Japanese spies attempting to penetrate China's maritime defences appeared in King Hu's *The Valiant Ones* (1974). In this film, the Ming Emperor Jiajing sends Yu Dayou to remove the enemies plaguing China's coast. Yu adopts a chess tactic in deploying his military forces, and the adversary finally retreats. In *Wong Fei Hung*, the hero's followers inform him about a conspiracy by Japanese spies acting in collusion with corrupt merchants. Wong therefore makes plans to arrest the villains. He leads his students in a battle against a Japanese knight using weaponry from Hung's school. While the battle is taking place, the spies steal back to Japan with the maps. In a moment of crisis for China, Wong uses his knowledge and wisdom, collaborates with his people, defeats the villains. He succeeds in combating imperialism and fighting against Japan's ambition to invade the marine territory of China.

Adapted from a Chinese literary classic, *The Water Margin: Booty Captured* shows Leung Chung-shu, the son-in-law of Choi King, giving an assignment to his general, Yeung Chi. Yeung Chi is to masquerade as a merchant to send a gift to the capital to congratulate Official Choi. Fearful of thieves along the way, Yeung forbids his subordinates to rest or drink wine. Sometimes, he kicks them, which leads to a great deal of resentment. In the end, Siu Koi and other strong fellows add a drug to the wine, causing all to become drunk and to collapse. The gift is then stolen. To Siu Koi and his counterparts, Leung Chung-shu, Ko Kao and Choi King are all corrupt officials who are out to fleece the people. Therefore, they regard their move to ruin the plan as an act of justice. Siu Koi and the other heroes have been mistreated by troops in the entourage of civil officials. For example, the family of Pak-shing, who sell wine, are so poor that they are on the point of starvation, but the government still demands that they pay taxes. To do so, they are forced to pawn their meagre garments for money. The soldiers even steal a jade figurine from them, a family heirloom. Without a doubt, the society is one in which both thieves and officials are robbers; thus, the logic that robbing Choi is a perfectly righteous act. The consciousness of official oppression and rebellion by the people is ubiquitous and unambiguous in the narrative.

The most memorable episode of *The Water Margin* is the sixth one. The representation of the female protagonist Pan Jinlian is completely different from the negative image of a lascivious lady of the original text. In the television-drama version, she is a woman who is courageous, expressive and ambitious in pursuing love. She once worked in a wealthy family as a maid. The master of the household was a lustful man. One night, he tried to rape Pan. Thinking quickly, she banged on a drum to call every person in the family. This behaviour scared the master away. He fled in the dark but was finally caught and beaten up. She marries Big Brother Wu, but loves his younger brother, Wu Song. However, Wu Song does not respond to her overtures, as he is an upright person who closely adheres to moral norms. Later, Pan is introduced by another lady to smart, spirited Xi Menqing. The lovers meet secretly and, eventually, Pan poisons her husband to death. Wu Song learns the news and vows to avenge his dead elder brother. First, he murders Xi; and then he rebukes Pan for being a lewd woman who does not keep to the path expected of women. Pan replies,

> If I am lewd, aren't men responsible for this? Every man can have more than one wife or concubine.... It is you who arouses the fantasies that make me lustful. Since I met Xi Menqing, it is as if I have become an entirely different person. I have enjoyed the kind of pleasure that I have never had before. Now that I have tasted such pleasure, I will not regret dying.

Wu then kills her with one thrust of his blade. In the drama, Pan is depicted as someone who is courageous enough to defy the constraints placed on women in a feudal society to pursue her own happiness. Thus, she is a pioneer in the movement for women's liberation in China, not a lascivious, evil lady as she has been cast according to traditional standards of morality.

The intense sense of nation and society seen in Clifford Choi's films arose out of his experience of studying in the United States. Choi chose to study literature, but because his western professors looked down on Chinese, they advised him to change his major to linguistics. Choi did not want to do so and debated the matter with the professors for some time. This happened in the late 1960s, when hippies and student movements flourished. All of this had a great impact on Choi. In addition, in 1971 and 1972, a dispute over the Diaoyu Islands flared up. Chinese in the United States held demonstrations in defence of China's claim over the Diaoyu Islands. This also incited a sense of national consciousness in Choi and stirred his first feelings of concern about the future of his nation. At about that time, he began to participate in community activities in San Francisco's Chinatown, in order to gain an understanding of the unjust treatment meted out to Chinese in a foreign land. All of these experiences directly or indirectly influenced the perspectives of the films that he would later make.

The Philosophy of Love: Trust and Openness

The Encore was Clifford Choi's first film. It is about two pairs of young lovers. One pair is grappling with the problem of a pre-marital pregnancy. Because of parental disapproval, they are prohibited from marrying. After the boy loses his job, he takes his girlfriend to get an abortion. Another pair, Danny Chan and Mary Yung Ching-ching, have a pure and romantic love that is punctuated by occasional quarrels and conflicts.

The film poses the questions encountered by the youth, such as love, study, family, the generation gap and so forth; and addresses them in a way that reveals the attitudes of the subjects. The closing sequence is a '1980's Amateur Singing Contest'. The contest is divided up into four sections: folk songs, avant-garde music, rock and roll and Cantopop. The male protagonist, Danny Chan, wins the championship in the last category with the song 'Encore', and the film has a happy ending. His girlfriend and parents are present to offer support, and the misunderstandings and conflicts between the two generations are resolved. The film depicts the attitudes of youth in a lively, natural and highly realistic way. It also provides an impressive yet unexaggerated, non-sensational portrayal of friendship, brotherhood and the bittersweet love of young people. Consider, for instance, the interaction between Danny Chan and Mary Yung. Meeting her in a library, Chan is struck by Yung's beauty. He gets her name and telephone number when they are in an elevator. Later, at home, with some trepidation, he gives her a call. The story is told in a natural and believable way and was very well received by a young audience.

No U-turn is a light comedy about young love. Different from the pure love portrayed in *The Encore, No U-turn* involves a triangular relationship. A taxi driver, Lam Kar-wah, encounters a salesgirl, Annie Liu, in a boutique. Later, Liu's cousin, who comes from a wealthy family, returns from the United States and begins pursuing her. Liu is trapped in a dilemma: should she choose the rich man who possesses a Rolls-Royce and wears fashionable clothes or the one from the working class? In the end, love conquers all, and Liu opts for Lam. The film spends a considerable amount of time depicting the differences between classes. For example, Lam is invited to a party thrown by Liu's cousin. All of the guests are rich businessmen, who drive expensive cars. Among them, Lam is a total misfit and is scorned. Finally, he leaves alone. After featuring in her cousin's fashion advertisements, Liu is given all of the designer clothing she has modeled. Liu has never owned such high-end clothing, and she is overjoyed. In the path of love, she is confronted with choices. In other words, she holds the initiative, which shows that women are no longer in a passive position. This is progress of a kind. In the end, Lam Kar-wah beats Liu's cousin in a car race and also gets the girl. These ideas or plots are perhaps clichéd; however, they offer the kind of mental fulfillment that poor people can obtain in only fantasy, not in reality. They thus help to somewhat lessen the impact of social conflicts and contradictions, while maintaining the strengthening of the existing order in society.

Debates about Youth Films

Clifford Choi's third picture, *Teenage Dreamers,* also centres on young people. The characters' views of love reflect the life of young people at a certain stage. Coincidentally, two films of the same genre appeared soon afterwards: *Lonely Fifteen* (1982) and *Once Upon a Rainbow* (1982).[20] The box office response to *Teenage Dreamers* and *Lonely Fifteen* was unexpectedly good,[21] thus arousing the attention of the public. Various newspapers and media outlets held debates on the so-called 'youth films', and two public seminars were organized in which experts and critics in education, culture and film took part.[22] In both seminars, the discussions were heated. At one point, Clifford Choi, who was one of the speakers, left to express his disapproval. The arguments of the two sides were as follows: Those who supported youth films did so because such films reflected various current social issues, for example, prostitution. Such problems existed already and had not been created by these films. If films were to only show something praiseworthy, it was unlikely that the reality would change for the better (Leung Nong-kong). Johnny Mak defended *Lonely Fifteen*, saying that it contained no obscene or violent elements. Furthermore, youth films exposed certain realistic problems in Hong Kong, particularly juvenile delinquency, to the audience, arousing public attention. Clifford Choi pointed out that the function of films was to reveal certain issues, while the job of providing follow-up action and solutions was one for social workers and educators. Those opposed to youth films questioned whether these movies were really representative of real life, and stated that if they focused on revealing problems but not supplying solutions, immature young people could easily be misled into wrongdoing. Szeto Wah (chairman of the Hong Kong Professional Teachers' Union) claimed that these movies offered no real help for social ills, but rather worsened them. They also smeared the image of certain positive figures. One teacher pointed to a scriptwriter who was present at the seminar and said that he had betrayed himself, like a woman who has sold her body (such a comment seemed to be a personal attack). Other teachers suggested that the Film Censorship Unit tighten its regulation to prohibit the release of such films, which provoked strong disapproval from many of those present. It was shocking to hear these intellectuals in a society that enjoys freedom of speech asking the government to use its political force to 'purify' the media and disregarding the danger of singularization of thought.[23] If intellectuals lack an open mind and tolerance for different opinions, is this not much more horrifying than the act of revealing the dark side of society? In the same seminar, however, Chan Man offered a constructive opinion. Chan declared that there was a need to respect the professionalism of film and freedom of creativity, which meant that there could be no uniformity of artistic representation. Moreover, he advocated that media criticism be made part of the curriculum in schools, to enhance the analytic capability of students. In fact, the causes of social problems were numerous and varied – a problematic social culture, an imbalance of wealth and the entire social structure – all had a bearing. These causes, not solely the film industry, also demanded our attention. Film-makers did not create these problems, but reflected them. Every member of the society shared the responsibility of finding solutions, and solving the problems would require the combined strength of the entire community.

The above debate on youth films is an example of the responses from society that were provoked by the New Wave films. The three waves of debate in the 1980s on films[24] were all set off by these new directors. This is evidence of the fact that New Wave members dared to tackle sensitive subjects that others might avoid.

From the Beginning to the Completion of Localization

Youth films did not begin to appear in Hong Kong only in the 1980s, but as early as the 1960s. They were a very early step in the localization of Hong Kong cinema. However, the productions of the 1960s were heavily influenced by western movies of the 1950s such as *Rebel Without a Cause*, *On the Waterfront* and *The Wild One*, and *West Side Story* in the 1960s.[25] The archetypal image of the rebellious youngster in these films had a profound influence on the Hong Kong youth movies of that period. Therefore, it was not difficult to see aspects of western popular culture such as Elvis Presley's music, the Beatles and go-go dancing in Hong Kong productions. Thus, genuine localization cannot be considered to have been achieved. Some of the Hong Kong youth movies of the time that can be considered somewhat representative include *Prince of Broadcasters* (1966), *I Love A-Go-Go* (1967), *The Joys and Sorrows of Youth* (1969), *Social Characters* (1969) and *The Teddy Girls* (1969).[26] These productions present an array of plots and motifs. The next generation rebels against money-minded parents who obstruct their love, as shown in *The Student Prince*. Delinquent behaviour among youth, such as engaging in kidnapping, blackmail, taking obscene photographs and rape, is common. It is chilling to view the twisted and depraved nature of human beings as shown, for example, in *The Joys and Sorrows of Youth*. Or as communicated in the film *Social Characters*, where parents oppose a youth romance and the youngsters then give themselves up to a life of decadence. Another example is seen in *The Teddy Girls*, which is about broken families that deprive their children of love, while a corrupt society causes young people to commit crimes. However, after encountering setbacks and difficulties in life, most of these young people repent, learn their lesson and pay for their wrongdoing. In many cases, the films close with a happy ending. This kind of ending is evident in *The Student Prince*: Ding Ying's father begs the forgiveness of the 'student prince', Tang Kwong-wing, and the movie ends with the union of the hero and the heroine. Another example is seen in *I Love A-Go-Go*, where Got Fong-fong finally leaves her wealthy biological parents to return to her adoptive father. Also, in *The Joys and Sorrows of Youth* the family of the millionaire Ng suffers the bitter consequences of his actions, which functions as a sort of redemptive compensation. In *Social Characters*, Tang Kwong-wing is the prodigal son who returns home after going astray. The last example is *The Teddy Girls*. After acts of vengeance, some of the girls are arrested and others return to the Girls' Home, where they are deservedly punished. There is a long, didactic speech in the film about family and society lying at the heart of the problem of youth delinquency.

As for youth films of the 1980s, *Teenage Dreamers* is about four schoolgirls. The plot centres on the relationship between Chow Sau-lan and Leslie Cheung. They become acquainted when both of them are acting in a play. They fall in love and develop a sexual relationship. Cheung is a playboy, who has a casual attitude towards relationships and is never faithful in love. Chow gradually learns of Cheung's irresponsible ways. Cheung gets involved in another love affair, this time with a western girl. In the final act of the play, Chow is full of devotion and kisses Cheung passionately. When the play is over, she comes to her senses and calmly parts from Cheung. *Lonely Fifteen* is a film about delinquent juvenile girls. The four girls come from the lower class and do not have their own independent personalities but are completely reliant on men for their existence. Of the four main characters, the first becomes a drug addict; the second is seriously injured in a car accident; the third commits suicide after being mistreated by a man; and the last is killed after being intimate with her boyfriend.[27] Another film, *Once Upon a Rainbow*, is about romance among young people participating in an acting training programme. The female protagonist, Tsui Kit, takes the initiative to pursue a classmate, Ng Siu-kong, who is the kind of young man who easily transfers his affections from one girl to another. Another female character, Chong Ching-yee, saves Tsui from being raped, by offering herself to the rapists. Chong thereafter no longer regards chastity as a means to secure a marriage. In all of the above three movies, women are the main protagonists. In *Teenage Dreamers*, Chow Sau-lan loses her virginity to Leslie Cheung after being deceived by him. But she does not fall into despair or anger; but gathers together her self-respect and lives in strength. Ending on a sad note, deprived of family warmth and school care and attracted by material temptations, all of the girls in *Lonely Fifteen* fall into depravity. *Once Upon a Rainbow*, on the other hand, is more equivocal and accommodating; the relationship depicted in the film is also more fragile.

All of these three films are 1980s productions and can be said to represent the growth of the young people of Hong Kong, from fantasy to disillusionment with love and from there to an understanding of life and of their society. They are genuine local movies. Even in the singing contest in *The Encore*, for example, the song that the male protagonist performs is a purely Cantopop one. This is a sign that, with the New Wave movies, the localization of Hong Kong cinema was complete. With regard to Clifford Choi's films, the protagonists in his *The Encore* certainly believe in love, but this changes in his later film *Teenage Dreamers*. As in the other two youth films, *Lonely Fifteen* and *Once Upon a Rainbow*, the protagonists in *Teenage Dreamer* come to reject blind faith in love. Instead, they hold a more open attitude. This is the result of the changing times.

The Cruelty of Reality and the Disillusionment of Dreams

Clifford Choi's first three films are relatively realistic. They depict everyday life, focus on details and do not have exaggerated plots. However, he began to use the technique of sensationalism in his film *Hong Kong Hong Kong*. By the time he got to *Devil and Angel*, he lost all restraint. *Hong Kong Hong Kong* is about a female illegal immigrant, Cherie Chung, who, in order to survive, becomes the secondary wife of a middle-aged carpenter, Kwan Hoi-shan. Later, she becomes acquainted with a Thai-Chinese boxer, Alex Man. Their fates being similar, they feel compassion for each other, which develops into affection. In the end, Chung falls down a staircase, which causes her to miscarry. Man carries the injured Chung and walks, symbolically, towards an uncertain future. The character Chung is an illegal immigrant who has no identity card and lives in a squatter area with other people of the same class. Men are the breadwinners and women are available to them, whenever they need, to satisfy their sexual desires. Thus, women are merely objects upon which men relieve themselves, and their bodies are the most ancient, primitive type of commodity for which they exchange the necessities of life. It is in such circumstances that Cherie Chung uses her body to survive. In the film, there is a scene of a beauty pageant on TV, in which the candidates display their attractive bodies. The allusion is that those women are no different from Cherie Chung;

they are selling their youth. Chung became Kwan's second wife only to be able to stay in Hong Kong and to survive. She is given five hundred dollars a month on the condition that she bears a son. In this way, Chung becomes a 'machine for producing offspring' for Kwan.[28] Likewise, Man engages in boxing matches merely for money. His body is also objectified and commodified, being converted into a 'machine for producing wealth'. On the boxing ring, Man is capable of winning, but his unethical boss, who is interested only in money, demands that he lose. Once, in fury, he swung his fist and defeated his opponent. However, he was accused of taking stimulants and stripped of his championship. This brought to an end his dream of going to the United States to box and to start a new life with Cherie Chung. This film uses the two protagonists' experience of selling their bodies to survive, to complain about the exploitation of the lower classes of Hong Kong society. It also expresses the worries and fears of the Chinese living in Hong Kong about the 1997 handover of sovereignty over Hong Kong to China. Through images of audacious sex, a bloody miscarriage and the last scene – the disappointment on the face of the dying Chung – the film expresses the physical and psychological trauma and the misery of Man and Chung's fates.

Big Brother centres on the male protagonist, Alex Man, who has been imprisoned for committing a robbery. He has just been released and is trying to pursue a new life, but encounters difficulties. Returning home from a jail, he is upbraided by his younger brother, Ng Doi-yung, for having lost the chance to enter university because he was forced to work to support the family when Man was in jail for seven years. Ng therefore tells his elder brother that he never wants to see him again. Man then visits a gangster, Kirk Wong (one of the New Wave directors), who had been his partner in the robbery, to ask for his share, which Wong had actually already spent. Wong humiliates him. Later, he gathers together a gang and smashes up Man's taxi, which Man relies on to make a living.

The policeman whom Man had injured during the robbery appears at Man's workplace. Man loses his job, and his future seems hopeless. The series of setbacks causes Man to realize how difficult it is to start a new life. Criminals (the dark side) suppress him, while policemen (the bright side) hinder him. Even his family offers him no understanding. In the eyes of the world, people who have committed crimes are considered incapable of changing, and they are not given a chance to do so. This is the sad message delivered by *Big Brother*. Man also encounters Ng Ka-lai, who was his neighbour in childhood and is now a superintendent in the police force. Also worth mentioning is a scene of a trumped-up robbery planned by the gangster Kirk Wong and a policemen, for the purpose of luring and then trapping Man. It takes place in the bank where Man's younger brother, Ng Doi-yung, is employed. The pair of brothers joins forces to kill the robbers. The policeman also dies, while Man's younger brother Ng is wounded. Only Man and Ng Ka-lai are unhurt. In this way, the conflicts of the narrative are resolved through the death of the villains. However, in real life, discrimination still prevails, as people's values and ways of thinking in fact remain unchanged.[29]

The film *Devils and Angels* deals with the most controversial of the realistic subjects explored by Clifford Choi – the Hong Kong government's declaration on 28 April 1987 that all illegal immigrants under the age of fourteen could apply for the right to stay in Hong Kong. The film takes that day as the ending of the story; the numerous happy-and-sad events prior to it, presented in flashback, are the focus of the rest of the film.

The narrative of *Devils and Angels,* which centres on three characters, namely Cecilia Yip, Nina Li and Ku Feng (a hawker), is developed along several plotlines, which converge in the end. The main characters, Yip and Li, are new immigrants from mainland China. Both of them are working as prostitutes in a nightclub. Both have daughters they hope to bring to Hong Kong. Driven by this wish, they endure the hardships of the unpleasant job. Li hopes for an early opportunity to marry a kind client, Wong Kam-sun, a Chinese-American. Then, he can support her for the rest of her life. Yip, on the other hand, has paid money to a snakehead, Kenneth Tsang, to bring her daughter to Hong Kong. When the amnesty is announced, Li and Wong are in a church, on the point of getting married. Unexpectedly, Li's daughter arrives from her hometown and suddenly appears at the wedding. However, Li denies that she is her daughter, as she fears that Wong will go back on his promise to marry her. But, finally, driven by motherly love, Li acknowledges her daughter and brings her to the immigration office in Wanchai. Meanwhile, the snakehead Kenneth Tsang, threatens and even rapes Yip and demands an extra fifty thousand Hong Kong dollars. Yip eventually kills Tsang with a cleaver. She then also takes her daughter to the immigration office. By highlighting the issue of young illegal immigrants, the film illustrates the priceless value of ethics and kinship. Furthermore, it castigates the evil of taking advantage of others in order to profit for ones self, as exemplified by Tsang.

Devils and Angels is even more sensational in style than *Hong Kong Hong Kong*. It recklessly and directly points out the cruel realities of society, revealing the dark side of human beings, such as their twisted nature, greed and abnormalities. This film can be considered the bloodiest and most passionate of Choi's films to date.[30]

Naughty Couple is a film Choi directed five years after making *Big Brother*. Adapted from a play of the same title, this story centres on a young married couple, Francis Ng and Anita Lee. They respectively lend their shared apartment to their boy/girlfriend as a meeting place for their trysts. As it turns out, an interior designer and a Filipino maid are involved. A series of misunderstandings, coincidences and mistakes are the source of jokes. This film, with a smooth plot, is basically at most a faithful re-creation of the stage performance. There are no breakthroughs in the film version.

Set in a school campus, Clifford Choi's *Grow Up in Anger* was clearly inspired by the turbulence that followed in the wake of the release of the youth films. The movie opens with a school principal severely criticizing youth films for demonizing family, education and teachers, and for being a poor influence on immature students. He vows to have this genre of films banned without exception. The principal's fury can be seen from this speech; the director's anger at being attacked in also evident. The narrative focuses on three students. The first, Ah Pan, has been expelled from school because he has been caught cheating in an examination. He then goes to work as an apprentice in a barber shop. The second, Man Kit, comes from a poor family. His academic performance is outstanding, and he has been relying on scholarships to continue his studies. Once, however, he failed an examination which cost him his scholarship. Depressed, he jumps from the roof in an attempt to commit suicide but fails. Only his legs are broken. He then begins a career in computing and later becomes wealthy. Nim Cho, the third student, is scornful of the hypocrisy of the school and its teachers. Although one instructor encourages him and he makes a renewed effort to apply himself, in the end he quits school. The film depicts the school as corrupt under a pleasing façade and the students as victims. The message conveyed in the film is that working is much better than studying, as working may lead to wealth. The film makes the mistake of oversimplifying and dichotomizing the problems that were raised. However, the director has certainly communicated the acuteness of his anger. In any case, any utopian image of school has certainly been shattered.

Family plays a key role in Choi's movies, particularly in his youth movies. It is most important in *The Encore*; however, its centrality in his films gradually declined, as is particularly evident in *Grow Up in Anger*. Conversely, the role of school went from being unimportant to very important.

The theme of challenge or competition repeatedly appears in Choi's films. There are the basketball games in *The Encore* and in *Grow Up in Anger*. There is the '1980s Amateur Singing Contest' in *The Encore*, in which Danny Chan wins the championship with the song '*Encore*'. In *No U-turn*, Lam Kar-wah participates in a car race. The film even closes with a cross-country race, in which Lam's competitor is also his rival in love. His competitor crashes his car, and, in the end, Lam triumphs in both the racing field and the sphere of love. In *Hong Kong Hong Kong*, Alex Man, a full-time boxer, defeats his opponent. However, his championship is stripped from him as he is accused of taking banned drugs. The scene of the stage performance of the play *Romeo and Julie*, in which two schools are participating, also has the flavour of competition. In *Devil and Angel*, Nina Li, Cecilia Yip and Ku Feng hear the news of the amnesty for child illegal immigrants and quickly bring their children to the immigration office to register them before the deadline. There is the sense here that they are competing with time. In addition, their action of obtaining residency for their children at all costs is an expression of the value of family and kinship.

Notes

1. Sin Nong. 'Costume Martial Arts Dramas with a Modern Façade – Interview with Kirk Wong'. *City Entertainment*. No. 69. 17 September 1981, p. 9.
2. Schatz, Thomas. *Hollywood Genres: Formulas, Filmmaking, and the Studio System*. New York: McGraw-Hill. 1981, p. 135.

3. Lam Lei. '*The Club*: the Pinnacle of Comic-Style Heroism.' *City Entertainment*. No. 71, October 1981, p. 37.
4. Lam Lei. '*Health Warning*.' *City Entertainment*. No. 123, p. 24.
5. Jiao Xiongping, ed. *Xianggang dianying fengmao, 1975–1986* (A View of Hong Kong Cinema, 1975–1986). Taipei Times Press. 1 May 1986, p. 37.
6. Wong, Kirk. 'Dialogue (I): Kirk Wong – Roger Garcia.' *Hong Kong Cinema 79–89* (20th Hong Kong International Film Festival). HK: Leisure and Cultural Services Department, Hong Kong Government. 12–17 April 2000, p. 62.
7. Wen Tianxiang. *Sheyingji yu jiaorouji – huayu dianying 1990–1996* (Camera and Mincing Machine – Chinese-language films 1990–1996). Taipei: Zhishufang Press. December 1996, p. 141.
8. Shek Kei. '*Organized Crime and Triad Bureau* – Hard-Boiled Cops and Valiant Criminals in a Fast-Rhythm and Terse Plot'. Ming Pao. 9 January 1994.
9. *Body Guard from Beijing*. 1994. Dir. by Corey Yuen. Eastern (HK) Film Production.
10. *My Father is a Hero*. 1995. Dir. by Corey Yuen. Win's Entertainment Ltd.
11. Law Kar, Ng Ho and Pak Tong Cheuk. 'The Change of Image of Chinese Cops (*Gongan*) in Hong Kong Films in the 1990s.' *Genre Theory in Hong Kong Cinema*. Oxford University Press, 1997, p. 155.
12. *Her Fatal Ways* I, II, III, IV, (1990, 91, 93, 94), dir. by Alfred Cheung.
13. *The Trail*, dir. by Man Chun, 1993, Kong Lung Film Ltd.
14. *The Untouchables*, 1987, dir. by Brian de Palma.
15. Bordwell, David. *Planet Hong Kong: Popular Cinema and the Art of Entertainment*. Cambridge: Harvard University Press, 2000, pp. 19–25.
16. The talented people from the Hong Kong film industry who have migrated to Hollywood include (non-performers) John Woo, Stanley Tong, Tsui Hark and Ringo Lam; and (performers) Jackie Chan, Chow Yun-fat, Sammo Hung, Michelle Yeoh and others.
17. *The Big Hit*, 1998, Kirk Wong's first Hollywood film.
18. *The Club* was originally a comedy, but as the director's first attempt at making a movie, Kirk Wong was not totally confident about being able to make a good comedy. For his first attempt as director, Wong preferred a genre that would be more promising in terms of box office return. That movie was *The Club*.
19. The drama series *Wong Fei Hung* consisted of thirteen episodes. It was a TVB production and was ranked at the top in terms of viewership.
20. *Lonely Fifteen* (1982, dir. David Lai, producer: Michael Mak). *Once Upon a Rainbow* (dir. Ng Siu-wan, a Cinema City production).
21. *Lonely Fifteen* earned over 10 million Hong Kong dollars at the box office, while the cost of production was 1.2 million. *Teenage Dreamer* had box office receipts of 5 million, but cost only 80 thousand to make.
22. The two seminars about 'youth films' were: (1) 'Film and Youth', released on Radio 1, Radio Television Hong Kong on the 1st and 2nd of May 1982. (2) 'A Panorama of Youth Films', held at the Hong Kong Arts Centre on 16 May 1982, which attracted a great deal of attention from the media. See 'A Panorama of "Youth Films".' *Chinese-Western Motion Pictures* (magazine). No. 28, 5 June 1982, 66-69; and Li Cheuk-to. 'We sit down together – Damn it! Start from the seminars about youth films.' *City Entertainment*. No. 87, 3 June 1982, pp. 3–5.

23. Ibid., Li Chek-to.
24. The other two controversies were over: the re-editing of Tsui Hark's *Dangerous Encounter – 1st Kind* (refer to the chapter on Tsui Hark) and the prohibition on the re-editing of Patrick Tam's *Nomad* (refer to the chapter on Patrick Tam).
25. *Rebel Without a Cause*, starring James Dean. *On the Waterfront*, starring Marlon Brando. *West Side Story*, starring Natalie Wood and Richard Beymer; a United Artists production.
26. *Prince of Broadcasters* (1966, dir. Long Kong), starring Tang Kwong-wing and Chan Chai-chung. *I Love A-Go-Go* (1967), starring Josephine Siao. *The Joys and Sorrows of Youth* (1969, dir. Chor Yuen), starring Tina Ti, Cheung Ching, Kenneth Tsang and others. *Social Characters* (1969, dir. Chan Wan), starring Lee Sze-ki, Tang Kwong-wing, Fung Bo-bo, Yi Lui and others.
27. Cheung Kou. 'What have *Teenage Dreamers/Once Upon a Rainbow/Lonely Fifteen* given us, after all?' *City Entertainment*. No. 85. 5 February 1982, p. 37.
28. Law Kar. 'Xianggang zhizao' (made in Hong Kong). *Baixing Zazhi* (The People). No. 52. 16 July 1983, p. 51.
29. Thomas Schatz. *Hollywood Genres: Formulas, Filmmaking, and the Studio System*. New York: McGraw Hill, 1981, p. 6.
30. Law Kar. 'Qinqing yu xiexing: Cai Jiguang de wenti zhizuo "Mogui tianshi"' (Kinship and conscience: the problematic work of Clifford Choi, *Devil and Angel*). *Baixing Zazhi*. No. 156. 16 November 1987, p. 56.

10

Studies on Non-Core New Wave Directors

Lau Shing Hon, Tong Kee Ming, Peter Yung and Dennis Yu

Lau Shing Hon

Lau Shing Hon was born in Macau in 1974. In 1968 he entered the State University of San Francisco in the United States to study film. After graduating in 1972, he studied at the Centre for Film Studies at the University of Southern California, then transferred to the Centre for Public Administration, where he earned his master's degree in 1974. When he returned to Hong Kong in 1975, he began work for Hong Kong Television and Commercial Television. He moved into feature film-making in 1979 and made his first picture, *House of the Lute*. Three films followed: *The Head Hunter* (1982), *Hunted in Hong Kong* (1983)[1] and *The Final Night of the Royal Hong Kong Police* (1999).[2] From 1986 to 1994 he worked for ICAC, directing the drama series *Vanguard*. He also became a well-known critic, writing *The Poetic Characteristics of Film* (Dianying fubixingji).[3] He is currently the head of the School of Film and TV of the Hong Kong Academy for Performing Arts.

His first feature, *House of the Lute*, was a self-financed, low-budget Category-III (erotic) movie. That his first film was self-financed made Lau Shing Hon, as well as Peter Yung, exceptions among the New Wave directors, most of whom had earned a reputation whilst working in television, where their works first came to the notice of critics. As for Lau and Yung, it was not until they had made their first film that their work attracted attention. Lau's choice of subject matter for his first film further set him apart from the other New Wave directors. Yim Ho's first feature was a light comedy, *The Extra*, featuring men of humble background who struggle to survive. Tsui Hark made a traditional, mysterious martial arts picture, *The Butterfly Murders*, with a science-fiction twist. Ann Hui directed a murder thriller, *The Secret*. Alex Chung produced a cop classic, *Cops and Robbers*, with fatalism as the main theme. Dennis Yu made an action comedy, *See Bar*, while Peter Yung shot a sensitive documentary-style film, *The System*. However, Lau Shing Hon opted to make a film focusing on sex, with audacious scenes of nudity and love-making.

Social Consciousness through Eroticism

House of the Lute is by no means a realistic picture; rather, it is an allegory. In a quiet mansion in the countryside, Kwan Hoi-shan, a gentleman who moved among the upper class of society during the colonial period, lives with his young second wife, Lok Pik-kee. One day, the young Simon Yam enters the picture. The hitherto orderly and tranquil household is turned upside down, the roles of outsider and host are reversed, and Yam manipulates everything in the house. This is an ordinary and conventional story, which is often found in foreign, particularly European, films. Examples are *Viridiana* (1961)[4] and *Tristana* (1970),[5] directed by the Spanish film-maker, Luis Bunuel (1900–1983). In *House of the Lute*, the old gentleman, Kwan, enjoys playing the *guqin*, a classical Chinese musical instrument, and chess and practicing calligraphy. These are all traditional pursuits of Chinese intellectuals. However, his legs are paralyzed and he needs to use a wheelchair. His teeth are also all artificial. These are symbols of the decline of the upper class. His second wife is a young, attractive 'prostitute', who has married for money. The young man Yam, who is from the lower class, has been hired by Kwan to do odd jobs. Other characters include a vulgar housekeeper and some extremely covetous tenants. It is obvious that all of the characters are greedy rascals. The plot centres on Yam, who is an outsider. His appearance in this secluded mansion foreshadows the end of the peace of the household. In addition, on his way back he steps on a dead crow and his shoes are bloodstained; this foreshadows a bloody story.

When Yam joins the household, he wants to learn chess from Kwan, who can easily beat him in the game. Kwan's wife tries to seduce Yam, parading naked before him. On the way back from the market, the two young people make unbridled love. Behind Kwan's back, they even make pleasure trips to various places around the city. After returning to the mansion, Yam's chess skills improve remarkably; in the end, Kwan loses to Yam. The intimacy between Yam and Lok becomes even more open. Kwan, unable to break up their relationship, commands Yam to leave, with three months of wages. However, Kwan's wife threatens to leave if Kwan interferes in her relationship with Yam. From then on, Yam dines together with Kwan; he is no longer a servant but the equal of Kwan in status. The significance of the film lies in the reversal of the master/servant relationship, the transgression of status and the breakdown of the classes. After they have fulfilled their sensual needs, Yam and Lok become even more ambitious. They are overwhelmed by wealth and desires, to the point of no turning back. This recalls the scene in *Viridiana* of the last supper. The blind and the lame, the lepers and the wanderers, take advantage of the nun's absence to celebrate wildly, buying their consciences and losing all grip on rationality. When the nun, who has endured hardships to adopt them and raise them, returns, each of them tries to sexually harass her. Here the evil, bestial and loathsome qualities of human beings are fully exposed. In the *House of the Lute*, Yam kills Kwan with the *guqin*. In a moment of terror and confusion, Lok mistakes Yam for her husband and stabs Yam to death with a hairpin. Lok is then arrested by the police. The story is not yet at an end: the housekeeper, Chan Lap-pun, now invites the tenants to enter the mansion to watch television. They sit in rows, enjoying everything the mansion has to offer. This scene resembles the one in Joseph Losey's *Servant*,[6] which ends in a reversal of the status of the master and the servant. Throughout the *House of the Lute*, the housekeeper, an old man and the tenants are voyeurs of events occurring in the mansion. They are especially delighted as the household in the mansion draws ever closer to devastation. In this, the movie also resembles the film *Tristana*, whose female protagonist watches her uncle die without offering a helping hand and with joy in her heart.

The scene of Yam trying to play Kwan's *guqin* is a sign that he is challenging Kwan's authority. When Kwan wants to find out what is happening, he falls down the stairs, an act that signifies the collapse of his status. The scene of Yam setting the *guqin* on fire recalls the one in Bunuel's *The Golden Age*,[7] in which a cross, and other sacred objects, are burnt. The notions of the upper class, the manipulation of the masters by the servants and the reversal of their roles have their roots in the works of these two forerunners in European cinema.

Besides symbolism, Lau Shing Hon has also adopted a hyper-realistic technique that blends fantasy and reality, in which it is difficult to distinguish between true and false, between fantasy and reality. After the death of Kwan, Yam takes on the role of master of the mansion. Lok prepares dinner for him, pours him tea and feeds him cakes. As the two of them are eating, Lok is frightened to discover Kwan's fake teeth in the bowl of soup. But Yam cannot see it in the soup; instead he sees it in the bowl of rice. In fact, these are hallucinations. The director makes frequent use of montage, with hand-held shots of the *guqin*. Yam is disturbed by some noise at night. He gets up to investigate. Monsters appear; frightened, he cries out. He wakes Lok up to ask her to find out what is going on. In the dark, a hand squeezes Lok's neck. Lok sees the face of her husband and immediately removes her hairpin and stabs him. She then discovers that she has instead stabbed Yam. This scene fully expresses Lok's unsettled psyche and her irrational behavior driven by her consciousness. However, the film takes an unusually calm approach instead of a deliberately sensational one, not allowing the audience to be overwhelmed by emotion. Rather, it tends to keep a distance from the audience, providing just enough stimulation to make them think.[8] This is the strong point of the film, and it is one that also distinguishes Lau from his New Wave contemporaries. Undoubtedly, the ways in which the characters, events, scenes, symbols and ideas are connected, as well as a tendency toward conceptualization, give the impression that the film has been 'assembled'.[9] But the messages communicated in this film were exactly those most lacking in Hong Kong cinema at that time, which makes this film significant.

Those aspects in the *House of the Lute* that represent traditional art and culture, such as the wearing of Chinese clothing, the playing of traditional Chinese musical instruments and Chinese chess, and the practicing of Chinese, are swallowed up by primitive eroticism and barbarian desires. Eventually, they cease to exist. In the end, the master of the mansion is murdered and the mansion is occupied by lower-class people. The film is clearly about the decline or total collapse of the colonial upper class and its substitution by a class of ordinary people.[10] The film appears to be tragically announcing the bankruptcy and disintegration of classical Chinese moral civilization, just as an elegant culture (as epitomized by Chinese chess and a Chinese classical musical instrument) is swallowed up by an ugly modern urban culture.[11]

The Embarrassment of the Impending Handover and the Collective Memory of Hong Kong People

The Head Hunter is an action movie about a killer. The male protagonist, Chow Yun-fat, is Vietnamese-Chinese. He has participated in the Vietnam War, during which he killed numerous people. After escaping to Hong Kong, he becomes an assassin for a criminal organization in the hope of being able to bring his family over from Vietnam. Such subject matter and characters are found in several Hong Kong movies of the time, for example, the television drama *The Boy from Vietnam* and the film *Story of Woo Viet*, both directed by Ann Hui. Compared to *The Head Hunter*, the *Story of Woo Viet* is deeper and the characters much more tragic. Chow Yun-fat stars in both films. In *The Head Hunter*, the female protagonist, Rosalind Kwan, is a journalist who befriends Chow Yun-fat while investigating a case involving the manufacturing of toxic gas. The friends then become lovers. Later Kwan unexpectedly discovers that her uncle was the behind-the-scenes leader in the case. Even more staggering was the discovery that Chow was the hated figure who had killed her father. These coincidences certainly make the story less believable. Under the control of the international criminal organization, Chow's fate is to be a killer for life. Because of this, he is unable to protect even his family. As for Hong Kong, it is the headquarters of the criminal organization, where toxic gas is produced and murders are committed. The toxic gas that is produced is supplied by criminal organizations in Southeast Asia. In other words, Hong Kong has a somewhat embarrassing reputation in the international arena. In an earlier film, *House of the Flute*, Lau portrayed Hong Kong as being neither a city nor a village; as half Chinese and half western.[12] Lau's next film, *Hunted in Hong Kong*, portrays Hong Kong as a paradise for crime. Again, Hong Kong is given a certain international character, interspersed with local traditions. The film contains such images as foreigners, sailors, Hong Kong people and fighters in black wearing Beijing opera masks; perpetuating the city's awkward image of being half-Chinese and half western or neither Chinese nor western. This film was made for a western audience and was not released in Hong Kong, thus accounting for the exotic scenes, which deliberately create an impression of China as a land of mystery and spectacle.

In Lau Shing Hon's work *One Body Two Flags*, the awkwardness of Hong Kong's position is especially evident. This is because the film is set at a critical point in Hong Kong's history: midnight of 30 June 1997 – the eve of the handover of Hong Kong to her motherland after a century of colonial rule by the United Kingdom. At such a moment, just like so many Hong Kong people, the male protagonist, a member of the Royal Hong Kong Police, faces the problem of identity brought about by the changes of flags. The first episode of the series *The Final Night of the Royal Hong Kong Police*,[13] *One Body Two Flags*, opens with the funeral of a Hong Kong policeman, Chan Man-fai, who has been killed in a police action on the eve of the handover. His spirit wanders in the funeral house, relating in first-person narration the story of his life. One week before, he had driven his cousin Chu Long-kee to the airport. His cousin was boarding a flight to Canada, where he was emigrating to. On the way to the airport, the film flashes back to the experiences of Chan and Chu. We are shown a range of events that occurred in the past: the widespread corruption in the police force in the 1960s, the leftist movement, the establishment of the ICAC in the 1970s, the attack on the ICAC in which Chu was the leader and so forth. Near the end of the film, Chan goes to the parking lot to pick up his car. He leaves in pursuit of a robber and is stabbed to death by the robber. The camera then cuts to the present in the funeral house. A number of policemen remove the national flag of the United Kingdom from the coffin, passing it to Chan's family, and then cover the coffin with the one of the Special Administrative Region of Hong Kong. They then salute and depart.

In the film, Chu is an experienced policeman whom Chan idolized as a child. He joined the police force under the influence of his cousin. In the leftist riots of 1967, the situation was chaotic, and bombs were going off everywhere. Chu uncompromisingly carried out the administration's policy of suppression. He responded to violence with violence, and often carried out severe punishments against the leftists. He hated the Communist Party and declared that if violence was not used to stop the leftists, Hong Kong would soon fall to the communists. In the 1970s, Chu was no different from many other policeman: immoral, overbearing and corrupt. In addition, Chu took a leading role in attacking the ICAC. He boasted that, in doing so, he rescued the property, which had been acquired through corruption, of quite a number of his colleagues. During the signing of the Joint Declaration between Britain and China, he suddenly resigned from the police force in order to run a business. Just prior to the handover, he leaves for Canada and urged Chan to also leave as quickly as possible. Chan was also corrupt, although not to the same degree as Chu. He still has a conscience. When he saw Chu beating up the leftists, he felt that this was unseemly behaviour and felt guilty that he could do nothing to stop it. On the eve of the handover, he gives his life for his job and becomes the last sacrifice of the Royal Hong Kong Police Force. His sins are cleansed through his death, which also redeems the police force. Many Hong Kong people who were born and raised in Hong Kong have said that their feelings on the eve of the 1997 handover were complicated and contradictory. The change of flag that symbolized the transfer of sovereignty has undeniably led to a problem of identification. The film expresses the possibly inerasable collective memory of the Hong Kong people brought about by their dual identities and the frustration they felt over the handover.[14] This film is a political work about the embarrassing psyche of an embarrassing person in an embarrassing place at an embarrassing point in time in the context of the transfer of sovereignty. Speaking broadly, the depiction is not of a single person, but of Hong Kong people as a whole.

Tong Kee Ming

Tong Kee Ming, Terry, whose family was from Nanhai in Guangdong Province, was born in Hong Kong on 29 July 1950. He graduated from the Chinese University of Hong Kong, with a major in art. He made an experimental movie, *Shimian maifu*.*[15] In 1975, he joined TVB, working first in the research unit and then in programme promotion. He then went to work for Commercial Television in 1978, where he directed *Liuxing Hudie Jian*. One year later, he transferred to Rediffusion Television and made a number of martial arts drama series, namely *Reincarnated, Dragon Strikes* and *The Silver Sword Killer*. In 1981, he moved to making feature films, with *Collies Killer* as his first project. His subsequent films include *Yellow Peril* (1984), *Hong Kong Graffiti* (1985), *Seven Warriors* (1989), *Gigolo and the Whore* (1991) and *Cash on Delivery* (1992). He began working for the ICAC in 1993 and directed the drama series *The ICAC Investigators*.

In July in 1978, Commercial Television shut down, largely due to a financial crisis and to a dispute over the control of its shares. Hong Kong's three television stations were now reduced to two, and the competition between TVB and Rediffusion Television became keener. The result was that TVB achieved a long-term monopoly, while Rediffusion (now ATV) constantly suffered from deficits. This situation persisted into the new millennium. When Commercial Television closed down, some directors, such as Tsui Hark and Patrick Tam, shifted to the film industry; while quite a large number of others transferred to Rediffusion, for instance, Terry Tong, Lee Wai-man, Michael Mak, Lai Shui-ching, Lai Tai-wai, Wong Tai-loi and others. *The Silver Sword Killer* was the first drama that Terry Tong directed in his days with Rediffusion. It was adapted from a martial arts novel written by Wong Ying who was famous for romantic, unusual plots. The drama depicts Shen Shengyi (Tsui Siu-keung), who, in order to make enough money to raise a family, is a righteous knight during the day and an assassin at night. He treats his wife, Leung Shuk-chong, coldly and transfers her affections to another man, Lau Wai-man, a comrade of Shen's. This triangular relationship is finally resolved through a fight between the two men. Although this is a martial arts costume drama, the content is quite modern, particularly that relating to the relationship between Tsui and Leung. Leung shifted her love to Lau, with whom she shared similar interests such as calligraphy, painting and playing the *qin*, a classical Chinese musical instrument. Tsui, on the other hand, was a swordsman with no knowledge of painting and calligraphy. The couple had little in common. Furthermore, Tsui was often absent from home. In the end, Leung kills herself with a sword. Lau also dies in the duel with Tsui. Before he died, he lamented, 'I kill many people because of her, but in the end what have I?' Having lost both a good friend and his wife, Tsui throws away his sword. In this vast world, he is lonely and miserable.

The Solitude of Killers and the Themes of Love and Death

Terry Tong's interest in lone killers persisted through his television and film-making periods. *Collies Killer* again pays homage to the killer-hero. In the film, the male protagonist, Chun Cheung-lam, is a killer, rising from a labourer in Sai Ying Pun (in the

Western District of Hong Kong Island) to becoming the boss of an international organization that carries out assassinations. A member of the older generation of assassins, Chun has the spirit of a traditional knight. He usually commands his subordinates not to kill the innocent. He has also not raised the rents for his apartments in five years. However, he has grown old and is not as quick as the younger people. For example, his subordinates are able to reassemble a dismantled gun in thirty seconds, which he cannot do. Later, he is secretly attacked by another gang, and, in one night, all of his subordinates lose their lives. The wounded Chun returns to his birthplace, Sai Ying Pun, to recover and wait for an opportunity to strike back. Sai Ying Pun was the base from which Chun initially rose up. Although he is the head of an enterprise, he never forgets to visit the place once a year. At this critical moment of his career and life, he took refuge and shelter there, as the safest place for him. The gloomy avenues, narrow alleys and old buildings of Sai Ying Pun are symbols of the traditional. They are in stark contrast with the skyscrapers and busy streets of Central, part of the modern urban culture of Hong Kong.

More significantly, warmth and compassion are to be found in Sai Ying Pun. Here, Chun encounters two women for whom he develops affection: one is a fortune teller, Jiao Jiao; and the other, Cecilia Yip, is the daughter of a tailor. When Chun returns to Sai Ying Pun to take refuge, he receives devoted care from Yip. Yip, with the utmost willingness, stays with him and is even willing to die for him. Before Chun leaves, they make love in the shadow of red flames. Then they go to the seashore. Chun shoots her in the back. Just before she dies, Yip turns and smiles at Chun and then collapses. She pleasantly accepts the shot from the man she loves. Not only is such a scene seldom seen in New Wave productions, but also in other Hong Kong movies. Tong has given a shocking and terrifying display of the unlimited power that men have always sought and of the exploitation that women have always suffered. This film is perhaps at the pinnacle of the vicious cycle of the myth of masculinities in Hong Kong.[16] It takes the male desire for authority and possession to the utmost extreme in intensity and horror.[17] The act of unhesitatingly killing the person one loves made this the most controversial movie of that time.

As with the preceding movie, Tong's second film, *Yellow Peril*, deals with the subject of killers. Chun in *Collies Killer* is a killer with no family, while Tang Kwong-wing in *Yellow Peril* is a man with a family. But they are in a similar dilemma: they are being pursued by enemies who want to kill them. The original idea behind *Yellow Peril* was to address the frustrations of Hong Kong people over the 1997 issue. It followed the release of Ann Hui's *The Boat People*, which touched on Hong Kong people's long-hidden fear of communism. At the time, the most ardent hope of Hong Kong people was to migrate to the United States; however, they were now forced to turn back to the ironic and ridiculous situation in Hong Kong.[18] Unfortunately, *Yellow Peril* did not live up to the expectations of the director. It failed to express the despair and the ridiculousness of the whole situation, containing as it does only chase-and-kill scenes, which are, at most, only exciting rather than illuminating. One reason for the failure was, of course, the insufficient support given to Tong by the production company. The company even opposed the direction in which Tong's film was going.[19] The hero of *Yellow Peril*, Tang Kwong-wing, migrates to the Untied States with his wife and son. The Chinatown there becomes the site of a power struggle between the Vietnam gang and the China gang. The Intelligence Agency (CIA) is on a campaign to eliminate the triads. It manufactures a murder case to implicate Tang. This forces him to flee back to Hong Kong to go into hiding. An ethnic Chinese staff member of the CIA arrives at Hong Kong and bribes and later murders an ethnic Chinese gangster in the Vietnam gang Kam Hing-yin. In fact, and in addition, the CIA staff member, the Vietnam gang and the policeman in Macau (Cheung Lui) are all ethnic Chinese, trying to kill one another and eliminate their opponents. This is precisely the tragedy of diasporic Chinese. The 'yellow peril' in this film refers to killings among the Chinese themselves. It is totally different from the original use of the term, which referred to the fear of white people, particularly Europeans, towards Chinese. What is most ironic in the film is that, although Tang and his entire family have migrated and settled in the United States, when his life is being threatened, he has to return to his homeland. Yet the feeling is one of helplessness and uncertainty and of the general preposterousness of the Chinese condition.

The Loves and Careers of Women

Of Terry Tong's two killer films mentioned above, the former is more romantic and the latter more realistic. In *Collies Killer*, the hero gains the love of two women, Jiao and Yip, who are willing to sacrifice themselves for him, thus fulfilling the masculine myth of complete domination. That the protagonist in *Yellow Peril*, Tang Kwong-wing, has a family corresponds to the fact that after Terry Tong married, he began to realize how important to him his family was. In the story, after Tang has fled to Hong Kong to go into hiding, his wife, Tong Lan-fa, hears that he has arrived. She is worried about her husband's safety and, therefore, returns to Hong Kong with his son to be with him in time of danger. Is this not an expression of support for the myth of masculinity? In as much danger as Tang, his mother and daughter in Hong Kong are also pursued by the villains. At the close of the film, the CIA staff member, Cheung Yik, kills Kam Hing-yin of the Vietnam gang. He hopes to eliminate Tang as well. At the critical moment, Tang's wife saves her husband's life. In the end, Tang shoots Cheung to death. In other words, the women in this film no longer give themselves up for sex or love. Rather, they are intelligent and brave. Tang Lan-fa, for example, protects their son and escapes from the killers. She shares a man's burdens: at the critical moment, she rescues her husband. Thus, in a masculine world, women have found their place.

Tong's next film, *Hong Kong Graffiti*, centres on four women: Olivia Cheng from Hong Kong, Chan Yuen-lai from mainland China, Ngai Shuk-kwan from Taiwan and Chor Yin-ling from Singapore. All ethnic Chinese, all of them are in Hong Kong for various reasons and all of them know each other. They each describe themselves, making up a picture of overseas Chinese women. Coming from different places, cultures, systems and backgrounds, they have of course developed different views on various aspects of life, particularly on love, career and their future. Olivia Cheng from Hong Kong, who is still single, is in love with her boss, Yeung Kwan. She is so competent that not only does her company value her highly, but rival companies are also interested in her. Chan Yuen-lai from mainland China is Cheng's sister-in-law. She has just obtained a divorce from her husband and moved to Hong Kong. She is penniless but extremely ambitious. Her aim is to earn as much money in as short a time as possible. Even her newly acquired English name, Plenty, demonstrates her intentions. In order to open a beauty salon, she entices away Yeung Kwan, whom Cheng loves. But when Chan encounters a richer man, she shifts to the new target. Ngai Shuk-kwan from Taiwan is Yeung's daughter, who initially dislikes Cheng but later becomes close friends with her. Chor Yin-ling from Singapore is an air hostess who has an open attitude towards love. She is willing to date men of any ethnicity, and also changes boyfriends frequently. If her boyfriend is disloyal to her, she will become depressed and attempt to commit suicide. This may happen as frequently as several times a month. But she soon finds a new lover. The focus of the film is on Chan. Her relationship with Cheng is depicted, as well as her careful plans. The film criticizes Chan's over-aggressiveness. Consider a conversation between Chan and Ngai: Responding to the accusation that she has behaved improperly by 'stealing' Cheng's lover, Chan defends herself, 'If Cheng has become destitute after losing your father, I will also become destitute when I lose your father. If you ask me to consider her, then who will consider me?' As for Hong Kong people, the film is full of satires: Hong Kong people are keen to follow crowds. But if they are at the rear of the crowd, they are afraid that they will lose out; if in the middle, they fear suffocation; at the front, they are afraid of being trampled. In other words, the film turns it attention to both Hong Kong people and mainlanders and is not one-sided.

Although Chan Yuen-lai is aggressive and selfish, there is still some kindness in her. When she meets a wealthier man than Yeung, she returns to Yeung the two hundred thousand Hong Kong dollars he has given her to open her business. In the end, the four women become reconciled, symbolizing the great wish for overseas Chinese to be united.

The concept for *Gigolo and the Whore* is taken from *My Fair Lady*.[20] A mainland girl who has come to Hong Kong is trained to be a high-class prostitute. The film is about both 'ducks' and 'chickens' (synonyms for male prostitutes and female prostitutes, respectively), and the story is told as a light comedy, making the film interesting but not obscene. The female protagonist, Claudia Lau, comes from mainland China. She applies to work as a waitress. However, she is humiliated by wealthy wives and such experiences cause her to become determined to make a lot of money from men. As far as she is concerned, she has nothing to lose and nothing to be afraid of. She becomes the disciple of a male prostitute, Simon Yam, and learns a full set of skills that will qualify her to become the 'queen of prostitutes'. When she is ready, she is introduced to a wealthy young man, Alex Fong Chung-shun, to become his mistress. At this moment, she realizes that she has fallen in love with Yam and also understands the truth that true love is not open for trade.

Women's persistence in love is the main theme in Terry Tong's *Cash on Delivery*. The central character is the male prostitute played by Simon Yam, who has retired from his career and is now in the antique business. The daughter-in-law of a wealthy man, Veronica Yip, takes a fancy to him. She asks Yam for some of his sperm. Later, she successfully becomes pregnant. However, she is unwilling to leave Yam and clings to him. Finally, she murders her husband and accuses Yam of having committed the crime. During the trial, the female prosecuting attorney, Sandra Ng, regards Yam with favour. After the case is settled, the wealthy head of the clan into which Yip has married discovers that Yip and her husband had conspired to deceive the family of funds through a pregnancy that would produce a child not of the family's bloodline. He leaves in a huff. Yam is released, free of guilt. The intimate affections between him and Ng remain. True love trumps class. The reunion of Yam, a former male prostitute, and Ng, a barrister, is proof of this. It also satisfies a male fantasy.

The Chivalrous Spirit and the Upholding of Justice

In an interview, Terry Tong stated the most memorable films in his childhood were *Shichinin No Samurai*, *Yojimbo*, *Akahige* and others.[21] Who would have imagined that, 35 years later, he would remake Akira Kurosawa's classic *Shichinin No Samurai* (1954). The same title as the original was first adopted for the remade version, but the film was later renamed the *Seven Warriors*.[22] In fact, as early as the 1960s, Hollywood has already remade the Japanese classic into a western, *The Magnificent Seven*. (1960) Tong's remaking of the film can be said to be a fulfillment of a childhood dream. The plot of Tong's version is largely similar to the original one, with the most noticeable disparity being the setting, which was from Warring States period in Japan to China in the 1920s. The latter was a time when warlords had divided up the country. Defeated soldiers became criminals. Soldiers and thieves could hardly be distinguished in a crime-ridden country. Ordinary people were helpless and suffered enormously. One village asked seven wandering warriors to guard them without pay. All of these seven heroes, except for Tony Leung Chiu-wai, have had actual experience in battle. They were Adam Cheng, Shing Fu-on, Jacky Cheung, Mok Siu-chong, Ng Ma and Lam Kwok-pan. Each of the warriors had served in different troops, and each had their own motives and talents. But in the end they are able to unite to defeat the villain, Law Lit, and secure the safety of the village.

Each of the characters in the film has a distinct personality; this was also the case in the original story. They are depicted in a cartoon-like manner, which lessens the tragic tone of the samurai image, and gives the film quite a modern sensibility. The plot is fairly fast-paced and the mood is lively. Perhaps it is exactly what Terry Tong has dubbed 'a nostalgic film with an urban rhythm'. In the film, the heroes mostly appear to be unruly and unmotivated. For example, Adam Cheng hides his head in the wine jug to forget his troubles. Moreover, each knight has his own motives. For example, Ng Ma intends to dig up some treasure; he is selfish and looks to his interests. Mok Siu-chong, for his part, is unwilling to kill local thieves, as he is not willing to sacrifice his life for nothing. But when the seven of them unite, they rise above themselves and become responsible, courageous and even ready to die for justice in front of their enemies. From them emanates a chivalrous spirit of upholding righteousness.

Although Terry Tong has not made many movies, his treatment of each film is meticulous. *Collies Killer* is sad in a romantic way. *Hong Kong Graffiti* is an exceedingly ambitious movie about the psyche of modern Chinese women. *Yellow Peril* describes the helplessness and despair of the diaspora and mixes a sense of the ridiculous and anger. *Gigolo and the Whore* and *Cash for Delivery* appear to be playful works with a great deal of eroticism; however, it communicates the thirst that people have for true love, and their persistence in looking for it. Despite the many pressures of film-making, including constraints on production from those who are financing the film, Tong still bravely strives to articulate his vision. Tong's spirit of loyalty to films and loyalty to his conscience is truly commendable.

Peter Yung

Yung Wai-chuen, Peter, was born in Hong Kong in 1949. In 1969, he entered the Los Angeles Art Centre in California and majored in photography, earning a bachelor's degree in 1971. He returned to Hong Kong in 1972. In each of the next two years, he held a one-man exhibition of his photographs. In 1975, he taught at the School of Communication of Hong Kong Baptist College. He then went to work for British Independent Television as a producer and photographer in the Hong Kong unit. He worked on the project *White Powder Opera*. In 1979, he made his first picture, a self-financed film, *The System*. This was followed by *Life After Life* (1981), *Journey to the Cossacks* (1982) and *Double Dealer* (1984). He is currently teaching at the School of Film and TV of the Hong Kong Academy for Performing Arts.

Peter Yung can be considered the other odd man out among the members of the New Wave. Like Lau Shing-hon, Peter Yung financed his first movie himself. Nor did he join a television station and undergo several years of training in directing, as most of the New Wave directors had, before embarking on a film-making career. Rather, Yung began with documentary-style photography. In 1971, he had discussed collaborating with an ethnic Chinese photographer, Jim Wong, to produce a documentary, *One Day in Locke*.[23] Because Wong suffered a heart attack, Yung completed the planned project alone. The documentary is a record of one day in the life of the oldest man in Locke. The film shows the hardship that several generations of Chinese there suffered. In 1974, Yung worked as a photographer for a director, Brian Blake, of documentary films. They went to Indonesia to shoot a film. It was at that time that Yung formally joined the ranks of documentary film-makers. In 1976, Adrian Cowell from British Independent Television arrived in Hong Kong to shoot a documentary about drugs called *White Powder Opera*. Yung was employed as an assistant producer and photographer. This gave him the chance to live with drug-addicted people in the Western District of Hong Kong Island. The shooting was done intermittently over one year and was mostly carried out secretly.[24] All of these experiences encouraged Yung to make his first film, *The System*.

Objects of Sacrifice under a Bureaucratic System

The System tells a story about the struggle between policemen and drug traffickers. The central character, Pak Ying, is a policeman who is completely devoted to the capturing of drug traffickers. He uses his informant, Shek Kin, to investigate the information given by the head of the gangsters, Lam Wai-kee. Unexpectedly, a traitor is found in the police force. In the end, there is a plot against both Pak and his informant Shek, and they die unjust deaths. The entire film is about the pursuits, fights and connections among the police, the head of the gangsters and the informant. This is a realistic account of how the Hong Kong police crack down on drug trafficking. Ironically, the police rely on informants who, if they are not drug traffickers themselves, will sooner or later participate in such a crime. Even more ironic is that any drug trafficker who is arrested can immediately win release by claiming to be an informant of certain superintendents of the Hong Kong police. It is not easy, therefore, to eradicate drug trafficking.

It is clear that Peter Yung devoted a great deal of effort to research when making *The System*. Certain facts such as the examination of drugs, drug trafficking routes, the fees paid to hire informants and the 'paparazzi' who chase the police are well understood by Yung and are represented realistically and in detail. Using a hand-held camera, Yung even shot some scenes of himself tracking drug traffickers, which required the use of a large amount of film.

> Editing these two scenes of secret tracking took about twenty days. As on-site shooting was adopted in Malaysia, with many people coming and going, it was difficult to control the filming. The scenes shot using a hand-held camera are mine. They were shot at several different sites, but this made matters overly complicated, and the results were not up to expectations. Therefore, the entire section of that film had to be discarded.[25]

This shows how difficult it is to capture, in a realistic manner, scenes of tracking the drug traffickers.

In order to adhere as closely to reality as possible, Yung gave up the idea of dubbing music; rather, he used direct recordings from the shooting site. Even certain sound effects were produced on site. This is a departure from the common practice in film-making, which is to dub the sounds later, for example, dialogue, music and sound effects such as doors banging, gunshots and even natural sounds. Although dubbing in a studio means that a sense of realism is lacking, the technique is widely applied in Hong Kong's film-making with very few exceptions.[26] Thus, the use of this technique differentiates New Wave directors from their contemporaries because in their television productions, virtually without exception, they employed direct sound recording.

The System exposes numerous problems in the government's bureaucratic system. Under the old government, two bodies were responsible for cracking down on drug traffickers: the police force and customs. The two units do not work together, but struggle against each other for superiority. Some are even so corrupt that they will collaborate with the criminals. In the police force alone, some senior officers (foreigners) are corrupt, and the dedicated junior policeman can do nothing to change the situation. The junior policemen may even be set up by their superiors and lose their lives. In the film, Pak Ying and Shek Kin are objects of sacrifice under such a system. Therefore, it is necessary to begin by altering the system, if the problems plaguing it are to be solved. Otherwise, even more policemen will lose their lives fruitlessly.

The Fate of the Solitary

The heroes in Peter Yung's films are chiefly the solitary and those without support. For instance, Pak Ying has almost no co-workers or friends that he trusts and on whom he can rely. Even his colleague, Chung Chi-keung, who goes through various crises with him, is later discovered to be an undercover policeman sent by Pak's boss to keep an eye on Pak's every action. The informant, Shek Kin, is even more reliable than Chung. When Shek brings Pak to meet Brother Wah, Pak shares his embarrassment and bitterness. There is a trust here that is absent between Pak and his superior and colleagues. In other words, the relationship between Pak and Shek is more genuine than his other relationships. The informant Shek is Pak's adversary at first, but they eventually become friends.

In a moment of leisure, Pak goes to Lantau Island alone and bird-watches. In this way, he gets away from his troubles and finds his long-obscured humanity. In one scene, he spends some time quietly thinking under an isolated lamp post and cleanses his soul. At that moment, he suddenly feels a sense of foreboding: 'Sooner or later, I will be tricked by somebody and die.' Feeling helpless, he turns on his tape recorder and verbally records his dilemma. This foreshadows his and Shek's impending death by being hacked in a car.

The film *Life After Life* is an amalgamation of computer technology, fashion shows, cosmology, Chinese traditional puppetry, reincarnation, fortune telling and auguries. The elements from both the East and the West are collaged in a flamboyant yet dazzling manner. But certain large and practical questions are raised: How can western technology and Chinese traditional superstitions, particularly the idea of reincarnation, be integrated? How can 'reincarnation' be rationalized? The film begins with three murders that took place in 1955 at the Exorcist Bridge. Twenty-six years later, the victims are reincarnated and restage the murders. In the film, George Lam, a designer, is hired from overseas by the government. He makes use of computer technology to produce impressive designs. In order to achieve a hybrid of East and West, he combines computer technology with Chinese traditional puppetry. The result is puppets that embark on a series of terrifying murders. Through shamanism and fortune telling, the mystery of the murders is gradually revealed. The firm plays with the audience, revealing the truth layer by layer and keeping the audience in suspense.

But, sometimes, the suspense is mere sensation unsupported by plot. With an underdeveloped plot, the dramatic effect is greatly weakened. The use of computer technology in film was novel at the time, but the puppet killers and superstitions did not help the story. In addition, the fortune telling, auguries and shamanism were nothing new. However, the combination of computing technology and puppetry was a new experiment and, therefore, definitely not a 'mistake'.[27]

The central character, George Lam, is a younger designer who was educated overseas. He borrows puppets to use in a fashion show. Although he lacks familiarity with puppets, he is somehow able to paint them in their original colours. Through cosmology, he contemplates life and the truth of the universe. He searches for a connection between the cosmos and his fate. There is a shot of the neurotic and helpless Lam standing in front of the stage, frustrated by a presentiment of misfortune. This scene is very similar to the one in *The System* of Pak Ying alone on Lantau Island. This situation of being solitary, helpless and close to death is even more evident in *Journey to the Cossacks*. The story is about an archeologist, Sze Wai, who returns to Xinjiang in northwest China. After the failure of his first dig, he embarks on a trip alone, following the instructions of a Kazakh girl. He encounters a sudden sandstorm, which causes both him and his horse to roll down a hill. His horse drowns in a swamp, while Sze can only stand by helplessly. Just when he discovers fragments of some old pieces, he is bitten on the hand by a poisonous snake. He immediately bandages the wound with a strip torn from his clothing, but the poison has already entered his system. Drenched in sweat, and with the sandstorm becoming increasingly severe, he collapses. When he struggles to stand up and walk, he falls down again. He finally faints and is covered by sand. He has reached the most critical moment of survival, but is helpless, lonely and isolated. This is a picture of utter despair.

This portrayal bears a certain resemblance to Peter Yung himself. He is a person who 'deviates from the normal.'[28] His philosophy that only when one is ready to face dilemmas will one be able to find the solutions to one's problems has influenced the personalities of his characters. But this persistence or stubbornness makes it difficult for him to 'survive' in the real world.[29] In *Double Dealer*, the young people are mostly social misfits in Hong Kong society. They have their own ways of thinking and their own ways of living. They are typical examples of people who are sandwiched between social norms and their own ways of living (the Chinese title of the film is, literally, *Sandwiches*). Their lives are composed of such marginalized deeds as, for example, fighting in the streets, taking drugs in toilets, speeding, dancing in discos, sleeping around and so forth. They are this way because they have done poorly in school and are unable to enter mainstream society. Thus, they have feelings of rebellion and vengeance, which drive them to smash expensive cars and to kidnap the children of wealthy families. They cannot help but take the path of delinquency. Such people have only a present but no future. They are moving, step by step, towards tragedy.

Peter Yung's *Journey to the Cossacks* was shot in Xinjiang province in China. Although he was not the first, non-leftist Hong Kong director to make films in the mainland, he was among the early ones to do so,[30] and he was the first among his New Wave counterparts. The film was made in collaboration with Sil-Metropole Organization Ltd and financed by Yung. It is about an archeologist, Sze Wai, who has gone to live in France. Sze goes to the desert in Xinjiang to search for historic pieces. His first dig fails. Then, under the guidance of a Kazakh, he succeeds in excavating some armour from the Han Dynasty. In the end, he chooses to stay in Xinjiang instead of returning to Paris. The plot centers on a stubborn intellectual, who leaves a capitalist society to go to China. He befriends Yao Wei, who works to promote exhibitions of Chinese antiquities abroad. The two develop an intimate relationship. However, Sze Wai disapproves of her view of cultural exchange as trade. In the end, they break up. Being obsessed with antiquities, Sze Wai is attracted to a Kazakh girl. Once, when he is dying, he is saved by the girl with blood from her beloved horse. What is more, she helps him to find the artefacts for which he has been searching. He also participates in the activity of *daoyang* ('contending for the sheep head') with the Kazakh people, living as part of their community. This film demonstrates the persistence and stubbornness of Sze Wai and the naivety of intellectuals in general.

Dennis Yu

Yu Wan-kwong, Dennis, was born in Hong Kong on 1 November 1950. In 1969 he entered the University of California, Los Angeles, in the United States, and earned a bachelor's degree in film four years later. In 1974, he spent one year doing graduate work. He returned to Hong Kong in 1975 and worked as an assistant to King Hu. In 1977, he joined TVB as a scriptwriter-director. His works include *CID*, *Seventeen*, *Black Report** and *Interpol*. In 1978, he founded Film Force Co. Ltd with Yim Ho, Ronnie Yu and others. They produced *The Extra*. In 1980, he made his first feature, *See Bar*. In the same year, he collaborated with Jeff Lau to establish Century Motion Picture and Distribution Co. Ltd. Then, he directed *The Beasts* and *The Imp*. His subsequent films include *The Comedy* (1984), *Musical Singer* (1985), *All the Wrong Clues* (1985), *Evil Cat* (1987) and *Tiger On Beat* (1989). He has now joined the commercial world and is engaged in real estate investment and online enterprises.

From Entertainment with Messages to Mere Entertainment

The 1977 drama *Seventeen: Summer Break* can be regarded as Dennis Yu's most remarkable work during his days in television. The story is about a female factory worker, Kong Ho-oi, with an elementary school education, who falls in love with a pre-university student, Lai Shui-ching, who is working in the factory as a summer job. Kong gradually discovers an immense discrepancy between them in living environment and thinking. When the summer comes to an end, so does their romance, as Lai enters university. The story is told from the points of view of the two young people. The main reason for this is to reveal the different mindsets and directions in life taken by these two people from different social classes. The girl loves reading popular novels such as the ones written by Qiong Yao and Yida and popular music such as that of The Wynners; while the boy is interested in the writings of Turgenev and Hemmingway, as well as in classical music, such as the compositions of Tchaikovsky and Chopin. For

Lai's sake, Kong studies in night school and borrows books from the library about the history of English literature. However, the gap between them cannot be filled. In addition, Lai's family is biased against factory workers. Lai's cousins and friends are all university students. The result is a wall that keeps Kong outside Lai's world. Most important of all, even Lai is unwilling to scale the wall that lies between them, so that there is no point of intersection between the two. Although the film is largely realistic, Lai is described as a lover of Tchaikovsky, Chopin and Turgenev, which is not representative of matriculated students as a whole. He has been raised to too lofty a height, so that he is more of a concept than a character. However, a vacation scene on an island is handled impressively well. The change in the two young people's relationship is demonstrated first by an embrace, then in the holding of hands, then in one sitting behind (not next to) the other and, finally, by the two of them sitting on two rocks, sitting separated by a stream of sea water. All of these actions symbolize their impending separation. In other words, the intellectual and spiritual differences between the two young people were growing ever greater. The device of metaphor is used very successfully here.

Dennis Yu also made use of metaphor in another episode of the *Seventeen* series: *Rainbow, a Beautiful Rainbow**. The drama is about a village girl who pursues her dream and joins a television station as a contract actress. Later, she realizes how complex the real world is. She uses a rainbow as a metaphor for her dream, which is neither practical nor substantial and which, therefore, has vanished into thin air.

All of Dennis Yu's television works intend to 'communicate certain messages to an audience to offer them both entertainment, and something else'.[31] However, in his first picture, the comedy *See Bar*, there is no message, only jokes. This is probably due to commercial pressure. What this film and Yu's television dramas have in common are that the main actors are television performers, such as Chow Yun-fat and Dorothy Yu and the scriptwriter Tang Wai-hung. In this film, Chow Yun-fat, who works in a garage, runs into a series of troubles. After taking part in a motorbike race with a subordinate of Big Head Shing, he is then pursued by killers. Over the gambling table, he also incurs the enmity of the boss of a loan enterprise, Pak Ying. In the end, he turns to See Bar (Roy Chiao) for help. See Bar arranges for Pak Ying to rob a bank, get caught and go to jail. The intention of the film is to put together all of the elements that will attract an audience: stunt driving, fights, tricks and jokes. However, the result is a fragmented plot. Narrative segments are simply put together in such a way that consistency and logic are lacking. Some parts, for instance, the plot to illegally bring in Vietnamese migrants, do not seem connected to anything. The entire film gives the impression of looseness, fragmentation and inconsistency, and these are its flaws. Some critics have called this film an 'assorted' production,[32] which does not sound unreasonable. Yu's style is characterized by liveliness, clarity and boisterousness. He made a first move into commercial cinema. His next comedy, *The Comedy*, which appeared four years later, was a great improvement. The jokes are frequent, inserted according to a precise calculation; the plot is fast-paced and there are no dull moments in the movie.

The Comedy shows three hooligans, Cheng Chuk-shi, Wong Ching and Wang Yu, who hang around in a train station swindling people. By chance, they meet the godfather of the gang, whose influence extends over 36 provinces. He invites them to a big hotel to participate in a competition to become the next godfather of the gang. Because the three hooligans are pursuing the godfather's daughter, other gang leaders mistake them for famous killers, and the three become targets for assassination. This film can be regarded as a large-scale production. Imitating Cinema City's comedies,[33] it contains numerous jokes and fast-paced action. Quick editing is employed to create scenes of hustle and bustle. The film contains tricks played by various gangs, gunplay, chases, singing and dancing, and struggles between cops and gangsters, all presented in a humorous manner. However, the actions and reactions of the characters are too uniform, which conveys a sense of rigidity. Occasionally, there are some creative scenes. For example, Cheng, Wong and Wang are disguised as a zebra and clowns when the detective, Paul Chun, arrives. Chun orders everybody not to leave, but his subordinate repeats his last syllable and thus utters, 'Leave'. Everybody quickly disappears. When Chun turns his head and sees that nobody is there he is furious. Another scene shows a poster on a wall of a beautiful woman. Chun presses on the breast of the woman and is struck by a current of electricity, which causes him to quickly withdraw his hand from the poster. As it turns out, under the poster is a button connected to an electricity source. Finally, there is a scene in which the three mobsters rescue a gang leader and his two daughters. One daughter, Tong Lan-fa, pairs up with Wong Ching, and another, Dorothy Yu, with Cheng Chuk-shi. Wong and Cheng promise to leave the underworld and live a stable life. Wang Yu is left, and he leaves alone by train. As he settles into his seat on the train, his two partners reappear. They would rather turn their backs on love and stability and together return to Guangzhou to continue the old life.

Dennis Yu's second film, *The Beasts*, is about a brother (Eddie) and a sister (Chong Ching-yee) who go camping with friends. The sister is raped and the brother is murdered. Their father, Chan Sing, decides to take the law into his own hands. He roams the countryside in pursuit of the 'beasts' who have harmed his family and kills them one by one. The philosophy of this film is that those who are in the habit of committing unjust deeds will surely perish. The numerous evil acts carried out by groups of young delinquents in the countryside included killing the villagers' chickens, stealing sweet potatoes and burying the villagers alive. They gang rape Chong, which causes her to lose her senses. Thus, she mistakes her father for a villain. Furthermore, they push Eddie, who has come chasing after them, down the hill; he is pierced by sharp bamboo sticks and dies. Suffering from psychosis, Chong is unable to recognize the rapists, who therefore go free. Chan Sing has no choice but to execute justice by himself. The scenes in which he kills the 'beasts' are violent and bloody. This is also a distinctive work of a new talent.

This movie is a carnival of violence, with scenes similar to those in *Deliverance*.[34] However, it fails to explore the implications of the irrational behaviour of human beings. Still, the narrative is orderly and clear. In the opening, two threads of action are placed in parallel. One shows a group of youngsters happily going for a picnic; they set up tents, start a fire and wash their clothes and dishes. Another shows a group of criminals appearing in the countryside. It shows that danger threatens the young people. The scenes of them enjoying themselves are interspersed with shots of the criminals spying on the young people, particularly the girls; and later, of the criminals teasing and raping Chong, who had gone alone to wash dishes by the river. Showing the tragic events unfolding one by one amidst the joyful moments certainly reinforces the intensity of the misfortune and violence. This is also an effect generated from the tight structure of the narrative. The development of the plot is also rational and persuasive. The director's approach is smooth yet terse, and the plot is presented clearly. Beautiful scenes of the countryside are also shown. The setting is skilfully employed to convey tension, as, for example, in the scenes of Chong being chased, Eddie being killed and Chan Sing avenging himself on the young delinquents. This is the most outstanding feature of the movie.

Fights between Humans and Demons, and the Deep Fears of Human Beings

The Imp is Dennis Yu's third picture, and his most successful one. Although the film shows influences from such Hollywood movies as *The Omen*, *Rosemary's Baby* and *The Exorcists*,[35] Yu has made it mesmerizing by adding local and Chinese traditional elements. It is a major work among both the New Wave and the genre of horror films in Hong Kong cinema as a whole. The central character, Chun Cheung-lam, is been born at a time and date in the Chinese character that is traditionally associated with ghosts. Chun works as a security guard in a building that is haunted by a group of ghosts. The spirits want to take over the fetus in the womb of Chun's wife, Dorothy Yu, and to be reborn. The story ends with Chun killing his son with an axe. These ghosts bring about the deaths of three of Chun's colleagues. The first victim, Uncle Hon, is Chun's boss. While at home, a sheet of old newspaper suddenly blows over his face and he falls down. Then, a pot of boiling congee spills over him and he dies. The second victim, Wong Ching, is having a midnight snack when he chokes to death on a chicken bone. The last victim, Cheng Chuk-shi, suspects that something strange is happening and resigns from his job. As he is driving home, a mist suddenly appears ahead; his car comes to a halt. Then, the car is lifted into the air and suddenly dropped. Both vehicle and driver are consumed in fire. A *fengshui* master, Ngok Wah, discovers that the ghosts are those who have died unjust deaths and who are trying to be reborn and are behind these tragedies. Coincidently, Chun's wife is expected to give birth at the very moment in the Chinese calendar most auspicious to ghosts. In addition, this moment will coincide with a full solar eclipse, which is when ghosts are most active. The ghosts have already entered Yu's body. If the rebirth is successful, Chun and Yu will become demons who bring peril to the world. Thus, the *fengshui* master urges Chun to hurry and destroy the ghosts before sunrise. The *fengshui* master is also defeated by the evil spirits; he is murdered when practicing Taoist rituals in an attempt to fight them. These scenes are mysterious and horrifying and provoke deep fear among the audience. In addition, the plot unfolds naturally and the narrative details are creative, making this a superior horror film.

Parallel editing is employed to juxtapose scenes of Yu in the hospital waiting to give birth and Chun struggling with the ghosts at his workplace. Just as Yu gives birth to her baby, Chun is lifted up into the air by the evil spirits and then dropped. The shot of Yu looking at the newborn baby is followed by the scene of Chun rushing home. Yu comes home carrying the baby. As she opens the door, Chun lifts up a chopper. Then the director cuts to a freeze shot. The implication is that Chun kills the baby that is possessed by the ghosts and that, at one stroke, this act will bring a clean resolution to the havoc caused by the accumulated anger of the numerous spirits of people who have died unjustly.

Evil Cat is a story about demons, which is characterized by the use of technology. Similar to *The Imp*, which describes a world disturbed by evil spirits, in *Evil Cat*, the phantoms are not the ghosts of human beings but a 400-year-old cat spirit. It also seeks to harm people and to enter their bodies. The demon cat causes a number of deaths. In this film, it is not defeated by a *fengshui* master or an axe, but by Maoshan, Taoist master. The Taoist master uses a sword made of cherry tree wood and a magic bow and three arrows that are over a thousand years old. In this story, the evil cat reappears once every 50 years to wreak havoc on the world. Master Lau Kar-leung and his disciple, Mark Cheng, join forces to conquer the devil using the magic bow and arrows. After undergoing countless difficulties, Master Lau dies, while Cheng, with the arrows, succeeds in killing the evil cat which disappears in a flash of blue. A science-fiction film with special effects, it employs computing technology and lasers. The film opens with a scene of construction workers digging a hole at the site. Suddenly, in a flash of blue, the evil cat appears in the sky. The cat, being active at night, murders a security guard in a building. Then, it approaches a company boss, Mr Fan, in the form of a blue light. The light changes into the shape of a cat (through computer animation) and takes possession of Mr Fan's body and then of Fan's secretary. Master Lau and Cheng rush over. They are invaded by the evil spirit. Lau commands Cheng to kill him in order to destroy the spirit. Cheng shoots an arrow shot at Lau, and Lau's body is destroyed in an explosion. A blue light flashes toward Cheng's girlfriend, Tang Lai-ying. Reluctantly, Cheng shoots an arrow at his lover. A flash of red pierces her, immediately followed by numerous blue flashes shooting up into the sky (laser technology). The flashes then turn into light beams, which are amazingly spectacular. The evil cat, who has turned into the light beams, disappears. Cheng holds his dead girlfriend in his lap; all is tranquil in the world.

The special effects in *Evil Cat* are excellent, but the plot is thin and somewhat clichéd. The way in which the evil spirit was defeated is very western and recalls *The Exorcist*. The only attractions are the spectacular special effects produced by the large-scale use of technology, which is a workable enough approach. However, the film suffers when comparison to some other similar works at the time. *Evil Cat* is not as natural, free in style, powerful in the use of technology and as mysterious in mood as *A Chinese Ghost Story*, which was released at approximately the same time. Furthermore, the film is not as interesting as two later works, *Happy Ghost 4* and *Fai and Chi: Kings of Kung Fu*, which incorporate human acting and animation. In fact, a sci-fi production with special effects also has to have new ideas and innovations; a strong story is also essential. Comparatively speaking, *Evil Cat* is greatly inferior to Dennis Yu's earlier film, *The Imp*.

To Live with Love

On the surface, *Musical Singer* is a musical but, in fact, it is a story about how to live. The narrative centres on an agent for singers, James Wong, who is only knowledgeable about the profession, not about how to be a person and how to manage financial affairs. The singers who signed under him leave, one by one, after becoming famous. Later, he trains a new talent, Law So, and succeeds in launching his career as a singer. As an experienced musician and agent, Wong has a unique way to coaching – he arranges for Law to perform in a noisy nightclub where no one listens attentively to his singing. Indeed, he is even booed off the stage. The frustrated Law has been taught a lesson by Wong: a price needs to be paid for success. Later, Wong orders Law to shout in the streets, to attract the notice of the public; this is to train him to develop a thick skin and to be bold. Wong's own problem is that he does not know how to behave as a person should; thus, although he is a good coach, he is not a good agent. It is the following words of advice from Law So's father, Roy Chiao, that help him to resolve his problem: Sincerity is the key to being a good person. It is rewarding to love others. Eventually, Wong apologizes to one of the singers who had left him, Anita Mui. His apology is accepted with a smile.

The action comedy *All the Wrong Clues* (1985) is a hybrid of Hollywood and Hong Kong elements. It contains some similarities to the Hollywood films *Police Academy* and *An Officer and a Gentleman*[36] and to the Hong Kong TV drama *Police Cadet I*. The film centres on the Systems Development Unit of the police force. The students there are undergoing harsh training but are both mischievous and funny. The film ends with a police action in which the students successfully defeat the criminals and rescue the hostages being held in a supermarket. This film resembles the youth films produced by Cinema City, although this time, the focus is not on the bodies of young girls, but on the masculine physique of the men.

Certainly, the film is not short of scenes of students horsing around, being scolded, punished and forced to undergo harsh physical training. There are naturally also scenes of girls being chased, which resemble those of Gere in *An Officer and a Gentleman*. In *All the Wrong Clues*, Mark Cheng chases a girl, Patricia Ha, working in a grocery. His trainer, Shek Tin, discovers this, and Cheng is punished by being forced to read his love letter aloud in the playground. This is a relatively creative scene, compared to other parts of the film, although it is somewhat familiar to a scene in Clifford Choi's *Grow Up in Anger*, in which a boy sends a love letter in class to a girl. The teacher intercepts the letter and reads it aloud in class. In addition, there are the scenes in which the students Lou Nam-kwong and Pang Kin-sun are assigned by their instructor to scrub the floor and to sweep the exercise yard. While humiliating, such tasks are effective in training new policemen. However, these scenes are nothing new to an audience and, thus, are insufficiently creative.

Notes

1. *Horatio I. P. I.* (1993) was a film made by Lau Shing Hon for Ken International Film Production in the United States. It has yet to be released in Hong Kong. Lau is a pioneer among Hong Kong directors who makes films for American film companies. He uses the technique of direct sound recording.
2. Originally named *The Final Night of the Royal Hong Kong Police: One Body Two Flags*. The project was financed with $900,000 from Hong Kong Arts Development Council.
3. *The Poetic Characteristics of Film* (Dianying fubixingji). Hong Kong: Cosmos Books, 1992.
4. *Viridiana*, 1961.
5. *Tristana*, 1970.
6. *The Servant*, 1963.
7. *The Golden Age*, 1930.
8. Tat Chun, 'Interviewing Lau Shing Hon', *Hong Kong Cinema 1980*. 4th Hong Kong International Film Festival. HK: Hong Kong Government. 3 April 1980, p. 178.
9. Gaolang. 'Zuhe dianying – *Yuhuo Fenqin*' (Combination Movies – *House of the Lute*). Li Youxin ed. *Dianying, Dianyingren Dianying Kanwu* (A Publication of Films and Filmmakers). Taiwan: Independent Evening News Press. March 1986, p. 194.
10. Tierya. 'Reality, Sensationalism, Flow of Sentimentality – Review of *House of the Lute* 3.' *City Entertainment*. No. 32, 10 April 1980.
11. Same as endnote 9.
12. Shek Kei. 'Start From The Head Hunter.' *Ming Pao Evening Paper*. 23 March 1983.
13. The full title of *One Body Two Flags* is *The Final Night of the Royal Hong Kong Police: One Body Two Flags*. The film is composed of two stories: *One Body Two Flags* and *Qingmei tiema* (not produced). It was financed by Hong Kong Arts Development Council.
14. Davis, Darrell. 'The Death of a Hong Kong Policeman: Lau Shing Hon's *One Body Two Flags*.' *Hong Kong Economic Journal*, 17 December 1999.
15. *Shimian maifu* was an experimental short film made by Terry Tong in 1976. Taking the form of chess animation, the film is accompanied by a Chinese musical score of the same title. It expresses the confrontation and antagonism between two armies. This work won the award for best experimental short film made that year.
16. Evans Chan. 'An Absurd Breed: *Collies Killer*.' *City Entertainment*. No. 89. 1 July 1982, p. 41.
17. Ho Man. 'The First Film of Terry Tong.' *City Entertainment*. No. 90, 16 July 1982, p. 35.
18. Fung Mei-wah. 'Interview of Terry Tong – May I be Me!' *City Entertainment*. No. 11. 1 March 1984, p. 18.
19. Ibid., p. 19.
20. *My Fair Lady* (1965). The film tells a story of how the male protagonist trains a village girl to masquerade as an aristocrat.
21. Pak Tong Cheuk, Law Kar and Cheung Chi-shing. 'Interviewing Terry Tong.' *After Twenty Years: a Retrospect of Hong Kong New Wave Cinema*. 23rd Hong Kong International Film Festival. HK: Contemporary Urban Council, 31 March – 15 April 1999, p. 143. These three films are by Japanese director Akira Kurosawa.
22. Chu Xin. 'Xianchang fangwen Tang Jiming "Qixiasiyi"' (interview with Terry Tong at the location of the shooting the *Seven Warriors*). *Dayinghua* (Big Motion Picture). Hong Kong: Hong Kong Motion Picture Press. No. 7. 1 October 1998, p. 15.

23. *One Day in Locke* is a documentary about one day in the life of this town where the residents are all Chinese. Refer to Chan Ting-ching, 'Peter Yung – From Documentary to Drama.' *City Entertainment*. No. 23, 22 November 1979, pp. 14–15.
24. Ibid., p. 15. *White Powder Opera* includes the self-narrated stories of a group of drug traffickers, some of whom were arrested, some imprisoned and some who had fled from Hong Kong.
25. Ibid., p. 16.
26. Only a few movies at that time adopted direct sound recording, namely *Lonely Fifteen*, *Ah Ying* and *Just Like Weather*.
27. When this movie was released, a senior member of the production company, Cinema City, said that allowing directors to make films that they wanted to make was a mistake. See Cheung Kou. 'What after all do *Teenage Dreamers/Once Upon a Rainbow/Lonely Fifteen* give us?' *City Entertainment*. No. 85. 6 May 1982, p. 14.
28. In an interview, Peter Yung honestly admitted that he is a deviant and a socially isolated person. See Nip Da. 'A Rebound from Near Death – An Interview of Peter Yung.' *City Entertainment*. No. 150, 12 November 1984, p. 14.
29. Ibid.
30. The first Hong Kong director to shoot a film in the mainland was Johnny To, when making *The Enigmatic Case* (1980).
31. Zhang Jinman. 'An interview: "Dennis Yu of Full Confidence"' (Xinxin shizu de Yu Yunkang). *Datexie* (Extreme Close-Up). No. 47, 9 December 1997, p. 37.
32. Yip Siu-yiu. '*See Bar*.' *City Entertainment*. No. 28, 7 February 1980, p. 29.
33. *All the Wrong Clues* by Cinema City. Dir. by Tsui Hark. 1981. See the chapter discussing 'Tsui Hark'.
34. *Deliverance*. Produced by Warner Brothers and directed by John Borman, 1973. This film was the second most popular movie in the United States that year, with box office receipts of 18 million Hong Kong dollars.
35. *The Exorcist*, produced by Warner Brothers and directed by William Frankin, 1974. *The Omen*, produced by 20th Century Fox and directed by Richard Donner, 1976.
36. *Police Academy*, produced by Ladd/Wanner Brothers, 1984. A crazy comedy, this movie was extremely popular and was followed by five serial episodes. *An Officer and a Gentleman*, produced by Paramount Pictures, 1982. It earned $52 million at the box office, making it the fifth highest-earning movie that year.

11

Contributions and Influence of the New Wave

In the 1970s the development of the Hong Kong television industry was rapid, reaching a peak in terms of both quantity and quality. This period is regarded as the 'golden age' of Hong Kong's television industry, when a new group of talented people emerged. In the decade following its beginnings in the 1960s, the industry transferred a significant pool of talent to the film industry, which turned the latter's fortunes around. This showed the existence of an intimate, reciprocal relationship between the two industries.[1] As soon as they entered the film industry, the New Wave talent had to find a way to survive. As a result, they chiefly produced genre films, unlike during their television days, when they were not under the pressure of the box office and were allowed to follow their interests and make dramas full of experimental flavour, for instance, Patrick Tam's *Seven Women, The Underdogs* and *Social Worker*; and Ann Hui's *CID, Social Worker – Ah Sze, Below the Lion Rock – The Boy from Vietnam, The Bridge* and others. This is not to say that genre films can never be works of quality. The prime example of this is Tsui Hark's martial arts drama *The Gold Dagger Romance I & II*, known for its particularly delicate portrayal of character, which he made for Commercial Television. It can be said that a genre film is jointly produced and jointly constructed by the audience and the director. In the discourse of genre, the focus is on the similarities among films with regard to theme, narrative structure, action, characters and image and visual-audio codes. This is precisely what lies at the basis of popular art. The New Wave directors were not able to go beyond the restrictions of mainstream commercial films, and the market and, thus, genre films were still their principal target.

Although there can often be a conflict between genre films and auteurs, the resources (including manpower) and support of a studio can also be very helpful. For potentially creative directors, the studio system was no constraint; conversely, it was a way for them to stand out from others. Consider Ann Hui's *The Secret*. Appropriating ideas from folklore and myth, it is a thriller with multiple points of view. In the film an equilibrium is achieved between suspense and the psyche of the characters, which was a departure from the generic mould. Her Vietnam trilogy is about the miserable destiny and the helplessness of diaspora Chinese in an era of change. It expresses sympathy and compassion for the weak. Tsui Hark's *The Butterfly Murders* makes use of modern technology to turn a martial arts legend upside down, showing creativity and creating excitement. His Wong Fei-hung series is an example of the kung fu genre. However, it hints at a cultural conflict between East and West. Tsui's message is communicated that modernization is the only path to prosperity for China. He called for the integration of the two cultures, with China absorbing the strengths of the West to offset her own weaknesses.

All of these are examples of genre films that have managed to rid themselves of the constraints of the genre and to display the personality of the auteurs. Yim Ho's *Homecoming, The Day the Sun Turned Cold* and *The Sun Has Ears* are all about the bewilderment that people feel in life, about self-commitment and, finally, about self-confidence and the ability to control one's fate. *Cops and Robbers, Man on the Brink* and *Imaginary Suspects Chatter Street Killer,* all directed by Alex Cheung, explore the reversal and ambiguity of good and evil in humanity, articulated on a philosophical level. Allen Fong in *Ah Ying, Just Like Weather, Dancing Bull* and *A Little Life – Opera* constantly sought to innovate, to blend life, reality and fiction. The subjects of his films changed from his family, to his friends, to a married couple and to artists, an indication of his concern about society and his persistence in pursuing his art. Each of Fong's films includes his personal experiences and views toward life. As for Patrick Tam, he stands out for his experimental use of colour, for example, in *Love Massacre*. He has also put a great deal of effort into mastering the technique of *mise-en-scène*, such as in *Seven Women* and *CID*. *Four Moments of Life* and *Social Worker,* on the contrary, show his efforts in employing montage. Tam is classified as a stylist or a metteur-en-scène, as argued in Auteur Theory. This is not to say that Tam does not have his own world-view – he does – but his style is what stands out. For example, *Seven Women No. 2, Four Moments of Life, Seven Women No. 1, My Heart is that Eternal Rose* and *The Sword* depict frustration, uncertainty and the inability to control one's fate. There is the sense that if one is not struggling in vain, then one is simply returning to the starting point.

The members of the New Wave burst into the dormant Hong Kong cinema scene with the vigour of the newly born. There was a great contrast between them and the industry. The former were a group of courageous, youthful directors who liked innovating and experimenting, while the latter was an inflexible industry, full of conventions, unable to keep things going as they were, and aging. The consequence was that the New Wave stole the spotlight and brought about a metamorphosis of the entire industry. All units in film production, including direct sound recording, post-dubbing, cinematography and art design, were on their way to being professionalized. The industry as a whole underwent a full-scale improvement. Every member of the New Wave made use of the opportunities, capital and marketing institutions offered by the industry to fully develop their talents. They were even able to give their insights on film and express their world-views in their genre films; Alex Cheung's cop movies and Tsui

Hark's science-fiction films are examples. They were able to go beyond the constraints of genre, to reinvigorate those genres. To paraphrase, the New Wave directors created extraordinary works in ordinary genres. The films, which were filled with meaning as well as being entertaining, showed the auteurs' personalities and visions. That is to say, these works had the popular appeal of a commercial genre film as well as uniqueness of an individual work. Where the New Wave differed from their mainstream counterparts was that, early in their film-making careers, members of the New Wave shot films for some independent production companies. The only exceptions were Tsui Hark (Seasonal Film Corporation), Patrick Tam (Golden Harvest Entertainment Co. Ltd), Allen Fong (Feng Huang [Phoenix] Motion Picture Co.) and Ann Hui in her later period (Shaw Brothers to make *Love in a Fallen City*, 1984), all of whom joined big studios. Therefore, the members of the New Wave were, relatively speaking, not greatly limited by the studio system. But they received relatively more pressure, both direct and indirect, from the box office. It was not until the growth of Cinema City and the expansion of the power of producers – a power great enough to manipulate the production of the film from start to finish – that the limitations from a large studio became oppressive.

The New Wave, Taiwan New Cinema and the Fifth Generation

Most of the members of the New Wave went overseas to study film in the early 1970s and then successively returned to Hong Kong in the middle of the decade within a two to three year period. In Hong Kong, they encountered a burgeoning television industry and the growing localization of programmes. They found a desperate demand for young, professionally trained directors. They began working in the rapidly changing television industry for several years and then moved to making feature films, which was their desired career. In other words, they naturally flocked to the industry without prior shared intentions or plans, and with no uniform agenda and no consistent ideology. Precisely because of this, they were not hemmed in and could let their imagination run wild, making films with a high degree of dash and originality. This reflects one of the advantages, as well as the characteristics, of Hong Kong's free, capitalist society. Film-makers can rely only on their own efforts. They do not receive government subsidies. Moreover, in the 1960s and 1970s Hong Kong's economy experienced dramatic growth. The society grew wealthier and the middle class prospered and expanded. This led to greater social diversity. A variety of interest groups sprang up. These developments were reflected in the New Wave films, which employed a range of novel styles and themes.

The Hong Kong New Wave and the Taiwan New Cinema, the latter of which arose in 1982, are very different in subject matter and content. The Taiwan New Cinema works are rich with historical memory and local experience. *In Our Time* (1982), *A Summer at Grandpa's* (1984), *A Time to Live, a Time to Die* (1985) and *Dust in the Wind* (1986) are examples. *In Our Time* consists of the works of four young directors, Tao Deshen, Edward Yang, Ke Yizheng and Zhang Yi, and is about four phases in life (childhood, the teenage years, early adulthood and adulthood). *A Summer at Grandpa's* is a record of the childhood story of the scriptwriter Zhu Tianwen. *A Time to Live, a Time to Die* is the autobiography of Hou Xiaoxian. And *Dust in the Wind* tells the story of Wu

Nianzhen. The style adopted by Taiwan New Cinema is principally realistic and, thus, makes heavy use of long takes. Less focus is placed on the narrative structure. This is very different from the approach of the Hong Kong New Wave, which emphasizes tense dramatic structures, quick yet precise montages, multiple perspectives and multi-layered modes of narration. The only Hong Kong New Wave director whose works are realistic is Allen Fong (for example, *Father and Son*), the others produce films that are primarily genre-based. This explains why Fong's work is so incompatible with mainstream cinema, dominated as the latter is by commercial movies.

In 1984, the Fifth Generation of film-makers, exemplified by directors Chen Kaige and Zhang Yimou, emerged in mainland China. They represent a generation that had suffered through the Cultural Revolution. Their works show a strong sense of personal consciousness, and the subject matter of their films is often drawn from history. They steer clear of the entanglements of politics or ideologies, focusing rather on showing primitive customs and the mysterious rituals of the northwestern part of China proper. Consider *Yellow Earth* (Chen Kaige, 1984) and *Red Sorghum* (Zhang Yimou, 1987). The former reveals a spectacular ritual of begging for rain, while the latter features a masculine and wild wine-offering song, and a marriage ritual that resembles a snake dance. These romantic images of an exotic Orient and distorted historical legends have attracted quite a few western viewers. Compared with Taiwan New Cinema and the Hong Kong New Wave, the Fifth Generation was the first to win awards at international festivals in the West (*Yellow Earth* won the prize for best cinematography in two festivals: The Festival of the Three Continents and the Hawaii International Film Festival in 1985; and *Red Sorghum* won the Golden Bear award at the 38th Berlin Film Festival). The films of the Fifth Generation tend to have exciting plots, unconventional narratives, be made in bold and unusual styles, take a cynical stance toward reality, and feature bizarre representational modes. All of these have helped the films earn acclaim in international film festivals.

Like the Hong Kong New Wave, the members of the Fifth Generation have no common manifesto. In this, they differ from the members of the Taiwan New Cinema, who issued a unified declaration at the nadir of Taiwan cinema, in 1987, entitled – 'Declaration of Taiwan cinema in the year 76 (of the Republican calendar): allowing alternative cinema space for survival'. In the statement, the film-makers point out that the Taiwan government, mass media and film critics were offering no active support to the development of film culture. Film was regarded as a commodity, not as part of the culture. This was leading to the impending death of alternative cinema in Taiwan.[2] The proclamation was an expression of their concern about the future of the New Cinema. It eventually served as an announcement of its termination.

Contribution and Influence of the New Wave

Moving from television to film allowed the New Wave film-makers to make use of practices that had worked well during their days in television when making films. Such practices included collective creation, the compilation of information, art direction, on-location shooting, not using 'canned music' and so forth. Responding to the demand for a vast quantity of television programmes of a high quality, virtually every station in

Hong Kong had to develop their own creative teams. Scripts were produced collectively. Programmes, ranging from the live show *Enjoy Yourself Tonight*, to situation comedies, or even long drama series, were assigned to individual teams to create. In Rediffusion Television, the long drama *Crocodile Tear* was the full responsibility of a particular team, with regard to ideas, narrative, plot and even details such as scenes in individual episodes. The results of the team's discussions were then passed on to scriptwriters to produce a script.[3] This same method was used by TVB with the long drama *A House is Not a Home* (1977). Even the hour-long drama *CID* (1977), a work of the film unit, was initially prepared by a few scriptwriters. An inspector then checked the result for character consistency and plot development.

The system of collective creation, which proved to be workable, went well with the tight schedules and needs of the television industry. Of course, this system had both benefits and drawbacks. The benefit was that the discussion, which allowed inputs from various sources, was usually inspirational and efficient. However, the members might have to compromise and the discussion was always changing, which made the outcome lack a personal, consistent style. The New Wave directors moved into feature film-making, bringing along the scriptwriters who had worked well with them, and just naturally continued to use a system that had worked well for them in the past. For instance, in Yim Ho's *The Extra*, the construction of the plot was done by a group of scriptwriters led by Yim. It should be remembered that Yim Ho was one of the few among the New Wave who could both write and direct. Another example was a film directed by the author of this book, *Marianna*, the script of which was created through the discussions of a team consisting of Kam Ping-hing, Ng Wai-wing, So Kin-wing and Lau Chun-wai. Because this mode of collective creation was extremely popular at the time, it was common to find in the film credits the item of 'scriptwriter' being shown as 'the creative team of xxx production company' instead of individual names.

The half of scriptwriting is the compilation of information. This grew in prominence in the late 1970s in television stations. Both RTHK's drama series in the early days, *Below The Lion Rock*, produced by Wong Wah-ki, and TVB's variety, *Enjoy Yourself Tonight*, had a formal production team who chiefly collected information relevant to the programme and coordinated the sites for shooting and the people involved.[4] In the late 1970s, the practice developed of having every single programme or drama supported by a professional research team early in the process of brainstorming and scriptwriting. Newspapers, magazines and books were the major sources of information. In an initial phase, the team provided the research outcome to the scriptwriters and directors for reference, and fieldtrips or interviews were then arranged for a more in-depth investigation. In making *Black Report*,* the scriptwriter-director Dennis Yu of the film unit of TVB visited a detention centre several times to interview the criminals there.[5] In this way, first-hand information was obtained. In the production of TVB's *CID*, the scriptwriter, Ma Choy-man, visited the Criminal Investigation Unit of the Kowloon headquarters of the police force for an entire week. He chatted with the policemen and followed them when they were investigating cases.[6]

The introduction by the New Wave talents of these practices into film-making was an attack on the frivolous, rigid approach to film-making in the industry. In the process of making *The Happening* (1980), Yim Ho spent a significant amount of time with teenagers, trying to understand their way of thinking. Kirk Wong visited nightclubs many times when he directed *The Club*. When Ann Hui made *Story of Woo Viet* and *The Boat People*, she and her scriptwriters interviewed a number of Vietnamese boat people in order to get a grasp of their past and present lives, as well as their dreams about the future. In short, the new breed of film-makers went to infinite pains to make their films convincing and real.

On-Location Shooting, Art Direction, Direct Dubbing and the Abandonment of 'Canned Music'

On-location shooting became a primary element of television dramas shot with film stock. The reasons for this are as follows:

1. A rapid increase in in-house programmes meant that there were not enough studies for shooting. Variety shows and long dramas were given priority for studio use, while new dramas such as anthology series shot with film stock had to look elsewhere for a place to do their shooting.
2. New Wave directors enjoyed on-location shooting because there was more space for the shooting, the mood was livelier, and there was more of a film atmosphere.
3. To capture a real environment, observe life and to draw material from life was, at a philosophical level, extremely valuable.

These dramas shot by the New Wave directors were actually features; they were released on the television screen only because of their relatively low production budgets. Furthermore, in order to popularize television, *yueyu* (Cantonese) was chosen as the 'official language' of the stations. This strategy alone had the direct effect of nearly bringing to a stop the production of Cantonese films in the early 1970s. However, the situation of the dominance of Mandarin films in the market could be corrected by restoring the production of Cantonese films. In 1973, *The House of 72 Tenants*, which had close ties with television, broke through the predicament. *The Hui Brothers Show* in 1974 and *The Last Message* in 1975, which were revisions of two of Michael Hui's comedies, the *Hui Brothers' Show* (1971) and *73* (1973), respectively, made Cantonese films popular. By the time of the New Wave period, nearly all productions were in Cantonese.

On-location sound recording is an essential part of television productions, including those shot with film stock. Its advantages are: 1. It saves time in that no post-production dubbing is necessary. 2. Voices and their textures are genuine and full of feeling, which highlights the atmosphere of the scenes. The young New Wave talents clearly understood the benefits of this practice and, when possible, made it a priority in their film-making. Among them, Allen Fong was an example of this practice, which was best illustrated in his *Ah Ying* (1983) and *Just Like Weather* (1986). This also contributed to the acclaim Fong's films earned. Moreover, the successes of Peter Yung's *The System* (1979) and Johnny Mak's *Lonely Fifteen* (1982) were aided by this practice.

With regard to background music, New Wave directors mostly hired musicians to perform musical arrangements and for dubbing instead of using 'canned music', as was more common. There are two advantages to using musicians to compose and dub music in films. First, the music and musical arrangements can match well with the theme and mood of the entire plot. Second, the music is more likely to fit precisely with shots, changes of scene and the characters' emotions. This practice and the concepts involved were also new to the Hong Kong film industry. Another modification was in art direction. Almost every single film had workers who were in charge specifically of art direction, which altered the convention that the props staff or the director himself should take on the task. Hence, the practice of being unprofessional was abolished by the specialized division of labour introduced by the New Wave film-makers. This brought about an important change in the Hong Kong film industry. It was exactly this kind of professionalism that facilitated communication with audiences at the local, national, regional and global levels.[7] Breaking through cultural barriers, the films could be easily accepted by different audiences, laying the foundation for the emergence of Hong Kong cinema in the international arena.

The Rise of Independent Productions and the Film Market

In the beginning of the 1970s, the Hong Kong film industry was basically still dominated by the two major studios, the Shaw Brothers and Golden Harvest, while independent film-making had declined. It was not until the mid- and late 1970s that independent film-making began to revive. *Binfen* Film and Pearl City Film were the most productive of the independent film-makers. In the early 1980s, independent production companies flourished. This was a big boost to the emergence of new directors and also expanded their room for development. Although some have argued that the independent production companies were no different from the big commercial enterprises in that both were commercial enterprises, at least they increased the demand for directors, which gave the new directors more opportunities to make films. This period coincided with the closing of Commercial Television in 1978 and the termination of TVB's film unit in 1980. Therefore, dozens of new directors moved into feature film-making within the space of about three years. With the exception of Patrick Tam's *The Sword* (1980) and Allen Fong's *Father and Son*,[8] their maiden films were the works of independent production companies. Thus, it is evident that the independent production organizations had a determining effect on the rise of the New Wave.

With only a few exceptions, independent production companies primarily created low-budget films because of their limited capital. At that time, it was standard for a film to cost about seven to eight hundred thousand Hong Kong dollars to make. A box office return of one hundred thousand for such a film was considered satisfactory. The theatres and production companies shared the revenue, with the latter taking 40 per cent. After subtracting 17.5 per cent for entertainment tax of 17.5 per cent, 15 per cent for distribution costs and 17.5 per cent for promotion costs, the actual income was only twenty thousand Hong Kong dollars. In other words, the production company would lose about sixty thousand, taking the upper range of estimated costs.[9] The losses had to be covered by income generated from overseas sales. By and large, the revenue gained from the Singapore-Malaysia region was three hundred thousand; from Taiwan, two hundred thousand; Europe and America, fifteen hundred thousand; and other regions, one hundred thousand, for a total of seventy-five hundred thousand dollars. Excluding the loss in Hong Kong, a film could generate a return of about one hundred and fifty to two hundred thousand. However, if domestic box office receipts were under eight hundred thousand, the film was at risk of running a loss. The philosophy of independent film-making was always to generate a large return from a small investment. Often, the production companies did not put out their own money, but relied on the deposit from overseas copyrights. A sum of about seven hundred thousand dollars in deposits from, say, Singapore, Malaysia and Taiwan was enough for the shooting to begin.

In other words, under normal circumstances Hong Kong could not support its own films, but depended on capital from overseas. This meant that the tastes of overseas audiences had to be taken into account. Thus, Hong Kong directors had to pay attention to both local and foreign viewers from different cultures and backgrounds, which added another layer of consideration. The potential influence of the source of the capital on the making of a film could not be ignored. This explains why Hong Kong New Wave directors, and Hong Kong directors in general, mainly made genre films. Genre films adopt conventions of film-making with which the audience is familiar. They rely more heavily on visual language than on verbal language, making them easier for overseas viewers to follow. When they first entered the Hong Kong film industry, the New Wave directors, while confident, were inevitably nervous about the box office response, as they all hoped to establish themselves in the industry.

Diverse Genres, Challenging Taboos and Breakthroughs in Narrative Mode

Facts prove the success of the New Wave film-makers. Their films became the focus of society and the favourites of the media, whilst the directors themselves even developed as a new force within the industry. Among them, each director had his/her own personality and made his/her own choices, as could be seen, for example, from their first films. Yim Ho's *The Extra* was a comedy portraying people in the lower classes of society. *The Butterfly Murders* (1979), directed by Tsui Hark, was a martial arts film with complex imagery. Alex Cheung's police flick, *Cops and Robbers* (1979), had a quick pace and strong rhythm. *The Secret* (1979), by Ann Hui, was a thriller that portrayed the horror, mystery and peculiarity of a society. As with his television works, Patrick Tam's *The Sword* (1980) was a martial arts feature that stressed form over content. *See Bar* (1980), produced by Dennis Yu, was a comedy. Clifford Choi's *The Encore* (1980) was classified as a youth film conveying extremely positive messages. Peter Yung's *The System* (1980) was a docudrama of the sub-genre of crime. *Father and Son* (1980), an Allen Fong film, was realistic in style. *The House of the Lute* (1980) was a Lau Shing Hon film with an erotic focus. *The Club*, directed by Kirk Wong (1981), was an action movie with sharp images. There were also Sin Wai-chu's youth film, *Cream Milk and Soda* (1981), Pak Tong Cheuk's *Baoche** (1981), Wong Chi's *The Crazy Corp* (1981), Ng Siu-wan's *Once Upon a Rainbow* (1982) and a wide variety of others films that were distinctive in style. Their emergence not only drew attention to Hong

Kong cinema, but also directly or indirectly facilitated the emergence of Taiwan New Cinema in the early 1980s. In 1980, a team of Hong Kong New Wave directors made their first trip to Taiwan to exchange views with other young directors there. Such a meeting inspired the young Taiwanese directors and energized Taiwan's stagnant film industry. In 1982, *In Our Time* was produced, marking the launch of Taiwan's New Cinema. This was followed by the rise of the Fifth Generation of mainland Chinese directors in the mid-1980s. Therefore, Hong Kong New Wave can be said to have been the pioneer in the emergence of a new kind of cinema in all three locations.

Daring to Address Taboo Subjects

New Wave directors were willing to make daring experiments in their creative work. Besides trying out a diversity of genres, they were also willing to venture into forbidden territory. Ann Hui was one example of this. In her *The Bridge*, a television drama, she had already dared to expose the indifference of the colonial bureaucracy to the feelings of the people. Her *ICAC: The Investigation* focused on the notorious corruption case of Peter Godber, the Superintendent of Police. However, as the completion of the film coincided with the police's attacks on the ICAC in 1977, the ICAC banned the film. It was not until 1999 that the film was released and shown in the Hong Kong International Film Festival. A ban was also slapped on the episode *ICAC: A Real Man*. Taking a humanistic perspective, the drama told of collective corruption in a police station in Lantau, which was reported by a brave new arrival, Wai Lit. In the end, all of the policemen who had been involved in the corrupt activities were tried and imprisoned. Likewise, the release of Tsui Harks' *Dangerous Encounter – 1st Kind* was prohibited by the Film Censorship Unit for political reasons. Following a storm of controversy, the authorities permitted a revised version to be released. In Patrick Tam's *Seven Women No. 1*, the scenes of high-school girls kissing and having sex caused the Film Censorship Unit to issue a warning to TVB. Another of Tam's films, *Nomad*, contained a lovemaking scene between the protagonists, set on a tram, that was fiercely criticized. The film nearly became the catalyst for the launching of a third 'clean-up campaign' in the film industry. Clifford Choi's *Teenage Dreamers*, together with *Lonely Fifteen* and *Once Upon a Rainbow*, which were released at about the same time, gave rise to seminars on 'youth films' because of their portrayals of the open attitude that young people had toward sex and violence. Choi even stomped out in the middle of a seminar to show his discontent towards certain points of view. It could be said that the three waves in Hong Kong cinema in the 1980s were all aroused by New Wave directors. This was all evidence of their courage and persistence in exploring taboo subjects and in daring to say what others did not.

Bold Innovations in Narrative Mode and Cinematic Language

Ann Hui's television work *Dragon, Tiger, Panther* had already abandoned the linear mode of narration that had traditionally been based on chronologically arranged sequence and, instead, adopted the approach of presenting multiple points of view. Even more self-conscious experiments with narrative style are evident in another of Hui's films, *The Spooky Bunch*, where the point of view constantly shifts between human and demon. Her later works, such as *Starry is the Night, Song of the Exile,*

Eighteen Springs and *Ordinary Heroes*, more aggressively cross-cut through time and space, sometimes in multiple layers. The layers of narration are sometimes even altered or reversed. In this way, the narrative paradigm itself becomes part of the content. Tsui Hark also demonstrated numerous experiments in his films in the dimension of cinematic language. For instance, a scene in *Dangerous Encounter - 1st Kind* involves a falling cat that is killed on an iron rail with a sharp point. It shows the potential of montage. *The Swordsman* and *The Blade* integrate illusion, the past and reality in an innovative way. There is a reversal of time and space in *The Chess, The Lovers, Twin Dragons* and *Love in the Time of Twilight*, particularly in the last, where there are three types of shifts - the most daring experiment in cinematic language at the time. Allen Fong also experimented with new film-making techniques. For example, in *Ah Ying*, over dinner in a restaurant, the heroine, Hui So-ying, and her boyfriend discuss their relationship. Without any script to follow, the young couple unreservedly express their feelings in an impromptu manner. This manner of allowing the story to unfold in its own way was a first in the history of Hong Kong cinema. Further evidence of Fong's daring was seen in the casting of *Just Like Weather*. All of the performers in that film were people from real life, telling their own story in front of the camera. In pursuit of verisimilitude, the director and his crew inject themselves into the characters' lives and into the film. In *Love Massacre*, Patrick Tam experimented with colour in narrative structure. Finally, there is the *mise-en-scène* of Patrick Tam and Yim Ho. As seen in *Four Moments of Life* and *Art Life*, their technique in this aspect is outstanding.

Novel Contents and Themes

The works of the New Wave directors are broad in vision and show vigour and novelty in theme and content. One example is the concern shown for the fate of individuals, particularly the overseas Chinese. Ann Hui's *The Boy From Vietnam, Story of Woo Viet* and *A Better Tomorrow III* are all about the tragic destinies of overseas Chinese in times of tumultuous change, who have been deprived of their right to make choices. Another of Hui's works, *Song of the Exile*, shows the contradiction between personal identity and the nation. Conflict and entanglement between individuals and the nation are likewise the focus in *Romance of Book and Sword I* and *II*. In addition, Tsui Hark's series *Once Upon a Time in China* expresses frustration over the country's future, and points out the need for China to make adjustments to and merge together elements of the cultures of East and West. Tsui's *The Shanghai Blues* and *The Swordsman* borrow from the past to satirize the present and express discontent with politics. Yim Ho presents the theme of the inability of the individual to escape from his/her environment, for example, in *CID: Wrongly Accused, The Happening* and *Buddha's Lock*. His *The Day the Sun Turned Cold* and *The Sun Has Ears* revolve around the ideas of embracing and re-embracing one's fate and overcoming the bondage within. In addition, the director's *Kitchen* is an impressive portrayal about the transcendence of the self. Another talented director, Kirk Wong, made *Health Warning*, a movie in a popular genre, to show the opposition between tradition and the world of the future. Notwithstanding Wong's failure, for a variety of reasons, to convey his messages as clearly has he might have wished, the director is worth respecting for his spirit of experimentation. In addition, Lau Shing Hon's *The House of the Lute* focuses on the decline of the aristocratic class of the colony, depicted from the approach of eroticism. The reversal of the status of the master and the servant illustrates the disintegration of the old social system.

The works of the New Wave earned the recognition of audiences, and a number of them have won critical and commercial acclaim. For example, Allen Fong's *Father and Son* (1981), Alex Cheung's *Cops and Robbers* (1980), Clifford Choi's *Hong Kong Hong Kong* (1983), Ann Hui's *The Boat People* (1982), Yim Ho's *Homecoming* (1983) and *Red Dust* (1990) and Tsui Hark's *Zu – Warriors from the Magic Mountain* (1983) and *A Chinese Ghost Story* (1987). Some were artistically so accomplished that they gained awards in various international film festivals. For example, Alex Cheung's *Man on the Brink* (1981) won Best Picture in the Golden Horse Awards in Taipei. Three of Allen Fong's films, *Father and Son* (1981), *Ah Ying* (1982) and *Just Like Weather* (1986), won Best Picture and Best Director in the Hong Kong Film Awards in 1981, 1982 and 1983, respectively. Yim Ho's *Homecoming* (1984), *Red Dust* (1990), *The Day the Sun Turned Cold* (1994) and *The Sun Has Ears* (1996) also prizes in the Hong Kong Film Awards, the Golden Horse Awards in Taipei, the Tokyo Film Festival (Best Picture), the Cannes Film Festival and other international film festivals. Thus far, Yim has won the most international awards of any Hong Kong director. In addition, Ann Hui's *Summer Snow* (1994) won the Best Actress award in the Berlin Film Festival.

Impact on the Hong Kong Television/Film Industries

Apart from simply entering mainstream cinema, the Hong Kong New Wave directors actually became the core of Hong Kong cinema in the 1970s and 1980s. In terms of breadth and depth, the influence of the New Wave can be said to be the greatest in the nearly one hundred years of the history of Hong Kong cinema. Their assault on the entire industry helped to turn around mainstream cinema. In this, they differed from those mainland and Taiwanese film-makers producing *xinwenyi dianying* (new literary-artistic films), who tended to be elitist and whose works were targeted for international awards.[10] Taiwan New Cinema, in particular, incorporated the subjects and contents that were relatively personal, which resulted in films of a higher level of artistry. But these films were not understood and accepted so well by the general public. The Cinema thus earned international acclaim but at the price of the vitality of its industry. Such a consequence was not expected. In Hong Kong, several directors, influenced by the New Wave, moved to the film industry, for instance, Stanley Kwan, Shu Kei, Yau Kin-kong, Alfred Cheung, Tony Au, Teddy Robin, Fong Ching-ling, Cheung Chi-shing, Fruit Chan, Wong Kar-wai and others. In his early days in the television industry, Stanley Kwan worked as an assistant to Yim Ho and Ann Hui. He followed Ann Hui as she entered the film industry. In 1984, Kwan worked independently and directed *Women* (1985), *Love Unto Waste* (1986), *Rouge* (1988), *The Centre Stage* (1990) and *The Island Tales* (2000). He became a leading director. Shu Kei also worked closely in television with Patrick Tam, Yim Ho, Ann Hui and others writing scripts for them. After his contemporaries moved into feature film-making, Shu Kei still worked as a scriptwriter for Yim Ho's *The Happening*. Later, he took on the role of director and made films such as *Sealed With a Kiss, Hu Du Men* and others. He was even involved in film distribution. As an experienced scriptwriter, Yau Kin-kong produced scripts for

Ann Hui's *Story of Woo Viet, The Boat People* and other films. He became prominent in Hong Kong cinema and also worked as an examiner of scripts for Century Motion Picture and Distribution Co. Ltd. In 1985, he made his first attempt to direct a film, *Tangchao Qilinan.** Alfred Cheung had been a scriptwriter for Ann Hui and participated in the project, *The Story of Woo Viet*. Later, he directed films such as *Let's Make Laugh* (1984) and *Her Fatal Ways* I, II, III, IV (1990–1994). These films proved that he was adept at scriptwriting and directing comedies.

In the 1980s, Tony Au began work for the New Wave directors in art direction. Moreover, he won the Best Art Director award in the Hong Kong Film Awards. He then directed films such as *The Last Affair* (1983), *Dream Lovers* (1986) and *Au Revoir Mon Amour/Till We Meet Again* (1991). Au and William Chang, who had also worked as an art director for many members of the New Wave, contributed to Hong Kong cinema by changing attitudes in the film industry towards art design, which had hitherto been overlooked. This ushered in a new era of visual spectacle in Hong Kong cinema. Teddy Robin was a film worker who can be considered to have grown together with the New Wave. He had already made experimental films with Alex Cheung in the 1970s. He then starred in Cheung's television drama *The Trio*. Later, he worked as a producer of *Cops and Robbers* and *The Story of Woo Viet*. He even directed his first feature, *The Legend of Wisely* (1987), in which Alex Cheung was his technical consultant. Fong Lin-ching once worked for Century Motion Picture as a scriptwriter and worked on the projects of *Nomads* and *Collies Killer*. Later, he directed *Tangchao Haofangnan** (1984), *Kawashima Yoshiko* (1990) and *Private Eye Blues* (1994) and co-directed *Floating Life* with Clara Law (1996). Cheung Chi-shing worked as a scriptwriter in Allen Fong's *Dancing Bull* and as a producer of other works such as *Ah Ying, Just Like Weather* and other films. He also partnered with Kirk Wong to write the scripts for *Crime Story* and *Taking Manhattan*. His subsequent directing projects included *I've Got You, Babe!* (1994), *I Wanna Be Your Man* (1994), *Love and Sex Among the Ruins* (1996) and *I Do* (2000). He was a creative director with great potential.

Fruit Chan, in the late 1970s, worked in TVB as a log keeper and as an assistant for the New Wave directors Stanley Kwan and Chan Mong-wah, then migrated to the film industry. Later, Chan developed a distinctive style and directed the movies *Finale in Blood* (1991), *Made in Hong Kong* (1997), *The Longest Summer* (1998), *Little Cheung* (1999) and *Durian Durian* (2000). Winning the awards for Best Picture, Best Director and Best Screenplay in the Hong Kong Film Awards, Chan became the most outstanding and most distinctive director of the 1990s. Wong Kar-wai worked as an assistant director and scriptwriter in Patrick Tam's *Final Victory*. He directed a handful of films such as *As Tears Go By* (1988), *Days of Being Wild* (1990), *Ashes of Time* (1988), *Chungking Express* (1995), *Happy Together* (1998), *In the Mood for Love* (2000) and other films. At present, he is regarded as the most prominent director in Hong Kong. His recent work, *In the Mood for Love*, also brought Tony Leung Chiu-wai the Best Actor award in the Cannes Film Festival. Furthermore, certain assistants to New Wave directors developed into leading members of the film industries of Taiwan and Southeast Asia. For instance, Lai Shui-ching became a famous director and producer of television dramas in Taiwan, and Ho Yat-fan became a well-known television producer in Malaysia. Another successful producer, Yuen Yan-hong, worked in the television industry in Singapore. In addition, Chan Kwok-hei, who once worked as an assistant scriptwriter for Patrick Tam, moved into advertising, as did Siu Yuen-chi, who was a director of photography in New Wave films. All of these people are now prominent in their own right. These talents in the film, television and advertising industries inherited the vigour, creativity and spirit of experimentation of the New Wave. Their achievements are not merely their own, but also redound to the glory of the New Wave. Moreover, the New Wave directors took the lead in various trends in cinema. For instance, the youth films and the female ghost films, exemplified by Ann Hui's works, prompted the rise of love comedies such as Cinema City's *Chasing Girls* (1981).[11] *The Story of Woo Viet* and *A Better Tomorrow* (with John Woo as director and Tsui Hark as producer) were the forerunners of films that used Vietnam to shed light on political crises[12] and led to the popularity of films featuring heroes. And, of course, Tsui Hark's series, *A Chinese Ghost Story*, became a model for high-tech ghost movies. He himself became a thorough 'technology auteur'. In 2000, directors such as Tsui Hark (*Time and Tide*), Ann Hui, Yim Ho and Allen Fong were still active in Hong Kong cinema. As for Kirk Wong, he has become successful in Hollywood.

Bringing Hong Kong Cinema to International Attention and Visual Education

In 1990s, quite a number of New Wave directors bade farewell to the film industry and turned to teaching about film and culture. Clifford Choi, Lau Shing-hon and Peter Yung have been teaching in the School of Film and TV of the Hong Kong Academy for Performing Arts. Pak Tong Cheuk joined the Department of Film and Television in the School of Communication of Hong Kong Baptist University. In 1998 and 1999, Patrick Tam was involved in examining scripts and training new scriptwriters in Malaysia. He returned to Hong Kong in 2000 and taught at City University, training students in creative media. Equipped practical industrial experience and professional knowledge, they are passing their knowledge on to the next generation. The situation now is radically different from that in the 1960s and 1970s, when no formal programmes about film and television were offered in tertiary institutions. Thus, the people who pursued formal training in this field were forced to study in North America or Europe. Furthermore, in recent years, the number of young people wishing to enroll in formal studies in film, television and the media at tertiary institutions has been increasing. However, there are not enough places for them. It can be predicted that, after receiving three years of professional training in a university, these students will develop as a central force in the film, television and media industries in Hong Kong and the greater China region. In other words, the members of the New Wave have made substantial contributions to the television and film industries of Hong Kong, Taiwan and Southeast Asia, as well as to education in the profession, in aspects as varied as their works.

The works of the New Wave have elevated the taste of audiences in Hong Kong and broadened their vision. Moreover, they transformed the entire make-up of Hong Kong cinema. In the 1980s to the 1990s, Hong Kong cinema flourished for a total period of fifteen years, the longest stretch of prosperity in the history of the industry.

Furthermore, Hong Kong films have been introduced to an international audience and have gained wide attention. 'Absent the New Wave, Western knowledge about Hong Kong cinema would probably still be at the stage of appreciating kung-fu movies. The New Wave brought Hong Kong cinema into the international arena. In this alone, their achievement has been great."[13] That is to say, the huge amount of effort put in by the New Wave in the 1970s and 1980s have lain a firm foundation for the Hong Kong film industry. They have helped Hong Kong movies as a whole to gain approval and recognition at the international level. They have also paved the way for several in the Hong Kong film industry, namely, Tsui Hark, Kirk Wong, Ringo Lam, Stanley Tong, Ronny Yu, John Woo and Yim Ho (in 2001), to migrate to Hollywood and to share their talent with the world.

Notes

1. American directors who first became involved in television industry and then moved into film-making have included Sidney Lumet, John Frankenhiemer, William Franklin and Steven Spielberg.
2. In early 1987, Taiwanese cultural and film workers led by Zhan Hongzhi, Hou Xiaoxian, Edward Yang, Wu Nianzhen, Xiaoye, Lin Huaimin, Ke Yizheng, Chen Yingzhen, Lai Shengchuan and Tao Dechen jointly signed the 'Declaration of Taiwanese Cinema'.
3. Yangzi, 'Wutaishan sandaqiaowang leitaizhan' (The Stage-Fight of the Three Major Diplomats of 'Five-Station Hill'). *Datexie* (Close-Up). No. 61, 12 July 1978, p. 4.
4. Lin Xuhua (oral narration). 'Dianshitai qingbaoju — ziliaoshouji de lishi yu renwu' (The Intelligence Agency of Television Stations — the History and Mission of Information Collection). *Datexie*. No. 62. 4 August 1978, p. 30.
5. Zhang Jinman. 'Xinxin shizu de Yu Yunkang' (The Fully Confident Dennis Yu). *Datexie*. No. 47, 9 December 1977.
6. Luo Weiming. 'Xinjingcha dianying — Wuxian de CID pianji' (New Cop Movies — TVB's CID Drama Series). *Datexie*. No. 61. 21 July 1978, p. 9.
7. Anthony King. 'Architecture, Capital and the Globalization of Culture', *Global Culture*. Mike Featherstone, ed. London: Sage, 1990, p. 398.
8. *The Sword*, directed by Patrick Tam, was a Golden Harvest production, whereas Allen Fong's *Father and Son* was produced by Feng Huang (Phoenix) Motion Picture Co.
9. Xue Zhixiong and Liu Fang. 'Tan Xianggang zhipian zhidu' (discussion on the film production system of Hong Kong). *Datexie*. No. 64. 1 September 1979, p. 5.
10. Shek Kei. 'Sense of Achievement and Crisis in Hong Kong Cinema in the 1980s'. *Hong Kong Cinema in the 1980s*. HK: 15th Hong Kong International Film Festival, 1991, p. 15.
11. Ibid.
12. Ibid.
13. 'An Overall Look at the New Wave', A Seminar on the Special Topic of Hong Kong New Wave Cinema. HK: 23rd Hong Kong International Film Festival. Venue: Lecture Hall, Hong Kong Science Museum. Time: 5:30 pm, 13 April 1999.

Filmography

Ann Hui

Title	Major Cast	Screenwriter	Producer	Company	Year
Dragon, Tiger, Panther	Lee Yan-Yee, Kwong Ngai, Shek Sau	Joyce Chan	Liu Fang-Kang	TVB	1976
Murder	James Wong, Wong Man-Wei, Ho Big-Kin	Yim Ho	Selina Leung	TVB	1976
Social Worker – Boy	Virginia Ng, Miu Kam-Fung, Ma Kim-Tong	Moyung Kit	Liu Fang-Kang	TVB	1977
Social Worker – Ah Sze	Cecilia Wong, Damian Lau, Ng Wai-Kwok	Joyce Chan	Liu Fang-Kang	TVB	1977
ICAC: Three Women	Damian Lau, Kwan Chung, Tin Ching	Joyce Chan	Rafael Hui	ICAC	1977
ICAC: A Real Man	Damian Lau, Kwan Chung, Wai Lit, Carol Cheng	Joyce Chan	Rafael Hui	ICAC	1977
ICAC: The Investigation	Damian Lau, Chao Hung, Lau Dan	Yim Ho	Rafael Hui	ICAC	1977
ICAC: The Ninth Clause	Damian Lau, Kwan Chung, Ng Mang-Tat	Yim Ho	Rafael Hui	ICAC	1977
Below the Lion Rock – The Boy from Vietnam	Tsang Chuen Shing, Li Guo-Song, Yau Hing-Fung	Wong Chi	Cheung Man-Yee	RTHK	1978
Below the Lion Rock – The Road	Wong Sun, Shirley Wong, Cheung Ying	Joyce Chan	Cheung Man-Yee	RTHK	1978
Below the Lion Rock – The Bridge	Gigi Wong, Wong Man-Lei, Carol Cheng	David Lam	Cheung Man-Yee	RTHK	1978
ICAC: Black and White	Damian Lau, Kwan Chung, Carol Cheng	Kam Kwok-Leung	Rafael Hui	ICAC	1978
ICAC: Steak Expense	Damian Lau, Kwan Chung, Mary Hon	Ngai Hong	Rafael Hui	ICAC	1978

Title	Major Cast	Screenwriter	Producer	Company	Year
The Secret	Sylvia Chang, Angie Chiu, Norman Chu, Alex Man	Joyce Chan	Lo Kai-Muk	Unique	1979
The Spooky Bunch	Josephine Siao, Kenny Bee, Lau Hak-Suen, Kwan Chung, Tina Lau, Chang Chin	Joyce Chan	Chui Po-Chu	Hi-Pitch	1980
The Story of Woo Viet	Chow Yun-Fat, Lo Lieh, Cherie Chung, Cora Miao	Alfred Cheung	Teddy Robin Kwan	Pearl City	1981
The Boat People	George Lam, Season Ma, Cora Miao, Andy Lau	Yau Tai On-Ping	Hsia Moon Jenny Chui	Bluebird	1982
Love in a Fallen City	Cora Miao, Chow Yun-Fat, Chiao Chiao, Keung Chung-Ping, Winnie Chin, Chung King-Fai	Fung Cho	Mona Fong	Shaw Brothers	1984
The Romance of Book and Sword	Da Shi-Chang, Zhang Duo Fu, Wu Chun-Sheng, Liu Chen-Xi, Guo Bi-Chuan, Ding Cui-Hua	Qin Xi-Xin	Shen Wen-Hui Guo Feng-Qi	Sil-Metropole Yeung Tse Kong	1987
Princess Fragrance	Da Shi-Chang, Ai Yi-Nuo, Zhang Duo-Fu, Liu Mei, Guo Bi-Chuan, Ding Cui-Hua	Qin Xi-Xin	Shen Wen-Hui Guo Feng-Qi	Sil-Metropole	1987
Starry is the Night	Brigitte Lin, George Lam, David Wu, Derek Yee, Gwok Chi Tung	Leung Suk-Wah	Mona Fong Hsu Feng	Tomson Shaw Brothers	1988
Song of the Exile	Maggie Cheung, Lu Hsiao-Fen, Waise Lee, Hsiao Hsiang, Tien Feng, Yang Ting, Kaji Kentaro	Wu Nien-Chen	King Hu Jimmy Wang Benny Chao	Cos China Film	1990
Zodiac Killers	Andy Lau, Cherie Chung, Suen Pang, Ishida Junichi, Tou Chung-Hua	Raymond To Wu Nien-Chen	Eric Tsang	Golden Harvest	1991
My American Grandson	Wu Ma, Huang Kun-Husen, Carina Lau, Suen Pang, Wang Lai	Wu Nien-Chen	Du Yau-Ling	Golden	1991
Boy and His Hero	Ko Chi-Kit, Kot Oi-Kwok, Yim Chun-Sing, Wong Lap-Man, Chiu Shu-Kei	Wong Siu-Dai	Damian Lau	China Entertainment	1993
Summer Snow	Josephine Siao, Chao Hung, Law Kar-Ying, Allen Ting, May Law	Chan Man-Keung	Ann Hui	Golden Harvest	1994
Ah Kam	Michelle Yeoh, Sammo Hung, Jimmy Wong, Ken Lo, Mang Hoi, Michael Lam	Chan Man-Keung Chan Kin-Chung	Catherine Hun	Golden Harvest	1996
Eighteen Springs	Anita Mui, Wu Chien-Lien, Leon Lai, Annie Wu	Chan Kin-Chung	Ann Hui Jimmy Wang	Mandarin	1997
As Time Goes By	Margaret Ng, Tsim Tak-Lung, Ann Hui	Ann Hui	Peggy Chiao	China Television	1997
Ordinary Heroes	Loletta Lee, Tse Kwan-Ho, Anthony Wong, Lee Kang-Sheng	Chan Kin-Chung	Ann Hui	Class	1999
Visible Secret	Eason Chan, Shu Qi, Sam Lee	Cheng Man-Wai	Ann Hui,	Media Asia	2001

Title	Major Cast	Screenwriter	Producer	Company	Year
Tsui Hark					
The Gold Dagger Romance I & II	Yeung Chak-Lam, Yau Tin-Lung, Candice Yu, Carol Cheng	Tang Ko, Tam Ling	Selina Leung	Commercial Television	1978
The Butterfly Murders	Chang Kuo-Chu, Hsu Siu-Ning, Michelle Mee, Jo Jo Chan, Lau Siu-Ming, Wong Shu-Tong	Lam Chi-Ming	Ng See-Yuen	Seasonal	1979
We're Going to Eat You	Norman Chu, Ko Hung	Tsui Hark Szeto Cheuk-Hon	Ng See-Yuen	Seasonal	1980
Dangerous Encounters of the First Kind	Lin Chen-Chi, Lo Lieh	Szeto Cheuk-Hon Chan Fonz Eddie Fong	Fung Wing-Fat	Fotocine	1980
All the Wrong Clues (For the Right Solution)	Teddy Robin Kwan, George Lam, Kelly Yiu, Karl Maka, Tang Kei-Chan, Mariann Wong	Raymond Wong Szeto Cheuk-Hon	Dean Shek Karl Maka	Cinema City	1981
Zu – Warriors from the Magic Mountain	Yuen Biao, Sammo Hung, Adam Cheng, Brigitte Lin	Szeto Cheuk-Hon Shui Chung-Yuet	Raymond Chow	Golden Harvest	1983
Aces Go Places III – Our Man from Bond Street	Sam Hui, Karl Maka, Sylvia Chang	Raymond Wong	Karl Maka Dean Shek Raymond Wong	Cinema City	1984
Working Class	Sam Hui, Teddy Robin Kwan, Tsui Hark, Joey Wang, David Wu	Anthony Chan	Tsui Hark	Cinema City Hong Kong Film Workshop	1985
Peking Opera Blues	Cherie Chung, Brigitte Lin, Sally Yeh, Cheung Kwok-Keung, Mark Cheng	Raymond To	Tsui Hark	Cinema City Hong Kong Film Workshop	1986
A Chinese Ghost Story I	Leslie Cheung, Joey Wang, Wu Ma, Lau Siu-Ming, Lam Wai	Yuen Kai-Chi	Tsui Hark	Cinema City Hong Kong Film Workshop	1987
A Better Tomorrow III	Chow Yun Fat, Anita Mui, Tony Leung Ka-Fai, Saburo Tokito	Edward Leung Dai Foo-Hiu	Tsui Hark	Golden Princess Hong Kong Film Workshop	1989
A Chinese Ghost Story II: The Story Continues	Joey Wang, Michelle Reis, Leslie Cheung, Wu Ma, Waise Lee	Lau Tai-Mok Lam Keeto Edward Leung	Tsui Hark	Golden Princess Hong Kong Film Workshop	1990
A Chinese Ghost Story III	Jacky Cheung, Tony Leung Chiu-Wai, Nina Li, Joey Wang	Roy Szeto Tsui Hark	Tsui Hark	Hong Kong Film Workshop	1991
Once Upon a Time in China	Jet Li, Yuen Biao, Rosamund Kwan	Tsui Hark, Yuen Kai-Chi, Edward Leung, Elsa Tang	Tsui Hark	Golden Harvest	1991
Twin Dragons	Jackie Chan, Maggie Cheung, Nina Li	Barry Wong, Tsui Hark, Joe Cheung	Ng See-Yuen	Hong Kong Directors' Guild	1991
The Banquet	Jacky Cheung, Eric Tsang, Stephen Chow, Maggie Cheung, Anita Mui	Tessa Choi	Ng See-Yuen Joe Cheung	Hitamin Ltd.	1991

Title	Major Cast	Screenwriter	Producer	Company	Year
Once Upon a Time in China II	Jet Li, Rosamund Kwan, Donnie Yen	Tsui Hark	Chan Tin-Suen Ng See-Yuen Ng See-Yuen	Tsui Hark Golden Harvest	1992
Once Upon a Time in China III	Jet Li	Tsui Hark Chan Tin-Suen Cheung Choi	Tsui Hark	Hong Kong Film Workshop	1993
Green Snake	Maggie Cheung, Joey Wang, Wu Hsing-Kuo, Zhao Wen-Zhuo	Lee Pik-Wah Tsui Hark	Tsui Hark	Seasonal	1993
Shanghai Blues	Sylvia Chang, Kenny Bee, Sally Yeh, Yu Ka-Hei, Tien Ching, Loletta Lee	John Chan Raymond To Szeto Cheuk-Hon	Tsui Hark	Hong Kong Film Workshop	1994
The Lovers	Nicky Wu, Charlie Yeung	Tsui Hark Sharon Hui	Tsui Hark	Golden Harvest	1994
Once Upon a Time in China	Zhao Wen-Zhuo, Rosamund Kwan, Max Mok Tai-Mok, Lam Keeto	Tsui Hark, Lau Ng See-Yuen	Tsui Hark	Paragon Films	1994
The Chinese Feast	Leslie Cheung, Anita Yuen, Kenny Bee, Zhao Wen-Zhuo	Tsui Hark, Leo Ng, Philip Cheng Tsui Hark	Raymond Wong Mandarin	Hong Kong Film Workshop	1995
The Blade	Zhao Wen-Zhuo, Xiong Xin-Xin, Sonia Su, Austin Wai, Moses Chan	Tsui Hark, Koan Hui, So Man-Sing	Tsui Hark	Golden Harvest	1995
Love in the Time of Twilight	Nicky Wu, Charlie Yeung, Eric Kot	Tsui Hark, Roy Szeto, Sharon Hui	Tsui Hark	Golden Harvest Era Hong Kong Film Workshop	1995
Tri-star	Leslie Cheung, Anita Yuen, Lau Ching-Wan		Tsui Hark	Cinema City Hong Kong Film Workshop	1996
Double Team	Jean-Claude Van Damme, Dennis Rodman	Lara Fox	Rick Nathanson Shi Nan-Sun	Mandalay Entertainment	1997
Knock Off	Jean-Claude Van Damme, Rob Schneider, Lela Rochon, Michael Wong, Carmen Lee	Steven E. de Souza	Shi Nan-Sun	Knock Films AW	1998
Time and Tide	Wu Bai, Nicholas Tse	Koan Hui Tsui Hark	Tsui Hark	Columbia Pictures Asia	2000
The Legend of Zu	Ekin Cheng, Cecilia Cheung, Louis Koo	Tsui Hark Li Man-Choi	Tsui Hark	One Hundred Years of Film Company Limited Hong Kong Film Workshop	2001

Title	Major Cast	Screenwriter	Producer	Company	Year
Patrick Tam					
Seven Women No. 1	Liao Yung-Hsiang, Wong Wan-Choi, Chow Yun-Fat	Lee Pik-Wah	Patrick Tam	TVB	1976
Seven Women No. 2	Miu Kam-Fung, Lo Yuen, Virginia Ng	Joyce Chan	Patrick Tam	TVB	1976
Seven Women No. 6	Meg Lam, Chan Lap-Bun	Joyce Chan	Patrick Tam	TVB	1976
Seven Women No. 7	Lisa Wang, Yu Yang	Joyce Chan	Patrick Tam	TVB	1976
Seven Women No. 3	Ivy Ho, Yeung Si-Dai, Lee Yan-Wing	Ivy Ho Joyce Chan	Patrick Tam	TVB	1976
CID: Four Moments of Life	Simon Yam, David Lo, Marx Cheung, Ho Big-Kin, Wai Yee-Yan, Wong Yuen-Sun	Joyce Chan	Patrick Tam	TVB	1976
The Underdogs: The Story of Ah Soon	Rover Tam, Yim Chau-Wa, Idy Chan	Shu Kei	Patrick Tam	TVB	1977
Social Worker No. 11	Wai Yee-Yan, Liao Yung-Hsiang, Damian Lau	Shu Kei Joyce Chan	Patrick Tam	TVB	1977
The Sword	Adam Cheng, Norman Chu, Jo Jo Chan, Wei Chiu-Hua, Tien Feng, Ko Hung, Hsu Jye, Lau Siu-Ming	Lau Tin-Chi, Lo Chi-Keung, Wong Ying, Patrick Tam	Raymond Chow	Golden Harvest	1980
Love Massacre	Brigitte Lin, Chang Kuo-Chu, Charlie Chin, Patrick Long, Deanie Ip, Tina Lau	Joyce Chan	Patrick Lung	David & David	1981
Nomad	Leslie Cheung, Ken Tong, Pat Ha, Cecilia Yip, Stuart Ong	Chiu Kang-Chien, Joyce Chan, John Chan, Eddie Fong, Kam Ping-Hing, Patrick Tam	Dennis Yu Jeff Lau	Century	1982
Cherie	Cherie Chung, Tony Leung Ka-Fai, Chor Yuen	Fung Lai-Chi, Joyce Chan, Roy Szeto, Patrick Tam	Selina Chow	Shaw Brothers	1985
Final Victory	Eric Tsang, Loletta Lee, Margaret Li	Wong Kar-Wai	John Sham	D & B	1987
Burning Snow	Simon Yam, Wong Kwong-Chun, Yeh Chun-Jen	Lai Ming-Tong	Kevin Chu	Tsai Mu-Ho	1988
My Heart is that Eternal Rose	Tony Leung Chiu-Wai, Joey Wang, Kenny Bee	John Chan Sammy Tsang	John Sham	Maverick	1988
Yim Ho					
CID: Wrongly Accused	Kwong Ngai, So Hang-Shuen, Wong Yuen-Sun	Yim Ho Shu Kei	Liu Fang-Kang	TVB	1977
Social Worker No. 3	Virginia Ng, Damian Lau, Yim Chau-Wa, Chiang Ko-Ai	Yim Ho	Liu Fang-Kang	TVB	1977
Seventeen: Art Life	Ringo Lam, Chan Juk-Chiu, Lee Wing, Teng Hsiao-Yu	Yim Ho	Liu Fang-Kang	TVB	1977

Title	Major Cast	Screenwriter	Producer	Company	Year
Seventeen: 1977	Damian Lau, Wong Chi-Ching, Lee Wing, Lee Tong	Joyce Chan	Liu Fang-Kang	TVB	1977
ICAC: Two Stories	Damian Lau, Ma Siu-Ying, So Hang-Shuen	Joyce Chan Yim Ho, Philip	Rafael Hui	ICAC	1977
The Extra	James Yi, Idy Chan	Chan, Ronny Yu	Yip Chi-Ming	Bang Bang Film Force	1978
The Happening	Yim Chau-Wa, Yim Chun-Wa, Ti Keung, Chu Siu-Ping, Yuen Lai-Sheung, Cheung Kwok-Keung	Shu Kei Yim Ho	Raymond Chow	Golden Harvest	1979
Wedding Bells, Wedding Belles	James Yi, Sidney, Lau Hak-Suen, Kwan Chung	Yim Ho	Raymond Chow	Golden Harvest	1981
Homecoming	Siqin Gaowa, Josephine Koo	Kong Liang	Hsia Moon	Bluebird	1984
Buddha's Lock	John X. Heart, Zhang Lu-Tong	Kong Liang	Zheng Hui-Li Johnston Wong	Shenzhen Highland	1987
Red Dust	Brigitte Lin, Chin Han, Maggie Cheung, Richard Ng, Josephine Koo, Yim Ho	Echo Chan Yim Ho	Hsu Feng	Tomson	1990
King of Chess	Tony Leung Ka-Fai, John Sham, Yeung Lam	Yim Ho, Tony Leung Ka-Fai	Tsui Hark	Golden Princess	1991
No Sun City	Maryann Ip, Lester Chan, Leung Yuen-Ching, Yau Kwok-Leung, Lau Wai-Yuen, Yim Ling	Yim Ho	Yim Ho	Cable Television	1992
The Day the Sun Turned Cold	Siqin Gaowa, Tsung Hua	Yim Ho Wong Zing-Dong Wong Zi-Bing	Yim Ho	Pineast	1994
The Sun Has Ears	Zhang Yu, You Yong, Gao Qiang	Yim Ho Mo Yan Yi Ling	Yim Ho	Moonhill International Limited, China Stars Inc. USA	1996
Kitchen	Jordan Chan, Tomita Yasuko, Karen Mok, Law Kar-Ying, Lau Siu-Ming, May Law	Yim Ho	Yim Ho Akira Morshige	Golden Harvest, Amuse	1997
Pavilion of Women	Willem Dafoe, Shek Sau, Luo Yan	Luo Yan	Luo Yan	Universal	2001

Allen Fong

Title	Major Cast	Screenwriter	Producer	Company	Year
Below the Lion Rock – The Wild Child	Wang Wai, Chan Lap-Bun	Wong Chi	Cheung Man-Yee	RTHK	1977
Below the Lion Rock – The Story of Yuen	Shirley Wong, Kwok Fung	Wong Chi	Cheung Man-Yee	RTHK	1977
Chau Chai	Li Kun, Li Pang-Fei	Liang Li-Jen	Cheung Man-Yee	RTHK	1977
Below the Lion Rock – The Extra Father and Son	Shek Lui, Chu Hung, Yung Wai-Man, Lee Yu-Tin, Cheng Yu-Or	Chen Chao Alfred Cheung Lee Pik-Wah		Fenghuang	1981

Title	Major Cast	Screenwriter	Producer	Company	Year
Ah Ying	Hui So-Ying, Peter Wang, Hui Pui	Sze Yeung-Ping Peter Wang		Fenghuang	1982
Just Like Weather	Lee Yuk-Guen, Chan Hung-Nin, Mak Chi-Kin, Chan Ting-Kwong, Allen Fong	Ng Chong-Chau Cheung Chi-Sing		Sil-Metropole	1986
Dancing Bull	Cora Miao, Lindzay Chan, Anthony Wong, John Fung	Cheung Chi-Sing	Willy Tsao	Dancing Bull	1990
A Little Life – Opera	Winston Chao, Yang Kuei-Mei	Chan Sai-Chit Chan Kin-Chung	Ann Hui Yao Wen-Tai	Edko	1998
Tibetan Tao	Ah Tao, Snow, Yh Ya, Si, Ta-Er-De	Allen Fong		Sil-Metropole	2000

Alex Cheung

Title	Major Cast	Screenwriter	Producer	Company	Year
CID No. 9	Wong Yuen-Sun, Ho Big-Kin, Simon Yam	Alex Cheung	Liu Fang-Kang	TVB	1977
The First Step: Facing Death	Lee Kwok-Lun, Nam Hung, Lau Dan, Lo Siu-Chi	Alex Cheung	Liu Fang-Kang	TVB	1977
Taxi Driver: The Car Thief	Eric Kam, Kenny Bee, Candy Cheng	Yip Chung-Han	Liu Fang-Kang	TVB	1978
Taxi Driver: The Trio	Eric Kam, Stanley Kwan, Leung Siu-Wah	Mo Kwok-Kwan Alex Cheung	Liu Fang-Kang	TVB	1978
Cops and Robbers	Wang Chung, Eric Kam, Cheung Kwok-Keung	Alex Cheung, Chan Kiu-Ying, Stanley Kwan, Lee Dun	Stanley Kwan	Pearl City Art Top	1980
Man on the Brink	Eddie Chan, Eric Kam, Callan Leung, Chic Lau	Alex Cheung William Cheung	Yang Chun	Century	1981
Twinkle Twinkle Little Star	Cherie Chung, James Yi	Alex Cheung, Manfred Wong, Sandy Shaw, John Au, Yuen Kai-Chi, Lawrence Cheng	Mona Fong	Shaw Brothers	1983
The Royal Thief	Bryan Leung, Fei Hsiang, Carroll Gordon	Alex Cheung	Mona Fong	Shaw Brothers	1985
Imaginary Suspects	Cheung Kwok-Keung, Kwan Ming-Yuk	Yuen Kai-Chi Alex Cheung	Stanley Kwan	Alan & Eric	1988
Framed	Alex Man, Simon Yam	Chong Koon-Nam	Yuen Sin-Kan	Hung Tai	1989
Midnight Caller	Diana Pang, Michael Wong, Ni Shu-Chun	Raymond Wong	Raymond Wong	Mandarin	1996
Made in Heaven	Ada Choi, Law Kar-Ying, Michael Tong	Chan Kam-Cheong Ho Tai-Tak Alex Cheung	Henry Fong	Skylark	1997

Title	Major Cast	Screenwriter	Producer	Company	Year
Kirk Wong					
The Club	Michael Chan, Norman Chu, Mabel Kwong, Erina Miyai	Tan Tien-Nan	Richard Cheung Yau Tat-Shing	Bang Bang	1981
Health Warning	Ko Hung, Johnny Wong, Ray Lui, Lam Hoi-Ling, Yuen Tin-Wan	Liu Wing-Leung	Ringo Wong	Bang Bang	1983
Life Line Express	Kent Cheng, Teddy Robin Kwan, Sandy Chan, Yam Hei-Bo, Ko Hung	Szeto Cheuk-Hon Lo Kin	Teddy Robin Kwan	Cinema City	1985
True Colours	Brigitte Lin, Raymond Wong, Tommy Ti	Raymond Wong	Raymond Wong	Cinema City	1986
Gun Men	Tony Leung Ka-Fai, Adam Cheng, Waise Lee, Mark Cheng, David Wu, Elvis Tsui, Carrie Ng, Elizabeth Lee	Nip Wang-Fung Gumby Law	Tsui Hark	Hong Kong Film Workshop	1988
Taking Manhattan	Lui Chi-Yin, Carrie Ng, Chen Jun, Alana Adena	Cheung Chi-Sing, Lai Kit, Raymond To, Colin Pahlow	Eric Tsang	Paragon Films Limited	1991
Crime Story	Jackie Chan, Kent Cheng, Christine Ng, Law Kar-Ying	Chun Tin-Nam, Chan Man-Keung, Chan Lai-Ling, Cheung Chi-Sing, Teddy Chen	Chua Lam	Golden Harvest	1993
Organized Crime and Triad Bureau	Danny Lee, Cecilia Yip, Anthony Wong, Elizabeth Lee	Lo Bing	Danny Lee Kirk Wong	Magnum Uniden	1993
Rock n' Roll Cop	Anthony Wong, Wu Hsing-Kuo, Carrie Ng	Lo Bing	Kirk Wong	Sky Point	1994
The Big Hit	Mark Wahlberg, Lou Diamond Philips, Christina Applegate, Avery Brooks, Bokeem Woodbine	Ben Ramsey	John Woo, Terence Chang, John M. Eckert	Tristar Picture	1999
Clifford Choi					
The Water Margin No. 6	Cecilia Wong, Shek Sau, Law Kwok-Wai	Raymond Wong	Beby Ng	TVB	1977
Wong Fei Hung	Kwan Chung, Lee Kuk-Wah, Ho Ka-Wai	Ng Ho, Stephen Shin, Raymond Wong	Beby Ng	TVB	1977
Encore	Danny Chan, Leslie Cheung, Yung Ching-Ching, Paul Chung	Manfred Wong Lawrence Cheng	Philip Chan	Fu Shan	1980
No U-Turn	Dominic Lam, Annie Liu	Clifton Ko	Karl Maka	Cinema City	1981
Teenage Dreamers	Leslie Cheung, Elaine Chow	Clifton Ko	Mona Fong	Shaw Brothers	1982
Hong Kong Hong Kong	Alex Man, Cherie Chung	Clifford Choi Hsu Mi	Mona Fong	Shaw Brothers	1983
North South East West	Tam Bing-Man, Lau Shui-Kei	Clifton Ko	Clifford Choi Lam Ching-Gai	Dragon Ray	1983

Title	Major Cast	Screenwriter	Producer	Company	Year
Devil & Angel	Cecilia Yip, Nina Li	Clifford Choi	Clifford Choi	Dragon Ray	1985
Grow Up in Anger	Wong Yiu-Fai, Ellen Chan	Terence Chang	Raymond Chow	Golden Harvest	1986
Big Brother	Alex Man, Carrie Ng	Tommy Hau	Clifford Choi	Dechance	1989
Naughty Couple	Francis Ng, Anita Lee	Szeto Wai-Kin	Raymond Wong	Mandarin	1994
Lai Man Wai (Father of the Hong Kong Cinema)		Law Kar	Clifford Choi, Law Kar	Dragon Ray	1998–2001
Lau Shing-Hon					
House of the Lute	Simon Yam, Kwan Hoi-Shan	Lau Shing-Hon	Lau Shing-Hon	Hung Wai	1979
The Head Hunter	Chow Yun-Fat, Rosamund Kwan	Szeto Cheuk-Hon	Kung Chuan-Kai	New Century	1982
Hunted in Hong Kong	Lawrence Tan, Rowena Cortes	Pat Dunlop, Lau Shing-Hon	Leonard L. Bianchi	Kent International Films Limited	1983
The Final Night of the Royal Hong Kong Police	John Chan, May Law	Lau Shing-Hon	Lau Shing-Hon	Make Hero	1999
Terry Tong					
The Silver Sword Killer	Norman Chu, Lau Wai-Man	Ng Ping	Johnny Mak	Rediffusion	1979
Collies Killer	Charlie Chin, Cecilia Yip, Chiao Chiao	Chiu Kang-Chien Chun Tin-Nam Eddie Fong	Dennis Yu	Century	1982
Yellow Peril	Alan Tang, Tong Lan-Fa	Lee Dun Chan Man-Kwai	Dennis Yu	Century	1984
Hong Kong Graffiti	Olivia Cheng, Chan Yuen-Lai, Ni Shu-Chun	Li Mo	Lo Wei	Lo Wei	1985
Seven Warriors	Adam Cheng, Jacky Cheung, Max Mok, Tony Leung Chiu-Wai	Sammy Tsang	John Sham	Maverick	1989
The Woman and Her Seven Husbands	Lu Hsiao-Fen, Chang Kuo-Chu, Wong Yeh, Siqin Gaowa, Chen Sung-Yung	Chan Man-Kwai Terry Tong	Lin Deng-Fei	Central Motion	1990
Gigolo and the Whore	Simon Yam, Carina Lau, Alex Fong	Or Lok Man Sandy Shaw	David Lam	David Lam	1991
Cash on Delivery	Simon Yam, Veronica Yip, Sandra Ng	Or Lok Man Zhang Jian	Zhang Jian Terry Tong	Hung Tai	1992
Peter Yung					
The System	Ringo Pai, Sek Kin, Chiao Chiao	Lee Sen, Peter Yung, Kam Ping-Hing	Peter Yung	Bunbun	1979
Life After Life	George Lam, Flora Cheong, Patrick Tse, Cheang Mang-Ha	Peter Yung, Benny Tam, James Lau	Karl Maka Dean Shek	Cinema City	1981
Journey to the Cossacks	Si Wai, To Yi Shun Koo Lai	Kwan Park Peter Yung	Peter Yung	Associate	1982
Double Dealer	Clare Wai, Leslie Cheung	Peter Yung	Peter Yung Adrian Cowell	Associate	1984

Title	Major Cast	Screenwriter	Producer	Company	Year
Dennis Yu					
Seventeen: Summer Break	Chiang Ko-Ai, Lai Shui-Ching, Wai Yee-Yan	Ho Hong-Kiu	Liu Fang-Kang	TVB	1977
See Bar	Chow Yun-Fat, Dorothy Yu, Ringo Pai, Chao Hung	Thomas Tang	David Tong	David & David	1980
The Beasts	Patricia Chong, Eddie Chan, Kent Cheng	Eddie Fong, Lee Dun	Stanley Kwan	Pearl City	1980
The Imp	Charlie Chin, Dorothy Yu, Elliot Yueh, Brigitte Lin	Kam Ping-Hing, Lee Dun, Cheung Kam-Moon	Jeff Lau	Century	1981
The Comedy	Kent Cheng, Dorothy Yu, Wong Yue, Tong Lan-Fa	Shek Wai-Man, Ng Cheuk-Hay	Dennis Yu Jeff Lau	Century	1984
All the Wrong Clues	Dean Shek, Mark Cheng, Bennett Pang, Anthony Tang, Pat Ha, Charine Chan	Ng Cheuk-Hay Lam Koon-Kiu	Dennis Yu	Paramount Cinema City	1985
Musical Singer	James Wong, Anita Mui, Russell Wong, Cher Yeung		Dennis Yu	Cinema City	1987
Evil Cat	Lau Kar-Leung, Joan Teng, Mark Cheng, Wong Jing, Hsu Shu-Yuen, Stuart Ong	Wong Jing	Dennis Yu	Cinema City	1987

References in Chinese

Books

Cai, Guorong. *Zhongguo jingdai wenyi dianying yanjiu* (A Study on Contemporary Literary-Artistic Films in China). Taipei: Film Library, 1995.

Cheng, Jihua, Li Shaobai and Ying Zuwen, eds. *Zhongguo Dianying Fazhanshi I & II* (History of Development of Chinese Cinema, Part I and II). Cultural Information Press, 1978.

Dai Pingan, et al., eds. *Xu Anhua de yuenan sanbuqu* (Ann Hui's Trilogy of Vietnam). Hong Kong: Qingwen shuju, 1983.

Deng Tu, ed. *Hong Kong Cinema Yearbook 1996*. Hong Kong: Hong Kong Film Critics Society, 1997.

Du Yunzhi. *Zhongguo dianying qishinian* (Seventy Years of Chinese Cinema). Taipei: Zhonghua minguo dianying fazhang jijinghui guojia dianying ziliaoguan, 1986.

—. *Zhonghua minguo dianyingshi* (History of Cinema in Republic of China). Taipei: xingzhengyuan wenhua jianshe weiyuanhui, 1998.

Gan Changqiu. *Xianggang jinji jiaocheng* (The Teaching Journey of Hong Kong Economy). Guangzhou: Sun Yat-sen University Press, 1985.

Gao Tianqiang. *Xianggang jinxi* (Past and Present of Hong Kong). Hong Kong: Joint Publishing Company Ltd., 1995.

Hu Peng. *Wo yu Huang Feihong* (Wong Fei-hung and I). Hong Kong: Sanyo, 1995.

Huang Jianye. *Renwen dianying de zhuixun* (The Quest of Films about Humanity). Taipei: Yuan Liou Publishing Co. Ltd., 1992.

Huang Zhuohan. *Dianying rensheng: Huang Zhuohan huiyilu* (Life of Film: Memory of Huang Zhuohan). Taipei: Wanxiang tushu youxian gongsi, 1994.

Huang Wulan, ed. *Dangdai gangtai dianying 1988–1992, I & II* (Contemporary Hong Kong and Taiwan Cinemas 1988–1992, I & II). Taipei Times Press, 1992.

—. *Dangdai zhongguo dianying 1993* (Contemporary Chinese Cinema 1993). Taipei Times Press, 1994.

—. *Dangdai zhongguo dianying 1994* (Contemporary Chinese Cinema 1994). Taipei Times Press, 1995.

Jiao Xiongping. *Taigang dianyingzhong dezuozhe yu leixing* (Auteurs and Genres of Films of Taiwan and Hong Kong). Taipei: Yuan Liou Publishing Co. Ltd., 1993.

—. *Shidai xianying* (A Manifestation of Times). Taipei: Yuan Liou Publishing Co. Ltd., 1993.

—, ed. *Xiangang dianyin fengmao 1975–1986* (A View on Hong Kong Cinema, 1975–1986). Taipei: Taipei Times Press, 1993.

—, ed. *Xianggang dianying chuanqi: Xiao Fangfang he sishinian dianying fengyun* (A Legend in Hong Kong Cinema: Josephine Siao and Turbulence in Cinema for Forty Years). Taipei: Variety Limited, 1995.

—, ed. *Xinyazhou dianying mianmianguan*. (A Panorama of New Asian Cinema). Taipei: Yuan Liou Publishing Co. Ltd., 1991.
Kuang Baowei, ed. *Xu Anhua shuo Xu Anhua* (Ann Hui on Ann Hui). Hong Kong: Hongye, 1998.
Kwok Ching-ling, ed. *Monographs of Hong Kong Film Veterans 1: Hong Kong Here I Come*. Hong Kong: Hong Kong Film Archive, 2000.
Lau Shing-hon. *Dianying fubixing* (The Poetic Characteristics of Film). Hong Kong: Cosmos Books, 1992
Law Kar, Ng Ho and Pak Tong Cheuk. *Xianggang dianying leixing* (Genre Films in Hong Kong). Hong Kong: Oxford University Press, 1995.
Law Wei-ming. *Luo Weiming dianying wenzhang* (Law Wei-ming's Writings about Film). Hong Kong: Zhenzheng chuangzao chuban, 1998.
Li Cheuk-to. *Bashi niandai xianggang dianging biji I & II* (Notes on Hong Kong Cinema in 1980s) I & II. Hong Kong: Chuangjian wenfu, 1990.
—. *Guanyiji: Zhongwei dianying bian* (An Anthology of Film Viewing from Another Perspective: Chinese and Western Films). Hong Kong: Subculture, 1994.
—. *Linli yingxiangguan: Jingshui bian* (Fluid Images: the Part of Well Water). Hong Kong: Subculture, 2000.
Li Hanxiang. *Sanshinian xishuo congtou* (To Speak from the Beginning for Thirty Years). Hong Kong: Cosmos Books, 1993.
—. *Yinghe shengxia* (All About the Galaxy). Hong Kong: Cosmos Books, 1997.
—. *Yinghai qianqiu* (The History of the Silver Ocean). Hong Kong: Cosmos Books, 1997.
—. *Yingcheng neiwei* (Inside and Outside the Studios). Hong Kong: Cosmos Books, 1997.
Li Tien-tuo, ed. *Dangdai huayu dianying lunshu* (Discourse of Contemporary Chinese-language Films). Taipei: Wanxiang tushu youxian gongsi, 1995.
—. and Liu Hsien-cheng, eds. *Yatai meijie tuzhi* (An Illustrated Guide of Media in Asia Pacific). Taipei: Yatai tuchu chubanshe, 1999.
Li Youxin. *Dianying, dianyingren, dianying kanwu* (Film, Filmmakers, and Film Publications). Taipei: Zili wenbao congshu, 1986.
—. *Gangtai Liuda daoyang* (Six Major Filmmakers in Hong Kong and Taiwan). Taipei: Zili wenbao congshu, 1986.
Lit Fu, ed. *Hong Kong Cinema Yearbook 1998*. Hong Kong: Hong Kong Film Critics Society, 2000.
Liu Hsien-cheng, ed. *Zhongguo dianying, lishi, wenhua yu zaixian* (Chinese Cinema, History, Culture and Representation). Taipei: Zhongguo dianying xhiliao yianjiuhui, 1996.
Lok Feng. *The Decadent City*. Hong Kong: Oxford University Press, 1995.
Ma Kit-wai, Eric. *Television and Identity*. Hong Kong: Breakthrough Ltd., 1996.
Mo Kai. *The Structural Changes and Economic Development of Hong Kong*. Hong Kong: Joint Publishing, 1993.
Ng Ho. *Xianggang dianying minzuxue* (The Ethnography of Hong Kong Cinema). Hong Kong: Subculture, 1993.
Po Fung, ed. *Hong Kong Cinema Yearbook 1997*. Hong Kong: Hong Kong Film Critics Society, 1999.
Sha Rongfeng. *Bingfen dianying sishinian* (Forty Years of Electric Shadows). Taipei: Guojia diangying ziliaoguan, 1994.
Shek Kei. *Shiqi yinghuaji: Xinlangchao borenlai (I)* (Shek Kei's Anthology of Film Reviews: The Vigorously Emergent New Wave, Part I). Hong Kong: Subculture, 1999.
—. *Shiqi yinghuaji: Xinlangchao borenlai (II)* (Shek Kei's Anthology of Film Reviews: The Vigorously Emergent New Wave, Part II). Hong Kong: Subculture, 1999.
—. *Shiqi yinghuaji: Cong xingsheng dao weiji (I)* (Shek Kei's Anthology of Film Reviews: From Prosperity to Crisis, Part I). Hong Kong: Subculture, 1999.
—. *Shiqi yinghuaji: Cong xingsheng dao weiji (II)* (Shek Kei's Anthology of Film Reviews: From Prosperity to Crisis, Part II). Hong Kong: Subculture, 1999.
—. *Shiqi yinghuaji: Bada mingjia fengmao (I)* (Shek Kei's Anthology of Film Reviews: The Charisma of Eight Masters, Part I). Hong Kong: Subculture, 1999.
—. *Shiqi yinghuaji: Bada mingjia fengmao (II)* (Shek Kei's Anthology of Film Reviews: The Charisma of Eight Masters, Part II). Hong Kong: Subculture, 1999.

—. *Shiqi yinghuaji: Shibaban wuyi (I)* (Shek Kei's Anthology of Film Reviews: A Variety of Skills, Part I). Hong Kong: Subculture, 1999.

—. *Shiqi yinghuaji: Shibaban wuyi (II)* (Shek Kei's Anthology of Film Reviews: A Variety of Skills, Part II). Hong Kong: Subculture, 1999.

Shu Kei, ed. *Hong Kong Cinema Yearbook 1994*. Hong Kong: Hong Kong Film Critics Society, 1996.

Sze, Stephen. *Shiwenhong de dianying pinglun* (Film Criticism by Stephen Sze). Hong Kong: Subculture, 1992.

—. *Shiwenhong de dazhong wenhua piping* (Mass Culture Criticism by Stephen Sze). Hong Kong: Subculture, 1992.

—. *Hong Kong Cinema Yearbook 1995*. Hong Kong: Hong Kong Film Critics Society, 1997.

Tay, William. *Wenhua piping yu huayu dianying* (Film Criticism and Chinese-language Films). Taipei: Editeur Rye Field, 1998.

Wang Ren, ed. *Hu Jinquan de shijie* (The World of King Hu). Taipei: Zhongguo dianying shiliao yianjiu hui, 1999.

Wen Tianxiang. *Sheyingji yu jiaorouji - huayu dianying 1990–1996* (Rolling Machines: Chinese-language Cinema 1990–1996). Taipei: Zhishufang chubanshe, 1996.

Yu Mo-wan. *Xianggang dianying bashi nian* (Eighty Years of Hong Kong Cinema). Hong Kong: Urban Council, 1994.

—. *Xianggang dianying shihua - wushi niandai 1950–1954* (History of Hong Kong Cinema - 1950s [1950–1954]). Hong Kong: Subculture, 2000.

Zhang, Che. *Huegu xianggang dianying sanshinian* (A Retrospect on Hong Kong Cinema for Thirty Years). Hong Kong: Joint Publishing Company Ltd., 1995.

Zhang, Zhendong and Li Chunwu, eds. *Xiangang Guangbo Dianshi Fazhanshi* (History of Development of Broadcasting and Television in Hong Kong). Beijing: China Broadcasting and Film Press, 1997.

Zhong Dafeng. *Zhongguo dianyingshi* (History of Chinese Cinema). Beijing: China Broadcasting and Film Press, 1985.

Zhu Ke. *Behind the Screen*. Hong Kong: Cosmo Books, 1985.

Special Issues, Serials and Magazines

Baixing (People). Bi-Weekly. Hong Kong: Baxing chuban youxian gongsi.

Border Crossings in Hong Kong Cinema. 24th HKIFF Catalogue, Hong Kong: Leisure and Cultural Services Department, 2000.

Breakthrough. Hong Kong: Breakthrough Press.

A Comparative Study of Post-war Mandarin and Cantonese Cinema: the Films of Zhu Shilin, Qin Jian and Other Directors. 7th HKIFF. Hong Kong: Urban Council, 1983.

Cantonese Cinema Retrospective, 1950–1959. 2nd International Film Festival (HKIFF). Hong Kong: Urban Council, 1978.

Cantonese Cinema Retrospective, 1960–69. 6th HKIFF. Hong Kong: Urban Council, 1982.

Cantonese Melodrama: 1950–1969. 10th HKIFF. Hong Kong: Urban Council, 1986.

Changes in Hong Kong Society Through Cinema. 12th HKIFF. Hong Kong: Urban Council, 1988.

Changjingtou zazhi (Long Shot Magazine). Taipei: Zongyang dianying shiye gufen youxian gongsi, 1987–1988.

The China Factor in Hong Kong Cinema. 14th HKIFF. Hong Kong: Urban Council, 1990.

Cinema of Two Cities: Hong Kong - Shanghai. 18th HKIFF. Hong Kong: Urban Council, 1994.

Chinese-Western Motion Pictures. Hong Kong: Chinese-Western Motion Pictures Press, 1982–1986.

City Entertainment. Bi-Weekly. Hong Kong: City Entertainment Press, 1979–1994.

Dangdai dianying (Contemporary Cinema). Beijing: China Film Archive. 1986–1997.

Dangdai wenxue (Contemporary Literature). Guangzhou: Huacheng chubanshe.

Database of Television Programs. Hong Kong: Radio Television Hong Kong, 1997.

Datexie Shuangzhoukan (Close-Up Biweekly) *20–64*. Hong Kong: *Datexie Shuangzhoukan she. 1976–1979.*

Dian guang huan ying: dian ying yan jiu wen ji (Electric Shadows: An anthology of writings about film studies). Hong Kong: School of continuing and Professional Studies, The Chinese University of Hong Kong and the television unit, Radio Television Hong Kong, 1985.

Dianying yishu (Film Art). Monthly. Beijing: Zhongguo dianyingjia jiehui, 1980-1990.
Early Images of Hong Kong and China. 19th HKIFF. Hong Kong: Urban Council, 1995.
Fifty Years of Electric Shadows. 21st HKIFF. Hong Kong: Urban Council, 1997.
Fifty Years of the Hong Kong Film Production and Distribution Industries: An Exhibition (1947-97). Hong Kong: Hong Kong Film Archive, 1997.
Film Appreciation Bi-Monthly. Taipei: Dianying ziliaoguan.
The First Generation Bi-Weekly. Hong Kong: New Generation Press, 1 June - 5 October, 1979. No. 89-94, 96-97 (including interviews of New Wave directors).
Hong Kong Annual Report. 1978-1987. Hong Kong: Hong Kong Government.
Hong Kong Cinema in the Eighties. 15th HKIFF. Hong Kong: Urban Council, 1991.
Hong Kong Cinema '79-'89 (combined edition). 24th HKIFF. Hong Kong: Leisure and Cultural Services Department, 2000.
Hong Kong Television Weekly. Hong Kong: Television Broadcasts Ltd., 1970-1985.
Influence Magazine 1-23. Taipei: Yingxiang zashishe, 1972-1988.
Juchang zashi (Theatre Magazine) 9: Special issue on Auteur Theory. Taipei, 1969.
Mandarin Films and Popular Songs: 40's - 60's. 17th HKIFF. Hong Kong: Urban Council, 1993.
Ming Pao Weekly. Hong Kong: Ming Pao Press.
Nanbeiji (North-South Poles). Hong Kong: Longmen wenhua shiye youxian gongsi.
Phantoms of the Hong Kong Cinema. 13th HKIFF. Hong Kong: Urban Council, 1989.
The Post-war Hong Kong Cinema Survey 1946-1968. 3rd HKIFF. Hong Kong: Urban Council, 1979.
A Report on the Symposium of Hong Kong Cinema. 21st HKIFF. Hong Kong: Urban Council, 10 April, 1997.
The Restless Breed: Cantonese Stars of the Sixties. 20th HKIFF. Hong Kong: Urban Council, 1996.
Seminar on Hong Kong New Wave. 23rd HKIFF. Provisional Urban Council, 3 April, 1999.
A Study of Hong Kong Cinema in the Seventies. 8th HKIFF. Hong Kong: Urban Council, 1984.
A Study of Hong Kong Swordplay Film (1945-1980). 5th HKIFF. Hong Kong: Urban Council, 1981.
Survey Summary of Television Viewing Ratings 1970-1980. Hong Kong: SRG..
Today Movies Magazine. Taipei: Jinri dianying zazhishe.
The Traditions of Hong Kong Comedy. 9th HKIFF. Hong Kong: Urban Council, 1985.
Transcending the Times: King Hu and Eileen Chang. 22nd HKIFF. Hong Kong: Provisional Urban Council, 1998.
Wah Kiu Annual Report. 1978-1985. Hong Kong; Wah Kiu Daily Press.
World Screen. Taiwan: World Screen Press.

References in English Books

Altman, Rick. *Film/Genre*. London: British Film Institute, 1999.
Bazin, Andre. *What is Cinema?* Vol. 1, Berkeley: University of California Press, 1967.
—. *What is Cinema?* Vol. 2, Berkeley: University of California Press, 1967.
Berry, Chris, ed. *Perspectives on Chinese Cinema*. 2nd expanded edition, London: British Film Institute, 1991.
Bordwell, David. *Planet Hong Kong: Popular Cinema and the Art of Entertainment*. Cambridge: Harvard University Press, 2000.
Bordwell, David and Kristin Thompson. *Film Art: An Introduction*. 4th ed. New York: McGraw-Hill, 1993.
Browne, Nick, et al., eds. *New Chinese Cinema: Forms, Identities, Politics*. Cambridge University Press, 1994.
—. *Cahiers du Cinema: 1969-1972, The Politics of Representation*. Cambridge: Harvard University Press, 1990.
Bywater, Tim and Thomas Sobchack. *An Introduction to Film Criticism: Major Critical Approaches to Narrative Film*. New York: Addison Wesley Logman, 1989.
Carrol, Noel. *Theorizing the Moving Image*. Cambridge: Cambridge University Press, 1996.
Caughie, John, ed. *Theories of Authorship*. London: Routledge & Kegan Paul, 1981.
Cawelti, John, G. *The Six-Gun Mystique*. Bowling Green, OH: Bowling Green State University Popular Press, 1970.

Dannen, Fredric and Barry Long. *Hong Kong Babylon: An Insider's Guide to the Hollywood of the East*. London: Faber, 1997.
Denzin, Norman K. *The Cinematic Society: The Voyeur's Gaze*. London: Sage, 1995.
Eberhard, Wolfram. *The Chinese Silver Screen: Hong Kong and Taiwan Motion Pictures in the 1960s*. Taipei: Orient Cultural Service, 1972.
Fonoroff, Paul. *At the Hong Kong Movies: 600 Reviews from 1988 till the Handover*. Hong Kong: Film Biweekly, 1998.
French, Philip. *Western: Aspect of a Movie Genre*. New York: Viking Press, 1974.
Fu, Poshek and David Desser, eds. *The Cinema of Hong Kong: History, Arts, Identity*. Cambridge University Press, 2000.
Graham, Peter. ed. *The New Wave*. London: Secker and Warburg, 1968.
Grant, Barry K., ed. *Film Genre Reader*. Austin: University of Texas Press, 1986.
Hammond, Stefan and Mike Wilkins. *Sex and Zen & A Bullet in the Head: The Essential Guide to Hong Kong's Mind-Bending Films*. New York: Fireside, 1996.
Henderson, Brian and Ann Martin, eds. *Film Quarterly: Forty Years – A Selection*. Berkeley: University of California Press, 1999.
Hillier, Jim, ed. *Cahiers du Cinema: The 1950s: Neo-Realism, Hollywood, New Wave*. Cambridge: Harvard University Press, 1985.
—. *Cahiers du Cinema: The 1960s: New Wave, New Cinema, Reevaluating Hollywood*. Cambridge: Harvard University Press, 1986.
Jarvie, I. C. *Window on Hong Kong: A Sociological Study of the Hong Kong Film Industry and Its Audience*. Hong Kong: Centre of Asian Studies, University of Hong Kong, 1977.
Kaminsky, Stuart M. *American Film Genre*. Chicago: Pflaum Publishers, 1974.
Kitses, Jim. *Horizons West: Anthony Mann, Budd Boetticher, Sam Peckinpah: Studies of Authorship within the Western*. Bloomington: Indiana University Press, 1969.
Kracauer, S. *The Theory of Film*. New York: Oxford University Press, 1960.
Lent, John A. *The Asian Film Industry*. London: Christopher Helm, 1990.
Leyda, Jay. *Dianying: An Account of Films and the Film Audience in China*. Cambridge, Mass: MIT Press, 1972.
Logan, Bey. *Hong Kong Action Cinema*. London: Titan Books, 1994.
Lu, Sheldon Hsiao-peng, ed. *Transnational Chinese Cinema: Identity, Nationhood, Gender*. Honolulu: University of Hawaii Press, 1997.
Mast, Gerald, Marshall Cohen and Leo Braudy, eds. *Film Theory and Criticism: Introductory Readings*. New York: Oxford University Press, 1992.
McArthur, Colin. *Underworld USA*. New York: Viking Press, 1972.
Metz, Christian. *Language and Cinema*. New York: Praeger, 1975.
Monaco, James, *The New Wave: Truffaut, Godard, Chabrol, Rohmer, Rivette*. New York: Oxford University Press, 1976.
Nichols, Bill. *Movies and Methods*. Berkeley: University of California Press, 1976.
Prince, Stephen, ed. *Sam Peckinpah's* The Wild Bunch. Cambridge: Cambridge University Press, 1999.
Sadoul, George. *Dictionary of Films*. Berkeley: University of California Press, 1972.
Sarris, Andrew. *The American Cinema: Directors and Directions 1929–1968*. New York: Da Capo Press, 1996.
Schatz, Thomas, *Hollywood Genre: Formula, Filmmaking and the Studio System*. New York: McGraw-Hill, 1981.
Server, Lee. *Asian Pop Cinema: Bombay to Tokyo*. San Francisco: Chronicle Books, 1999.
Solomon, Stanley J. *Beyond Formula: American Film Genres*. New York: Harcourt Brace Jovanovich, 1976.
Stam, Robert, Robert Buroyne and Sandy Flitterman Leuis. *New Vocabularies in Film Semiotics*. London: Routledge, 1972.
Stokes, Lisa Odham and Michael Hoover. *City on Fire: Hong Kong Cinema*. London: Verso, 1999.
Tam, Kwok Kan and Wimal Dissanayake. *New Chinese Cinema*. Hong Kong: Oxford University Press, 1998.

Teo, Stephen. *Hong Kong Cinema: The Extra Dimensions*. London: British Film Institute, 1997.
Tobias, Mel. *Memoirs of an Asian Moviegoer*. Hong Kong: South China Morning Post, 1982.
Tudor, Andrew. *Theories of Film*. New York: Viking, 1974.
Warshow, Robert. *The Immediate Experience*. New York: Atheneum, 1977.
Weisser, Thomas. *Asian Cult Cinema*. New York: Boulevard Books, 1997.
Wollen, Peter. *Signs and Meaning in the Cinema*. London: Martin Secker & Warburg, 1969.
Wood, Miles. *Cine East: Hong Kong Cinema Through the Looking Glass*. London: Routledge, 1998.
Wright, Will. *Six-Guns and Society: A Structural Study of the Western*. Berkeley: University of California Press, 1975.
Zhang, Ying Jin and Zhiwei Xiao, eds. *Encyclopedia of Chinese Film*. London: Routledge, 1998.

Serials

Asian Cult Cinema. Miami: Vital Books, 1996–. Bimonthly continues.
Asian Trash Cinema. Houston: Asian Trash Cinema, 1994–1995. Quarterly.
Bright Light. Cincinnati. OH: Bright Lights Film Journal, 1993– . Quarterly. No. 13 (1994) is a special issue on Hong Kong Cinema.
Hong Kong Film Magazine. San Francisco: Hong Kong Film Magazine, 1995– . Quarterly.
Hong Kong Films. Hong Kong: Hong Kong, Kowloon and New Territories Motion Picture Industry Association, 1991–. Annual, Chinese and English, First volume is 1989/1990. *Post Script*. Vol. 19, No. 1. Texas: Post Script, 1999. Special issue on Hong Kong Cinema.

These/Dissertations

Cheung, William. 'An Evaluation of the New Wave Cinema in Hong Kong through the Study of Four Directors: Patrick Tam, Allen Fong, Ann Hui, Tsui Hark.' Ph.D. dissertation, University of Hong Kong, 2000.
Chu, Wing Ki. 'The Representation of Space in Contemporary Hong Kong Cinema Nostalgia Films.' M.Phil. thesis, Chinese University of Hong Kong, 1998.
Chu, Ying Chi. 'Hong Kong Cinema and National Cinema: Coloniser, Motherland and Self.' Ph. D. dissertation, Murdoch University, 2000.
Ho, Chui Fun Selina. 'Ann Hui as a female Filmmaker: In search of Hong Kong Culture.' M.A. thesis, University of Hong Kong, 1998.
Lau, Kwok Wah. 'A Cultural Interpretation of the Popular Cinema of China and Hong Kong, 1981–1985.' Ph.D. dissertation, Northwestern University, 1998.
Leung, Grace Lai Kuen. 'The Evolution of Hong Kong as a Regional Movie Production and Export Center.' M.Phil. thesis. Chinese University of Hong Kong, 1993.
Ma Ka Fai. 'Hero, Hong Kong Style: A Structural Study of Hero Films in Hong Kong.' M.A. thesis, University of Chicago, 1990.
Ng, Hoi Shan Crystal. 'Rewriting Louis Cha's Classical Characters in Filmic Representation in Response to the Political and Cultural Mutation of Hong Kong 90s – Wong Kar Wai and Tsui Hark.' M.A. thesis, University of Hong Kong, 1998.
Tan, See Kam. 'Dangerous Encounters: New Hong Kong Cinema and (Post) Coloniality.' Ph.D. dissertation, University of Melbourne, 1997.
Walsh Lau, Man Yee Eliza. 'In Search of Identity: Hong Kong as Seen Through Its Cinema from 1950s to the Early 1980s.' M.Phil. thesis, University of Hong Kong, 1996.
Wong, Shuk Han Mary. 'New Chinese Cinema and Feminine Writings.' Ph.D. dissertation, University of Hong Kong, 2000.
Yang, Ming Yu. 'China: Once Upon a Time/Hong Kong: 1997. A Critical Study of Contemporary Hong Kong Martial Arts Films.' Ph.D. dissertation, University of Maryland, College Park, 1995.
Yu, Gwo Chauo, 'China, Hong Kong and Taiwan: The Convergence and Interaction of Chinese Film.' M.A. thesis, University of North Texas, 1993.
Yue, Andrey Ing-sun. 'Pre-Post-1997: Postcolonial Hong Kong Cinema, 1984–1997.' Ph.D. dissertation, La Trobe University, 1999.
Yung, Dominic Yuk Yu. 'Mainlanders in Hong Kong Films of the Eighties: A Study on Their Changing Depiction.' M.Phil. thesis, Chinese University of Hong Kong, 1991.

Acknowledgements

During the collecting of materials for this work, Ms Chan Po-chu, the manager of the programme section of Hong Kong Television Broadcasts Limited, generously lent me more than ten drama series, Mr Yu Mo-wan from the Hong Kong Film Archive made available to me many videotapes and magazines, and Mr Law Kar of the Hong Kong International Film Festival supplied me with many films and special issues of the Festival To all of them, I give my heartfelt thanks. I also give special thanks to Mr Lee Ho-cheung, who helped me with the task of verifying information.

In the writing of this work, I relied on Prof. Leonard Chu's constant guidance and the invaluable comments from my colleagues Dr Yu Xu, Dr Xiao Xiaosui, and Dr Steve Guo. I am particularly indebted to Prof. Wong Kin-yuen for his many constructive suggestions. I would like to thank Dorothy Lau for translating the book from Chinese to English; it is a lot of work and I am grateful for her tremendous efforts. I would also like to thank Dr. Ian Aitken for his invaluable help in reading the English-language manuscript of this book, and for helping to copy-edit the work into its English translation. Thanks are also due to Josephine Khu, Judy Chan and the editors of Intellect Press. Finally, I thank my wife, Yuk-man, for her tolerance, understanding, and support. Without her help, this book would never have seen the light of day.